Creating a Common Table

IN TWENTIETH-CENTURY ARGENTINA

Creating a Common Table

IN TWENTIETH-CENTURY ARGENTINA

Doña Petrona, Women, & Food

Rebekah E. Pite

THE UNIVERSITY OF NORTH CAROLINA PRESS   CHAPEL HILL

This volume was published with the assistance of the Greensboro Women's Fund of the University of North Carolina Press.
Founding Contributors: Linda Arnold Carlisle, Sally Schindel Cone, Anne Faircloth, Bonnie McElveen Hunter, Linda Bullard Jennings, Janice J. Kerley (in honor of Margaret Supplee Smith), Nancy Rouzer May, and Betty Hughes Nichols.

The paper in this book meets the guidelines for permanence and durability of the Committee on Production Guidelines for Book Longevity of the Council on Library Resources. The University of North Carolina Press has been a member of the Green Press Initiative since 2003.

Library of Congress Cataloging-in-Publication Data
Pite, Rebekah E.
Creating a common table in twentieth-century Argentina : Doña Petrona, women, and food / Rebekah E. Pite. — 1 [edition].
pages cm
Includes bibliographical references and index.
ISBN 978-1-4696-0689-7 (hardback : alk. paper) —
ISBN 978-1-4696-0690-3 (pbk. : alk. paper)
1. Gandulfo, Petrona C. de. 2. Cooking, Argentine. 3. Cooking—Argentina.
4. Women—Argentina—Social conditions—20th century. 5. Feminism—Argentina—History—20th century. I. Title. II. Title: Creating a common table in 20th-century Argentina.
TX649.G36P58 2013
641.5982—dc23
2012034766

The epigraph (p. vii) is from Margaret Sayers Peden, ed., *A Woman of Genius: The Intellectual Autobiography of Sor Juana Inés de la Cruz* (Salisbury, Conn.: Lime Rock Press, 1982), and is used with permission of the publisher.

Frontispiece (p. iii): Petrona C. de Gandulfo (far right) and fellow *económas*, ca. 1930. Courtesy of Archivo General de la Nación.

cloth   17 16 15 14 13   5 4 3 2 1
paper   17 16 15 14 13   5 4 3 2 1

To my mother,

LINDALEA PITE LUDWICK,

and my grandmother,

SARA SKOLNICK PITE

And what shall I tell you, lady, of the natural secrets I have discovered while cooking? I see that an egg holds together and fries in butter or in oil, but, on the contrary, in syrup shrivels into shreds; observe that to keep sugar in a liquid state one needs only add a drop or two of water in which a quince or other bitter fruit has been soaked; observe that the yolk and the white of the egg are so dissimilar that each with sugar produces a result not obtainable with both together. I do not wish to weary you with such inconsequential matters, and make mention of them only to give you full notion of my nature, for I believe they will be occasion for laughter. But lady, as women, what wisdom may be ours if not the philosophies of the kitchen?

—SOR JUANA INÉS DE LA CRUZ, MEXICO CITY, 1690

CONTENTS

Acknowledgments, xi

INTRODUCTION Setting the Table, 3

CHAPTER ONE
The Elevation of Cooking in Turn-of-the-Century Argentina, 23

CHAPTER TWO
Creating a Public in Buenos Aires and Beyond, 55

CHAPTER THREE
Expanding Consumption and Middle-Class Domesticity, 91

CHAPTER FOUR
Professionalizing a Thriftier Homemaker, 121

CHAPTER FIVE
Shifting Priorities and Entertaining Inequalities, 151

CHAPTER SIX
Cooking in and out of the Spotlight, 183

CONCLUSION Keeping the Table Set, 219

Notes, 229
Bibliography, 279
Index, 309

ILLUSTRATIONS

Map of Argentina, 2

Petrona Carrizo on estancia in Santiago del Estero, ca. 1910, 36

Advertisement for Primitiva's gas services in the magazine *Plus Ultra*, 1928, 47

Meeting for sales division at Primitiva with salesmen and *ecónomas*, ca. 1928, 49

Petrona C. de Gandulfo conducting an early demonstration for Primitiva, ca. 1930, 51

Petrona C. de Gandulfo and fellow *ecónomas* presenting a culinary demonstration on stage, ca. 1936, 60

Audience for Primitiva demonstration in Rosario featuring Petrona C. de Gandulfo, ca. 1936, 61

Primitiva advertisement in the magazine *Revista Aconcagua*, 1931, 63

Illustration of dishes from *El libro de Doña Petrona*, 1934, 73

Petrona C. de Gandulfo on Radio El Mundo, ca. 1935, 81

Petrona C. de Gandulfo promoting meat for the Junta Nacional de Carnes, ca. 1938, 87

The Eva Perón Foundation distributing Christmas sweet bread and cider in Rosario, ca. 1950, 93

Portraits of Petrona C. de Gandulfo from *El libro de Doña Petrona*, 1934, 1935–40, 1941–47, 97

Elba A. with her copy of *El libro de Doña Petrona*, 2004, 98

Petrona C. de Gandulfo's identification card for Gas del Estado,
ca. 1946, 107

Cover of Peronist fifth-grade textbook, *The Argentine Woman at Work*,
1950, 125

Television recipe pamphlet from *Viernes Hogareños* (Fridays at Home),
1958, 144

Cover of Argentina's television guide, *Canal TV*, featuring Petrona C.
de Gandulfo, 1959, 150

Images of Petrona C. de Gandulfo and Juanita Bordoy from a
newspaper article in *Mar Tiempo*, 1983, 168

Petrona C. de Gandulfo and Juanita Bordoy on the set of *Buenas Tardes,
Mucho Gusto*, 1973, 171

Photographs of Doña Petrona and family in the magazine *Gente*,
1969, 177

World Cup Cake on the cover of *El libro de Doña Petrona*, 1979–80, 185

Petrona C. de Gandulfo and Juanita Bordoy making World Cup Cake on
television, 1978, 185

Unión Feminista Argentina Mother's Day flyer, ca. 1970, 191

Photograph of Petrona C. de Gandulfo and Juanita Bordoy at home,
1986, 216

ACKNOWLEDGMENTS

This book, like any good meal, has benefited from many busy hands and keen minds. From its inception, Sueann Caulfield helped me to craft and consistently improve the manuscript, generously reading countless drafts and providing sage advice at every turn. For over a decade now, she and Rebecca J. Scott have served as incomparable mentors, inspiring me with both their scholarship and their examples. Jeremy Adelman, Gillian Feeley-Harnick, María Cotera, and Jeffrey Pilcher have likewise been there from the beginning, helping me to sharpen my analysis and push my project in fruitful directions. So too, my fellow Latin Americanists and Women's Studies scholars at the University of Michigan (especially Sarah Arvey, Mónica Burguera, Tamar Caroll, Marie Cruz, Erika Gasser, Juan Hernandéz, Kathy López, Edward Murphy, and Tamara Walker) have provided important advice and friendship. Historians Gabrielle Hecht, Nancy Rose Hunt, and Carol Karlsen, as well as my friend Verónica Miranda, also merit special mention for their early suggestions and support.

It has been my good fortune to find a vibrant and welcoming intellectual community in Argentina as well. Paola Alonso, Mirta Lobato, and Hilda Sabato provided valuable feedback on my preliminary project in 2002, recommending that I might find a home in the Gender Institute (IIEGE) at the Universidad de Buenos Aires. The director of this institute, Dora Barrancos, warmly welcomed me into its scholarly community shortly thereafter. Ever since, she has graciously shared her advice, her experiences, and her contacts with me. Through the IIEGE, I befriended fellow historians Andrea Andújar, Valeria Pita, and Cristiana Schettini Pereira, and over the past decade we have explored numerous archives, combed book fairs, and enjoyed lively mealtime discussions together. I also had the good fortune to meet historians Paula Bontempo, Isabella Cosse, Karina Ramacciotti, and Alejandra Vassallo, with whom I have enjoyed close collaboration and friendship ever since. I am also grateful to Paula Lucía Aguilar, Marcelo Álvarez, Eduardo Archetti, Anahi Ballent, Claudio Belini, María José Billarou, Paula Caldo, Gastón Lazarri, Oscar Chamosa, Eduardo Elena, Katharine French-Fuller, Francisco Liernur, Valeria Manzano, Natalia Milanesio, José Moya, Inés Pérez, Luisa Pinotti, Ricardo Salvatore, Carlos Ulanovsky, and Oscar Traversa for sharing their work and ideas about food, home economics, consumption, and domestic work in Argentina. Fernando

Rocchi deserves special mention for his advice and for putting me in touch with the newspaper archive at *La Nación* and at the television cooking channel Utilísima. I am also grateful to my friend Carolina Brunstein for facilitating my research at *El Clarín*'s newspaper archive. For her assistance with my research, I thank Gabriela Gómez, and for their transcriptions of oral histories, I thank María José Valdez, Carolina González Velasco, and Horacio Mosquera.

To put it simply, this project would not have been possible were it not for the collaboration of Marcela Massut, the granddaughter of Doña Petrona C. de Gandulfo. In May 2002, Marcela arrived at our first interview at a café in Buenos Aires with an old suitcase filled with some of her grandmother's papers and photographs. In the ensuing years, she has generously invited me on countless occasions to her catering business and to her home to comb through her grandmother's materials. She also has shared her personal stories with me in three formal interviews and in many more informal conversations over lunch, a cup of tea, or a round of *mate*. I thank Marcela for her generosity and her permission to reproduce her grandmother's materials here. I also thank Jorge Tartarini for graciously sharing his recent high-quality scans of much of this material.

Approximately eighty other Argentines generously shared their oral histories with me. I will be forever grateful to them (the majority of whose names I have shortened to protect their privacy) for telling me their stories. Several of my early interviews were facilitated by sociologist Susana Batista. I also wish to thank Franci La Greca for inviting me to discuss food history in the oral history workshop she regularly convenes on the outskirts of Buenos Aires. In addition, I express my deep appreciation to Sergio Raimondi and the staff at the Museo del Puerto Ingeniero White for organizing a magical week filled with interviews and a debate on Doña Petrona.

My ability to write this book was also enhanced by the generosity of other archivists and friends. In particular, I wish to recognize archivists Marta Inés Orgueria at the Museo de la Ciudad, María Rosa at the Facultad de Medicina, and Gabriel Taruselli and his colleagues at the Archivo General de la Nación for their assistance. Gabriel has not only guided me in the archive, but, even more important, he and his wife, Marisa, and their son, Juan, have become like family. Similarly, Aldo, Lupe, Vicki, and Mariano Favia have made Buenos Aires feel even more like home; they have also showered me with moving research-related gifts, including Aldo's late mother's copy of *El libro de Doña Petrona* and a rare first edition of this cookbook. Additionally, Gustavo Gallo and Juan Di Benedetto at Canal 13 made it possible for me to watch Doña Petrona's extant television cooking segments, and the Asociación de Ecónomas graciously invited me to attend its cooking lessons and consult its files. The hardworking staff at the Biblioteca Nacional, Biblioteca Tournquist, Facultad de Derecho, INDEC, Instituto Juan Domingo Perón, and Museo del Cine also deserve my gratitude for their assistance with my research.

Opportunities to share my work with other scholars have likewise proved crucial to the development of this project. For inviting me to present my work at conferences or their institutions, I thank Sandra Aguilar Rodríguez, Paulina Alberto, Oscar Chamosa, Eduardo Elena, Jan Longone, Jocelyn Olcott, Valeria Pita, Jeffrey Pilcher, Cristiana Schettini Pereira, Lenny Ureña, and Tamara Walker. I also wish to express my appreciation to fellow historians of Argentina Oscar Chamosa and Valeria Manzano, for their careful reading of and suggestions on an early version of the manuscript. Likewise, I am deeply grateful to Ann Farnsworth-Alvear for her inspiring book and her insightful suggestions on mine. In addition, I thank my dear friends and colleagues Paulina Alberto, Emily Musil Church, and Tamara Walker for the time and thought they put into responding to various drafts of the manuscript, as well as for providing crucial emotional support. Further, I am fortunate that Elaine Maisner, in her capacity as senior executive editor at the University of North Carolina Press, was eager to work with me on this project. In addition to generously offering answers to my numerous queries, she secured two wonderful readers. Since both shared their names, I am able to offer my heartfelt thanks to Elizabeth Hutchinson and Christine Ehrick for the tremendous time and thought they put into their reader's reports and the numerous ways in which they helped me to improve the manuscript. So too, I extend my appreciation to Dorothea Anderson, who copyedited the manuscript with great care. At UNC Press, I also thank Dino Battista, Caitlin Bell-Butterfield, Ron Maner, Beth Lassiter, and Vicky Wells for generously sharing their time and expertise.

Of course, this book would not exist without crucial institutional support. From 2000 through 2007, the University of Michigan provided a rich learning environment and also funding to support my archival trips, conference participation, and writing. In turn, a Fulbright-Hays Doctoral Research Grant allowed me to conduct research in Argentina in 2003 and 2004, and the Fulbright staff in Argentina (especially Norma González and Laura Moraña) and fellow grantees (especially Ivonne Wallace Fuentes) helped make it a particularly rewarding experience. Since joining Lafayette College in 2007, I have also benefited from generous financial support to attend conferences, revise my manuscript, and conduct additional research in Argentina. My colleagues at Lafayette in the History Department and across campus have been extremely supportive. In particular, I thank our previous department chair, Deborah Rosen, and current chair Joshua Sanborn for being so generous with their time and advice. In addition, I extend my thanks to my multitalented colleague Paul Barclay for creating the map at the beginning of this book. I also thank my friends Carrie Rohman, Paulina Alberto, and Jesse Hoffnung-Garskof for their book-related advice, and Seo-Hyun Park for reading my manuscript. For their technical help with my illustrations and files, I thank Jason Alley, Eric Luhrs, and Kelly Smith; and for securing me many, many books through interlibrary loan, I thank Karen Haduck. For their assistance in their capacities as capable and enthusiastic undergraduate Excel scholars, I express my gratitude to Amalia Berardone and Thomas Brinkerhoff.

My final thanks go to my friends and family. To my friends, thank you for helping me to appreciate the importance of belonging to an intimate and lively community of friends, whether in Madison, Connecticut; Amherst, Massachusetts; Barcelona, Spain; Washington, D.C.; Ann Arbor, Michigan; Buenos Aires, Argentina; Easton, Pennsylvania; or somewhere in between. No words can fully express my gratitude to my mom, Lindalea Pite Ludwick. Since I was a little girl, she has modeled a love of learning, an appreciation for social justice, and an interest in Latin America that has inspired me. She has not only served as a role model but has also generously offered herself as travel companion, crucial domestic helper, and tireless reader, who has been willing to edit countless drafts of my papers (including this manuscript). My father, William J. Pite, also deserves credit for supporting my education and encouraging me to explore important questions about the world. In addition, I extend my deepest appreciation to my grandparents, Sara and Edward Pite, for their unflagging support. I am particularly grateful to my grandmother for encouraging me to write an undergraduate thesis at Amherst College. (For expertly advising this thesis, I thank Jeffrey Rubin.) My sister, Jessica Pite McNamara, and my mom also deserve credit for my interest in studying food, due to the countless meals we have enjoyed together and the ways in which making them has emphasized both the pleasure and the power dynamics that can surround food preparation. So too I offer thanks to my extended family and lifelong friends for sharing many delicious meals and the ups and downs of life and of writing this book with me.

Last, but certainly not least, I wish to thank my husband, Christopher Eckman, who will now finally have the chance to read this book! I am deeply grateful to him for enthusiastically sharing all the adventures along the way—from living in Argentina in 2003–4, to combing book fairs with me for potential sources, to planning the logistics of traveling with and caring for our children on subsequent research trips. To our children, Sofia and Elijah, thank you for your love and your laughter, and for giving me a deeper understanding of the pleasures and challenges of caring work. I hope that your lives will be filled with curiosity, good health, dear friends, and, of course, delicious food.

Creating a Common Table

IN TWENTIETH-CENTURY ARGENTINA

Argentina

SETTING THE TABLE

In 2002, a wizened bookseller in Buenos Aires pushed a copy of *El libro de Doña Petrona* into my hands. "This is the cookbook you are looking for," he explained. "It is the bible of the home." Not being sure what this meant, I purchased the book, determined to find out. After some preliminary research, I discovered that this cookbook, first published in 1934, had since enjoyed over 100 editions. People in Buenos Aires explained to me that it "was in every Argentine home." I wondered if this could possibly be true. And what might this cookbook, the claims about it, and the woman who wrote it, tell us about twentieth-century Argentina?

The Woman behind the Cookbook and a New History of Argentina

The woman who authored Argentina's most influential and revealing twentieth-century book was Petrona Carrizo de Gandulfo. Petrona Carrizo was born toward the close of the nineteenth century in the northwestern province of Santiago del Estero to a mother of Italian and indigenous heritage and a father of Spanish descent.[1] As part of an early wave of migration, this common woman moved from her province to the capital city of Buenos Aires in the late 1910s with her future husband's family. In 1928, she took a position as an *ecónoma* (corporate home economist) for the British gas company Primitiva to lead demonstrations of their new gas stoves for small neighborhood crowds in Buenos Aires.[2] By the 1930s, she had already begun to establish herself as a culinary professional in Buenos Aires and beyond. In addition to giving live cooking presentations for Primitiva in front of thousands of enthusiastic women, she began to pen her own magazine column, host a national radio program, and publish the first editions of her cookbook. With the arrival of television in Argentina in 1951, Doña Petrona became the first to cook on air, boosting her already considerable popularity to new heights. This entertaining brunette became famous for her elaborate dishes, provincial accent, matronly figure, didactic tone, and bossy treatment of her assistant, as well as her responsiveness to fans—she even gave her telephone number out on air. Doña Petrona continued to cook in the spotlight through the 1980s, cementing

3

her status as Argentina's leading domestic expert over the course of her seven-decade-long career.

During the twentieth century, many Argentines embraced Doña Petrona's approach to cooking, which emphasized the idea that the modern home-maker should follow specific recipes to make abundant and artful cosmopolitan meals. People across the country flocked to her live performances, clipped her magazine columns, tuned into her radio program, and watched her cook on television. Many wrote or called her for advice. Most dramatically, people purchased her cookbook in record numbers. First published in 1934, *El libro de Doña Petrona* became one of the three best-selling books in Argentina, along with the Bible and the 1872 epic poem *Martín Fierro* about a gaucho of the same name.[3]

So, at its simplest level, this is a story inspired by the tremendous popularity of a cookbook and the woman behind it. But this is not a biography. Due to her focus on food as well as her tremendous popularity and longevity, Doña Petrona's story allows us to consider understudied dynamics of daily life in twentieth-century Argentina and the leading role of women within them. Food mattered to all Argentines, and many dedicated a significant portion of their day to getting, cooking, and serving food. But which women (and to a lesser extent, which men) cooked and how they did so changed over time. In other words, the relationship between people and cooking—like other relationships—has a history.

For Argentines, dreams of progress and modernity, which had seemed so promising during the first half of the century, would be routinely crushed by economic and political crises that erupted during the second half of it—literally determining what and how people could afford to cook and eat. What remained fairly constant was the extent to which food purchases dominated a typical family's budget, often taking half of working-class families' monthly wages and a third of their middle-class counterparts' earnings.[4] Since the early twentieth century, corporations, government leaders, and mass media outlets in Argentina understood and capitalized on the leading role that female homemakers played in buying food and other consumer goods. During moments of expansion and crisis, public and private figures pinned their hopes on women's abilities to cook and consume effectively for their families and their nation.

As a result, turning our attention to Doña Petrona, her fans, and the literally thousands of stories surrounding them expands our understanding of the history of gender and daily life in twentieth-century Argentina. Because Doña Petrona was so talented at reshaping herself in response to changing demands, analyzing her career allows us to perceive changes and continuities in women's lives, not just at the level of discourse and imagery, but also in social practice. By using Doña Petrona as a starting point to ask broader questions about women's domestic and extradomestic experiences, we can better appreciate the central role that women played in "modernizing" Argentina as caretakers, consumers, and conveyors of new patterns of sociability. We can also appreciate the tremendous impact of the growth of the mass media and consumer culture on the gendered dynamics of daily life. As in other capitalist industrializing societies, twentieth-century leaders in Argentina promoted men's incorporation into the paid workforce and women's domesticity—defined here as home life and devotion to it. Therefore, in exploring the career of Doña Petrona, a woman who stood at the nexus of the domestic and public realms, we see women's experiences, contributions, and sense of belonging more broadly.

Culinary Celebrity

With the growth of the mass media and the publishing industry, other famous cooks and cookbook authors emerged across the globe during the nineteenth and twentieth centuries. While prior to this period male chefs had published the great majority of cookbooks for other professionals, during this era a number of women began to issue cookbooks directed to female homemakers and housekeepers. In the West, this trend began in European countries, including England and Denmark. Some books enjoyed remarkable success.[5] In England, for example, Mrs. Beeton's cookbook and domestic advice manual, *The Book of Household Management* (first published in segments from 1859 to 1861), flew off the shelves, selling around a third of a million copies by 1888. Like Doña Petrona's subsequent success, Mrs. Beeton's popularity stemmed from her ability to tap into the desire for "expert" domestic advice among the emerging middle classes in England.[6]

In Latin America, the processes of industrialization and urbanization that enabled such editorial success and culinary celebrity would come later. The first cookbooks published in Latin America came out in the mid-nineteenth century and reached small elite audiences and their cooks.[7] Many countries never had a central figure like Mrs. Beeton, and those that did were nations, like Argentina and Mexico, that had sufficient resources to support internal consumption during the early twentieth century. In Mexico, for example, Doña Velazquez de León, who founded a cooking school in Mexico City and wrote several popular cookbooks, reached the height of her popularity during the mid-twentieth century.[8] Interestingly, in contrast to Doña Petrona's (and Mrs. Beeton's) enduring fame, Mexico's most famous mid-twentieth-century cook is no longer a well-known figure there. Petrona C. de Gandulfo's uniqueness within the Americas stems from her particularly successful effort to establish and maintain herself at the top of her profession for so long. Argentine journalists called *El libro de Doña Petrona* "the best-selling book in Latin America."[9] Despite the difficulty of confirming such a claim, its very utterance speaks to the tremendous popularity that Doña Petrona enjoyed during her career, as well as the sense of Argentine greatness that surrounded her success.

Tellingly, Doña Petrona's closest counterparts can be found not in other Latin American nations but rather in the United States. At the start of the twentieth century, Argentina and the United States vied for hemispheric dominance. With rapidly expanding economies and policies aimed at stimulating immigration, both succeeded in attracting an unprecedented number of Europeans to their shores.[10] This high proportion of immigrants accounted for the lack of a clear shared culinary repertoire and contributed to the desire for extrafamilial "expert" advice. The expansion of public education and mass media made it possible for large numbers of people to follow such advice. For its part, Argentina claimed the best-educated and most-literate populace in Latin America.[11]

Yet, due in part to Argentina's more concentrated media market, Doña Petrona's success compares to not one, but all the major legends of home cooking in the United States put together. Like Fanny Farmer, who established the importance of specific measurements in her late nineteenth-century cookbook and cooking school in Boston, Doña Petrona pioneered the (less-exact) codification of Argentine home cooking.[12] Like Betty Crocker (who was not a real person but rather a U.S. marketing invention), Doña Petrona successfully promoted many early commercial products as "trustworthy."[13] Like Irma Rombauer, who wrote the top-selling 1936 cookbook, *The Joy of Cooking*, Doña Petrona's signature cookbook far outsold its competitors.[14] In turn, Julia Child (and not Rombauer) established herself as the most popular culinary celebrity in the United States, with her lively French cooking lessons on public television starting in the 1960s. And so too, like Julia Child, Doña Petrona used television to reach a broad and enthusiastic national audience, as well as to promote her other endeavors.[15]

Following in the footsteps of Julia Child and Doña Petrona, a growing number of cooks and domestic experts have sought fame and fortune in the United States and Argentina during the last few decades. Most were women, but a few men also established themselves as culinary celebrities. In the United States, first Jacques Pépin and later Emeril Lagasse made names for themselves and their cookbooks as television personalities; in

Argentina, Gato Dumas did the same.[16] Mirroring the long-standing association of men with the most profitable and respected aspects of cooking, most were "chefs" who had cut their teeth in professional kitchens. In turn, their most popular female contemporaries were not chefs but entrepreneurs, namely Martha Stewart and Rachel Ray, who parlayed their knowledge about cooking and decorating into multimedia empires—such that the most apt final comparison to Doña Petrona in the U.S. context would be to these two female icons, who have successfully branded themselves, along with their domestic advice, on television shows and in cookbooks and magazines. Many decades earlier, the pioneering Doña Petrona built a multimedia empire around her own name in Argentina. She used this name to establish herself as the most popular and commercially supported culinary figure in twentieth-century Argentina.

A History of Argentine Exceptionalism?

Doña Petrona's allure stemmed from both her engaging personality and the attractiveness of the types of food that her background enabled her to present to the Argentine public. Petrona's recipes retraced her path from the northwestern province of Santiago del Estero to the capital city of Buenos Aires. In *El libro de Doña Petrona*, she codified a version of Argentine cuisine that combined the sensibilities of provincial home cooks with indigenous and Spanish culinary roots, the influence of the cuisine brought by immigrants (most from Italy and Spain), and the self-conscious internationalism of elites in Buenos Aires, who celebrated French cuisine. In contrast to her reflection of Argentina's culinary diversity, she provided relatively few recipes for beef, despite the fact that Argentines prided themselves on having the highest level of per capita beef consumption in the world. Given the Argentine preference for simple preparations of beef with some salt for adornment, she did not seem to think that women needed a recipe to grill meat on the stovetop, nor men to grill it outdoors.[17] She preferred to steer her fans toward more elaborate preparations.

In addition to the role of the food itself, Doña Petrona's success also spoke of the saliency of her gendered performance and the ideas about domesticity she presented to the public. Because Doña Petrona's cookbook not only included recipes for pâté, pasta, paella, and empanadas but also modeled changing gendered patterns of "respectable" domestic behavior, her vision resonated with, and helped define, the sense of Argentina as a middle-class nation. Women in Argentina, who enjoyed greater access to education than did women in many other parts of Latin America, played a key role in cementing such status—primarily through their domestic roles rather than their professional ones. Capitalizing on such expectations and experiences, Doña Petrona established herself as an author and purveyor of middle-class domesticity.

This points to yet another way in which Doña Petrona can help us uncover new ways of looking at Argentine history. In Argentina and elsewhere in Latin America, the middle classes have been understudied in relation to their historical importance.[18] This oversight stems, in part, from the difficulty of locating these "middle classes." It may also be the unintended consequence of the important shift by recent generations of scholars from studying the elite to researching the lives of the poor majority. Whatever the reasons, this omission has prevented historians from fully understanding the actions, motivations, and aspirations of a group of actors central to these nations' histories in the twentieth century.

In Argentina, in particular, the role of the middle class—a great number of whom turned to Doña Petrona for domestic advice over the course of the twentieth century—is an essential and almost inescapable topic. National and foreign observers alike have repeatedly declared Argentina to have possessed the largest and most influential middle class in Latin America.[19] Nevertheless, a self-conscious middle-class identity actually emerged there only in the 1920s and 1930s, around the same time as in other South American nations.[20] In Buenos Aires, as in other cities across mid-twentieth-century Latin America, people constructed and asserted their middle-class status by referring to not only political and economic criteria but also gender-specific ideological and behavioral characteristics. The family and the home were particularly important constitutive spaces of class identity.[21] Starting during the 1930s, numerous women aspiring to "respectable" or "middle-class" status turned to Doña Petrona for domestic advice about how to "properly" cook, set the table, and serve a meal. In the process, they helped establish their families and their nation as consisting of a civilized and modern middle class.

Looking back, Argentines often recall that their country had entered the twentieth century as one of the wealthiest and most optimistic nations in the world. The rich soils of the pampas provided fertile ground for the production of beef and wheat, and exports of these products, together with early industrialization efforts, enabled the national economy to prosper during the late nineteenth and early twentieth centuries.[22] This boom lined the pockets of cattle barons and estancia owners and allowed for the emergence of a sizable urban middle sector. At the same time, it impoverished the poor majority. The Great Depression and the world wars then revealed the vulnerability of Argentina's liberal economic policies to the vagaries of global markets and politics. At the beginning of the twentieth century, well-off residents of Buenos Aires had reveled in depicting their city as the "Paris of South America," but by the century's end, they despaired of their country's increasing resemblance to the poverty-stricken nations of Paraguay and Bolivia, with whom it shares borders.

This was quite a fall for the South American nation that had often sought to present itself as better off than its Latin American neighbors. However, the decline was neither as neat nor as linear as such a comparison might at first suggest. During the early twentieth century, as Argentina began to turn away from a liberal agro-export model and as industrialization brought hopeful migrants (including Petrona) to cities, urban dwellers witnessed the uneven benefits of this modernization. Juan Perón won the presidency in 1946 by highlighting such inequalities and promising to raise working-class Argentines' standard of living. Following four years of expanding access and benefits, President Perón began to encourage more careful consumption as the post–World War II surpluses of money dried up and the economy fell into crisis. After a military coup removed him from office in 1955, new generations of leaders rolled back many of his state programs and implemented economic policies that were based on the premise that the "free market" would best resolve Argentina's economic woes. Such policies expanded the variety of goods that Argentines could purchase, but they also made Argentines' ability to consume these new items, along with old standbys, more uncertain. As in other large, industrializing, twentieth-century Latin American nations, most Argentines (including many of those who identified as "middle class") had difficult and unstable relationships with the growing economy. During the second half of the twentieth century, economic and political crises would become an unfortunate feature of daily life.

What was unique about Argentina within Latin America, therefore, was the endurance of its (and others') sense of its exceptionalism in a region plagued by economic inequalities and crises and inhabited by poor and mixed-race majorities. This book joins other recent scholarship in arguing that Argentina's white and middle-class identities were both deliberate and overlapping constructions.[23] In step with late nineteenth-century elites' whitening projects, Argentina (along with neighboring Uruguay and southern Brazil) did in fact attract a large number of European immigrants to its shores during the period from 1870 to 1930. And these largely southeastern European immigrants would come to outnumber the native-born population, changing the demographic makeup of the country, and especially its capital.[24] Nevertheless, despite the appearance of a sizable "white" population of European descent, recent scholarship has emphasized the predominance of Argentines' indigenous and African roots.[25] Such diversity also made its way to the dinner table, where Argentines sat down to meals shaped by people from all of these backgrounds.[26]

As a woman from northwestern Argentina with both European and indigenous roots who sought to make a name for herself in Buenos Aires and beyond, Petrona did not directly address her racial or ethnic identity until late in her career. However, paying attention to Petrona's changing self-presentation provides key insights into how overlapping ideas of ethnicity and race could be expressed through amorphous class and regional identities. When she arrived in Buenos Aires from Santiago del Estero, Petrona's contemporaries likely considered her to be a *criolla* (creole), a term that conjured up rural settings, oral cultures, and lower social status in the capital.[27] Unlike many from other parts of Latin America, mid-twentieth-century Argentines never widely adopted the term *mestizo/mestiza* to describe locals with mixed indigenous, European, and/or African heritage. As Oscar Chamosa explains, "There is no consensual term for 'mixed race' in Argentina, and many rural people referred to themselves as '*paisanos*.'" Indeed, contemporaries also used the term *criollo/criolla* not only to refer to those of Spanish (and, less commonly, African) heritage born in the Americas, but also to signal acculturated Argentines with mixed or indigenous ancestry.[28] However, by the 1960s and 1970s, *lo criollo* would take on a new, more implicitly mestizo valence with the emergence of a more Latin American (and less European) identity among urban, middle-class Argentines. As we shall see, in keeping with these shifts, Petrona first sought to establish her urban respectability and distance herself from the provinces by touting her European training and cuisine in Buenos Aires during the period from the 1930s to the 1950s. Then during the 1960s and 1970s, she began to tout her *cocina criolla* (creole cooking) and her provincial identity as a *santiagueña* (as a woman from Santiago del Estero was known).

Making Modern Amas de Casa

Even as twentieth-century Argentines tended not to speak directly about race, many spoke openly about their gendered expectations for women and men. Most believed that properly modern men should work outside the home for wages and that properly modern women should be *amas de casa* (loosely translated as housewives, or more accurately in this context, as homemakers).[29] This had not always been the case. During the nineteenth century, the majority of women in Argentina described themselves as "economically active" workers to census takers, in spite of their responsibilities for domestic matters as well.[30] And paid domestic work had not yet been fully feminized, as both poor women and poor men regularly worked as domestic servants.[31] However, throughout the twentieth century, around three-quarters of Argentine women consistently characterized themselves as *amas de casa* (and those with the means to do so employed paid female domestic help).[32] This sharp statistical decrease in the percentage of "working" women should not be taken at face value, as it speaks to the ways in which twentieth-century census takers in Argentina (as elsewhere in Latin America) undercounted women's ongoing economic contributions in an industrializing economy.[33] Nevertheless, this dramatic statistical drop in "economically active" women reveals an increasingly negative perception of women's remunerated work.[34] Consequently, while the census registered a growing number of women entering the workforce from the 1940s on (with the most significant increases during the 1960s), the mainstream model of domesticity continued to celebrate women's unpaid homemaking above all else until the early 1980s.

Despite the praise for and ubiquity of female homemakers, these women are largely absent from most histories. In focusing on women in their capacity as *amas de casa*, this project joins others that suggest that focusing on women's gendered experiences, rather than writing a history that puts equal weight on women and men, has important payoffs.[35] This is crucial because so many women's experiences (and, especially, their domestic experiences) remain unknown. Even as past scholarship has tended to overlook women's common domestic roles, some of it has implicitly suggested their importance. For example, histories of women's industrial labor in Argentina contrast the masculinizing taint of such work with the feminizing ideal surrounding women's housework.[36] In turn, studies of the modernization of Argentina's major commodities illuminate the male-dominated production of wheat and beef for the market but generally overlook the female-dominated consumption and preparation of these (and other) foods.[37] With the notable exception of Paula Caldo's recent book on turn-of-the-century female cooks, studies of food in Argentina have tended to confirm but not deeply analyze the major role that women have played as the primary home cooks and consumers in twentieth-century Argentina.[38]

By turning our attention to women's domestic leadership then, we gain a gendered history from a new angle. While most female-centered histories of Argentina, and indeed of Latin America, have focused on women's experiences as factory workers, political figures, or members of social movements, most women have also or exclusively worked in the home. In other words, while recent scholars have revealed women's significant presence in the supposedly male domains of politics, the factory, and social movements, they have not paid nearly as much attention to women's more common domestic roles. This is certainly true in comparing the scholarship on First Lady Eva Perón and Doña Petrona, who were arguably the two most influential women in twentieth-century Argentina. Whereas hundreds, if not thousands, of articles and books have been written about Eva Perón, Doña Petrona's attention to domestic matters as opposed to politics has largely rendered her—and the *amas de casa* to whom she directed her work—outside of history.[39]

This book illuminates the ubiquitous and understudied domestic roles that women played, echoing the gendered division of labor in twentieth-century Argentina. That is, most Argentines expected that domesticity was the purview of women, and many more women than men took responsibility for shopping, cooking, cleaning, and caregiving on a daily basis—even when these women also worked outside of the home or were paid to do this work in someone else's house. As we shall see, men also played key domestic roles as heralded providers for and beneficiaries of women's domesticity. And just as women's femininity was measured by what they could cook (or manage their paid help to cook) in the kitchen, men's masculinity was (and still is) measured by their prowess in making a proper *asado* (beef barbecue) outdoors.[40] Nevertheless, manning the *asado* largely took place on Sundays or special occasions, whereas women tended to assume responsibility for food preparation every day.

While many women surely felt this responsibility as an obligation more than a privilege, a large number of women actively sought out a culinary education with Doña Petrona. As we shall see, Doña Petrona's unprecedented popularity stemmed in large part from numerous women's interest in locating themselves within a community that valued their domestic contributions and enabled them to seek advice from an "expert." Doña Petrona was both a "self-made" woman *and* a woman made by other women who lobbied for a figure who publicly validated the importance of their own domestic roles.

Searching the Past for Women and Food

Because Petrona C. de Gandulfo, like many of her peers, focused on women's domestic roles, writing her story and other women's stories requires various kinds of historical sources to overcome the lack of traditional sources in the public archives. Homemakers, their domestic help, and food often appear at the margins, if at all, in governmental repositories. However, Petrona's prolific career production provides a useful starting point, especially as she left behind a substantial (but still far from complete) collection of cookbooks, publications, articles, photographs, personal papers, radio and television transcripts, and a few recordings.[41] Writing a history of Doña Petrona without these materials, many of which are held by her granddaughter, Marcela Massut, would be nearly impossible. For example, Doña Petrona's unpublished memoirs provide the best access to her voice and to perspective on her career. In this 102-page document, which she wrote with a biographer in the late 1980s, she shared unknown details about her life and reveled in particular accomplishments, conceding, for example, that she would "laugh when reminded that my book outsold *Martín Fierro* on the continent."[42]

As do her memoirs, Doña Petrona's quotes in the many newspaper and magazine articles written about her over the course of her career illuminate her self-conscious presentation of herself to the Argentine public. For instance, Doña Petrona was careful to point out that she never worked as a *cocinera*, or cook, for any family. In 1985, she was quoted as saying, "I never wanted to be anything other than an *ecónoma*. No one, except my friends, can say that they had Doña Petrona in their kitchen at any time."[43] How journalists responded to such statements, and the woman who made them, also reveals their changing perspectives on this national icon. First introduced to the public by a journalist as *una mujer sencilla* (a simple, unpretentious woman) in the 1930s, by the twilight of her career Doña Petrona was described as a "diva" and a figure linked with the "abundance" of the past.[44] Such a shift spoke to how far Doña Petrona had come as well as how far Argentines felt their country had declined.

Other sources enable us to consider how everyday Argentines related to Doña Petrona's example and domestic advice. For instance, Doña Petrona's printed responses to her magazine column readers during the 1930s and the 1970s demonstrate Argentine women's interest in and eventual questioning of her expertise. In 1935, for example, Carola C. de Milesi wrote to ask Petrona C. de Gandulfo about using fish tail to make jelly, to which Petrona emphatically responded, "You should not put fish tail in the quince jelly. I will send you a good recipe to prepare it."[45] As in this case, during the first half of the twentieth century, fans who turned to this *ecónoma* were instructed to replace traditional techniques (like using fish tails to thicken preparations) with "modern" recipes that might call for store-bought ingredients like gelatin. Some forty years later, readers seemed more comfortable using recipes and packaged products but expressed concern that Doña Petrona's recipes were too time consuming and costly for the current moment. For example, in September 1974, a self-described *mujer del pueblo* (common woman) wrote in: "Reading an edition of the magazine (that says it is in the service of women) I wondered, what women?" She went on to argue that "the foods of señora de Gandulfo are not for every budget."[46]

These kinds of colorful printed reactions to Doña Petrona's advice are unfortunately limited to her columns from the 1930s and 1970s. The magazines in which they are published also tend to reveal more about how people in cities lived than their rural counterparts. Mass media outlets with which Doña Petrona collaborated tended to take the experiences of relatively well-off urban women as the norm. Living and working in the capital, Doña Petrona also focused her early attentions on *porteños* (residents of Buenos Aires), many of whom were recent internal migrants like Petrona or first- or second-generation immigrants. But she also made a point of reaching out to "provincial cooks." Her radio and television programs made their way across the country, and she regularly answered letters from provincial fans in her magazine column and on television. She even took her show on the road, giving live performances in other Argentine and South American cities (especially in neighboring Montevideo, Uruguay) during the course of her career.

Despite the fact that most of the letters that Petrona C. de Gandulfo received were neither published nor preserved, the memory of Doña Petrona continues to run deep throughout much of society. Even today, a home-cooked meal is often associated with Doña Petrona ("Ay, if only Doña Petrona could see this!" someone might remark about a particularly good or bad meal). A number of people also continue to reiterate the bookseller's claim that *El libro de Doña Petrona* is "the bible of the home."[47] More than one cabdriver proudly told me about giving his wife a copy of the cookbook as a wedding gift, and several people across the country broke into an emphatic imitation of her famous command to her assistant, Juana Bordoy, on television: "¡Juanita, alcánzame la sal! [Juanita, get me the salt!]" As a result, many of the stories that follow are shaped by what Argentines at the start of the twenty-first century remember about this icon and the changing role of cooking and consumption in their own lives.

I found contemporary Argentines eager to talk about these topics. In addition to hundreds of informal conversations from 2000 to 2011, I taped formal interviews with forty-six individuals from 2002 through 2004. I also helped lead two larger oral history workshops on Doña Petrona and cooking, in which a total of forty people participated. The first was held in the middle- and working-class neighborhood of Villa Luro, on the outskirts of Buenos Aires; and the second took place in the largely working-class port city of Ingeniero White, ten hours to the south. Doña Petrona became most popular in these places at different times. Whereas *porteños* began seeking Doña Petrona out in the 1930s and especially during the 1940s and 1950s, most people living in Ingeniero White became enamored with her once she was on local television in the 1960s and 1970s. This was about not only differing access, but also technology, as many residents of this small port city did not get access to natural gas until the 1950s and to television in the 1960s and after. As in this case, people in the capital and then other major urban areas had the earliest access to the technologies that Doña Petrona used to broadcast her cooking lessons and to cook.

While I address these temporal and spatial distinctions when possible, this book narrates a history that focuses on the lives of the urban women to whom Doña Petrona directed herself and who responded in the greatest number to her call. Throughout her career, Doña Petrona's main fan base consisted of women who lived in or near cities and who were relatively well-off or upwardly striving *amas de casa*. But, as we shall see, there were others who were interested in her too. Starting in the 1920s, businessmen were particularly keen to reach new generations of female consumers and paid Petrona C. de Gandulfo to tout their products. In turn, numerous men (like the taxi drivers I spoke with) bought her cookbook for the women in their lives or, as children, listened to her on the radio or watched her on television. In addition, a number of female domestic servants across the country shared with me that they had consulted *El libro de Doña Petrona*, often at the behest of their employers, to learn how to "properly" set the table or make an unfamiliar dish.

The majority of my interviewees were older women in their seventies and eighties who had experienced the ups and downs of the mid-twentieth century alongside Doña Petrona. Some were domestic servants; a few worked outside of the home; most were self-defined *amas de casa*. But I also made a point of seeking out men as well as younger women, both of whom often had different relationships to cooking and to this star. Most of the people I interviewed were enthusiastic about Doña Petrona and therefore interested in speaking with me about her.

Several people I spoke with were not fans of Doña Petrona and pointed out the distance of her story from their own lives. In northwestern and northeastern Argentina, for example, I met a number of women of indigenous descent who had never heard of Argentina's most famous culinary expert. They told me they had learned to cook from their female friends and relatives. And in the port city of Ingeniero White, I spoke with a cook who had heard of Doña Petrona but began our conversation by stating, "Doña Petrona never mattered to me."[48] She went on to explain that she had had little time or money to follow Doña Petrona while raising her brothers and sisters during the 1970s on the typical subsistence diet of the Argentine poor—the herbal infusion *mate* and crackers. For her, and for other poor Argentines, food and cooking were not about artistry and adventure but rather about sustenance and survival.[49]

When considered in light of one another, the memories that Argentine women and men from a variety of backgrounds have shared with me illuminate their understanding of the links and disconnects between their individual experiences and the transformations of their society.[50] These stories become even more meaningful when analyzed together with the printed materials, recordings, manuscripts, government documents, and secondary sources. This is particularly the case because memories involving food seem to linger after others fade. For example, in describing the disillusionment that surrounded Juan Perón's second term as president, a couple now in their eighties recalled the "really bad" brown bread they had had to eat because all of the "good wheat" was being sent abroad.[51] Some five decades later, their memories echo in the letters that Argentines had originally written to President Juan Perón in 1951 and 1952 to decry (among other things) such food shortages.[52] However, in contrast to memories of resignation, these letters reveal the hope that many Argentines still possessed in this period, suggesting that if the Peronist government followed their advice it might be able to fix the problem and bring white bread back to Argentina.

Argentines' memories of the transformations and, as in this case, failures of their society have often been measured by the availability of certain foods—especially bread and beef. In addition, their memories of the past have been shaped by what has happened since. When Argentines sat down with me in 2002–4 to talk about Doña Petrona and home cooking in Argentina, they did so in a country in which poor people were picking through the trash to find something to eat. The drama of this setting and the nostalgia it tended to generate does not render such evidence ahistorical, but rather it allows us to ask questions about changes and continuities over time.[53] In comments about scarce bread under Perón and elaborate meals prepared with *El libro de Doña Petrona*, we can almost feel the sorrow and the hope that marked patterns of daily life in Argentina during the twentieth century.

The story I tell here traces the history of women, food, and Doña Petrona's career over time. As this is a social history that explores changes and continuities in daily life, I have adopted a chronological approach. I have not foregrounded the typical political periods that garner the most scholarly attention (that is, the 1946–55 Peronist era and the 1976–83 military dictatorship's "Dirty War"), but rather I have considered them in the midst of other social and economic trends. The chapters open with key points of inflection in Doña Petrona's trajectory, which often coincided with significant changes in the socioeconomic possibilities of other Argentines (and especially those of women). Many of these occurred around the start of a particular decade. As we shall see, Petrona began to establish herself as a culinary celebrity in Buenos Aires in the early 1930s; started working with a publisher to market her cookbook in 1941; began broadcasting a cooking program on the brand-new medium of television in 1951; joined a popular televised women's variety show in 1961; and began to publish many fewer editions of her cookbooks during the early 1970s. In turn, major socioeconomic trends such as the 1929 depression and the 1949 economic boom time reversal influenced changing patterns of consumption and domestic behavior during the early 1930s and 1950s, respectively. While such economic shocks occurred around the turn of decades, a number did not map directly onto them. History rarely proceeds so neatly. Therefore, each chapter depicts how things both changed and stayed the same over the course of decades that many twentieth-century Argentines (including my interviewees) have grouped in their heads.[54] As a result of this organizational strategy, we can appreciate the ways in which gendered dynamics of Argentines' lives were impacted and not impacted by specific political leaders, events, policies, and trends.

Because food was at the heart of Doña Petrona's success and appeal, each chapter begins with a recipe that touches on the relationships among gender, cooking, consumption, and social relations at the time. For example, I begin with *pastelitos*, or quince-filled pastries, which were the first thing that Petrona appears to have learned to cook as a child. In chapter 1, I trace her journey from reluctantly cooking *pastelitos* for her mother's boarders in early twentieth-century Santiago del Estero to proudly presenting public cooking lectures before thousands of eager women for the English gas company Primitiva in late 1920s Buenos Aires. I argue that her and other women's shift from avoiding to embracing the kitchen reflected changing gender norms and a growing appreciation for cooking in an urbanizing society.

During the ensuing decades, Petrona C. de Gandulfo would use the burgeoning mass media to position herself as a relevant and responsive national domestic expert. Chapter 2 opens in 1930, with her promotion to head *ecónoma*, and explores her growing impact across the radio airwaves, in magazines, and with the early editions of her first cookbook, *El libro de Doña Petrona*. During the 1940s, her popularity continued to expand, along with that of the radio, and her cookbook moved beyond Buenos Aires. Such personalist, mass media success preceded and foreshadowed that of Juan and Eva Perón; it also benefited from the Peronist government's expansion of the right to consume to the working class. Nevertheless, as we shall see, the Peronist era led to the consolidation rather than the repudiation of the middle-class patterns of domesticity that Doña Petrona had come to represent. Along with the economic challenges of the 1950s, *El libro de Dona Petrona* and other efforts to professionalize *amas de casa* would reach their pinnacle during this decade.

The professionalization of *amas de casa* would be followed by the professionalization of middle-class women, forcing Doña Petrona to shift her approach to remain relevant during the 1960s. She did so now on a bigger and more immediate stage—television. This medium and her on-air relationship with her assistant, Juanita Bordoy, enabled Doña Petrona to reach new heights of popularity and become the object of new types of critiques.[55] As more people began to question women's domestic roles, new debates swirled around the meanings of domestic work. During the period immediately preceding and during the 1976–83 military dictatorship, women's "traditional" roles as consumers and cooks became cause first for public critique and then for celebration.[56] As we shall see, an unintended fallout from this gruesome chapter in Argentine history included the widespread acceptance of a much less domestic model of womanhood during the rest of the 1980s, as Doña Petrona gradually withdrew from public life.

Creating a Common Table

Gendered ideals and practices played a leading role in the process of modernizing the Argentine market and forming ideas about the nation. During the late nineteenth and early twentieth centuries, the male gaucho took center stage in popular literature and the national imaginary.[57] By the mid-twentieth century, another gendered figure had emerged as the linchpin that held society together: the urban middle-class woman. Argentina's triad of best-selling books (the Bible, *Martín Fierro*, and *El libro de Doña Petrona*), then, reflect a broader trend. While the Bible's popularity speaks to Argentina's enduring Catholic heritage, and *Martín Fierro* confirms the significance of rural, native-born masculinity in the making of Argentina, the success of *El libro de Doña Petrona* reveals the prominent role that urban women played in the formation of the national imaginary during the mid-twentieth century.

The urban woman's role and ideas about what made her "modern" changed with the times. When Doña Petrona began her career, the modern woman was widely characterized as a technologically savvy urban homemaker. By the time she retired, mainstream images of the modern woman had transformed to depict her as a well-educated, middle-class professional. These shifting notions reflected the importance and changing appreciation of women's contributions to modernizing their country's economy and securing its middle-class status. They were first heralded as consumers (but not generally recognized as workers), and later they were imagined as middle-class professionals with important domestic *and* extra-domestic obligations.

By the 1980s, many agreed that the version of domesticity that Doña Petrona represented was out-of-date. Some celebrated and others lamented the fact that women no longer seemed to have the time, the resources, or even the desire to cook like Doña Petrona. Nevertheless, as the conclusion will attest, Doña Petrona remains a central referent for Argentines even today, recently inspiring a new televised cooking program and a museum exhibition in her honor. Her continued power to represent the bounty and the possibility of Argentina points to the enduring appreciation of home cooking and plentiful food there. It also highlights the significance of the *mesa familiar* (family table) in Argentina's process of forming a sense of community through shared eating practices, a phenomenon anthropologists refer to as "commensality."[58]

Most scholars have analyzed commensality as a literal sharing of food by people in the same place, mostly seated at the same table but also in other shared settings (for example, around an earthen pot or at a banquet).[59] But the history I narrate here reveals a broader conception of commensality that emerged with the growth of a mass media environment in Argentina, and likely in other "modern" nations that have widespread media access as well. That is, starting in the 1930s, commensals in Argentina were not only people who sat down together to eat but also those who imagined they shared a common cuisine and set of domestic practices with other people they did not know.

To be sure, print capitalism—in the form of Doña Petrona's cookbooks and magazine column—played a role in creating what Benedict Anderson has famously labeled an "imagined community" in Argentina. But in contrast to Anderson's vision, this sense of community did not emerge in the period leading up to independence, but rather during the course of the twentieth century. Nor was it overtly nationalistic.[60] Most significant, it was spread not solely by men and print, but also by women, radio, television, social gatherings, and a culinary celebrity.[61]

Over the course of the twentieth century, the idea of sharing food at a common table—which was at once physical and symbolic—became a poignant metaphor for national belonging in Argentina. In this book, I use the term "common table" to refer to the development of a shared repertoire of dishes and patterns of sociability that helped create a sense of national identity. In creating a common table over the course of the twentieth century, participants decided which people and which traditions might properly be deemed Argentine. As we shall see, who and what was included changed over time, while the desire to live up to the latest iteration of "modernity" remained constant for many with middle-class aspirations.

Doña Petrona did more than any other single person in Argentina to define and distribute ideas about Argentina's common table. Whether in her cookbook or on her television program, she shared specific ideas not only about what and how women should cook, but also about how they should set the table and serve family and guests. In the late 1940s, President and First Lady Juan and Eva Perón encouraged the urban working classes to join this metaphorical national table and enjoy its abundance. Yet, even during this era, people across Argentina did not share the same ability or desire to join this table—making the common table more of a myth than a reality for the poorest sectors of society. That is, even as commensalism defined group identity through inclusion, it also did so (and continues to do so) through exclusion.[62]

Therefore, the enduring twentieth-century notion that *El libro de Doña Petrona* had found its way into "every Argentine home" reveals the domestic construction of an exclusionary Argentine national identity. Those who asserted this idea constructed a national "us" composed of Argentines, who, while they could not actually sit and dine together, could all own the same cookbook and enjoy similar meals from it. Within Argentina, people who did not know about this cookbook, could not afford to purchase or cook with it, or were uninterested in doing so were left out of the national imaginary by those who imagined it in "every Argentine home." Specifically, the rural indigenous and *mestizo* poor and those who worked as domestic servants were frequently not able, invited, or imagined to take a seat at Argentina's metaphorical common table. In turn, the cookbook owners, a sizable and relatively (but not exclusively) privileged group, came to represent the nation.

Doña Petrona and her cuisine became a powerful symbol of a gender- and class-specific version of "Argentine-ness" during a period of modernization in which an imagined national unity began to supersede distinctions of region and country of origin. Her preeminence illuminates the persistence of the ideal in which upward social mobility through consumption was a goal for many Argentines. Petrona's career was born of the Argentine dream for progress through capitalist consumption—a dream that would be repeatedly challenged by chronic political and economic crises during the second half of the twentieth century. Such crises manifested themselves strongly in people's daily lives, especially when they found themselves unable to eat the same things as their social "betters" or to cook like Argentina's leading culinary icon. Nevertheless, Doña Petrona and the ideal of middle-class domesticity she had come to represent would not fade into oblivion. As we shall see, over the course of the twentieth century a great many Argentines worked to create lives filled with food, family, and friendship—a triumvirate that remains at the heart of daily life in Argentina.

CHAPTER ONE

THE ELEVATION OF COOKING IN
TURN-OF-THE-CENTURY ARGENTINA

Pastelitos de Dulce (Quince-Filled Pastries)

Place on the table, in the form of a crown, 500 grams of flour; in the middle put 100 grams of butter, one cup of water, a pinch of salt and form a dough that is neither too hard nor too soft; smooth it out and allow it to rest for a moment. Then stretch it, leaving it at the thickness of one finger, spread it with 50 grams of soft butter, sprinkle flour on it and fold it in half; spread it with butter again and fold it so that it is folded in four; stretch it with the rolling pin and cut it into very thin strips that are six centimeters wide; cut this, forming squares, put a little bit of melted quince paste, wet the borders with water, cover it with another square and form the pasteles. Fry them in warm lard at first and hot lard after, submerging them frequently with a spoon.

Prepare a syrup: Put in a pan 400 grams of refined sugar, cover it with water, add a small bar of vanilla and let it boil for a few minutes; dip the pastelitos in the syrup and dust them with sprinkles. It is necessary to allow them to come to a boil in the syrup. The quince paste has to be melted over heat.[1]

As a child, Petrona Carrizo prepared *pastelitos de dulce*. As this 1934 recipe in the first edition of her cookbook attests, there were many steps. First the cook mixed, kneaded, and smoothed the dough. Then she covered it with butter. After that she folded the dough a couple of times to give the pastry layers. Then she cut the dough into squares, at which point she dabbed some melted quince paste in between two squares and sealed the edges. The next step was to fry the *pastelitos* in a pot of increasingly hot lard. And the final steps called for making a simple syrup and then dunking the fried pastry into it and covering the *pastelitos* with sprinkles.

Despite her childhood expertise at preparing this tasty and complicated treat, Petrona did not publicly describe it as the start of her cooking career. In numerous interviews with the media, she proudly mentioned that she began her culinary career in the late 1920s as an *ecónoma* (corporate home economist) for the English gas company La Compañía Primitiva de Gas and trained as a student at the French culinary institute Le Cordon Bleu around the same time. In turn, she seemed to revel in declaring that she never learned to cook as a child or young woman. Describing her reluctance to enter the kitchen, she remarked, "My mother owned the best boarding-house [*pensión*] in Santiago del Estero and she called me [into the kitchen] many times to watch how she cooked, but I didn't pay attention; it was not interesting to me."[2] She repeatedly told reporters, "Not even a lasso could get me into the kitchen."[3]

Notwithstanding her public disavowal, Petrona did enter the kitchen, according to her niece, Olga, and her unpublished memoirs. Apparently Petrona's mother cajoled her daughter into making *pastelitos*. Petrona's quince-filled pastries "opened up like a flower," Olga recalled, "even though she did not like to make them and cried when forced to do so."[4] Her expertise at making these complicated and tasty *criollo* treats replicated the experience of many generations of women across Argentina, especially in the northwestern provinces, where they were (and still are) a popular treat.[5] This familiarity is evident in Petrona C. de Gandulfo's recipe—the cook must know how to make pastry dough that is "neither too hard nor too soft." At the same time, she suggested that even experienced cooks would benefit from more precise, modern measurements in specifying, for example, the exact number of centimeters for each strip of dough.

What can we learn from this story about a girl who did not like to cook and ended up pursuing a cooking career? And why was she so eager to avoid the kitchen in the first place? As we shall see, Petrona's journey from despairingly making *pastelitos* in Santiago del Estero to proudly leading cooking classes for Primitiva in Buenos Aires is a story that speaks to more than one woman's personal history. Indeed, it is a story that, when taken together with others, reveals the constraints and opportunities that women in Buenos Aires navigated with a gendered modernization of the economy that celebrated men's paid extradomestic work and women's unpaid domestic roles. During the late nineteenth and early twentieth centuries, Argentina's booming liberal economy lined the pockets of wealthy families while further impoverishing the poor majority. At the same time, it also enabled a much smaller number of urban dwellers to carve out a new respectable middling status and a belief in progress. Most families earned this respectability through men's white-collar work and women's homemaking. But it was an open question which aspect of homemaking respectable women should focus on. As we shall see, marketers, mass media outlets, home economists, and many women gravitated toward the culinary arts. In so doing, they elevated the status of cooking from something associated with servants and poor women at the turn of the century to an endeavor worthy of "respectable" women's attention by the 1920s.

Santiago del Estero

Little is known about most ordinary people's lives in turn-of-the-century Santiago del Estero.[6] While her subsequent fame shed light on her provincial origins, Petrona's early life is no exception. In the late 1980s, Petrona C. de Gandulfo enlisted the help of a writer, Oscar Alberto Cejas, to compose a history of her life, which, among other things, provided a narrative about her childhood. However, she never published this document. According to Marcela Massut, her grandmother did not like the way in which it portrayed her as being very provincial and unrefined, or as she apparently put it, *del campo* (from the countryside).[7] This dissatisfaction is telling, as throughout her career she would seek to craft a public image that was decidedly more urbane and cosmopolitan than country bumpkin. However, as a migrant from the provinces (even one from her province's capital city), that was not always an easy task. As Buenos Aires asserted its dominance and superiority over the rest of the nation, *porteños* tended to dub common people from the "interior" as inferior and even "barbaric." Most famously, during the mid-nineteenth century, writer (and future president) Domingo F. Sarmiento lastingly divided Argentina into the "civilized" city and the "barbaric" interior.[8]

Petrona Carrizo was born on the outskirts of the provincial capital of Santiago del Estero during the last decade of the nineteenth century. She claimed her birth year to be 1898, although it was probably a little earlier, in 1896 or even as early as 1890.[9] Named Petrona after San Pedro, the saint who shared her birthday, she was the sixth of seven children (five girls and two boys). She spent her early childhood on a *quinta* (small rural estate), which she described in her memoirs as "spacious and comfortable," with various rooms and a patio surrounded by fruit trees.[10] In contrast, the vast majority of *santiagueños* lived in humble one-room dwellings that dotted the dry scrubland of this province.[11] These modest dwellings and their inhabitants shaped the predominant view within Argentina of Santiago del Estero as being particularly rural and poor.

Petrona's parents played a large role in securing what she later described as a "comfortable" home.[12] Her mother, Clementina Ramasco, oversaw the household and raised her children with the help of a wet nurse. According to

Petrona, her mother's father came from Piedmont, Italy, and her maternal grandmother was native to the province. As such, Clementina represented one of the contemporary uses of the term *criolla* in Argentina (*mestiza* in most other parts of Latin America) due to her combination of indigenous and European ancestry.[13] While Petrona never met her mother's parents, she described frequent visits from her maternal great-grandfather with his "unmistakably indigenous features," who would arrive on horseback from the hills of Serra de Guasayán bearing sacks filled with dried cobs of corn.[14] In turn, Petrona's father, Manuel Carrizo, died when she was just six years old, leaving her with only a vague memory of a "tall, good looking Basque man who, according to what was said, was a tireless traveler."[15] Perhaps, if the *quinta* was as "comfortable" as Petrona's memoirs suggested, he worked as a relatively successful traveling merchant. Still, it is unclear that Petrona's mother and father were actually married.[16] If this was the case, characterizing her father as a traveler might have been part of an effort to preserve a greater veneer of respectability for the Carrizo family.

In any case, the Carrizos were not among the poorest *santiagueño* families. This was a family that did not have to put their children to work (at least for the time being) and sent their children to public schools, something that just under half the population in this province was able to do.[17] Petrona described herself as not being that interested in school when she attended the primary school of Zorilla de Santiago. Still, there were some bright moments. In her memoirs, she proudly recalled a paper she wrote based on a romanticized provincial history entitled *Madre de ciudades* (Mother of Cities), the nickname her provincial capital claimed as the oldest continuously populated city in (what would become) Argentina. Some eight decades later, she remembered her description of how "the small farms and homes kept popping up, of the magnificent countryside offered by the plains, and of vegetation that members of the expedition had not seen the likes of before." She also recalled her teacher's public praise for her decision to end this paper with a popular Quechua sign-off, "Allita Chayay, Heraccochi."[18] As this anecdote suggests, Petrona grew up surrounded by provincial patriotism in a place where Quechua, the language of many indigenous Andeans, was commonplace and where, at the same time, the European "founding fathers" were celebrated as heroes in public schools.[19] In addition, her strong memory of this paper shows her precociousness as well as her interest in underscoring her (provincial) urbanity.

Despite the initiative Petrona showed on this paper, when her mother encouraged her to become a teacher she was not interested. She later explained in her memoirs, "I thought teachers' destinies were to remain permanently single, and since the tenderest age, I dreamed of getting married."[20] Whether or not Petrona actually felt this way at the time, marriage promised women a measure of respectability, especially in the provinces, where common law unions predominated among all but the top echelons of society.[21]

Like other girls educated in Argentine public schools during the first decade of the twentieth century, Petrona had been encouraged to prepare herself for domestic life. Whereas late nineteenth-century politicians and home economists had focused their attentions on educating elite women about home economics, by the early twentieth century, state officials along with bourgeois women had begun to target poorer women and girls in Argentina through less-expensive publications and public education.[22] In 1884, Argentine politicians mandated that girls learn home economics and related skills like sewing and knitting in public school. As a corollary, boys were at first required to learn basic military and agrarian skills and later, by 1907, manual labor.[23] This was part of a larger effort to address gendered tensions about men's and women's proper roles in a modernizing nation in which both sexes were entering the growing industrial workforce in significant numbers.[24] Boys were encouraged to develop skills for extradomestic work that would financially support their families, while girls were taught to become well-informed *amas de casa* (homemakers) who would buttress their husbands' wage labor with their own unpaid industriousness at home. Male politicians sought to encourage this gendered division of labor not only by passing a gender-specific curriculum but also by making women's workday two hours shorter than men's eight-hour limit in 1907.[25]

The Argentine government also sought to standardize and assume greater control over the home economics curriculum around this time— seeking to definitively replace religious orders and charitable societies, which continued to dominate domestic training.[26] Well-educated Argentine women often took a leading role in these early initiatives, sometimes linking their efforts with other campaigns to improve women's legal status, like their counterparts in the United States.[27] In 1902, Cecilia Grierson, an influential feminist and the first certified female doctor in Argentina, established the Escuela Técnica del Hogar (Technical Domestic School) in Buenos Aires.[28] In the following years, a handful of other professional home economics programs linked to public universities appeared.[29] Still, the state focused most of its efforts on younger girls in public schools. Clotilde Guillen, in her capacity as the first official inspector of home economics, played a significant role. After a 1904–5 research trip to Europe, Guillen returned to Argentina advocating a familial, as opposed to an individualist, approach to home economics in which students worked together to complete a domestic task.[30] In addition, she focused on establishing kitchens and cooking courses in schools, as well as expanding the instruction on cleaning, ironing, and puericulture (or infant care), for both girls and their teachers, especially in working-class communities.[31] Guillen and other home economists saw girls' education for these tasks as critical. A 1905 home economics textbook explained that home economics was "indispensable in forming mothers who directly influenced the education of citizens."[32] In this updated iteration of republican motherhood, a broader group of women were now deemed responsible for educating their male relatives for citizenship.

The rationale for women's domestic training stemmed not only from moral and political imperatives but also from health-related beliefs. Experts sought to teach girls and women proper domestic hygiene to keep their families healthy and, as Diego Armus has shown, to stymie the spread of diseases like tuberculosis.[33] In step with other hygienic thinkers, male educator Angel Bassi characterized public schools as ideal places to further young girls' scientific "preparation for the home." In 1914, he published a new text directed to public school teachers on what he labeled *ciencia doméstica* (domestic science). He drew on his role in teaching this material at the Universidad de la Plata, as well as from the expertise of his wife, Emilia Durione y Sesia.[34] With a "soft" version of eugenics in vogue, Bassi argued that changing behavior (for example, how people cooked and ate) would improve the vitality of the population.[35] Therefore, he recommended that girls learn to cook with a focus on hygiene and nutrition rather than on taste and tradition. During this time, scientific experts like Bassi argued that women's responsibility for maintaining their families' well-being was "natural" and long-standing, but, at the same time, undermined this claim by insisting that women needed to be trained to fulfill the responsibility properly.

Home economics education proved to be simultaneously empowering and constraining for girls. On the positive side, it emphasized women's power over their homes and families and justified more thorough and extensive education for women across Argentina, as Marcela Nari has demonstrated.[36] At the same time, by focusing women's educations on domestic science, educators restricted to the home the space in which it was socially acceptable for women to exercise power, providing a scientific rationale for men's and women's inequality.[37] The very teaching of home economics also denigrated the basis of traditional female knowledge, which had been passed down orally for generations, as being insufficient and out-of-date.

Like that of other young girls in public schools across Argentina during the first decades of the twentieth century, Petrona's public education should have included the study of home economics.[38] While we do not know exactly how she felt about it, her negative reactions to her mother's entreaties to cook suggest her lack of interest. She later explained that when her mother tried to lure her into the kitchen by explaining "that men were attracted to women who knew how to cook," she retorted that "when I get married I am going to have a cook."[39] As she would in her subsequent career, Petrona sought to emulate elite women who had other poorer women cooking for them, rather than those who cooked for others or even for their own families.

Petrona was not alone in her reticence to cook, or in her association of cooking with low status and servitude. For example, in 1907, Dr. J. B. Zubiar, an Argentine physician and member of the National School Council, decried the fact that girls in public schools were less than enthusiastic about the home economics curriculum because they considered this subject to be dishonoring.[40] In turn, he lamented the fact that boys sought to avoid woodworking class, "with the general idea among them that such work is lacking in personal dignity and social status."[41] Like the boys, the girls Zubiar wrote about seemed to believe that learning how to cook, clean, and sew at school would prepare them for a life of servitude rather than one of respectability. Such ideas were shaped by their local experiences as well as by the idealized images of elite, "nonworking," white women in their textbooks, as well as in other books and magazines that began to be more widely read during this time.[42] They were also echoed in the private school curriculum, which until 1920 taught elite girls how to manage service personnel rather than how to cook and clean.[43] This educational distinction highlights the class-specific versions of domesticity that circulated in early twentieth-century Argentina. While elite girls were expected to learn how to manage domestic servants, the rest were expected to know how to serve their families or their better-off counterparts.

This distinction was informed by the history of domestic work in Argentina. Since the colonial era, elite women had managed other poorer women and men (often slaves or dependents), who did domestic tasks for little or no money.[44] Even with the shift toward more consistently paid domestic servants by the late nineteenth century, the low wages and subservient positions marked these workers as socially inferior. In an early twentieth-century society in which the majority of women were now considered *amas de casa*, elite women's lives differed from those of other women primarily because they did not have to do the domestic "dirty work." While cleaning was (and still is) by necessity a messy undertaking, during this era cooking was as well, due to the smoke, heat, and residue of cooking using coal or firewood. As a result, kitchens were often found in the back or basement of urban homes or outside in rural areas—neither of which fit with the idealized interior spaces reserved for the female elite—making this a space that Petrona and other girls seeking "respectability" wished to avoid.

Writing It Down: Early Elite Cookbooks

While turn-of-the-century girls were interested in distancing themselves from the ranks of servitude, cooking could still inspire appreciation and even respectability in the proper context. Elite women testified to their own interest in cooking and other domestic arts by taking the time to write down their recipes. For example, on my 2003 visit to her *criollo* restaurant, La Cupertina, Cecilia Hermann showed me her collection of handwritten recipe books from her female forebears from the mid-nineteenth century through the mid-twentieth.[45] As members of an elite family residing in the northwestern provinces of Tucumán and later Córdoba, Cecilia's maternal relatives acted as domestic managers responsible for overseeing staffs of at least four domestic servants. They composed their own handwritten manuscripts and used them to instruct their servants on the proper ways to cook and do housework. Their manuscripts suggest the wide variety of topics on which they had expertise, including cooking, hygiene, and household accounting. Cecilia explained, "They combined in these domestic books everything that was important for women [to know]."[46] It is telling that such essential female knowledge foregrounded cooking and health-related information that would literally sustain the family, as well as the economic know-how to manage the family budget.

A much smaller number of authors than represented by these elite women and their handwritten domestic books published cookbooks in Argentina around the turn of the century. Most cookbooks in circulation in Argentina prior to and even during this time came from Europe and were written by male chefs for a professional audience of other chefs and male or female cooks working in elite homes. In 1887, Francisco Figueredo, who had himself cooked for elite families in Buenos Aires and other South American cities, used his experience to release the first cookbook published in Argentina, *La cocina y la pastelería de América* (American Cooking and Pastry). He later explained that "no one had thought of doing it, not here [Buenos Aires], nor in Montevideo, Chile, or Brazil."[47]

A few years later, two elite women authored their own cookbooks, but, in contrast to those of male chefs like Figueredo, their efforts were socially risky undertakings. In 1890, writer Juana Manuela Gorriti published a compilation of recipes entitled *Cocina ecléctica* (Eclectic Cuisine). Gorriti was nearing the end of her career as a renowned writer, and she used her literary influence to publish this compilation of recipes from friends and acquaintances—175 women and one man, the majority of whom came from Argentina, Peru, and Bolivia, signed their recipes.[48] The geographic diversity of this cookbook reflected Gorriti's own life story. Born into an elite political family in the northwestern Argentine province of Salta, Gorriti spent much of her life exiled in Bolivia and Peru. Her decision to publish this cookbook was what two literary scholars have aptly labeled a "dangerous act," because she was stepping out of her prescribed role. As a woman, she was entering (yet again) the male world of publishing, and by focusing on cooking she was entering into the "dirty" work of the kitchen, a social role beneath her.[49] This compilation of recipes suggests that these risks were worth taking to Gorriti and her elite friends, in order to publicly honor the meals they had cooked, or at least shared, during their lives.

Around the turn of the century, two more elite women authored cookbooks, but in contrast to Gorriti, both chose to hide their identities. Publishing her cookbook the same year as Gorriti, Susana Torres de Castex published her 1890 cookbook, *La perfecta cocinera argentina* (The Perfect Argentine Cook) under the pseudonym Teófila Benavento. A member of *porteño* high society who regularly traveled to Europe, Castex's choice to use a common alter ego and to refer to the perfect female cook in the title reflected her desire to educate but also to distance herself from those women who worked as *cocineras* for other families.[50] This trend would repeat itself over a decade later with the 1914 publication of *La cocinera criolla* (The Creole Cook) by "Marta." The author, Mercedes Cullen de Aldao, was an elite woman who laid claim to two of "the most exalted last names" in the province of Santa Fe.[51] Like Susana Torres de Castex, Mercedes Cullen de Aldao hid her upper-class identity and instead conjured up an image of an everyday *cocinera criolla*, simply named "Marta."

While it is interesting to note that two of the four early cookbook authors in Argentina were from the provinces, all of these cookbooks were primarily available in the capital, where they were printed and sold. As a result, cookbooks (like other books) were easier to find in Buenos Aires than in the countryside. But that did not mean that there were no cookbooks in the provinces. In 1920, a congregation of nuns published *El arte de cocinar* (The Art of Cooking) in the province of Tucumán, and the book became quite popular there.[52] Further, both before and after this publication, elite provincial families, many of whom regularly traveled to Buenos Aires and Europe for business and leisure, owned, and expected their cooks to use, cookbooks published abroad or in the capital.[53]

Nevertheless, the great majority of early twentieth-century Argentines never possessed a cookbook. This was certainly the case in Petrona's community. In her memoirs, she recalls two older neighbors, Mamita Cleme and Mamita Avila, who would prepare delicious *tortillas del campo* made with flour, lard, salt, and water and cooked over a *parrilla* (open-air grill)— a recipe they knew by heart.[54] In her own home, Petrona recalled how she first learned to make the recipe for *pastelitos* (which began this chapter). Her mother sat her down on a bench in the kitchen in front of a *brasero* (small stove) to teach her to make *pastelitos*. Petrona recalled what happened when it was time to fry them: "Totally ignorant, I was all of ten years, I went outside of the orthodox methods, and submerged them too long."[55] This mistake actually proved fortuitous and was the reason Petrona's *pastelitos* had "opened up like a flower." Like many cooks before her, Petrona had inadvertently changed a recipe she had learned from watching someone else, and in that way she had made it her own.

The Provincial Capital and the Estancia

Just one year after this cooking experiment, Petrona's widowed mother moved her seven children into the provincial capital of Santiago del Estero. While late nineteenth-century visitors from other cities had decried this small city's muddy streets, clay homes, and lack of "modern" amenities, in her memoirs Petrona marveled at the "wide, tree-lined streets."[56] Indeed, the liberal era in Argentina that began in the 1870s ushered in a period of modernization for this provincial city of around 20,000 people.[57] After the train tracks crossing the province were completed in 1876, rail lines brought new technologies and goods from Buenos Aires and beyond. Under Governor Absalón Rojas (1886–89), the city of Santiago gained square blocks, planned streets, and electric lights.[58] In 1889, an enthusiastic Italian visitor championed the speed and extent of this "progress," celebrating the new market, buzzing commercial center, and renovated homes filled with products from Europe and the capital. He emphasized his particular appreciation for the renovated kitchens, which, in his view, "reveal[ed] a step forward in the manner of eating." Citing writer Brillat-Savarin's famous aphorism, "Tell me what you eat and I will tell you what you are," he argued that this new manner of cooking and eating embodied "true progress."[59]

While he did not specify what such elites were eating, it was likely French fare, or at least *criollo* dishes dressed up with French names and served at elegant, well-set tables.[60]

But such "progress" was far from universal. While a small number of elites could update their homes and their culinary habits, the great majority of *santiagueños* were at or just above the level of subsistence. Among those living in the capital, most would have been unable to construct a new kitchen or to cook with imported foods. This trend was even more pronounced in rural areas, where common women cooked outside over a *fogón*, a semiprotected fire pit—a practice that continues even today in the poorest areas. On a daily basis since the colonial era, provincial women prepared bread and filling one-pot soups or stews made with hominy, squash, and meat spiked with *ají* (hot pepper). For big occasions, like weddings, people in the northwest often celebrated with spicy beef empanadas.[61] During the late nineteenth century, as the numbers of immigrants and imports from Europe grew steadily, Italian foods like noodles eventually found their way into many a commoner's soup pot across the country. And while elite families sat down to a well-set table with several courses and the flatware to match, as late as 1943 folklorist Orestes di Lullo noted that even when the rural poor had a table, they usually used it to prepare food (kneading dough, cutting meat, or making cheese) rather than to eat.[62]

In addition to growing social distances around the table, the wealthy minority exploited the work of the growing rural poor. During this era, an increasing number of *santiagueños* would work in their province to fell trees that would be exported en masse via the new train tracks, severely damaging the topography of the province. Others would provide their seasonal labor to wealthy provincial figures, especially the sugar barons in the neighboring province of Tucumán.[63] In turn, some would harvest alfalfa to feed mules and horses across the country, and a number would work on estancias that would ship the best beef to wealthier consumers elsewhere.[64] Those outside of the growing liberal export economy continued to raise corn or wheat for their own consumption.[65] While poor women and children worked in all of these endeavors, many dedicated long days to gathering firewood and food as well as cooking and caring for their families and, if they had them, some sheep.[66]

Petrona's mother was fortunate to find another way to provide for herself and her family. In an entrepreneurial move that addressed the lack of lodging or eating establishments in the provincial capital, Clementina Ramasco set up a *pensión* in the center of the city.[67] As a woman with seven children (most of whom were adolescent girls), this undertaking represented one of the few ways she could support her family and keep them together. The most likely alternatives would have been domestic service, which would have paid too little, or marriage, a difficult proposition with so many children. Petrona would later say of her mother: "She was good looking, decidedly young when she was widowed but as a spirited woman she knew how to confront this situation."[68]

Clementina Ramasco put herself and her children to work doing domestic work for profit. Ramasco and her children served a largely male clientele that passed through or lived in the capital of Santiago del Estero and needed a place to stay or wanted home-cooked food to eat. Her grandson (Petrona's nephew, affectionately known as "Goyo") explained, "I know that my grandmother was kind of demanding and all of the girls helped out. One washed, another ironed, another cleaned the house, and the other helped to cook."[69] Petrona was not the cook; that job fell to her older sister, Carolina.[70] In turn, Petrona and her younger brother, Gregorio (also known as "Goyo," like his son), delivered foods, including empanadas and *pastelitos*, to the *pensión*'s customers.[71] And despite their work at the boardinghouse, all of the children would continue to go to school.

Despite her apparent reticence to become a teacher, Petrona attended the Colegio Normal Manuel Belgrano, a prestigious local public school that trained female teachers.[72] Just as this fifteen-year-old was finishing her second year of high school, one of the *pensión*'s most loyal clients would come to play a pivotal role in the unfolding of her life story. A local army lieutenant who regularly ate lunch at the *pensión* asked for her hand in marriage.[73] Her mother was enthusiastic about this match with an army lieutenant, a position that enjoyed a great deal of social status in Santiago del Estero. But Petrona felt otherwise. Two months before their scheduled nuptials, she boldly wrote another one of her "courters" and asked if she could escape with him to avoid the wedding. He apparently accepted, and the two took an overnight train to his family's ranch, leaving behind a scandal in Petrona's hometown.[74]

In her memoirs, Petrona pointed out that when she and her companion disembarked from the train, there was no other option but to present her as "wife and mistress of the establishment [*patrona*]."[75] (Of course, there were other options—she could have been presented as a girlfriend or a domestic servant, neither of which would have appealed to the status-conscious Petrona.) But, according to her memoirs, Petrona Carrizo and Leandro Antonio Taboada lived as common law husband and wife, as did many in the provinces. Still, marriage was expected among elites, and the Taboada family represented the elite family par excellence in Santiago del Estero.

During the mid- to late nineteenth century, three Taboada brothers had controlled the province and received national attention for their exploits: General Antonio Taboada for his military might, Manuel Taboada for his 1851–71 governorship of Santiago del Estero, and Gaspar Taboada for his ranching fortune.[76] For her part, the fifteen-year-old Petrona had felt brazen enough to approach this "twenty-something with powerful and very old roots" because she had heard about the presumed "illegitimacy" of his parents' marriage.[77] Apparently, because Leandro's parents were known to have strayed from elite norms of propriety, she figured their son might be willing to do the same.

At the estancia, Leandro and Petrona's division of labor also diverged from elite gender conventions. During Leandro's frequent trips to Buenos Aires, Petrona would help manage this large 15,000-hectare ranch with some 5,000 head of cattle. She rode horses, tended sick animals, and carried firearms, as we can see in a photograph she sent to her mother, apparently after they reconciled. Looking defiantly at the camera, she wears boots and a coat with a long skirt that was both suitable for rural work and a marker of her femininity. Her hands finger a pistol and a shotgun, and her relaxed pose suggests her confidence in this role. Looking back, she explained in her memoirs that she was more than up for the challenges that working on the ranch posed: "I was as capable as suitable and willing."[78] In other words, Argentina's future culinary superstar spent her time at the estancia outdoors rather than in the kitchen.

Like most estancias, the Taboada ranch must have enjoyed the services of a paid domestic staff. While Petrona never addressed this directly, she did mention in her memoirs that, a couple of years into her stay there, Leandro arrived with a young woman and her baby, "to keep her company." Such an act seems unusual, unless this woman and eventually her daughter were brought to do the housework, or unless Leandro had fathered the child. However, the mother became ill and died, leaving her daughter, Beatriz, behind. Petrona explained in her memoirs: "The little one stayed under our charge, we raised her [*la criamos*] as if she were ours."[79] Like her assistant, Juanita Bordoy, Beatriz would come to play an enduring role in Petrona's family as a domestic helper and as a daughter-like figure who would eventually follow her to Buenos Aires.[80]

Petrona seemed eager to avoid domestic work herself, but as a wife eager to please her husband she also began to show the glimmers of a new appreciation for cooking. "Jealous" of her husband's appreciation for their friend Juanita's *panqueques* (crepes), Petrona asked for the recipe. She later explained, "A little while after that I wanted to surprise my husband

Petrona Carrizo on estancia in Santiago del Estero, ca. 1910.
Courtesy of Marcela Massut.

and I decided to make them myself." But as with the *pastelitos*, Petrona inadvertently changed the recipe, adding too much butter to the pan. As a result, she ended up frying up *tortitas* (little cakes). In a sign of what was to come, when Leandro entered and asked if she had made *panqueques*, she responded, "No; they're *tortitas* that I know how to make." In her memoirs, she would refer to these *tortitas* as "the first recipe of her life."[81]

Petrona's success with this recipe would not lead her to focus on cooking, especially as she was eager to convey the status of a *patrona* rather than a *cocinera*. As a common law wife without a powerful last name (she was not "de Taboada" after all), whether Petrona could legitimately claim and maintain this status was an open question. Like other elite men, Taboada was apparently unwilling to "marry down" and to confer Petrona with the marital status so central to defining a woman's honor. At the same time, since Taboada lived with her as a common law wife, he presumably took her virginity, compromising her desirability as a marital partner for the future.[82]

There is little remaining information other than her memoirs about her time on the Taboada estancia, but in this document she hinted that her common law husband's frequent absences were cause for concern about their relationship. On one particular occasion when she thought he had stayed too long in Buenos Aires, she went to visit him, selling two cows to pay her train fare. The trip there provided her a new perspective on the long, dry zone of quebracho and carob trees that made up most of her province. In contrast, in Buenos Aires there was so much to see, and most of it was man-made. After her husband got over his initial shock of seeing her there, he took her to visit "stores, boutiques, theaters, clubs, etc. etc."[83] But after a few weeks, he told her she must go back to the ranch. She recalled the epiphany she had on her train ride back, "that I was really a woman who took on and took charge of business matters."[84] Perhaps without this experience she would never have had the vision or the confidence to promote her future career.

But Petrona's career as an *ecónoma* was still more than a decade away, and in the immediate aftermath of this trip to Buenos Aires, her interest in living and working on the estancia apparently waned. As she later explained, "In the end, the tiredness, the exhaustion, and the monotony of an existence without alternatives, led my husband to contract the services of a ranch manager" to take up her work.[85] The new manager was Oscar Gandulfo, who arrived with his mother and sister. A year later, when Leandro accompanied his sister to Milan to train as a singer, Petrona fell for Oscar and confessed her love to him. The feeling was apparently mutual, and they traveled together to Buenos Aires with his mother and sister. Once there, Petrona sent Leandro a long message explaining what had happened and renouncing the allowance he had periodically sent her.[86] Like other chapters in her provincial life, Petrona never publicly discussed her common law marriage or her subsequent separation from Leandro Antonio Taboada. She also never publicly spoke of her time on his ranch. In fact, establishing herself as a respectable woman in early twentieth-century Buenos Aires would require an entirely different set of experiences. And, despite her initial willingness to buck tradition in Santiago del Estero, she (like many other famous female contemporaries) would promote women's domestic roles above all others once she found her place in the spotlight.

Making It in Buenos Aires

Petrona Carrizo moved to Buenos Aires around 1916.[87] She was part of a larger trend of migration, in which rural Argentines began to move to urban areas, and especially to the capital city.[88] During the first twenty years of Petrona's life, the capital's population had almost doubled, from 1.5 million people in 1895 to nearly 3 million by 1914.[89] But, as opposed to Petrona's experience and the subsequent internal migration that fed this and other Latin American cities, immigrants from Italy, Spain, and Eastern Europe provided the great majority of population growth in turn-of-the-century Buenos Aires. Some two-thirds of the city's residents in 1895 had been born abroad, and foreigners continued to make up around half of the largely young and predominantly male population when Petrona arrived.[90] During the early decades of the twentieth century, Buenos Aires earned the reputation of a new urban "Babel," where people in the streets spoke a multitude of languages.

Petrona's first few years in Buenos Aires coincided with the economic challenges brought on by World War I, including high inflation, unemployment, and declining real wages. The city was full of tension and filled with strikes. State officials used police power to quell workers' protests, most dramatically in the "Tragic Week" of 1919, which left protestors dead in the streets. During this era, domestic critics of Argentina's philosophy of economic liberalism began to champion a turn toward nationalism and industrialization as the paths toward greater economic independence. Contemporaries directed their macroeconomic suggestions about the benefits of building national industries toward the male decision makers in Argentina. At the same time, they stepped up their campaigns to convince Argentine women that it was their duty to economize in their own homes for their families and their country.

Female philanthropists and home economists frequently took the lead, focusing their efforts on poor women, based on the belief that through them they could influence their entire communities.[91] During the 1920s, female members of the right-wing Liga Patriótica (Patriotic League) set up over fifty factory schools for female workers to teach them domestic and vocational skills, along with a strong sense of nationalism.[92] A few years earlier, public home economist María Luisa Mégy had explained that "widespread progress has made life much more complicated and demands greater aptitudes and an improved intellectual culture from women." She continued, "We well know that there are entire neighborhoods of this city [Buenos Aires] where things at home are going pretty badly due to idleness, sometimes, but in many other cases due to ignorance."[93] Like their bourgeois predecessors in the puericulture and hygienic movements, Mégy, members of the Liga Patriótica, and their peers criticized poor women's failings but failed to recognize how economic challenges contributed to them.[94]

In contrast to Mégy's sense of the "idleness" and "ignorance" of certain poor neighborhoods, most people in Buenos Aires were working hard to better their lot in life. Many had come to Argentina's capital for this very reason. The political and economic climate had begun to open up with the passage of universal suffrage for men in 1912, the election of the first nonaristocratic president, Hipólito Yrigoyen, some four years later, and the expansion of the bureaucracy and the service sector. Consequently, a number of people who secured nonmanual jobs began to seek to distinguish themselves from their poorer counterparts. Such folks would not yet label themselves as "middle class,"[95] but a growing number sought to establish themselves as "respectable" citizens with more similarities to the traditional elite, the *gente bien*, than with their poorer counterparts. Some had an easier time than others, as people tended to find their place on the new social hierarchy based on their wealth, job, and education, as well as by their skin color, place of origin, manners, and overall "culture."[96] In other words, the parameters for respectability were partly based on economic criteria and partly on physical and social attributes. As we shall see, women's proper exercise of their roles as mothers and homemakers would come to play a larger and larger role in determining whether families could claim respectability.[97]

As with the linguistic "Babel," the culinary "Babel" of early twentieth-century Buenos Aires reflected the broad ethnic diversity and class consciousness of the local population. There was no clear shared repertoire of dishes, no "common table," for those who lived in and around the capital. Immigrants from Italy, Spain, and Eastern Europe brought their regional foodways with them to Buenos Aires. Italians, most from southern Italy, brought pasta, polenta, and pizza, as well as a tendency to eat more vegetables than meat. Like their Italian counterparts, Spanish immigrants, especially those from Galicia, were linked with the smell of garlic, which seasoned their soups and stews. Both of these main immigrant groups, together with those from Eastern Europe, mostly ate the food of the poor—starchy dishes or soups filled with pasta, corn, or potatoes—replacing hard-to-find ingredients with local staples.[98] In turn, internal migrants, many of whom came from the northwest, brought spicy corn-based dishes with both indigenous and early Spanish roots. In a tight urban environment in which neighbors in tenement houses and nonelite neighborhoods could smell, watch, and see what other people were cooking and eating, culinary distinctions and even prejudices were in the air. At the same time, a process of culinary mixing began to take place. By the early twentieth century, Italian macaroni had found its way into Spanish soups and *criollo* stews, and beef had become a staple in immigrants' and migrants' diets.[99]

During this period of massive migration, Argentine elites used food and other cultural markers (like architecture, furniture, clothing, and even prostitutes) to distinguish themselves from their poorer counterparts. Like many of their Latin American peers, including elites in Brazil and Mexico, members of Argentine high society turned toward Europe, and specifically toward France, for cultural sophistication in the late nineteenth and early twentieth centuries. Since 1850, French chefs had moved to other parts of Europe and the Americas to both encourage and benefit from such ideas, creating a culinary empire of sorts. In an era of Eurocentrism and eugenic thought, Argentines sought out French food and other luxuries associated with Europe to present themselves as transplanted and civilized Western Europeans (and not, it should be noted, the less culturally and biologically esteemed Southern Europeans, who made up most of Argentina's immigrant population).[100]

Previous generations of elites had enjoyed *criollo* fare like *puchero* (a traditional dish with boiled beef and vegetables) at simply set tables, regularly sharing bowls, glasses, and spoons; but by the 1890s, *porteño* elites sat at formally set tables replete with silverware and glassware.[101] For special occasions, they dined on French dishes that called for ingredients like prawns and cognac, even as they continued to eat standard *criollo* specialties for everyday meals.[102] In emulating the French manner of cooking and eating, the *porteño* elite sought to elevate themselves above the peoples and foods of Argentina's indigenous and *mestizo* interior. This culinary distancing reflects the ambivalence of nation making—that is, even though such elites did not publicly celebrate provincial foods, many did publicly celebrate other elements of provincial culture, including the male gaucho and folkloric music, as authentically Argentine during this time.[103]

In contrast to the Argentine provinces and countries like Mexico, which had small elites and large, poor populations, in Buenos Aires, social distinctions were less personal and harder to cement. As a testament to their awareness of this social proximity, wealthy *porteños* built new urban mansions that put more vertical distance between the servants and themselves. Kitchens and servants' quarters were now found in the tight confines of the basement, with dining rooms, reception halls, and bedrooms far above.[104] To staff these kitchens, *porteño* elites sought out cooks who could serve their families and guests French haute cuisine. To train these cooks, the French chef Germain Mairet established a local branch of the famed French culinary institute Le Cordon Bleu in the capital in 1914.[105] French food also dominated the menus of social institutions patronized by elite men, including the Jockey Club.[106] Whether in elite homes or in the kitchen of the Jockey Club, cooks (most from Argentina) did not simply borrow French and other international foods, but rather adapted them to Argentine circumstances.[107] Petrona did not report on what she ate during her early years in Buenos Aires, but it is unlikely that it was French haute cuisine. In all but elite homes, cooking centered on tradition, sustenance, and, ideally, abundance, as opposed to variety and fancy presentations.[108]

Petrona's descriptions of this period suggest the tensions that surrounded "respectability" for provincial Argentines who had recently arrived there, especially women. As a previously "married" single woman who was separated from her family and living with her boyfriend's family in the big city, Petrona Carrizo's standing in society was uncertain. She felt this acutely when the Gandulfo family decided to move to a new neighborhood in Flores, and none of them (including Oscar) told her anything about their plans. She later recalled wondering, "What did I represent in this house?" Unsure, she moved in with a couple from Germany whose son was a good friend of Oscar's and contemplated becoming a driver for the new public buses that had begun to traverse Buenos Aires.[109] Despite her previous and subsequent bravado, Petrona did not take this or another less conventional path. Instead, she sewed clothes, a typical way in which many Argentine (and other Latin American) women made money in the informal domestic economy.[110] She also waited for Oscar to propose to her. Eventually he did, and she gained the honorable "de" of a married woman as well as the name for which she would become famous—Petrona C. de Gandulfo—during the mid-1920s.[111]

The newlyweds' future did not seem to portend fame or financial success. Oscar was out of work, and Petrona made only a little money doing piecework. The 1920s were generally a period of economic recovery after the economic challenges of the World War I era, but the types of mid-level jobs they desired were often offered to those with more education or professional experience—and many of these were European descendants who had grown up in the capital.[112] Despite Oscar and Petrona's previous experiences managing a ranch, it was their friend raised in the city by German parents who was offered a position as an estancia manager. He took Oscar and Petrona with him, but their stay was cut short because, as Petrona later explained, their friend, "like most *porteños* . . . was ignorant of the norms of the countryside" and lent out the estancia's horses against the owner's instructions. The owner apparently expressed regret to Petrona that he had not hired her instead.[113] But it was relatively unlikely that an estancia owner would have hired an unknown woman directly.[114]

Back in Buenos Aires, Oscar and Petrona's lack of economic resources initially forced them to move in with the Gandulfos in their apartment in Flores. But soon, with the help of his brother Emilio, Oscar Gandulfo was able to benefit from the expanding government bureaucracy, landing a job with the postal service. This allowed him the prestige and the modest salary of a government employee.[115] In their new two-room apartment on Calle Alsina, Petrona knit *batas* (housecoats) for a store that paid her the modest sum of one peso each. Beatriz came to live with them from Santiago del Estero and did the cooking. "I should recognize," Petrona conceded in her memoirs, "that I never liked to cook, but Beatriz, already an adolescent, covered these duties." Petrona also recalled that when Oscar bought her a cookbook, she "only opened it on one occasion."[116] Whether this was true or hyperbole, it is clear that Petrona did not seek out a culinary education until she saw its potential for helping them improve their life in the capital.

Justifications for Work

In 1928, Petrona C. de Gandulfo applied for a position as an *ecónoma* working for the British gas company Primitiva in Buenos Aires. As she later explained to a journalist, "One day Primitiva publicly sought twenty young women, preferably *amas de casa*, to whom it would award a scholarship for a home economics course. They picked some, including me."[117] Primitiva then sent these women to study at the French culinary academy Le Cordon Bleu. Now under the leadership of an Italian immigrant named Angel Baldi, the academy taught mostly female and a few male cooks how to make

French cuisine, as well as Italian and other local favorites, for private families. Starting in the early 1920s, Le Cordon Bleu had also begun offering separate classes for "*señoras* and *señoritas*," suggesting a new respectability for this undertaking as long as it was kept separate from those who cooked for a living.[118] Despite her previous lack of interest in cooking, Petrona apparently excelled in the professional classes and "happily was chosen" to become one of Primitiva's demonstrators.[119]

Fifty years after the fact, Petrona C. de Gandulfo remembered well how her new husband's family disapproved of the idea that she would get a job instead of fulfilling her "natural" role as a full-time *ama de casa*.[120] She recalled that her husband had an accident and lost one of his two jobs, leaving them with but 180 pesos a month in salary, only a little more than the average male manual laborer.[121] "We were dealing with a bad financial situation; the money that came into the house did not cover anything."[122] Despite her husband's accident and small income, the fact that the Gandulfo family was, as she later put it, "of a certain standing" meant that they were appalled by the idea that she would work for wages.[123] There were legitimate ways of climbing the social scale (mainly through men's career advancement), and women's work was not one of them.[124]

Doña Petrona later described how her "need" to contribute to the household budget was not simply a matter of survival but also a pursuit of upward social mobility. For example, in a 1983 interview, she explained that her husband's job at the post office did not allow them to "progress" because his salary was quite small.[125] In another interview, she remarked, "I liked to live well and [getting a job] was the only way to pay for my needs."[126] In the time she had spent living in Buenos Aires, her definition of "living well" had certainly grown and changed. Like other migrants who experienced the rapidly growing consumer culture of the 1920s, Petrona marked her family's "progress" in large part by the way they could afford to live and the things they could afford to buy.

Just two years earlier, Petrona would have been legally obligated to get her husband's permission before she could take the job. In a nod to social expectations and the legal code that had mandated spousal approval for married women's employment, she asked for her husband's permission to take the job at Primitiva.[127] Like other women who wished to work during this era, Petrona probably pointed to necessity and the hope for progress as her primary motivations, as they represented the only socially accepted reasons for women to work outside of the home.[128] Still, Oscar Gandulfo was not convinced by either rationale, as his sense of respectable gender roles apparently trumped a desire for more income. "I applied for the job against the wishes of my husband and all of the Gandulfo family," Petrona later explained.[129] As a concession, she agreed to let one of her husband's aunts accompany her to the first interview at Primitiva so that she, "a young lady" (now in her early thirties), would not be alone with the men who worked there.

Petrona concluded that the Gandulfos' attitude reflected a larger societal view: "The employment of women outside of the home was looked upon badly and left one open to ill-intentioned gossip."[130] This perspective stood in contrast to her previous experience—her mother's boardinghouse had supported the family.[131] It also diverged from the reality that large numbers of Argentine women were employed during this period, and most, as historian Mirta Lobato has shown, were working out of economic necessity.[132] In 1914, just over a quarter of women in Argentina identified themselves as workers to census takers—a figure that surely underestimates women's participation in the labor market.[133] Most held low-paying and low-status jobs as domestic servants or factory workers or doing piecework at home—making some 30 to 50 percent less than men, based on the rationale that their work was supplementary to men's.[134] The ideal of the nonworking woman illuminates the double bind faced by Petrona and other women who aspired to a "respectable" status but had to work—and at the same time had to not work—to secure this status.

While Argentine women had always participated in the labor force in significant numbers, what was new in the early twentieth century was the simultaneous decrease in their officially recognized participation, as well as their growing numbers in industrial and commercial jobs. The former caused many prominent members of society the most concern. For example, in 1920, Senator Augusto Bunge acknowledged that women's industrial work was a "modern necessity" but urged his peers to remember that women's most important role was motherhood.[135] Like many contemporary physicians and other politicians, Bunge feared that extradomestic work harmed women's reproductive systems as well as their ability to take care of others—and thus Argentina's future labor force.[136] Male leaders' increasingly negative perception of women's extradomestic work was accompanied by their attempts to discourage and even to undercount female labor; census statistics registered women's official participation in the Argentine labor market at an all-time low between 1920 and 1940.[137]

At the same time, during this era a small number of women, like Petrona C. de Gandulfo, entered the workforce in new, specifically female, professional careers that enjoyed a measure of respectability. Sales clerks, telephone operators, nurses, social workers, and *ecónomas* joined teachers in jobs considered appropriate and even respectable for single women of the emerging middle class to pursue. Still, as Dora Barrancos has noted, most people expected respectable women to leave the workforce when they got married.[138] Fortunately for Petrona, her job suffered from neither the working-class nor the masculine associations of factory labor, nor the social inferiority associated with domestic service. Instead, it enjoyed the relative esteem of teaching, along with the new sheen of technological and scientific authority. Essentially, she and her fellow *ecónomas* would use the new technology of gas stoves to teach private and traditionally feminine domestic tasks in public. They would serve as ambassadors to other "modern women" of the 1920s, who were now expected to combine traditional skills like sewing and embroidering with beauty, manners, "economical" consumption, and a new modern way of cooking.[139]

Selling Home Economics

Even before hiring Petrona C. de Gandulfo and her fellow *ecónomas*, Primitiva had sought to convince such women to modernize by purchasing its products. This was part of a larger strategy by business executives to target and celebrate female consumers in Argentina and much of the world during the 1920s and 1930s.[140] In the challenging economic climate that followed World War I, many corporations (along with home economists) in Argentina seemed to believe that women were their best hope. While public home economists continued to tell women that they needed to economize to maintain the strength of their families and their nation, corporations also began to get in on the act, promoting their products as "economical" to female consumers eager to save money and time.

Primitiva was neither the first nor the only corporation to turn to home economics as a way to sell its products in Argentina. For example, in 1923, the Argentine frozen meat company Sansinena, which un-self-consciously branded its products under the name La Negra (The Black Woman), released a home economics manual. The company's logo showed a black woman holding sausages in what seemed to be a "nostalgic" reference to domestic slave servants (like Aunt Jemima in the U.S. context). This depiction reminded women that they did not have such help and should buy new products to compensate.[141] Like contemporary home economists who worked for the state, La Negra's spokesperson, Luis Barrantes Molina, expressed anxiety in this manual about the growing difficulty and importance of domestic tasks for urban women. He explained, "When the wife cannot avoid luxury for social reasons and does not know how to economize or flavor her foods, nor sew her clothes at home, the [male] household head . . . has to struggle intensely to obtain resources." He concluded that this "distress" could lead to mental illness or even temptations associated with a loss of "honor."[142] In other words, like public home economists, La Negra's corporate spokesperson encouraged women to economize (and to buy La Negra's economical frozen meat products) by warning them that they could lose their honor or their man if they did not.

In hiring and putting its female *ecónomas* out front in 1928, Primitiva would take a more positive approach to reach female consumers with a new corporate spin on home economics. But in the years leading up to this effort, this gas company did not yet directly embrace home economics. Formed in 1910 as a merger of British gas interests hoping to compete with the growing electrical industry, Primitiva only definitively shifted its focus to residential consumers in 1920 after it lost the contract for gas lighting in Buenos Aires.[143] Given consumers' legitimate concerns about the safety of gas, Primitiva's representatives had their work cut out for them. Starting in 1923, they launched a two-pronged campaign to capture the consumer market, commencing house-to-house visits and an advertising campaign.[144] During the 1920s, stand-alone advertisements definitively replaced classified advertisements and began to target women. As Fernando Rocchi has revealed, advertisers hoped to build female consumers' brand-related expertise so that they could reach them directly with their sales pitches and render retailers less influential in purchasing decisions.[145]

During the mid-1920s, Primitiva's advertisements celebrated the time, money, and happiness that its products would bring women and their families. For example, a set of ads placed in the magazine *Caras y Caretas* in 1926 contrasted "the happy wife" whose husband installed a gas heater with the "disgusted wife" whose husband had forgotten to do so.[146] In this way, Primitiva suggested that the man of the house would make the decision to install gas, even if it was at the urging of his wife.

In 1928, Primitiva began to target women much more directly and intensely. Now Primitiva's advertisements celebrated the dramatic and transformative impact that gas stoves could have on women's lives and contrasted gas with the inferiority of other cooking methods. For example, Primitiva ran an advertisement in 1928 in *Plus Ultra* that presented side-by-side illustrations of a woman with her "jailer," depicted as a giant coal monster, next to her "liberator," represented by a gas stove. The caption referred to gas as the breath of a "good fairy," a metaphor that Primitiva began to regularly employ to emphasize the magical qualities of cooking with gas.[147] As

SU CARCELERO

SU LIBERTADOR

Advertisement for Primitiva's gas services in the magazine Plus Ultra, *1928.*

in this case, Argentine advertising tended to play up the magical and liberating potential of products and did not generally employ the educational marketing popular in the United States. Argentine advertisers sought to sell romance along with technology.[148]

Corporations like Primitiva primarily sought to sell the romance of their products to relatively well-off families who could afford them. Like others during the 1920s who promoted the new nonessentials (such as a radio or a fashionable store-made dress), Primitiva suggested that the purchase of its product improved the owners' social status as well as their lifestyle.[149] For example, in 1928, Primitiva placed an ad in the magazine *Plus Ultra* with four images that depicted the impact of gas on a well-off family. Two images at the top of the page replayed familiar tropes: on the left, a woman sat reading next to a gas stove—she did not need to work while the food was cooking. On the right, a family was gathered before a gas fireplace—equating gas with familial bliss. In the bottom two images, a domestic servant was also pictured; however, as opposed to the family of consumers, she was busy working. On the left, she was serving the home owners and their guests at a formally decorated table, and on the right, she was bathing their children with warm bathwater.[150] Thus, these four images suggested the different impact of gas on members of the household—the *patrona* would gain leisure and the family more togetherness, while the maid would continue to work, albeit in a more efficient manner.

Starting in 1928, Primitiva would complement this print campaign by replacing its house-to-house visits with free cooking demonstrations in its stores across Buenos Aires. In a way, it was surprising that the British company had not tried this sooner, as the gas industry in Britain had successfully used professional female demonstrators (nicknamed "Lady Demons") to sell their gas stoves to female consumers since the turn of the century.[151] And in neighboring Chile, the gas industry had recently tried a similar experiment, joining forces with Lucía Vergara Smith (author of the 1916 cookbook *Cordon Bleu*) to run a series of cooking classes for them.[152] In Buenos Aires, chef Angel Baldi had offered popular classes at his Cordon Bleu since the early 1920s.[153] Primitiva would copy liberally from Baldi's format by asking its female demonstrators to prepare a full meal, pass around a sample for each attendee, and raffle off the meal at the end of the presentation.

The gas company would also put its own stamp on these demonstrations by labeling the women who would demonstrate their gas stoves *ecónomas*. This term feminized the original Castilian term *ecónomo* (male administrator or accountant), with its roots in the Greek term *oikónomos*, which combines the Greek words for home and distribution.[154] While the feminized version of this term also occasionally appeared in other Latin American countries during the early twentieth century, it became much more common in Argentina and Uruguay.[155] Starting in the late 1920s, corporations and consumers there used the term *ecónoma* to describe domestic experts who worked for businesses like Primitiva (and not home economists who worked for the state and its public schools). In characterizing its demonstrators in this way, Primitiva shied away from the exclusively male-dominated world of chefs as well as the denigrated status of *cocineras* and the explicitly commercial association with sales. Instead, it sought to capitalize on the scientific authority and femininity associated with home economics. In contrast to past iterations of home economics, however, this commercial version was based on culinary rather than scientific training. The *ecónomas* working for Primitiva had learned how to cook at the Cordon Bleu and how to do so "economically" from their employers, who, at the end of the day, aimed to sell their products. The *ecónomas* were all women, whereas the rest of the executives at Primitiva were all men.

Gas was still a new fuel during the 1920s, one that some *porteños* were eager to incorporate into their homes and others viewed as inaccessible or

Meeting for sales division at Primitiva, with Petrona C. de Gandulfo and other ecónomas *on the right, ca. 1928. Eager to stand out from the outset, Petrona donned a black dress with an elegant large white collar and pearls. Courtesy of Marcela Massut.*

untrustworthy.[156] Ofelia F., an Argentine woman of British descent, recalled that many of her neighbors in a relatively well-off section of Buenos Aires quickly snapped up Primitiva's gas stoves soon after they were introduced.[157] They were among the lucky few, as most people in Buenos Aires could not afford these new stoves, and gas services were unattainable outside of the capital city. Most Argentines continued to cook with other less expensive fuels, including coal, firewood, and kerosene.[158] Even within the capital city, a number of those with sufficient resources chose not to buy gas stoves. Some elite families preferred the taste of foods cooked over coal or firewood and, since they employed servants to do the cooking, did not feel compelled to switch to this new, cleaner technology. Others were afraid that the gas cylinder might explode. Ofelia explained, "There were people who did not want to use gas and they made do with coal. . . . Two out of ten held out [in our neighborhood]. . . . They were afraid of gas because of the explosions."[159]

To convince potentially skeptical buyers, the *ecónomas* planned their performances with dramatic flair to emphasize the safety, ease, and economy of cooking with gas.[160] They stood before viewers in crisply starched outfits with clean white aprons, suggesting how much cleaner cooking could be with a gas stove. Then they demonstrated that with only twenty cents' worth of gas, or a cubic meter, one could prepare a complete meal, with a beef dish, a fish entrée, and a quince tart or apple pie for dessert.[161] After putting all of these dishes into the oven, Petrona recalled, "I would close the door with a padlock (like the Great Houdini) and I would say to the people: I'll be back in an hour and a half." When she returned, she removed the food, which she claimed would be cooked perfectly, and displayed it to the audience.[162] During the process, she noted that the people sat silently, watching her actions as if she were performing magic.[163] In describing the impact of these performances, current-day *ecónoma* María Cristina Dillon explained that for contemporaries like her grandmother, who were used to cooking with coal or firewood, this "was revolutionary."[164]

This revolution was not only about technology. It was also about a new way of learning how and what to cook. After the presentations, women would approach the *ecónomas* to ask not only about gas stoves but also about what dishes to make.[165] Inspired by training at Le Cordon Bleu, the menu represented a cosmopolitan departure from the one-pot meals that many Argentines were accustomed to eating. The baked beef echoed the Argentine love of this ubiquitous protein, and the fish (which few *porteños* ate) reflected the *ecónomas'* training in continental cuisine from the other side of the Atlantic. In turn, the desserts incorporated a new, European twist on traditional pastries like *pastelitos*, by baking rather than frying them. The stylized presentation of all of these dishes suggested the potential artistry of the home cook. The *ecónomas* explained how to present and garnish savory dishes and how to decorate elaborate desserts like tiered cakes. In this way, they suggested that cooking with a gas stove was not about the drudgery of providing obligatory nourishment to others but rather the art of creating beautiful dishes that appealed to the eye as well as the stomach.

Women's interest was evident at these early demonstrations and also in the marketplace. In fact, Primitiva was quite successful at expanding its market in conjunction with this promotional campaign targeting women through advertisements and live performances. From 1920 to 1926, the company had only minimally expanded its customer base, by about 10 percent. But over the next four years (the last two of which included the *ecónomas'* demonstrations), Primitiva doubled its customer base, reporting a total of 70,000 consumers and 48,870 devices sold by 1930.[166] Using a name that underscored deep-rooted tradition, Primitiva succeeded in branding its products as modern and desirable.

Even the president seemed to take note of this success, or at least that of *ecónoma* Petrona C. de Gandulfo. The sweet-toothed Yrigoyen commissioned some desserts from her, including quince and apple tarts, to share with his friends at his personal residence.[167] But if men increasingly requested such treats, they did not pursue a culinary education themselves

Petrona C. de Gandulfo conducting an early demonstration for Primitiva (note chain on right of gas stove to lock it while food cooks), ca. 1930. Courtesy of Marcela Massut.

unless they intended to work as professional cooks. In contrast, nonprofessional women eagerly sought out such an education when offered it for free by Primitiva. Despite its previous association with servitude, by the late 1920s, *señoritas* and *señoras* across Buenos Aires flocked to the cooking demonstrations led by Primitiva's *ecónomas*.

The growing popularity of cooking was shaped by new ideas of "modern" homes that began to circulate during this time. The recent shift to cleaner fuels like gas and electricity led to a reimagining of the "modern" home that moved the kitchen into the home's interior. The installation of gas and electricity required infrastructure and money, and it was feasible only for wealthy families in Buenos Aires.[168] Still, the placement of kitchens in the interior of the home with smaller coal or kerosene stoves also began to be replicated in the more modest outlying neighborhoods of Buenos Aires during the early twentieth-century construction boom.[169] Further, outside of the city, the expanding mass media began to present Argentines with vicarious experiences of this new, urban marriage between modernity and domesticity.

The modernization of cooking highlighted at these presentations in the capital emphasized the positive associations among women's education, the growth of technology, and the aesthetics of food and succeeded at drawing a sizable and enthusiastic female audience. By this point, many "respectable" women were convinced that learning how to cook did not necessarily undermine class standing and could even enhance it. New corporate and media portrayals of "modern" products and "modern" women played a key role in this change in attitude. In addition, this generation of urban women, many of whom had been separated from relatives by immigration and migration, lacked informal daily cooking tutorials and were accustomed to learning new skills in educational settings. Women eager to continue their studies found this forum to be both serious and socially acceptable. By paying attention to food's taste and quality and also to its presentation, the *ecónomas* suggested the potential artistry of home cooks. Perhaps a gas stove could cook unwatched, but an educated woman was needed to make the meal come together artfully.

Conclusion

By the late 1920s, Petrona C. de Gandulfo had established herself as a corporate home economist. It was a fortuitous turn of events. Her early twentieth-century trajectory from her mother's boardinghouse, to a common law marriage in Santiago del Estero, to the big city as a single (and presumably deflowered) woman accompanying her new boyfriend's family could have led to many less successful endings. During the liberal export boom, wealth was further concentrated in the hands of elite families (like the Taboadas), who passed down their possessions to their legitimate children. Most common women who migrated to Buenos Aires found themselves among the working poor, laboring as domestic servants or manual laborers and earning little money or respect. A small number of women, like Petrona, found honor in marriage and respectable, if still not totally desirable, female employment.

For its part, the male executives at Primitiva hired *ecónomas* in recognition of the fact that women were taking an ever larger role in household purchasing decisions and had a growing interest in the culinary arts. As photographs and descriptions of these early demonstrations and Primitiva's sales figures attest, many women in Buenos Aires in a position to do so began to seek out a culinary education. Petrona C. de Gandulfo later described the crowds who gathered at her first neighborhood presentations for Primitiva as "women, interested as I never could have imagined, in everything related to gastronomy."[170] Having avoided the kitchen at all costs as a child in Santiago del Estero, Petrona now seized the opportunity to teach other women the culinary arts in Buenos Aires. Her desire for upward social mobility and the opportunity to become a respected performer in a public setting intersected with the contemporary modernization of domesticity and gender roles—enabling her to overcome her previous disdain for cooking.

Petrona C. de Gandulfo never forgot the stigmas associated with cooking for a living that she grew up with, however, and after becoming a star she was careful to publicly point out that she never worked as a *cocinera* for any family.[171] In referring to herself as an *económa* throughout her career, she would distance herself from the biases that continued to relegate female cooks in private homes to the bottom ranks of the social scale. In crafting a public story about her career that began with her British employer and French culinary training rather than with her earlier experiences grudgingly learning to cook and willingly working outside on a ranch in Santiago del Estero, she claimed a professional and social status in the capital superior to the lowly one associated with domestic help and the provinces. The French culinary institute where she and her fellow *económas* trained had made a similar distinction by offering separate classes for *señoritas* and *señoras* since the early 1920s.

The elevation of the culinary arts during the course of the early twentieth century, therefore, was accompanied by a clearly marked differentiation between women who cooked for pleasure and those who did so for a living. While early twentieth-century girls had rejected cooking classes in public school in an effort to maintain their respectability, by the late 1920s *señoritas* and *señoras* in Buenos Aires actively sought out a private culinary education. By this point, cooking, in contrast to cleaning and other domestic tasks, had begun to emerge as a respectable and even prestigious endeavor for modern women to pursue, in the right context. Relatively well-off urban women's interest in education and technologies that would help them improve their domestic lives, together with corporations' desires to sell domestic products to them, helps to explain this shift.

The confluence of these desires offered women a brand of consumerist citizenship that emphasized their main domestic and economic roles. As eager and influential consumers, women (and the corporations who targeted them) extended the domestic realm beyond the confines of the home to the marketplace. Nevertheless, even as cooking presented women with new opportunities for consumption and social mobility, it also steered them away from other public pursuits. Further, the new commercial pitch touting women's "economizing" was built on an inherent contradiction, as it encouraged women to spend money in order to save it. Indeed, talk of economizing went hand in hand with a growth of consumerism and a belief in progress in the period bridging World War I and the worldwide depression.

As we shall see in the next chapter, women's roles as consumers, as well as their interest in cooking and in forging a larger culinary community, would continue to grow dramatically during the 1930s. Corporations would both create and respond to this interest. For its part, Primitiva would put Petrona C. de Gandulfo on an ever-larger stage to promote its products. In turn, this ambitious *ecónoma* would use the burgeoning mass media to reach larger and larger audiences. As she expanded her repertoire, Petrona C. de Gandulfo would build her career on women's desire for advice from and connection with other women, especially in their supposedly private and individual capacity as modern homemakers.

CHAPTER TWO

CREATING A PUBLIC IN
BUENOS AIRES & BEYOND

Copa "El Hogar" ("*El Hogar*" Sundae)

Put a generous scoop of plain ice cream in one part of a cup, on the side, pineapple ice cream, and on the other side strawberry ice cream; in the middle, and on top of the three, make a tower of whipped cream, decorating with a ridged pastry sleeve; adorn it with small pieces of pineapple and strawberry.

This is generally made in champagne glasses.

All of the ice creams should rest for at least an hour in the machine with plenty of ice and salt. They should always be prepared so that they come out creamy.

It is possible to mold ice creams, once they are made, in a mold with a top so that water cannot get into the container, which is [filled] with lots of ice and rock salt; in order to de-mold it later, run the mold through cold water.[1]

Inspired by the interest and persistence of her fans, Petrona C. de Gandulfo would publish her first cookbook, *El libro de Doña Petrona*, in 1934. Along with a thousand other dishes, she included the above recipe for a decorative homemade ice cream sundae named in honor of the magazine *El Hogar*. It was a dessert that required the type of technology that this magazine touted and the time that the magazine imagined Argentine women had at their disposal. In order to prepare each of the three flavors of ice cream, one needed an ice cream maker, and presenting the sundae properly called for a pastry sleeve and champagne glasses. Because of these requirements, together with the reality that most Argentines were just starting to enjoy such ice cream–based treats at cafés and bakeries, few of her readers would actually have prepared a recipe like Copa *El Hogar* at home.[2]

Petrona C. de Gandulfo's decision to name a recipe in her cookbook after the magazine that sponsored her reveals the ways in which corporate branding and the expanding mass media were beginning to change Argentina's food and domestic landscape. For centuries, most of what women had known about cooking, cleaning, and curing had been passed down to them orally or through familial manuscripts that passed from generation to generation. For Argentine women who grew up during the 1930s and afterward, this type of local and familial domestic education was augmented by the information provided by experts and advertisers in magazines, radio broadcasts, and cookbooks.

Still, at the start of the decade, there was no definitive domestic expert or text. Petrona had found a career as a corporate home economist during the late 1920s, but she was not yet well known. She was one of fifteen or so *ecónomas* (corporate home economists) working for a British gas company to promote its products in Buenos Aires to small neighborhood groups. How then did Petrona establish herself as an iconic corporate home economist, with a cadre of sponsors, a local following, a popular cookbook, and fans across the country, by the late 1930s? And more important, what does this tell us about women's roles in the rapidly expanding consumer and media market?

As we shall see, over the course of the 1930s, businesses, mass media outlets, government officials, and women (including Petrona) joined forces to create a public culinary community. Companies like Primitiva, magazines like *El Hogar*, and government organizations, including the Junta Nacional de Carnes (National Meat Board) sought to reach a largely female public eager to buy their products. Urban women sought out socially acceptable public spaces in which to continue their educations, socialize with other women, and celebrate their domestic roles. They also pursued the opportunity to develop a relationship with a domestic expert. Petrona responded to these desires and carved out a career that would allow her to continue to personally "progress." Eager to succeed in the public arena but without challenging gender norms, she nurtured her relationship with female fans, attributing her rising career trajectory to their requests rather than her business acumen. Urban women's interest in the modern cooking lessons, entertainment, and relationships that Petrona and her sponsors fostered transformed daily life in Buenos Aires and, to a lesser extent, elsewhere in Argentina over the course of this decade.

A Larger Stage

At first glance, Petrona's entry into the consumer market might have appeared untimely. In 1929, just her second year as an *ecónoma*, the worldwide economic depression shook Argentina. Inflation and unemployment increased while salaries and public spending decreased. Perhaps even more important, this external "shock" to the liberal agro-export model reinforced and strengthened the economic lessons of World War I, exposing Argentina's vulnerability on the world market and beginning a shift toward nationalism and import substitution industrialization (ISI). This shift would take place under the auspices of a series of conservative military governments supported by the traditional elite. Unknown to people at the time, the 1930 coup toppling democratically elected President Hipólito Yrigoyen would initiate the military's efforts to control political life for the next five decades.

"The Infamous Decade," as it has come to be known, was noteworthy for not only its political corruption (especially electoral fraud) but also its conservative social views. The government and its aristocratic supporters, who dominated the political scene from 1930 to 1943, were outspoken about their desires to restore traditional social hierarchies, including gender hierarchies, in Argentina. Many sought to roll back some of the newfound social freedoms of "modern women," who they feared were becoming too autonomous and corrupted through their exposure to coworkers, movies, books, and increased public socialization. Nevertheless, even conservatives seemed to recognize that they could not entirely force women back in time, and feminists gained widespread political support in their struggles for the vote in 1932, even though Argentine women would not win suffrage rights until 1947.[3]

As they had been since the turn of the century, "respectable" women of the 1930s were expected to be unremunerated *amas de casa* dedicated to their homes and their families. *El Hogar* explained in 1931, "The man contributes money from work and the woman ... doubles the value of it and brings well-being to the home."[4] But there were changes afoot as well. During the 1930s, the number of girls who went beyond primary school grew more dramatically than the number of boys. And in the cities, women attended new professional schools for teaching and administration, as well as the university, in growing numbers. The number of young women who worked for wages before becoming mothers started to increase as well.[5] In Buenos Aires, the ratio of women to men nearly equalized as the number of foreign-born male immigrants declined and the number of female migrants from the Argentine provinces increased in response to the Great Depression.[6] The population of the capital city swelled to more than 2.4 million residents by 1936, with around two-thirds of that number native born.[7] As internal migrants' and women's presence in the capital grew alongside industry, so did their role in the economy as workers and consumers.

It was unclear what role Petrona would play in the expanding consumer market at the bleak beginning of 1930. But later that year, Primitiva offered her the position of heading the home economics division, replacing her female British boss.[8] She again sought her husband's approval. By this point, Oscar Gandulfo had apparently become more accepting of her extradomestic work, even encouraging her to accept the promotion if she considered herself "capable of fulfilling this role."[9] She did. She later explained that her acceptance of this promotion was inspired by patriotism and not professionalism—the other candidate was Chilean. Such a rationale highlighted her commitment to her country during a moment of growing nationalism. It also allowed Petrona to deflect the threatening notion that she was a businesswoman who was interested in climbing the corporate ladder.[10] Nevertheless, in hindsight, it is clear that Petrona began actively pursuing career advancement during the early 1930s.

Even as the Argentine economy was still suffering from the depression, Primitiva was joining forces with the magazine *El Hogar* to increase their respective and overlapping audiences. Since 1904, *El Hogar* had provided families with advice about topics ranging from homes to literature, giving a growing number of upwardly striving Argentines "a window" onto the lives of the elite.[11] And it was in this spirit that *El Hogar* and the head of publicity at Primitiva organized a new series of cooking classes in May 1931 in the magazine's recently inaugurated lecture hall. This was an era in which *porteños* began to frequent such grand halls and theater culture began to thrive, but this was apparently the first time that such a space was used for a promotional initiative explicitly aimed at a female audience.[12] In announcing this new initiative, *El Hogar* explained that its hall would be used for not only "high literary and artistic events" but also meetings of a more "practical nature."[13] It emphasized the respectability of this practical approach by labeling this series "lectures on home economics" rather than "cooking classes," because, as one of the managers explained to Petrona, they wished "to give it more prestige."[14]

Petrona later conceded that she "did not really consider herself ready" to present in front of such a large and prestigious group. She recalled that the inaugural ceremonies at *El Hogar* included "all of the most important personalities" from Buenos Aires—the so-called gold list.[15] After a speech by writer Josué Quesada, Petrona C. de Gandulfo and fellow *ecónoma* G. María Pirés de Burguez took the stage in front of a packed auditorium. Both were nervous and tongue-tied as they began to cook a three-course meal. Soon after, the mayonnaise separated for one of the dishes, and they could not get it to emulsify. Petrona decided to add some cold water, which turned out to be a "saintly remedy" and a self-described turning point in her career. Despite the fact that their boss told them immediately after their presentation that they were very "shy," *El Hogar* invited them back to repeat the same menu, due to the interest of those unable to attend the first presentation.[16]

Women's intense interest in these lectures convinced *El Hogar* and Primitiva to expand their offerings. The magazine asked Petrona and her colleague to give classes three times a week. Its hall held 270 people, and from the first class on, it was regularly filled to capacity.[17] Like the smaller neighborhood classes, these demonstrations were free, but in the emerging spirit of what future businesspeople might label "cross-promotion," the magazine now required readers to mail in coupons from its pages to reserve a seat. The majority of attendees at *El Hogar*'s series of lectures were women who could afford to consume nonessentials. Petrona described the audience at her first performance in *El Hogar*'s hall as "the most distinguished aristocracy" and "from the highest social echelon."[18] More women from the middle sectors would attend subsequent classes, but numerous photographs reveal that most wore dressy outfits with hats, with a number sporting furs.[19]

Petrona later contrasted the formality and elitism of the demonstrations she gave in lecture halls to the informality and more common nature of the first smaller classes she had given in the neighborhoods for Primitiva. She described the attendees at the first neighborhood classes as relatively "modest" and interested in whether gas could save them money over coal. She contrasted these presentations with the "halls where they did not let people in without a hat," explaining that the "ladies with the hats did not want the cooks sitting next to them."[20] In fact, these *señoras'* complaints eventually led to an official policy in which cooks and other women "without hats" were sent to sit in the back and eventually the balcony above the main seating area.[21] This policy expanded upon the separate nonprofessional curriculum established at Le Cordon Bleu in the previous decade. Growing numbers of "respectable" women could now learn to cook without associating their culinary education with those compelled to cook for money.

In contrast to attitudes of some *señoras*, Petrona later made clear that she sought to appeal to a broad audience. After recounting the rationale behind the seating arrangement, she explicitly rejected the classism of her audience, proclaiming in 1970, "I am an ordinary person [*soy muy popular*]."[22] No doubt this self-definition stemmed in large part from her provincial upbringing and lack of aristocratic status, which by 1970 had become badges of honor. To the elite women who had initially watched her cook, she was likely perceived to be quite *popular*. Her provincial accent,

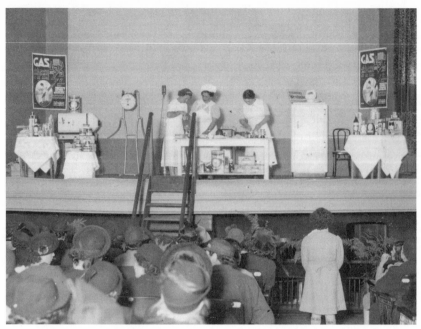

Petrona C. de Gandulfo (center) and fellow ecónomas *presenting a culinary demonstration on stage, ca. 1936. Courtesy of Marcela Massut.*

together with the very fact of her employment, suggested that she was not from an elite background. But this nonelite bearing likely contributed to her success, as members of the emerging middle classes could relate to her and elites would expect a common woman to cook in the first place. She later credited these presentations with establishing her style, which she described as "natural" and unstudied.[23] Through this experience, she gained the confidence to use her regular speaking style in public: "I talked as I was used to talking and I was very successful."[24]

From May to December 1931, thousands of women and girls came to watch Petrona and her fellow *ecónoma* cook on stage. *El Hogar* reflected and fed into this popularity by reproducing numerous images and descriptions of its popular "home economics" classes in its pages.[25] The magazine's coverage emphasized the large number and intense interest of the fans—many of whom regularly came once per week. On 22 May 1931, for example, photographs of the rapt audience were accompanied by the caption, "Observe the expression of profound interest on all of their faces, and it will be sufficiently convincing that the modern woman is just as suited to making a dish as dancing the Charleston or playing tennis."[26] The kitchen

Audience for Primitiva demonstration in Rosario featuring Petrona C. de Gandulfo, with "ladies" down below and cocineras in the balcony, ca. 1936. Courtesy of Marcela Massut.

was the modern woman's "kingdom," a writer in *El Hogar* explained, and like her U.S. counterpart (who, the writer pointed out, frequently lacked domestic service), the Argentine woman was eager to rule in this domain.[27] As in this case, media outlets frequently linked modernity to the United States and Europe, pointing to the transnational circulation of ideas about gender and consumption during this era.

Women in Buenos Aires attended these classes because they tapped into a desire for cosmopolitanism and modernity and also provided one of the few socially acceptable venues in which they could publicly gather with their peers to discuss issues relevant to their everyday lives. As *El Hogar* explained at the close of the 1931 session, "The familiar environment that has always existed in EL HOGAR's lecture hall has created solid friendships among many of the attendees." The author continued, "And so we have contributed not only to the well-served table in *porteño* homes, but also to a new orientation for women's social lives."[28] While some women had the means and desire to play tennis or dance the Charleston, many others could gather with other women for entertaining and informative cooking classes that were at once modern and unthreatening to the conservative gender norms in vogue at the time.

This echoes trends elsewhere in Latin America. As Barbara Weinstein suggests, women in 1940s and 1950s São Paolo, Brazil, were likely drawn to cooking, sewing, and child-rearing courses due to their social acceptability. But whereas 1930s Argentine audiences tended to be better-off women who were principally instructed in the culinary arts, the Brazilian students who studied such topics in the following decades were working-class women who worked as "unskilled" laborers in industrial settings.[29] Likewise, in Colombia, cooking and ironing classes were directed toward a similar population of poor women.[30] And as we shall see, in Argentina, the Peronist government would later target working-class women with its more popular and broader domestic instruction.

The growing interest in cooking among "respectable" women in early 1930s Buenos Aires was thus relatively unusual and stemmed from the emergence of a sizable middle sector eager to consume new patterns of domesticity. During the 1930s, magazines and their sponsors stepped up their celebrations of the new lives that these women could lead in "modern" homes equipped with the latest technology and with separate rooms for different purposes.[31] Most Argentines still did not live in such "modern homes," but a growing number could see them in popular magazines like *El Hogar*, *Para Ti*, and *Vosotras*.[32] Companies and media outlets began to present even more dramatic portrayals of how domestic technological advancement would transform women's roles. For example, Primitiva placed an advertisement in *Revista Aconcagua* in 1931 depicting a woman in midair, taking "an ideal leap" (*un salto ideal*) from a dark and dirty kitchen, sullied by previous cooking methods such as coal and firewood, to a bright and clean one with a gas stove.[33] The woman in this advertisement now literally leaped into a better life through her own volition, rather than that of an angel or her husband, both of whom had figured more prominently in the advertisements of the previous decade.

In Buenos Aires, this vision of domestic empowerment proved alluring to many women who could afford to pursue it. By the early 1930s, cooking elegant meals on a gas stove had become a mark of prestige and a way to fulfill one's "natural" role as a modern woman. For example, Ofelia F., the woman of British descent whom we met in the previous chapter, recalled that she and her mother attended Petrona's classes. Her mother, who, like others of her generation, "hated to cook," attended the neighborhood classes for free as a result of buying a gas stove from Primitiva. Ofelia, who for her part was eager to learn how to cook, later went to the demonstrations cohosted by *El Hogar*. She recalled that at age seventeen she clipped an ad from *El Hogar* and went to watch Petrona and her fellow *ecónomas* prepare "elaborate French-style dishes," including desserts and appetizers—in other words, "all of the most useful foods." When asked whether she also

Primitiva advertisement in the magazine Revista Aconcagua, *1931.*

learned how to make popular provincial dishes like empanadas and locro (a traditional Andean stew made with hominy, squash, beans, potatoes, hot peppers, and, sometimes, beef), she replied, "No, with Petrona we didn't have any of that. How strange, if I think about it," because she was "from the provinces [*provinciana*]."[34]

This provincial *ecónoma* commanded respect through her French-inspired recipes and also her didactic tone. A very serious school-like atmosphere prevailed in the hall. Ofelia explained that "there was no talking; when [Petrona] entered it became silent" and women began taking notes.[35] At home, Ofelia continued to take seriously her duties as a student, practicing the dishes on the weekend with the recipes that appeared weekly in *El Hogar* as a guide. For her, and for thousands of other attendees, the links between media outlets and businesses were changing the ways in which they learned about cooking and entertaining; in-person tutorials were augmented by professionals' public lectures and magazine columns that celebrated a more modern and elegant approach to such domestic tasks.

El Hogar's printed coverage of these conferences included the recipes for the dishes prepared and also the names of the high-society ladies in attendance.[36] In contrast, during this first series of cooking classes the magazine devoted little attention to the *ecónomas* who led them.[37] By the end of this series, in December 1931, *El Hogar* sought to remedy this "injustice" by devoting an article and some photographs to the two teachers "who had earned their students' applause and our sincere endorsement." The journalist explained that Petrona's delivery and background, as much as her tasty recipes, were central to her popularity: "La señora de Gandulfo . . . always brings to mind the marvelous fresh, native charm," continuing that "she tells a joke that never flops, and immediately, without a transition, she becomes very serious and provides a very important warning about the cooking of a particular dish." The author concluded that this style, together with her frequent smiles, sharp mind, and responsiveness to the attendees, led them to "love her as if they had known her for a long time."[38]

In turn, Petrona's counterpart, G. María Pirés de Burguez, was depicted as "calmer, more meticulous." In comparison to her more engaging colleague, she was said to have a "more objective approach to her profession." The public "respected" her for her knowledge, but they did not seem as attached to her as they were to the "señora de Gandulfo" (as she was referred to here). These women had different personalities and approaches, and they played different roles during the presentations themselves. La señora de Burguez went through the crowd to display the cooked items, while señora de Gandulfo stayed on stage cooking and entertaining the crowd.[39]

In addition to taking the leading role in the cooking classes for Primitiva and *El Hogar*, Petrona was now authoring a recipe column for the magazine to accompany the live performances. Her name was initially absent from the recipes that *El Hogar* published in the pages of the magazine. However, when the summer break came in 1932, she accepted the offer to continue her column but also requested the modest fee of sixty pesos for each column and brazenly asked that she be permitted to sign her page. When challenged by a manager at *El Hogar* on why she wanted to use her name, she explained, "Up until today I made recipes from different cookbooks, but if you let me sign my name, then I will create my own."[40] Apparently it was a convincing argument—by the following year, she had begun to sign her columns "Petrona C. de Gandulfo," presenting a range of fancy cosmopolitan and creolized recipes in *El Hogar*.

This move represented a major shift in the place that food and food-related experts occupied within women's magazines. As Gastón Lazzari has demonstrated, over the course of the early twentieth century, information about food had become increasingly prominent in women's magazines. In 1931, when Petrona began to collaborate with *El Hogar*, both this publication and the popular women's magazine *Para Ti* began to dedicate separate columns to cooking, taking recipes out of general household advice columns and extending their food-related content beyond practical concerns and health matters. By allowing Petrona to sign her column in 1933, *El Hogar* helped start a new trend that would emphasize the individuality and theatricality of the cook—a trend that would continue to accelerate throughout the twentieth century.[41] That same year, Primitiva published an advertisement in *El Hogar* picturing Petrona C. de Gandulfo, whom it deemed a "celebrated lecturer" and whose handwritten note endorsed the "easy and efficient" nature of cooking with modern gas stoves.[42]

The growth of the mass media thus allowed corporations and media outlets to grow their businesses together and helped create national celebrities. When asked what she considered her initiation into fame, Petrona later explained, "My big debut was in *El Hogar*."[43] In her lectures staged by this magazine, she cooked live in front of thousands of women.[44] Their numbers and enthusiasm far exceeded what this magazine had imagined possible. "We should confess," *El Hogar* wrote in a 1933 article, "that we never thought that today there were so many ladies who worried about how to prepare a dish or present a well-served table."[45] Such "ladies" were mostly full-time homemakers and their daughters, or the family's domestic help, but starting in 1933, female teachers were encouraged to attend a new class offered at a later time to accommodate their schedules.[46]

Through her collaboration in the hall and the pages of *El Hogar*, Petrona began to establish her reputation and share her recipes with a much broader national audience. Nevertheless, she had not yet established herself as Argentina's premier domestic expert. The same year that she started signing her column, 1933, *Para Ti*, the only magazine explicitly directed to a female public, sang the praises of her mentor, Angel Baldi. With two decades of culinary experience and over 2,800 pupils, Chef Baldi (and not Petrona C. de Gandulfo) was presented as "the best qualified person in the country to direct, write, and illustrate" *Para Ti*'s new cooking column.[47]

Taking to the Air

Petrona had increased her name recognition, but she had yet to fully set herself apart from other culinary experts. She would start to do so by actively pursuing a larger fan base through the expanding mass media. In November 1933, Petrona seized on the growing popularity of radio broadcasting in Argentina and began broadcasting a cooking program with Radio Prieto.[48] She later explained that the popularity of her live performances and magazine columns permitted her "to rent space on the radio, and with the support of some firms, enter into all households."[49]

Since its arrival in Argentina during the 1920s, radio had begun to link people through shared aural experiences and a new form of entertainment and information. Early radio broadcasts were held in public places; by the end of this decade, as the price of radios declined and their numbers increased, Argentines listened to the radio in the privacy of their homes or in the semiprivacy of patios. As in the United States, radios became common in Argentina during this era, more so than anywhere else in Latin America and most places in Europe. As the number of radios grew during the 1930s, it became a particularly effective means of creating and reaching a mass audience—especially for an *ecónoma* in step with increasingly conservative gender norms.[50]

As in other aspects of public life, men predominated on radio broadcasts, gendering this new "soundscape" male.[51] But women also had a significant presence. Most sang and acted, but a select few led talk shows directed to a male and female audience. For example, Tita Armengol served as announcer for Radio Argentina in 1927, and Silvia Guerrico hosted a popular evening variety show, *Cartel Sonoro*, from 1931 to 1935.[52] As historian Christine Ehrick has shown, women actually had greater opportunities to speak about intellectual and political issues during this early era of radio than they would for a good while. As radio "professionalized" during the early 1930s, in large part by becoming more male in spoken content, criticism of more political and intellectual female radio personalities like Guerrico mounted.[53] At the same time, the entertainment press lauded programs like Petrona's. The magazine *Sintonia*, for example, praised the "truly practical goal" of her new initiative in 1933.[54] As opposed to other female radio personalities who were disparaged for participating in a purportedly male domain, Petrona was complimented for sharing female-appropriate content that encouraged her listeners to focus on domestic pursuits.

Petrona's program represented a relative novelty on the radio and a new and public way of conveying information about cooking. In announcing her program, *Sintonia* explained that it filled an important gap, because "one of the least cared for aspects of radio broadcasting by most stations is that of culinary recipes delivered by a specialist."[55] A survey of broadcast content commissioned by the military government in 1933 (in preparation to censure this medium) reiterated the small amount of airtime given to cultural programming of any variety. At this point, when listeners turned on the radio they generally expected to hear music (especially tango), which represented over half of the broadcasting.[56] Still, Petrona did not host the first radio cooking program. Chef Antonio Gonzaga (who also cooked for the Argentine Congress) had started broadcasting a program at the end of the 1920s.[57]

Radio provided a less-expensive and more-direct source of mass advertising than print media or live performances.[58] As a result, advertisements blanketed the airwaves, covering nearly 10 percent of airtime, which helped companies create a desire for their products and, at the same time, frustrated listeners.[59] Radio programs had originally targeted undifferentiated audiences, but by the 1930s radio executives (and their sponsors) began to recognize that women were more likely to be at home and able to listen to the radio during the day, and they directed some daytime programming specifically to women.[60] For their part, advertisers eagerly supported "women's" programming, like afternoon fashion programs and the increasingly popular radio soap operas, to target their primary consumers.[61] In keeping with this trend, Petrona's radio show benefited from substantial commercial support, on Radio Prieto in 1933 and later when she made her first move, to Radio Mitre, the following year.[62]

By tuning into Petrona's radio program during her first years of broadcasting, radio listeners throughout Buenos Aires (as well as those outside the city who could tune into this channel) could share the experience of listening to a live cooking demonstration.[63] Some listened in the living room, others in the kitchen, and others at a neighbor's house.[64] As with Petrona's live performances, they would learn not only about particular ways to cook but also about proper gender roles. Listeners heard about how to make a roast or a flan and also received beauty tips and suggestions about how to organize their time and their domestic tasks. They also heard pitches for new domestic products targeted to women. Petrona later explained, "My radio programs and my classes were always really fun. . . . I spoke of different things of interest for the home."[65] She also responded to her listeners' questions. Her monologue was interrupted only by advertisements and the presence of an announcer who read the recipe ingredients.[66] As with her magazine column, in this new venue Petrona and her sponsors were able to expand her public beyond those who had the proximity and the means to attend her live performances.

The Cookbook

In 1934, one year after she began signing her magazine column and broadcasting her first radio program, Petrona published her recipes in a cookbook.

She later attributed her decision to do so to the persistent requests of her fans—an explanation that deflected any potential criticism about her ambition and, at the same time, recognized the crucial role that women's interest had played in her decision. In her memoirs, she explained: "The women in attendance at my classes, along with those who knew me from public life, asked me, over and over, to publish a book, to such a point of persistence, that, little by little, I began to put together ideas." This "firm and obstinate action" of her followers, she concluded, was the decisive factor that led her to complete the book.[67] She later explained to a journalist: "I started to write [this cookbook] a ton of times, but, for one reason or another, I always abandoned it. In the end, people's insistence was so overwhelming that I ended up hiring a girl to type it up." She said that she became fully committed to printing it only after the manuscript was in hand.[68]

But this was no easy feat. In fact, the "worst part" of the process, Petrona later explained, was trying to find a publishing house willing to take on her book.[69] Apparently, even as corporations like Primitiva and media outlets like *El Hogar* recognized women's growing importance as consumers, their peers in the publishing world had yet to realize women's interest in buying books—especially cookbooks. Petrona was therefore initially unable to find a publisher who wanted to fund her cookbook, and she resorted to borrowing money from a relative and a printing house to cover the expenses.[70]

It was money well spent. With the publication of her cookbook, Petrona would begin to establish herself as "Doña Petrona." She later explained that this was not her original intent. After she decided to publish her cookbook, she went to consult Luis J. García, the head of the Centro Azucarero (Sugar Center), about the title, and he recommended "El libro de Doña Petrona" in lieu of her idea "El arte del buen comer" (The Art of Good Eating).[71] Although she eventually elected to follow García's advice, she conceded that at first she was resistant, "because [doña] was a very old-fashioned term and I was very young."[72] Petrona was in her late thirties at the time and not yet a mother—not that young but not grandmotherly either. She was nevertheless convinced by García's argument that the use of the word "doña" tapped into the profound symbolism of "the family table" and "fit exactly with the idea of the kitchen and the symbolism of the *ama de casa*."[73] By titling her book in this way and including "Petrona C. de Gandulfo" on the front page, she took the next step in her personal rise from commoner to honorable status, claiming in gilded letters the full respectability of a married woman with two honorifics—doña and de—in her title. At the same time, this decision allowed her to personally link herself with her cookbook—at a time when the best-selling U.S. cookbook, *The Joy of Cooking* (first published in 1936), became much better known for its title than for its authors, Irma S. Rombauer and Marion Rombauer Becker.[74]

Petrona consulted her contacts in the business world not only about the title for her cookbook but also about its price. Explaining to Ortiga Ankerman, the director of the publishing firm Atlántida, that she hoped to sell it at five pesos, he apparently responded, "For this sum they will not buy a single copy! Now they ask you for it, but later, you will see what happens!"[75] Showing both her pride and her business acumen, she decided that she would not drop but rather increase the price, to seven pesos. This was a significant sum. It represented about one-tenth of the money needed to feed a working-class *porteño* family of five during the course of a month, the same type of family who spent at least half of its income on moderately priced foods like meat, bread, and potatoes.[76] But as her pricing attests, Petrona was not directing her cookbook at an audience that struggled to make ends meet, but rather at one that could afford to buy luxury items. She later explained the rationale behind her decision: "More than an impulsive act, it was [based on] the faith [I had] placed in my work."[77] Some of her sponsors seemed to share her faith. Like many other contemporary cookbooks, the first edition of *El libro de Doña Petrona* included advertisements to help cover printing expenses. While Primitiva was notably absent, Levarol baking powder, Cordero brand wine, DairyCo products, Flit bug repellent, and a local store that sold cooking molds all placed advertisements in the first edition.

The publication and price increase were risky propositions on borrowed money, and Petrona later admitted that even she had her doubts. But this strategy for the printing, titling, and pricing of her cookbook would prove to be tremendously effective. Petrona proudly recalled the "lines of women that would form, from my home on the second floor, up until the end of the block," to purchase the first edition of her book.[78] She claimed that despite the fact that there was no publicity or bookstores involved with her first edition, "news moved quickly, and the exclusively female public" proved to be eager buyers.[79] Despite her disavowals, she did promote her cookbook, as a 1934 advertisement in the magazine *Rosalinda* attests.[80] With such publicity helping her cause, Petrona sold the first print run of 5,000 copies in around two months.[81] This success from largely going it on her own convinced her that she had an interested public and encouraged her to retain control over the publishing process. She would continue to print and sell at least a portion of her own cookbooks throughout her career.[82]

The actual contents of *El libro de Doña Petrona* revealed her desire to present her cookbook as classy and complete. In the first edition of *el gordo* (the fat one), as this cookbook would come to be known, she included a prologue, fifteen pages of general suggestions, ten recommended menus, a list of twenty-five cocktails, several illustrations of the food, and approximately 1,000 recipes, on a total of 414 pages. She also included several pages of suggestions about how to organize the dining room and how to set and serve the table.

From where had she drawn all of this information? As Jacques Pépin has famously quipped, writing a cookbook is, in part, "an exercise in plagiarism."[83] By necessity, cookbook authors often borrow recipes, generally without crediting the sources.[84] For her part, many of Petrona's recipes and pieces of domestic advice stemmed from her training at Le Cordon Bleu and her presentations for Primitiva. A small number she credited to someone in her life, such as Locro de Maíz "Mamita Cleme," a version of the classic Argentine hominy stew made by an elderly neighbor in Santiago del Estero, and Suprema de Pollo a la Carolina, a chicken dish created by her older sister. In addition, as she had admitted to the manager at *El Hogar*, prior to signing her column in 1933, she had looked to other cookbooks for her recipes. While her cookbook collection from this period no longer exists, it included cookbooks from abroad; her friend and Argentine ambassador Tomás Le Bretón had previously brought cookbooks to her from his travels to the United States and Europe.[85] Undoubtedly, Petrona also would have been aware of the handful of Argentine cookbooks and consulted at least the two with the most editorial success. *La perfecta cocinera argentina* by "Teófila Benavento," first published in 1890 and popular with elites in Buenos Aires, had reached its thirty-first edition by 1931. In turn, its more provincial successor, *La cocinera criolla*, first published in 1914 by "Marta," had reached its eighteenth edition by 1928.

Therefore, *El libro de Doña Petrona* was not actually the "first" cookbook published in Argentina—as many Argentines claim—nor even the first to have success. Rather, it was the first to go beyond elite households and successfully target Argentine *amas de casa* of the middle class and, eventually, the working class. Petrona suggested that if the "good homemaker" (*buena ama de casa*) cooked with it regularly, she could make this book her own comprehensive guide to domestic life. While Petrona unconditionally expected such women to dedicate themselves to their homes, she did not expect them to be experts in cooking or other domestic tasks. In the prologue, she explained that this cookbook would allow "the biggest novice" to make "the most exquisite dishes" due to the clarity and simplicity of the recipes.[86]

The media helped her to make this case. For example, in 1934, the journalist who reviewed her cookbook for the Argentine newspaper *La Nación* assured readers who were likely unfamiliar with this type of text that there was "no doubt" that it would help all women to prepare "exquisite dishes." The reviewer continued: "[Señora] Gandulfo has composed this treatise with the clarity necessary so that even a beginner can put her theory into practice." The cookbook author was deemed "a simple, straightforward woman" (*una mujer sencilla*). The reviewer did not discount her for this common background but rather claimed that it was part of the book's merit. "[Señora] Gandulfo" was congratulated for employing "the terminology current to our environment," which, in contrast to cookbooks with exotic recipes and complicated terminology, made her recipes "something more than a theoretical aspiration."[87]

The expectations of both the author of this cookbook and the journalist who reviewed it were shaped by the specificity of women's roles in Argentina, especially in the capital. Young urban women's lifestyles were changing as they spent more time studying and socializing and less time doing domestic chores at home. Their increasing education, literacy, and employment meant that they often lacked, or, perhaps even more important, felt they lacked, the knowledge to run a home and be a "good" homemaker. At the same time, Argentine women's relatively high levels of literacy and education meant that they were capable of learning these kinds of skills through reading about them. In contrast to many other Latin American nations at this time, free primary education in Argentina had by 1930 drawn two-thirds of children into public school classes. Almost all second-generation immigrants residing in Buenos Aires by the mid-1930s were literate, even though their parents sometimes were not.[88]

But what kinds of culinary education would an *ama de casa* in 1930s Argentina benefit from? In addition to knowing how to set and serve an elegant table, Petrona suggested she should know how to cook, present, and serve food in a modern way. She preached a recipe-and-measurement type of cooking and implied by contrast the inferiority of previous cooking methods, which relied principally on approximations and received experience. In addition to providing a chart for converting common measurements in cups and tablespoons to grams, she enjoined her reader to use exact quantities and quality ingredients and to follow the baking instructions to "the letter."[89]

While such instructions emphasized a more "scientific" approach to cooking, the recipes and the illustrations often celebrated the art of presentation. Petrona encouraged readers to shape, mold, and decorate dishes to make them more appealing.[90] As with the sundae recipe for *El Hogar* that opens this chapter, she emphasized the importance of decorative flourishes that women could create. Thumbing through her cookbook, one is struck by the hand-drawn color illustrations that depict piped potato roses, hard-boiled eggs fashioned into bunnies, fruit pyramids, and cakes built to resemble houses, soccer fields, and churches. Several people I spoke with recalled how they would flip through these illustrations as children as if they were looking through a picture book. By visually demonstrating the aesthetic appeal of stylized food, Petrona incorporated the artistry for which she had become famous as a demonstrator for Primitiva. Championing the contemporary notion that the human transformation of natural things could improve them, she emphasized the artistry of the modern woman who prepared such creations.[91]

Petrona applied this modern culinary artistry to a wide range of dishes and recommended that her readers do the same. Reflecting Argentina's history and her own background, Petrona's recipes crossed class, ethnic, national, and regional boundaries—ranging from French haute cuisine to Italian and Spanish fare to *criollo* home cooking. Therefore, even as Petrona included some explicitly nationalistic recipes, such as a cake with an Argentine national flag, along with some typical *criollo* cuisine, like empanadas, she presented French, Spanish, and Italian dishes as equally important for Argentine *amas de casa* to master.[92] Such variety is evidenced by just one page of illustrations of dishes from her cookbook. French vol-au-vents shared the page with Italian-style pizza, two dishes with local fowl (Pichones Rellenos a la Cacerola, a stuffed young partridge in a stylized casserole, and Martinetas en Bella Vista, a roasted bird indigenous to the region), and two versions of empanadas (one from her native province of Santiago del Estero and the other popular in Buenos Aires). In this way, *El libro de Doña Petrona* was less self-consciously nationalistic than other contemporary cookbooks published in places with longer-standing shared culinary traditions like France, India, and Mexico.[93]

Petrona's eclectic approach reflected the transnational complexity of national identity in Argentina during this time. In fact, the combination of recipes in this cookbook expressed the self-conscious internationalism of elites in Buenos Aires, who often sought to define Argentina as a cosmopolitan nation of European immigrants. Her inclusion of *criollo* dishes, as well as the creolization of many foreign preparations, mirrored the ways in which European foods and identities were transformed in Argentines' daily lives. *El libro de Doña Petrona* did not simply assemble French, Spanish,

Illustration of dishes from Petrona Carrizo de Gandulfo, El libro de Doña Petrona, 1st edition, published in 1934. Courtesy of Marcela Massut.

and Italian recipes but rather tailored them to the local environment. For example, Doña Petrona added *dulce de leche* (South American milk caramel) to the Spanish flan and filled one version of her Italian cannelloni with *humita*, a traditional creamed corn eaten regularly in northwestern Argentina. Given such culinary mixing, Argentine cuisine (like that of the United States) is best understood as a combination of immigrant and regional specialties, as opposed to a singular cuisine of its "own."[94]

Nevertheless, if Argentina did lay claim to a unique culinary tradition, it would stem from the preponderance of beef in the diet. Petrona did include a substantial number of recipes with red meat—sixty-four in all. However, she actually underrepresented beef in her cookbook in comparison to its ubiquity on tables across central Argentina.[95] In contrast, she provided some ninety recipes for chicken and fish, two foods that were often quite expensive or difficult to obtain.[96] There are several possible explanations, including her interest in emulating European preferences for fish and fowl and the Argentine preference for simple preparations of beef.[97] The most celebrated dish, *asado*, consists of beef ribs that men have traditionally cooked outdoors over an open fire or a grill. Petrona did not include a recipe for an outdoor *asado* in her cookbook, despite the tremendous status and popularity of this preparation. Instead, she elected to include a recipe, Asado al Horno, which is a version of this dish made in the oven. By moving the cooking process indoors, Petrona adapted a traditional dish to the new technology of the gas stove that she promoted for Primitiva. At the same time, she reinforced men's expertise and authority over the classic way of making this celebratory meal outside and asserted women's expertise and authority with this dish (and others) in the kitchen.

Petrona asserted the *ama de casa's* authority not only over the kitchen but also in the household, especially over servants who might work for her. Most notably, when describing "the most general indications for how to serve a table," she stated that the servant should be instructed to pass the rolls, serve the wine, and clean off the table before dessert in order to preserve the "charm" of the table and the evening.[98] She also suggested that the homemaker might match the clothing of the domestic servants to the colors in the dining room if they were not dressed in the traditional black and white.[99] As opposed to the *ama de casa*, who was imagined to be responsible for the smooth management of her home, the help was described as an accessory to be decorated and to do the more mundane housekeeping tasks.

In Buenos Aires, where wealthier families resided in greater numbers, most households (and many of Petrona's fans) did not have regular paid domestic help. One sociologist estimated that in 1936 only one in ten families employed a full-time servant.[100] More, but not most, had part-time help. Therefore, by specifying how to use domestic help and to serve a table elegantly, Petrona was divulging the details of how to be refined to an audience that might not already know the protocol. For example, in highlighting the importance of the dining room in family sociability, Petrona emphasized that it was the responsibility of the *buena ama de casa* to ensure that the table was "clean, comfortable, and elegant, even in its simplicity," and specified that she allow at least sixty centimeters between each chair at the dining room table.[101] As elites and those working for them would presumably already know how to "properly" set a dining room table and serve a multicourse meal, this approach spoke to the experiences and desires of the growing number of people who aspired to respectability.

By the mid-1930s, more people in the capital were in a position to follow Doña Petrona in emulating elite patterns of consumption and etiquette, due to new domestic arrangements, educational opportunities, and the growth of white-collar jobs. Inspired by studies of the middle class in Europe, Argentine sociologist Gino Germani concluded in 1942 that nearly half the population in the Argentine capital was "middle class" as of 1936.[102] Germani argued that the growth of the urban middle class had had the most dramatic impact on changing Argentine society during the previous fifty years.[103] Historians have subsequently argued that Germani overstated this success and sense of a "middle-class" identity prior to the 1940s,[104] and Germani himself admitted the difficulty in determining who belonged to this "middle class." In contrast, he described his relative ease in identifying members of the upper class—whom he characterized as business, political, and cultural leaders, along with wealthy heirs and property owners—and the lower class—whose very work as *obreros* defined their working-class status.[105] Argentina possessed a clear upper and lower class, but the middle class was in formation.

Like people living during the 1930s, Germani recognized that class status stemmed not only from economic standing but also from patterns of consumption and behavior. While defining professional activity, economic position, and urban location as the keys to middle-class status, Germani also explained that ultimately it was a "value judgment" based on "a shared kind of lifestyle, upbringing, education, taste, manners, customs, ideas, and tendencies, or in other words, by a combination of objective and subjective conditions."[106] Writing eight years later, scholar Sergio Bagú echoed this perspective by detailing the "spiritual expansion" of the middle class after 1930. Bagú described this group in large part through its interest in literature, books, concerts, and exhibitions. In addition to emphasizing how shared cultural appetites reflected and legitimated status, he noted that members of the urban middle class often lived in smaller, nuclear families. He emphasized that this domestic pattern was quite different from the larger family size that predominated among the urban rich and poor, as well as among their rural counterparts.[107]

As urban migration and the ideal of upward social mobility grew during the 1930s, women's proper exercise of their roles as mothers and homemakers played a growing part in determining whether their families fit the nascent middle-class model of respectability. Due to the changes in family composition, such urban women were now more likely to be solely responsible for household tasks like cooking, which might have been shared among female relatives in earlier years or in rural settings. As a result, many began to seek out domestic advice, and a growing number looked to Doña Petrona.

During the mid-1930s, even those who could not afford to purchase *El libro de Doña Petrona* were increasingly likely to hear about the emerging star behind it. The growing number of venues in which Petrona appeared led to countless opportunities for publicity and cross-promotion. For example, after *El libro de Doña Petrona* was released, *El Hogar* ran an advertisement in its magazine that announced that "the luxurious cookbook '*El Libro de Doña Petrona*' is already for sale."[108]

In 1934, *El Hogar* also incorporated a new section that further linked her magazine column to her live performances, entitled "Al margen de las conferencias" (Alongside the Lectures).[109] This column had originally been intended for the "readers from the interior," so that they could collect and practice the menus prepared live in Buenos Aires.[110] This new initiative allowed fans across the country to get Petrona's responses to their questions in print. It also provided *El Hogar* with a new selling point and Petrona with a new means to foster her relationship with her fans. In turn, this correspondence provides us with a unique window into how women during the mid-1930s related to this emerging culinary figure, and to the new patterns of domestic modernity that she endorsed.

From June 1934 through November 1935, letters poured in to *El Hogar* from all over Argentina, evidencing the massive interest and growing geographical reach of this *ecónoma*. Fans' letters were not printed, but her responses were. Of the more than 400 letters to which Petrona publicly responded in *El Hogar*, some 60 percent were from people who lived in the province of Buenos Aires, the majority of these from the capital. But they also wrote from Rosario and Córdoba (Argentina's second- and third-largest cities) and other provincial capitals and, to a lesser extent, from provincial towns across the country.[111] In addition, a dozen or so other South Americans received published responses.[112] Most letter writers seemed to belong to the emerging middle sectors—they were women who did not use two last names like elites but still had access to the magazine and the time and skill to write.[113] They were also an ethnically diverse bunch—many had Spanish and Italian surnames and others were of British or Middle Eastern origin.[114] Almost all were women. Of the hundreds of printed responses, only one was directed to a man (who wrote with a query about how to grill fish outdoors).[115] As in the Primitiva demonstrations, women and girls were invited and eager to take the lead in this public culinary community.

The responses published in *El Hogar* shed light on the relationship between Petrona and the women who wrote to her, as well as on the changing culinary landscape. Most queries revolved around a common culinary challenge, such as how to fix a mayonnaise that had separated, how to make proper *hojaldre* dough, or how to prevent raisins from falling to the bottom of a dessert. The recurrence of these particular topics points to the novelty of mayonnaise, French-style pastry, and British-style desserts at the time. Likewise, many correspondents wrote to ask how to improve their ability to cook using the oven. The *ecónoma*'s replies to such queries reveal her teacher-like dedication to her fans and her desire to maintain an ongoing conversation with them. For example, in a reply to Angélica P. De Cossi of Rosario in August 1934, she explained: "This biscuit, señora, turned out so dry, without a doubt because you left it too long in the oven; use the exact measurements, practice it again and write me back."[116] She reassured many a nervous letter writer that it was no bother to receive and respond to these questions; in fact, she said, "it was a pleasure."[117]

For their part, the women expressed the urgency of their queries by writing back if this *ecónoma* did not answer quickly enough. Petrona regularly asked her readers for their patience, pointing to the large number of letters she received on a daily basis and promising to mail someone a recipe in the near future or to reprint it in an upcoming column. At times adopting a sterner tone, she reiterated *El Hogar*'s stated policy that the letters would be answered "strictly in the order they were received."[118]

While most writers seemed concerned about getting quick replies and accurate information, a handful expressed concerns about economizing or a lack of equipment. By the mid-1930s, the effects of the 1929 depression had abated, with salaries and prices stabilizing in Argentina. Nevertheless, only a select group of urban Argentines had the money and the access to buy gas stoves, new pots and pans, and the unique ingredients that Petrona touted. Still, some people with more limited resources turned to her for new ideas about cooking. For example, in January 1935, Doña Petrona responded to Aurelia from Lomas de Zamora about how to reuse the leftovers from *puchero*, the classic and modest Argentine one-pot meal. She advised her to cut all the ingredients (beef, potatoes, onion, pepper, and tomato) into fine slices, sauté them in oil with three eggs, and serve the mixture with fried bread. "It depends on your skill," she explained, "that with little expense, you can present different menus to your relatives."[119] This reply is revealing on many levels. It shows that a woman with relatively limited resources might turn to Petrona for help, even as most women in such circumstances did not. In addition, it sheds light on this *ecónoma*'s public stance that the skill of the *ama de casa* rather than the resources of the family determined the variety of its diet. At the same time, it establishes a newfound appreciation for variety—someone who made *puchero* regularly was looking for something new to do with it.

By the mid-1930s, Petrona had begun to establish herself as a key figure who could help women negotiate Argentina's culinary diversity and modernity. To be sure, many continued to ask their neighbors, friends, or in-laws how to make a particular dish with which they were unfamiliar. But others looked to "Doña Petrona," as a number of her fans now called her.[120] Women's letters showcased their interest in and their confusion about food and drink with which they were not familiar, as well as their willingness to ask an expert for help. For example, in January 1935, Petrona demystified the nature of the Italian antipasto plate for Celina M. Costa de Marquis, of Ciudadela, and suggested some ingredients for making one.[121] On other occasions, she explained how to make British-style tea and the traditional jams that were made in the provinces to readers apparently not familiar with such preparations.

In her role as the lead culinary expert for *El Hogar*, this *ecónoma* was a gatekeeper to a new, more commercial way of cooking, and she took this role quite seriously. On several occasions, she encouraged fans to subscribe to and save all of the recipes she published in *El Hogar* for easy consultation.[122] And other times she directed them to a particular product or type of establishment to buy something they needed to make one of her recipes. In July 1934, for example, she explained to señora de Sehwam that she should add a heaping tablespoon of Royal baking powder for her dessert to turn out right.[123] On other occasions, she encouraged readers to buy copper pans for making sweets or canned pineapple for a particular dessert.

Her column in *El Hogar*, which ran until 1936, highlighted not only her ability to successfully present cooking lessons to large audiences but also her interest in responding individually to women who had questions for her about the brand of modern cooking she endorsed. But why did she publish her replies in *El Hogar* rather than just respond directly through the mail? Through publishing this correspondence, both *El Hogar* and its leading culinary expert could develop and display the relationship between Petrona and her fans. "Your letter does not seem strange to me," she assured an anonymous correspondent in August 1934, "given that I have countless female students with whom I maintain ongoing correspondence; they share their progress, etc. And they maintain anonymity."[124] As in this case, other fans or potential fans could see that even women reticent to reveal their identities were eager to approach this *ecónoma* for cooking advice.

This column also reveals how much fan feedback and praise meant to Petrona, especially during this early phase of her career. For example, in response to Elvira F. de Bibolini, from Formosa, she exclaimed in August 1934, "It made me very happy that you had success with these desserts; your encouraging little letter is a true stimulus for my work, and thanks to these encouraging words from my students, I continue forward along the chosen path."[125] As she would throughout her career, Petrona stressed that she actively continued in her profession due to the interest of the women who enthusiastically sought her out.

Measuring and Moving

While the letters pouring into *El Hogar* assured Petrona that women were following her magazine column and the sales of her cookbook gave her the confidence to reissue it in 1935, the success of her radio program at first seemed harder to gauge. Shortly after taking to the air, she organized a contest in which she asked listeners to send in their collections of the recipes she had presented. She announced that she would award a prize for the most complete entry. To her delight, "the quantity of notebooks and folders was so large, with details as complete as in the original [recipes], that it was necessary to get extra personnel to classify the entries."[126] She later recalled that some of her listeners even included illustrations to clarify the details of a recipe she had shared. As a result of the quantity and quality of the entries, Petrona decided to give out multiple prizes, including a large number of her cookbooks—seizing on yet another opportunity to promote it. As a result of this experience, she became convinced that her radio programs were working. This was the last such contest she organized, explaining: "It was enough already, it was more than convincing, the proof and the genuine interest of my listeners."[127]

Petrona was not the only one who was convinced by the possibilities of radio to reach large audiences. By the mid-1930s, there were over 1 million radio sets in Argentina, or about one for every ten people.[128] Programming had diversified, and, in the still-small culinary realm, a handful of male chefs and female *ecónomas* now broadcast programs on different stations. For example, *ecónoma* Ida P. de Ruiz presented a home economics program directly from General Electric's Buenos Aires headquarters, starting in May 1935.[129] Like Primitiva before it, General Electric now used professional home economists and the expanding mass media to promote its electric stoves.

In 1935, the brand-new station Radio El Mundo asked Petrona to join its lineup. The British interest Editorial Haynes, which also owned the magazine *El Hogar*, had founded this station as an extension of its print empire.

She agreed but was less than thrilled. "Against my wishes," she recalled in her memoirs. "I had no other alternative but to abandon the firms that had sponsored me to entirely dedicate myself to the Board of Directors coming from the magazine [*El Hogar*]."[130] Petrona seemed particularly frustrated that this move cut into her autonomy as well as the money she could make. "Relatively new and modern," historian Robert Claxton explains, "Radio El Mundo was the most powerful station in Argentina" and the first station to deliberately seek a national audience.[131] It did so by promoting its magazine and radio station as well as its rising stars (like voice comic Niní Marshall and radio actress Eva Duarte) across the country. Located in the "heart of the entertainment district," it built an auditorium that allowed people to watch the radio broadcast live.[132] Wrapped in a fur stole with a carefully coiffed hairstyle and an elegant hat, Petrona embodied modern elegance before the microphone.

When her first year of broadcasting ended at Radio El Mundo, Petrona asked for a raise, but it was denied.[133] Soon after, she moved to Radio Argentina and then shortly thereafter to Radio Excelsior, which presumably let her negotiate directly with her sponsors, an important matter, given that most radio stations did not pay their performers much money.[134] Petrona had broadcast on Radio Argentina on Tuesdays, Thursdays, and Saturdays at 6:30 P.M. On Radio Excelsior, she moved to an earlier and exclusively weekday slot at 2:30 P.M. on Mondays, Wednesdays, and Fridays.[135] In this way, she and her sponsors were able to reach her target audience of female listeners during or right after lunch.[136] Like Petrona, Radio Excelsior had ambitions to reach a large public. Directing "its programs to the middle classes," it sought "to unite the greatest number of listeners on the soil of South America."[137]

Petrona expanded her audience beyond Argentina's capital by means of the radio and her magazine column, and also by traveling to Argentina's second-largest city. In 1936, she gave a live performance in Rosario. She had no trouble drawing a large crowd—more than 1,500 spectators came to watch her cook live at the Imperial Theater.[138] As this was her first performance in the city, women's interest had apparently been piqued by what they had seen and heard of her in the magazines and on the radio. By the mid-1930s, Petrona had established herself as a culinary expert with name recognition that extended beyond Buenos Aires.

If Petrona's move to Radio Excelsior was likely inspired by her desire to break away from Editorial Haynes, it seems her move to the magazine *Caras y Caretas* was also caused by this split as well as by this prestigious magazine's willingness to make her a headliner. In 1936, *Caras y*

Petrona C. de Gandulfo on Radio El Mundo, ca. 1935. Courtesy of Marcela Massut.

Caretas proudly announced "important news" for *dueñas de casa*. Starting in August, "the renowned instructor of the culinary arts, señora Petrona C. de Gandulfo, would collaborate exclusively" with this magazine. This collaboration would entail a series of lectures held in significantly larger public locations (with seating capacity for some 1,000 people), as well as recipes and tips published in the magazine. Reflecting the increased prestige of both this *ecónoma* and cooking by this point, *Caras y Caretas* titled this series of lectures, "El arte de cocinar por Petrona C. de Gandulfo" (The Art of Cooking by Petrona C. de Gandulfo). In contrast to *El Hogar*'s series of lectures, "*El Hogar*'s Home Economics Course," *Caras y Caretas* put Petrona's name (and not its own) first.

Along with the initial announcement, *Caras y Caretas* ran a picture of crowds of women outside the hall unable to attend a previous lecture at the Imperial Theater in Rosario, visually demonstrating both Petrona C. de Gandulfo's popularity and the service they were providing through this new "effort . . . in homage to [our] readers."[139] Like *El Hogar*, *Caras y Caretas* encouraged new readers to purchase its magazine by including within it a coupon that allowed them to attend the lecture for free. The magazine instructed readers to claim their tickets by mailing the coupons either to

Caras y Caretas or to La Compañía Primitiva de Gas, evidencing yet again this new type of synergy between mass media outlets and corporations.[140]

For her part, Petrona paid homage to her new sponsor by preparing a lacy white cake covered with pale pink roses that she dubbed Torta "Caras y Caretas" (*Caras y Caretas* Cake), first in her magazine column and soon thereafter in her cookbook.[141] Yet again echoing her strategy at *El Hogar*, she encouraged readers to regularly purchase the magazine in order to collect all the recipes. She was now even more specific about how they should do so: "I recommend that you cut out the pages with the details and collect them together with the page of the color recipes. To bind them together, later, stick two pages back-to-back with a strip of gummy paper."[142] This suggestion put a new mass media twist on the more traditional practice of compiling handwritten manuscripts of recipes and other domestic advice.

As we learned previously, some women (including Ofelia) had saved and regularly consulted the recipes from *El Hogar* starting in the early 1930s. Many made similar manuscript books with this new column from *Caras y Caretas*. For example, señorita Gardella, a single woman who lived with and cooked for her brother's family in Rosario, assembled Petrona's recipes from *Caras y Caretas* along with others published in *El Hogar* during the 1930s. She passed on her carefully crafted hardcover book to her niece, who eventually donated it to the women's library at the Universidad de la Pampa.[143] Like previous handwritten manuscript recipe books, Gardella's compilation of magazine recipes was passed down as a family heirloom. But in contrast to its predecessors, the content was more homogenized, if still selected and sometimes modified by the creator of the book.

Caras y Caretas thus provided a new venue for women to gain access to Petrona's printed recipes and also helped promote her radio show and her popularity. Toward the end of August 1936, the magazine ran an announcement stating that "the señora Petrona C. de Gandulfo gives radio talks about the art of cooking . . . *exclusively* on Radio Excelsior."[144] And the following week, it reported that fans had sent "thousands of letters" to Radio Excelsior in response to her broadcasts, revealing yet again this *ecónoma*'s popularity and her responsiveness to fan mail, as well as the growing number of linkages between traditional and newer forms of mass media.[145]

The magazine also contributed to Petrona's media presence by running photographs of the previous sessions each month in its pages. This *ecónoma* consistently wore pearls around her neck or elegant dresses with large collars partially covered by fancy embroidered aprons with her initials on them, thus protecting her clothes while also conveying her sophistication.

She was not a humble cook but instead an elegant and respected culinary educator.

As with the previous series at *El Hogar*, women's interest derived from Petrona's artistic approach to food as well as the educational and social nature of the classes themselves. *Caras y Caretas* referred to Petrona as a *profesora* (a term used to refer to an upper-school teacher or college professor) who was presenting "an academic topic."[146] The magazine regularly included pictures of women taking notes and pointed out how this act showcased their commitment.[147] Like *El Hogar* before it, *Caras y Caretas* also noted the social function its classes played. In August 1937, for example, it explained that the hall "continues to be a 'rendez-vous' for distinguished enthusiasts of the noble culinary arts."[148] For many women, this meeting point presented them with an opportunity to enjoy a legitimate and even prestigious outing with other women.

As before, these conferences primarily drew female members of the upper and middle sectors of society, along with their cooks. Although the attendees all seemed to be female and the coupon specified that only "ladies" (*damas*) were invited to attend, a photograph from September 1936 shows a group of young girls watching from the balcony.[149] A couple of months later, the magazine explained that the "distinguished female public" was "of all ages," "old and young women" alike.[150] Photographs reveal that most of the women, like the *económa* who taught them, came finely dressed, many with chic hats and furs. Captions accompanying photos of the audience emphasized "the select and numerous female spectators" who continued to attend over the years.[151]

Almost all the lectures were held at La Liga Argentina de Damas Católicas (the Argentine Catholic Ladies League), which had a traditionally conservative and privileged membership. Further, the demonstration was augmented by this group's charity efforts, namely a well-supported raffle of one of the dishes to benefit the Patronato de la Infancia (Children's Foundation), an organization that focused on orphans.[152] Such charity work provided a respectable outlet for women's public initiatives and a means to begin to build the welfare state, as Donna Guy has demonstrated.[153]

For her part, Petrona had a vested personal (and not just commercial) interest in the success of these conferences. As was the case with most celebrities during this era, Petrona's growing number of female fans knew little of her personal life, and especially of her and her husband's struggles with infertility. As one journalist from Santiago del Estero later put it, "Without the blessing of natural children," Petrona and Oscar apparently chose to adopt at some point during the mid-1930s.[154] Petrona later recalled in her memoirs: "The arrival of my only son Marcelo fifty years ago brought happiness to our lives. I have seen few children so beautiful and well behaved as him."[155]

Nevertheless, while she shared the joy of Marcelo's arrival with her would-be biographer, Oscar Alberto Cejas, Petrona apparently did not mention that she had adopted her son. In his prologue, Cejas wrote, "It would be admirable if her grandchildren, great-grandchildren, and those who with the passing of time share her bloodline, conserve the spirit, the strength, and the moral principles of their predecessor."[156] As his reference to a shared bloodline suggests, neither on this occasion nor during many other interviews did Petrona publicly speak about this adoption. Like her time on the Taboada estancia, it seems that adoption was a topic that did not fit with the ideal model of womanhood that circulated in early twentieth-century Buenos Aires.[157]

With all of Petrona's financial success, during the mid-1930s the recently expanded family was able to move to Olivos, a wealthy suburb of Buenos Aires. In fact, their new house on Malaver Street stood just across from the presidential residence. They now enjoyed the size and location of an elite *porteño* household. They also bought their first car, which Petrona apparently loved to drive—and which Oscar did not. One of Petrona's favorite public anecdotes occurred at some point during the 1930s when she was driving fast and nearly crashed with another driver, who as it turned out was the soccer star Angel Labruna. "Why don't you learn to cook instead of drive!" he apparently exclaimed after they both got out of their cars. Petrona calmly handed him her card, and he called her later to apologize.[158] Petrona seemed to relish the irony that she both confirmed and challenged his expectations of what a woman should do with her time.

Government Involvement

Petrona clearly had moved up in the world—from a northwestern migrant unsure about her future in the big city, to a woman who faced questions from her husband's family about her decision to work, to a culinary celebrity who had made enough money to buy a car and a house next to the president's. While women's interest, corporate backing, and the expansion of the mass media had enabled this remarkable journey, the government also began to play a small role during the late 1930s. In 1938, the National Meat Board commissioned Petrona to promote underused cuts of meat, as part of its ongoing desire to "popularize the cooking process for each type of cut, in order to awaken interest for fibrous and older meat."[159] This initiative spoke to the Argentine state's mounting interest in food and domestic consumption. Whereas corporations had capitalized on the home economics movement in the late 1920s and early 1930s to sell their products to female consumers, in the late 1930s public interests began to use corporate sales strategies to promote internal consumption for national industries. The Peronist government would certainly become much better known for such initiatives, but the National Meat Board's previous collaboration with Petrona C. de Gandulfo demonstrates an earlier state involvement in trying to foster domestic consumption.

The national government became increasingly interested in the question of what its populace was eating during the mid-1930s. Building on the development of nutritional science and international attention to food in the previous decade, Argentine politicians and doctors began to speak and write about the relationship between food and health. In 1935, Emilio J. Schleh, a delegate of the Argentine Association of Biotypology, Eugenics, and Social Medicine, complained that despite the fact that Argentines "live surrounded by abundance," a significant portion of the population had a deficient diet. He continued, "Neither public powers, nor private institutions . . . nor individual concern, have until today made the necessary effort so that everyone in all social classes and all latitudes of the country can count on sufficient resources and shared accessibility to them."[160] The director of the state-supported National Institute of Nutrition, Dr. Pedro Escudero, also pointed out in 1935 that Argentine doctors had focused on disease without considering how inadequate diets and too much work had led to illness and death.[161] Dr. Escudero initiated several campaigns to study working-class families' current eating practices and to educate Argentines about "fundamental dietary laws."[162] He was convinced that nutritional deficits stemmed more from a lack of knowledge than from a lack of resources.[163]

Some three years earlier, the National Meat Board had commissioned Dr. Escudero to look at how to increase domestic meat consumption of less desirable cuts of meat in Argentina. Founded in 1933, the board sought to provide a formal organization to link Argentine meat producers and help them to market their products.[164] In addition to setting up a network to better store and distribute meat, the board charged itself with educating Argentine consumers, whom it envisioned as providing the "safest" and potentially largest source of future profits. The board explained that it aimed "not only to strengthen the situation of this industry, but also to improve the dietary conditions of some poor and distant regions of the country."[165]

This focus on the domestic market bespoke a dramatic shift away from the export-oriented focus of the past—a shift that was particularly telling in an industry that had served as a pillar of Argentina's export economy.[166]

To address both the commercial and the dietary issues, Dr. Escudero suggested and received permission to create the Comisión para el Estudio y Propaganda de la Carne (Commission for the Study and Promotion of Meat). Under Escudero's leadership, this commission adopted a "strictly scientific" approach, which included the establishment of a meat laboratory where official cuts, best cooking techniques, and nutritional values were established. Like Petrona C. de Gandulfo, Escudero made use of new media venues to share his conclusions, including conferences, brochures, and the radio.

The National Meat Board shifted to a more commercial approach after partnering with Petrona C. de Gandulfo. In 1938, she released a cookbook for the board entitled *Los cortes de carnes y su utilización: Recetas culinarias preparadas por la señora Petrona C. de Gandulfo* (Cuts of Meat and their Utilization: Culinary Recipes Prepared by Mrs. Petrona C. de Gandulfo). Around the same time, Petrona began to give live presentations about how to best cook with less popular cuts of meat. Speaking to a mixed-sex crowd in person and on Radio Excelsior, she was joined by another female *ecónoma* and a couple of male butchers. (Meat and masculinity remained tightly linked.) Still, Petrona addressed the new cookbook she published to women and included recipes for cooking various cuts of beef, veal, lamb, and pork indoors. While it started off with a few fancy French recipes such as steaks au gratin, steaks *a la maitre d'hotel*, and fan (*abanico*) of hot and cold tongue, the majority of the dishes were simple, typical *criollo* preparations, such as *puchero, carbonada criolla* (beef stew with vegetables, tomatoes, and peaches), *milanesa* (breaded beef cutlet), and *parrillada* (grilled beef innards, ribs, and steaks). While Petrona deemed some of these recipes too simple for inclusion in *El libro de Doña Petrona* (such as the ubiquitous *milanesa*), others, like *bifes de lomo a la maitre d'hotel*, were clearly modified repetitions.[167]

In this new cookbook, Petrona C. de Gandulfo offered more specific and even somewhat scientific instructions. For example, at the beginning of this text she specified that "to make a good *puchero*, in which the meat is substantial, it should be put in boiling water, because in this way the fibers will contract and they will not lose their properties."[168] In addition, she included a separate ingredients list in the National Meat Board's cookbook, making these versions of her recipes easier to follow than in her original

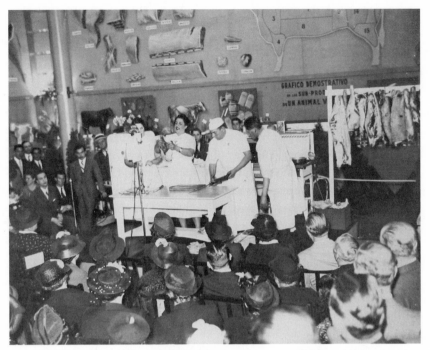

Petrona C. de Gandulfo promoting different cuts of meat for the Junta Nacional de Carnes, live and on Radio Excelsior, ca. 1938. Courtesy of Marcela Massut.

cookbook. Because she was asked to focus her instructions on how to cook with tougher cuts of meat, many of the preparations in *Los cortes de carnes* required that the meats be cooked in some type of liquid, as was the case with the *puchero* recipe.

Petrona's attention to proper cooking techniques in the cookbook she wrote for the National Meat Board reflected a larger governmental concern about whether Argentines knew how to cook and eat properly. President Roberto M. Ortiz, a member of the Radical Party elected to the presidency in 1938, replacing the military governments that preceded him, reiterated several times that dietary problems represented "one of the most serious preoccupations" of his government.[169] Ortiz himself was a diabetic treated privately by Dr. Pedro Escudero, so he had firsthand experience with the links between food and health.[170] As president, Ortiz's preoccupation with food in Argentina was part of a larger concern about the inadequacy of the global food supply, which would become increasingly apparent with the start of World War II in 1939.

Conclusion

By the late 1930s, corporations and homemakers were joined by Argentine politicians and medical professionals who recognized the importance of food. As director of the National Institute of Nutrition Pedro Escudero remarked in 1938, there was a new awareness in Argentina that food had "the highest place in family life and society" because it was "the basis of existence."[171] Advances in nutrition science, combined with changes in the global political economy, encouraged politicians to become more involved in promoting specific foods and food-related behaviors in Argentina. As leaders shifted their focus inward, they became more preoccupied with increasing domestic consumption of nationally produced goods such as beef. Such initiatives would pave the way for many of the Peronist platforms that would follow—and also expand Petrona's potential audience.

This *ecónoma* had already made significant inroads during the 1930s. Her early success in championing a new modern style of cooking was made possible by the growth of the consumer market, the mass media, and urban women's sense that they needed and wanted to learn more about the culinary arts. Petrona proved herself to be a savvy businesswoman—by asking to sign her magazine column, buying radio space, and promoting her cookbook. She did so at the behest of women who demonstrated their keen interest in these endeavors. In looking back on her career, she underplayed her ambition and instead emphasized her desire to meet women's needs rather than to create and profit from them. Her corporate and government sponsors were more direct in their desire to use her to help sell their products to women. In turn, the women who contacted her seemed more interested in the information and relationships with her and other women that she could provide than the things she could sell. Nevertheless, to follow her instructions "to the letter" required acquiring new things—from a gas stove to a magazine to a particular brand of baking powder.

As the consumer market expanded, young, urban women, many of whom had spent more time studying and socializing outside of the house than had previous generations, began to look outside their homes for domestic advice. Even as the majority of women across the country continued to learn how to cook from female relatives and friends, a significant number of relatively well-off urban women began to turn to new sources of information. Their earliest choices included a handful of cookbooks aimed at professionals or culinary advice columns in magazines like *El Hogar* or *Para Ti*. By the early 1930s, live demonstrations and radio broadcasts expanded the venues for a public culinary education.

By the middle of the decade, Petrona C. de Gandulfo and her sponsors had used these venues and this interest to make her into a new type of figure—a public domestic expert. Women began to turn specifically to her for expertise and advice, as they did to brand-name products. She and her fans had begun to set a common table, even if it was not yet widely disbursed. By establishing herself as a common culinary referent for people in diverse circumstances, this *económa* began to dramatically widen the scope and homogenize the content of common private tutorials. Petrona began to play a significant role in disbursing new ideas about food—by emphasizing the importance of mastering a cosmopolitan repertoire, by using new technologies and products to make baked desserts and stylized dishes, and by explaining how to set an elegant dining room table.

This modern approach to cooking resonated with the changing dynamics of urban daily life. Some seven decades later, her granddaughter, Marcela Massut, suggested that her grandmother sought to provide Argentine women, who had formerly learned to cook from previous generations, with "another way to cook, to serve a meal, [and] to take care of the home."[172] Many were interested. In cities across Argentina, women followed her magazine columns and hundreds received published responses in the mid-1930s. Growing numbers listened to her on the radio, and thousands of women in Buenos Aires and Rosario attended free, live cooking lectures. Those who could snapped up her 1934 cookbook. She would go on to sell out five additional editions of at least 5,000 copies each over the rest of the decade.[173] As the editors of *Caras y Caretas* pointed out in 1937, Petrona C. de Gandulfo was "achieving a success without precedent."[174]

Nevertheless, while her live performances, radio program, and magazine column began to give her a national presence and ushered in the era of cooking as entertainment, her cookbook's influence did not yet extend much beyond the capital city and the well-to-do. The household of the governor of the province of Jujuy came to possess the sixth edition of *El libro de Doña Petrona* in 1939, and his staff proceeded to regularly refer to it, but most Argentines still did not own this or any other cookbook.[175] In the next chapter, we shall see how Petrona began to establish her cookbook as the "bible of the home" during the 1940s. It is a story not only about a successful cook and her book, but also about the changing dynamics of consumption and social mobility during this decade.

CHAPTER THREE

EXPANDING CONSUMPTION
& MIDDLE-CLASS DOMESTICITY

Pan Dulce de Navidad (Christmas Sweet Bread)

FIRST PREPARATION:
Put on the table, in the form of a crown, 200 grams of flour; in the middle, 100 grams of fresh bread yeast and a little lukewarm water; knead it to form a dough that is neither too soft nor too firm, knead it well, put it in a bowl, cover it with flour, put a towel on top and leave it like that in a lukewarm place until it rises.

SECOND PREPARATION:
Put on the table, in the form of a crown, 500 grams of flour; in the middle put the first preparation, add a little lukewarm water and form the dough; knead it well, put it in a bowl, put a towel on top and leave it like that in a lukewarm place until it rises again.

THIRD PREPARATION:
Repeat the procedure with an equal quantity of flour as the second time, that is to say, 500 grams, put it in a lukewarm place and let it rise for the third time.

Put on the table, in the form of a crown, two kilograms of flour; in the middle [put] the preparation with yeast and 600 grams of butter; knead this yeast mixture with the butter until they are well combined; add a dozen whole eggs, a cup of cognac, three tablespoons of orange blossom water, a little bit of fine salt and 800 grams of ground sugar; knead it well adding to it, if necessary, lukewarm water; form a dough that is neither too soft nor too firm and work it over well until it is smooth and soft. Open it up at this point, adding 250 grams of raisins, 100 grams of sugared cut-up orange peel, 50 grams of almonds and 50 grams of pine nuts; knead it well so that the fruit is well distributed, put it in a bowl or large platter, cover it and leave it until it rises. At this point, cut it into pieces weighing one kilogram or one kilogram and 100 grams, form them into balls, put them on separate pans, cover them and leave them until they rise. Score them with a razor blade, paint them with beaten egg and put them in the oven to cook at a moderate temperature. The pans should be buttered and floured.

Details: So that the bread is light and spongy it is necessary to work it a lot, in other words, knead the dough a lot and also let it rise well. If you let the yeast rise too long, it will spoil. If it needs more water or milk, add it; do the same with flour.[1]

Introduction

Even today, many Argentines celebrate the Christmas and New Year's holidays by sharing some *pan dulce de navidad* with friends and relatives. While many people buy it at bakeries, others still make it at home. Those who prepare it themselves sometimes proudly mention that they made it "with Doña Petrona." Over the course of the twentieth century, Petrona's recipe became the standard for homemade Christmas sweet bread in Argentina. As her recipe from the 1930s suggests, the person following it would need a significant amount of time and resources. Petrona instructed the cook to start the first preparation at seven in the morning, the second around the middle of the day, and the third step in the evening.[2] The cook would need the entire day to make this bread, which also required the skill to determine the proper texture for the dough, how long to knead it, and how long to bake it in the oven, as her instructions presupposed this expertise. In addition, this recipe required costly ingredients, like almonds, pine nuts, cognac, and a dozen eggs.

After taking office in 1946, President and First Lady Juan and Eva Perón capitalized on the tremendous symbolic value of food by distributing millions of loaves of *pan dulce* and bottles of cider as a gift to Argentine citizens to celebrate the Christmas holiday. In so doing, this populist government enabled working-class families who might not have had the time or the resources to follow Petrona's recipe (or to buy *pan dulce* at a bakery) the chance to take part in this ritual celebration. Many did, and large crowds gathered to claim their holiday gifts. This act, which invited the working class to enjoy the fruits of the common table, provided a tangible representation of the Peronist pledge to promote social justice in everyday life. When Argentines recall this gesture today, some mention that it made them feel as if they were part of a national family. This was a sentiment that the president and first lady worked hard to promote. Both in this act and in

The Eva Perón Foundation distributing Christmas sweet bread and cider in Rosario, ca. 1950. Courtesy of Archivo General de la Nación.

many others, the Peronist propaganda machine portrayed Juan Perón as the father and Eva Perón as the mother of the nation.[3]

Juan and Eva Perón were not the first to adopt a parental position to generate public support or to use the media to do so. During the 1930s and early 1940s, Petrona C. de Gandulfo established herself as an increasingly well-known motherly figure. As we have seen, she reached urban women who wished to learn how to cook in a modern manner through her live performances, magazine columns, and radio programs. In Argentina then it was not only populist politicians but also commercial figures who gained national favor and influence by establishing a sense of familiarity with citizens and by expanding the terms of citizenship beyond the political to the economic and social realms.

Both prior to and during the Peronist expansion of consumption, Petrona C. de Gandulfo worked hard to continue to expand her audience. But her ability to do so was not a foregone conclusion. During the early 1940s, she promoted a model of privileged domesticity that, at first glance, might seem to be threatened by the Peronist government's celebration of the working class and its growing control of the media during the second half of the decade. Nevertheless, as we shall see, while this populist government would seek to demote her, it would also extend the patterns of the common table she had set. In addition, while the Peronist government would usurp a number of private initiatives, it would not replace them entirely, allowing Doña Petrona and her sponsors to continue to shape consumer desires. This chapter reveals how first Doña Petrona, and then the Peronist government, together with a growing number of Argentines, expanded a model of middle-class domesticity and expected a broader range of women to implement it during the course of the 1940s.

Reaching Out

Since the early 1930s, Petrona (and her sponsors) had used the mass media to establish herself as one of Argentina's leading domestic experts. Her live cooking demonstrations drew thousands of women in Buenos Aires and Rosario, and her presence on the radio and in magazines enabled her to reach beyond Argentina's largest cities. Still, most of her fans were relatively well-off women who owned a radio, or could afford to buy a cookbook, or were interested in subscribing to a fancy magazine. However, during the 1940s, the major expansion of the radio, along with Petrona's attempts to provide some less-expensive recipes in print, allowed her to reach a broader, and more modest, demographic.

The radio would become the most popular appliance in Argentina over the course of the 1940s, with nearly half the population possessing one across the country—a figure that rose to 82 percent in Buenos Aires.[4] With the expansion of this technology and Radio Excelsior's network, many more Argentines could listen to Petrona's culinary program across the country than during the previous decade. Petrona later remarked, "In that moment, the radio was as massive as television is today [1991] and this helped my popularity among women to grow."[5] Food journalist Miriam Becker echoed this sentiment, explaining, "I found out about her like all the people of my generation, from her books and her unmistakable radio style that began with a classic 'Good afternoon, dear (female) friends' [*Buenas tardes, queridas amigas*]."[6]

Petrona further expanded her audience through a new partnership with the popular magazine *Para Ti*.[7] In contrast to her previous magazine partners, this magazine was explicitly directed to women and reached a broader and more modest demographic.[8] Starting on 15 October 1940, Petrona C. de Gandulfo became the signatory on a column called "Para el menú" (For the Menu). There was surprisingly little fanfare. Her first recipes appeared with her signature but no explanation of her collaboration; it was not until the following year that she was described as being in charge of *Para Ti*'s culinary section.[9] In this new, more popular venue, Petrona published recipes for elaborate preparations and also for some homier and less-expensive dishes. For example, she dedicated one column to recipes using the inexpensive Italian staple polenta and another to favorites from northwestern Argentina, including empanadas and *pastelitos*.[10]

While Petrona's presence on Radio Excelsior and in *Para Ti* helped increase the demand for her advice, it was the editorial expansion of the 1940s that enabled her to sell her cookbook to a broader public. As the Spanish Civil War raged, from 1936 to 1939, numerous Spanish publishing professionals fled to Argentina, enabling it to become one of the preeminent publishers in the Americas.[11] Petrona seemed to recognize this potential, and even as she retained editorial control and the bulk of the profits for herself, she elected to work with the Argentine publisher Atlántida (which also owned *Para Ti*) in 1941. In publishing her cookbook with Atlántida, Petrona traded her exclusive profits for wider distribution across Argentina. Lifelong book distributor Isay Klasse explains that by the early 1940s both Atlántida and Doña Petrona envisioned the benefits of their collaboration: "The firm Atlántida entered into a relationship with Doña Petrona because where there is a magazine for children and for women there can also be a cookbook; in addition [this firm] offered her the great advantage of putting advertisements in their magazines, which reached from the lower to the upper middle class. It was the market that Doña Petrona needed, and for the first time, she gave up the sale of [some of] her books to Atlántida."[12] Like the recollections of others from the time, Klasse's recollections linked middle-class women with the primary responsibility for, as well as interest in, topics pertaining to children and food.

As a result of this collaboration, the number of editions of *El libro de Doña Petrona* in circulation increased dramatically. With Atlántida publishing and distributing a portion of her books, Petrona released twenty-one new editions from 1941 to 1949 and sold over 128,000 copies—more than tripling her production of the previous decade.[13] As we shall see, this book would sell quite well during the Peronist era; but even before Perón took office, the collaboration between Petrona and Atlántida paid off by almost doubling her previous solo production. From 1941 to 1945, twelve new editions were brought to market, amounting to more than 70,000 copies.[14] A growing number of other cookbooks would appear over the course of the 1940s, but they proved little match for *El libro de Doña Petrona*, whose author enjoyed a larger presence in the media.[15]

Atlántida not only helped Petrona to expand her sales but also convinced her to modify and streamline the layout and printing of her cookbook. The ninth edition, which was the first that Atlántida printed, used a smaller font to fit more text on each page, and its index had two columns rather than one. In addition, the difficult-to-print fold-out pages, which had provided step-by-step photographs of certain processes like how to make empanada and pastry dough, were replaced by easier-to-print pages consistent with the rest of the text. Notwithstanding the techniques implemented to save space, the ninth edition was thirty-one pages longer than its predecessor. These additional pages were filled with around 300 new recipes, many, in the sections on appetizers and desserts, useful for entertaining. Petrona did not remove any previous recipes but simply added new ones, as she had done and would continue to do in other editions.

In addition to streamlining the publication of her cookbook, Atlántida also helped Petrona update her self-presentation. The new photograph at the beginning of the ninth edition suggested a more confident and polished image. In the first edition, she had included a photo of herself in which she looked sternly at the camera. She replaced this photo in the second edition with one in which she gently smiled, a braid crowning the top of her head— giving her a more traditional, even provincial look. In the new photograph for the 1941 edition with Atlántida, Petrona looked straight at the camera and smiled brightly, her hair framing her face in short waves, conveying a more modern, urbane appearance.[16]

Petrona's collaboration with Atlántida also led to an increase in new advertisements. The ninth edition, printed with Atlántida, incorporated an updated Primitiva advertisement along with those from new local businesses, including Casa D'Huicque, which sold coffees and teas, Julia R. Esteves, which sold materials for bakeries, and the upscale British department store Harrod's, one of the "cathedrals of the new religion of consumerism," which had opened in Buenos Aires in 1914.[17] Eager to disseminate this doctrine, Petrona included an advertisement for Harrod's in her cookbook, and she continued to give live cooking demonstrations there during the 1940s. As consumer culture continued to expand during the early part of this decade, businesses proved eager to link their products to this cookbook and its author.

The ninth edition also included a promotion for Petrona's new cookbook, *Para aprender a decorar* (Learning How to Decorate). Also published in 1941 by Atlántida, this thin, beautifully illustrated book focused exclusively on decorating cakes and other desserts.[18] Although it would never have the success achieved by *El libro de Doña Petrona*, the first print run of 10,000

Portraits of Petrona C. de Gandulfo from El libro de Doña Petrona: *1934 (left), 1935–40 (middle), and 1941–47 (right). Courtesy of Marcela Massut.*

copies sold out quickly, and it would become one of her most-sought-after books.[19] Yet again Petrona and her sponsors used her mass media presence to help this effort. For example, in June 1942, *Para Ti* included her new decorating cookbook on its list of "six interesting books for women."[20]

The success of *Para aprender a decorar* helped to establish Petrona's reputation as a skilled culinary decorator and *the* definitive resource for dessert recipes for celebratory occasions like birthdays, weddings, and anniversaries. Several middle- and working-class Argentines I spoke with described how they used *Para aprender a decorar* or *El libro de Doña Petrona* to prepare their children's birthday cakes. A woman named Elba, who grew up in the province of Santa Fe and later moved to Mendoza and eventually to Buenos Aires, described how she had done just this. "The cake for my oldest son's first birthday, which was the merry-go-round [cake], I got from *El libro de Doña Petrona*." Pointing at the picture proudly, she explained, "I did it just the same, light blue, exactly as it is in this book."[21] Other women I spoke with mentioned that they had made her cake with a soccer field or a clown for one of their children's birthdays.

The growing emphasis on desserts reflected the greater ease of baking with the newly available gas stoves. It also tapped into the new respect for cooking as a form of artistic expression worthy of study. In her memoirs, Petrona claimed that she single-handedly succeeded at ending the tradition of elite *porteño* families ordering their wedding cakes from England. She proudly stated, "It was I who eliminated [this practice], as my wedding cakes, produced, designed and decorated with a unique style and originality, replaced those that had arrived from London."[22] In fact, Elba had used Petrona's recipe to bake and decorate her own wedding cake with a friend's

Elba A. with her copy of
El libro de Doña Petrona, *which is turned to the page with the wedding cake she made from it. Buenos Aires, 2004. Photograph taken by author.*

help. "I made the cake for my wedding. And with the pillars, looking at the book, a friend, who was my husband's cousin, decorated it for me. She did the white part, and afterward we put the rings, the charms together [on top]."[23]

Petrona's recipes for British-style cakes played an important role in stimulating the local production of elaborate cakes by dedicated home cooks like Elba and her friend, as well as professional bakers. But the ongoing struggle of World War II clearly did as well. In the spring of 1940, with the Germans occupying much of Europe, the British established a naval blockade in the Atlantic, effectively sealing off Argentina's primary trade partners in Europe. Argentina maintained its neutrality, despite U.S. pressure and its subsequent decision to boycott the Argentine economy starting in 1942. Argentina's grain exports to continental Europe dropped dramatically, while beef exports to England, its main trading partner, increased. At the same time, imports screeched to a halt.[24] It was not a time for Brits to be shipping cakes across the Atlantic; instead it was a time for Argentina to once again consider its vulnerability on the world market.

This vulnerability was something many Argentines increasingly presumed the current government would be unable to overcome. Having replaced the more liberal president Ortiz in 1940, former vice president Ramón Castillo and his government earned notoriety for their role in fraudulent elections and ineffectual economic policy. In 1943, for the second time in Argentine history, the military staged a coup. Military leaders argued that they would more aggressively fight communism, arm Argentina to protect itself against the United States and an increasingly militarized Brazil, and intervene in the nation's economy.[25] But after taking power, the military leadership fractured into two distinct camps, one favoring a more liberal and conciliatory approach toward the United States and the other rejecting such conciliation and championing nationalism and industrialization. Juan Perón belonged to the latter camp. He made his way through the ranks, establishing himself as minister of labor and then minister of war, eventually becoming vice president in 1945. It was still unclear at this point if he would play an enduring role in Argentine politics.

With the direction of national politics in question, Petrona's personal life took a devastating turn. Her husband, Oscar Gandulfo, became ill, and in 1943 he passed away. In her memoirs, she recalled the loneliness and the sadness of the period following his death. She described the enormous pain she felt at the loss of her "true love," her companion, with whom she had shared the ups and downs of their path from "subsistence to prosperity." A number of her friends helped her through this difficult time.[26] She also seemed to find some solace in her career. Despite her tremendous personal grief, Petrona continued to offer re-editions of her first cookbook, and people continued to buy them.

Cities had grown dramatically in the previous ten years, and none more than Buenos Aires, which had gained over a million new residents, most of them from small towns in the provinces.[27] In 1945, Petrona released a new edition of *El libro de Doña Petrona* that incorporated a new section directed to those living in modern urban homes. While most recent internal migrants struggled to get by, she offered her advice to families well enough off to set themselves apart—many of whom were the children or grandchildren of European immigrants. She suggested that the famous aphorism, "Tell me *what* you eat and I will tell you who you are," should now be changed to, "Tell me *how and where* you eat and I will tell you who you are."[28] She spoke to the "how" by continuing to provide specific instructions on how to set a table and serve a meal. She emphasized the "where" by continuing to instruct the *buena ama de casa* in how to give the modern dining room "all the attention it deserves." Relating the decoration of the dining room to the identity of the homemaker, she wrote, "No other room will reflect your personality as fully."[29] Such advice spoke to the growing importance of sociability at the table, as well as the growing expectations that women should dedicate themselves to realizing it.

As the birthrate fell and the country continued to industrialize, politicians and health officials stepped up their efforts to steer women toward the domestic realm. As World War II drew to a close, some warned that women's extradomestic work was threatening Argentina's future. For example, the prominent Alejandro Bunge Institute issued a 1945 report that explained, "We think the essential problem is that women, who abandon the home to work in jobs not suited for them and compete successfully with men because they accept lower salaries, threaten the family hierarchy . . . and challenge their patriotic duties of motherhood."[30] Like previous generations, those who issued this and similar warnings clearly stated that women belonged in the home and not the workplace, for both their families' and their nation's well-being.

Buying into It

Doña Petrona's advice continued to use the carrot much more than the stick to direct women to the home and to domestic pursuits. She celebrated what women could achieve in the home and even began to loosen up some of the domestic "rules," such as how to set a table, in the 1945 edition. Nevertheless, she also emphasized the importance of the incorporation of the personal touch of the young homemaker (*joven dueña de casa*), making it clear that although women could have flexibility in decorating, they should still focus on this kind of activity. As before, she did not presume that her fans would know how to decorate or to cook in this modern manner. For example, she included a chart with two weeks' worth of daily menus, aimed at women unsure of how to combine different foods or how to entertain. Because she was making significant changes to this 1945 edition, Petrona also added many new recipes for appetizers, poultry, meats, eggs, and desserts for multicourse meals. Several people I spoke with suggested that this inclusivity was a key part of what made this cookbook so successful. As one person explained, "This [book] is like a kind of encyclopedia. If one didn't know about a particular dish someone mentioned, you knew that you would find it in *El libro de Doña Petrona*."[31]

Petrona released some significantly modified editions, as in the 1941 and 1945 editions, but most of her re-editions tended to have only minor changes. For example, revising the twelfth edition in 1943 for the thirteenth edition, Petrona penciled in minor corrections on just 21 of the 515 pages. Her attention to detail is clear; her notes generally correct typos or clarify procedures. Her main substantive change was a testament to the impact of commercialization—to thicken dishes she now replaced flour and potato starch (*chuño*) with cornstarch (*maizena*), which was becoming popular during this time.[32]

As Isay Klasse explained, Petrona generally did not have time for major changes because of the consistently high demand for her cookbook.[33] Luis La Cueva experienced this demand firsthand as a young man selling books at El Ateneo in the mid-1940s. One of the largest publishers and bookstores in Buenos Aires, El Ateneo attempted to keep a steady supply of *El libro de Doña Petrona* in the store to meet consumer requests. Luis explained that they would receive 500 copies at a time to sell to individual customers as well as to other smaller bookstores in Buenos Aires and the provinces. He recalled that Doña Petrona's cookbook "would sell to such an extent that we put them in a pile in the basement, where we would keep replacements, and we bound the pile with rope so that it would not fall. . . . We sold them by the ton, as we were selling them to the provinces as well."[34] He noted that most of his customers were women buying this "mid-priced" book for weddings, birthdays, and New Year's Eve for their friends and family members. Some men also got in on the act. Luis himself said that he "gave it as a gift count-less times to people who were going to get married."[35]

During the course of the 1940s, *El libro de Doña Petrona* became a classic gift for young girls as well as for about-to-be married women across Argentina. This trend reflected Argentines' increasing possibilities for consumption, as well as the saliency of the idea that women should know how to cook and would benefit from learning how to do so from an expert, in addition to or in lieu of advice from their friends and relatives. For example, as Ofelia F. explained, her husband bought her *El libro de Doña Petrona* during the early 1940s so that "she could learn how to cook."[36] This sentiment existed despite the fact that she had cooked since she was little and, as we saw previously, had, as a teenager during the 1930s, faithfully attended, practiced, and compiled the culinary lessons that Petrona C. de Gandulfo led in *El Hogar*'s hall.

Several women who would later become *económas* also spoke publicly of having such an experience themselves. For example, *económa* María del Carmen recalled being given *El libro de Doña Petrona* as a gift from her fiancé in 1942. "One day my mother suggested that we invite my future parents-in-law over to meet my parents," she recalled, "and I had to cook [with *El libro de Doña Petrona*] in order to show my merits."[37] *Económa*

Emmy de Molina suggested the ubiquity of this trend: "What *ama de casa*, recently married woman, or fiancée did not receive *El libro de Doña Petrona* on the day of their [big] event? In it one found every kind of recipe, from the most simple and economic up through the most elaborate and costly."[38] More often than not, Argentines who came to own this cookbook during the 1940s (and after) were relatively well-off women who had received it as a gift for a special occasion or rite of passage.

For her part, Emmy de Molina, whose upper middle-class family resided in Buenos Aires, not only became a recipient of this cookbook but also experienced the weight of expectations that cooking and caring for her family should be her ultimate goal. Emmy's daughter, Pelusa Molina, explained that at some point in the 1940s after her mother got engaged, "her parents went on a trip, and she stayed at home with her brothers, who were studying with some male friends from the university and they asked her to prepare them something." They were horrified to learn that their sister did not "even know how to make a fried egg." They called their grandparents, who promptly sent Emmy to a technical school to learn how to cook. Interestingly, Emmy's grandmother could not teach her to cook as "she was raised in a family with high social standing, with domestic help, and she didn't go in the kitchen."[39]

But times had changed. Even well-off women were expected to know how to cook in 1940s Buenos Aires. Despite Emmy's desire to be an artist, her family put greater emphasis on ensuring that she received the proper culinary training to become a wife and homemaker. For her part, Emmy would eventually translate this training into a career as an *ecónoma*, becoming one of Petrona's most trusted colleagues.[40]

Some women were thrust into this domestic role, but many others clearly sought it out. For example, Elba, the woman who had used *El libro de Doña Petrona* to make her own wedding cake, described her excitement in receiving *El libro de Doña Petrona* as a gift on the birthday before her wedding in 1944. Earlier that decade, Elba had begun a manuscript collection of recipes from magazines, her friends, and eventually her future mother-in-law's edition of *El libro de Doña Petrona*.[41] Once in possession of this cookbook, she replaced her recipe cut-outs with this text. She used it to figure out how to "set the table well" when she had guests over to eat or a birthday party for one of her children. A huge fan of *El libro de Doña Petrona*, she "oohed and aahed" as we looked through the cookbook together sixty years later, recalling particular recipes she enjoyed or tips she appreciated. She stopped to marvel at some of her favorite recipes, including those for stuffed cannelloni; Vitel Tonne, a cold meat dish popular for Christmas and New Year's; and the thumbprint cookies called *pepitas*.

In a sense, Elba's familiarity with this cookbook had made it her own. Like women who had previously kept manuscript books, for Elba and others, *El libro de Doña Petrona* could evoke a feeling of ownership. Even more than Elba's previous collection of recipes from magazines and other sources, its character as a bound book further distanced this kind of text from handwritten manuscripts. The information within was therefore more standardized for the many women who began to cook with it. Petrona and those who cooked with her or like her had established a common (if still not widely distributed) table.

Women's desire for experts and printed material for domestic advice was something that a growing number of commercial entities worked hard to promote. While the British gas company Primitiva had launched Petrona's career based on such a desire, the U.S. brand Royal now sought to link its baking powder to Argentina's leading *ecónoma*.[42] In 1945, Royal asked her to create a free pamphlet with ten recipes using its baking powder. The company placed numerous advertisements in newspapers and magazines touting this pamphlet and the company's relationship with its author. For example, a November 1945 ad in *La Nación* pronounced that "Royal is pleased to offer you the favorite recipes of the popular and famous culinary authority, la señora Petrona C. de Gandulfo." Royal also began to put advertisements (and a cut-out for requesting the booklet) next to Petrona's recipe columns in *Para Ti*.[43] By linking its product to Petrona, this international company sought to encourage local women to buy its product, apparently with success. According to several Argentines I spoke with, Royal's small, free booklet was among the most common for women to have and bake with at home.[44]

Getting Involved: The Peronist Government

Corporations would continue to play a major role in marketing their products and emphasizing women's roles as consumers, homemakers, and cooks during the second half of the 1940s. But with the 1946 election of Juan Perón, the government would become a much more significant figure in directly shaping the dynamics of the marketplace and of daily life. In the post–World War II period, leaders of various political persuasions agreed upon the merits of industrialization but disagreed about who should benefit from these processes and how they should be implemented. Juan Perón gained enough electoral support to win the presidency based on his stance that the working class should be among the primary beneficiaries and that the state should control the distribution of these benefits.

This novel approach spoke to a deep-seated frustration of the poor about the lack of benefits they had gained with the modernization of Argentina's economy. As we have seen, liberal policies led to a national boom that benefited a small wealthy minority, helped create a substantial urban middle class, and further impoverished the poor majority. Perón's ability to begin to address poor people's plight as minister of labor (1943–45) had won him significant working-class support, which manifested itself in the massive march for his release from jail on 17 October 1945.[45] Perón had also sought out the support of the middle class as minister of labor in 1944. Like others at the time, Perón (who came from a middle-class background himself) initially seemed to feel that the middle class was noble for being "right in the middle" (*justo medio*) and therefore essential to maintaining the social equilibrium.[46] However, after taking the presidency with working-class support, Juan Perón celebrated the workers and "the shirtless ones" (the *descamisados*) and not the middle class as the backbone of Argentine society.

Elected with the support of these so-called inferiors, Juan Perón responded to working-class demands for greater social and economic parity by extending citizenship rights beyond the political to the social and economic realms. He made "wage raising" a right to be claimed and negotiated on an annual basis by most industrial workers.[47] From 1946 to 1948, Perón supported policies that led to a 20 percent increase in the real wages of workers.[48] As Eduardo Elena has demonstrated, he also implemented policies and broadcast propaganda that made the right to consume across social class lines a central part of the "new Argentina" he sought to create.[49] By reducing food and housing costs, which represented most families' primary expenditures, Peronist policies created more expendable income for more Argentines.[50] The government subsidized beef, oil, sugar, and flour and set limits on the prices for these staples. It also established open-air markets in Buenos Aires where food was sold at reduced prices. In addition, it continued the rent freeze that had been initiated in 1943. Such policies created changes that people could appreciate in their everyday lives.[51] For example, in Daniel James's life history of Doña María Roldán, Roldán (a female meatpacker, union activist, and Peronist) fondly recalled Perón's first presidency, not only for advancements in social justice but also for material improvements that enabled her to buy some meat for supper or buy a new dress.[52]

The Peronist measures that allowed for such "improvements" were quite successful at first and, despite growing inflation, translated into a 7 percent increase in consumer spending during Perón's first two years in office.[53] The government publicly championed this feat and the idea that Argentine citizens, even relatively poor ones, all had a right to enjoy things like *pan dulce*, a juicy steak, new clothes, or a trip to the movies. But, as historians Juan Carlos Torre and Elisa Pastoriza have argued, although the Peronists radically redrew the social hierarchy, they did not promote a new cultural identity for Argentina.[54] Instead, the government suggested that the poor deserved to emulate the rich.

First Lady Eva Perón took a leading role in conveying this message. Eva Perón had played a relatively small role in Juan Perón's rise to the presidency, but once her husband took power, Evita (as she would come to be known) established herself as a key figure in national politics. As a former radio and film actress, Argentina's new first lady was adept at using the media to highlight her efforts. The government flooded the state-controlled media with images of Evita giving out sewing machines and soccer balls to grateful recipients. Not everyone agreed that the government should distribute such "handouts" to the poor. Many better-off Argentines expressed anxiety about the ways in which Peronist policies allowed their presumed social inferiors to socialize and consume like them.[55] In seeking to distinguish themselves, many became more self-consciously middle class.[56] Some labeled Perón's followers "little black heads" (*cabecitas negras*), emphasizing the superiority of their own education, comportment, and white skin to that of darker-skinned migrants. In particular, they (along with elites) scoffed at how Eva Perón, an illegitimate commoner, dared to dress in the elegant gowns and jewels that had once been the sole preserve of the upper echelon. But for the first lady, this ridicule was overshadowed by working-class adoration of her and the image of upward social mobility that she was able to convey.[57]

The Peronist government's decision to extend citizenship rights to include the right of the poor to consume was quite deliberate. The government aimed not only to sustain working-class support but also to build a national market that would absorb Argentine-made products. Touting a "third way" of organizing the economy that departed from both free market liberalism and communism, Perón installed a planning state that sought to control the market and temper the forces of unfettered capitalism. The government sought to tame the "immoral market" through wage hikes, price controls, and supervision and also nationalized several industries that had been under foreign ownership.[58] Perón argued that by buying back businesses from private businessmen and foreigners, Argentines could buy back their national sovereignty. Most famously, he made such promises tangible by nationalizing the previously British-owned railroad.

Petrona had built her career in the liberal "free market" with the support of international corporations, especially the British gas company Primitiva. On 5 March 1945, the military government nationalized this company.[59] In 1946, Perón acquired several other formerly private gas companies and formed Gas del Estado. Petrona was initially retained by this public entity, as can be seen on her new identification card. By the end of 1946, *El libro de Doña Petrona* included an advertisement heralding the state's ownership of gas services in Argentina. In contrast to the previous four-page advertisements by Primitiva, Gas del Estado's one-page advertisement was relatively simple, with only one illustration and little text. In the foreground, a woman holds a platter of food made in a spotless kitchen with a gas stove; the headline reads, "Ensure the success of your recipes. . . . Use Gas, the unbeatable fuel."[60]

The simplicity of this advertisement belied the dramatic changes that the state's acquisition of gas interests would have on expanding gas consumption in Argentina. In 1945, prior to the transition, private gas companies served 85 percent of the 255,000 gas consumers in Argentina. By 1949, the situation had more than reversed itself, with the state registering 96 percent of the now 384,000 users. During that period, the government had invested significant resources—some 50 million dollars and a lot of propaganda—into constructing a natural gas pipeline dubbed the "Presidente Perón."[61] With the pipeline up and running, by 1951, the state had once again almost doubled the total number of gas consumers, registering 700,000 across the country.[62] By creating favorable conditions for the manufacture and purchase of gas stoves, it enabled this Argentine industry to nearly triple.[63] At the same time, Peronist policies stymied the competition posed by electric stoves by placing additional restrictions on their manufacture and adding fees to their purchase.[64] While such tactics dramatically increased the number of people who had gas services in greater Buenos Aires, most Argentines outside this area continued to live without access to gas. Many continued to cook on *cocinas económicas*, fed with coal, kerosene, or firewood.[65] Nonetheless, Peronist propaganda celebrated its expansion of gas services "as one of the most significant indexes of the progress of our day."[66]

In addition to advertising in *El libro de Doña Petrona*, Gas del Estado asked both Petrona C. de Gandulfo and Angel Baldi (her former culinary instructor at Le Cordon Bleu) to sign a document publicly demonstrating

Petrona C. de Gandulfo's identification card for Gas del Estado, ca. 1946. Courtesy of Marcela Massut.

their support for gas as a cooking fuel. In a piece of propaganda published in 1946, both touted their experience with gas and its ease, security, efficiency, and affordability.[67] The Peronist regime's decision to seek out Petrona (and her mentor) as a "collaborator" from the inception of Gas del Estado reflected its recognition of her importance and influence with consumers. In a more private interaction, Juan Perón also apparently asked Petrona to make a cake for a birthday celebration at his private residence in their shared neighborhood. Petrona agreed, but asked her son, who delivered the cake across the street, not to ever tell anyone that she had baked Perón a cake.[68] As she would throughout the course of her career, Petrona sought to convey a public persona that distanced itself from and, at the same time, bridged political divides.

Doña Petrona, along with other women in the public eye, now shared the stage with a first lady eager to take the political spotlight. Eva Perón did not yet seem very interested in competing with Doña Petrona during the late 1940s, but she would seek to place other major female public efforts (especially those of suffragists and charity groups) under her purview. In early 1947, Eva Perón began campaigning on the radio and in other venues for the government's passage of female suffrage. She distinguished herself from feminists by parodying them as manly, elitist, and antinationalist.[69] In contrast, she suggested that those who now stood with Perón for female suffrage were supporting women's traditional roles.

Eva Perón made clear that the Peronist government called women into the political realm not to become more like men but rather so that they could use their womanly approach to help moralize and domesticate it.[70] As she explained to a group of women gathered for a speech in support of female suffrage in February 1947, "Your home, like mine, friend, is the soundbox [*caja de resonancia*] of the country, and anything that cannot be discussed, criticized, accepted, or rejected at the family table, does not count among the preoccupations of the country." On another occasion, she explained that women wanted the vote to defend "the family table and the right to a less difficult destiny." According to this new Peronist logic, because the home was the "center of the country" and the "family table" was the place where matters of national concern were discussed, women (who were in charge of both the home and the family table) were entitled to vote as well as to be elected.[71]

After the Peronist government passed female suffrage into law in September 1947, Evita continued to suggest that women themselves had earned this right. Women's hands, she explained, were "not new in struggles, work, and the repeated miracle of creation."[72] In expressing this sentiment, the first lady, like many of the Argentine feminists who preceded her, emphasized a maternalist rationale for women's right to vote.[73] Like a smaller number of previous suffragettes, Eva defended women's right to vote based on their work—both outside and inside the home.[74] The first lady, however, did not give any credit to the feminists who had fought for this right for decades. Instead, she shifted the credit and patriarchal authority to Perón, encouraging Argentine women to be faithful to the man who had incorporated them into politics. "Thanks to General Perón," she told a crowd of supporters, "all women are appreciated as much as they deserve to be appreciated." Both at home and in the "national consciousness," Eva Perón explained, women had finally acquired the respect they merited.[75]

During the 1940s, women not only gained the right to vote but also found new opportunities to pursue ongoing education and work, both before and during Peron's first presidency. More women attended secondary and professional schools, studied at the university, and entered the job market.[76] Perhaps most significant, given the pace of industrialization, women entered manufacturing jobs at a faster rate than men. Women continued to be especially dominant in particular industries like textile manufacturing, where they made up half of the workforce, and the garment industry, where they composed nearly 70 percent of the workers.[77] Their overall representation in Buenos Aires, where industry was consolidated, was higher than elsewhere in Argentina, reaching nearly a third of the workforce. This trend was also shaped by more women's entry into the "professional" realms of the economy dominated by men. By 1947, women had increased their presence in law, medicine, and other professions and composed more than 20 percent of government employees in the capital, up from 14 percent in 1914, a trend that would continue to accelerate.[78]

While women in Argentina had become more likely to work for wages before having children, they also became less likely to be employed during their childbearing years.[79] Women's withdrawal from full-time work to focus on mothering was something they were encouraged to do by a wide range of actors—government and media outlets, families and friends, and even the Catholic Church. Pope Pius XII encouraged the adoption of a family wage in Catholic countries across the globe so that men could support their families and women could return to their "proper calling" in the domestic realm.[80] In Argentina, male-dominated unions and the Peronist government agreed to wage raises, which made it feasible for more working-class men to support their families and more working-class women to become unpaid homemakers. Despite women's increasing educational (and to a lesser extent, professional) opportunities, around three-quarters of women continued to be identified as unremunerated *amas de casa* on both the 1947 and the 1960 censuses.[81]

Still, a number of female migrants to the capital came without male partners and little financial support. In response, the Peronist government established three Hogares de Tránsito (Transitional Homes) in 1948 and the Hogar de la Empleada (Female Employees' Home) in 1949 to house female migrants and their children in Buenos Aires. It is telling that these initiatives focused on women and their children, who the state suggested needed its protection. Such protection was both paternalist and maternalist in nature.[82] In the name of Argentina's first father, Juan Perón, Eva Perón assumed a motherly role. She set up the ground rules for the residents, not only restricting men from entering these homes but also imposing a strict curfew of 10:00 P.M. She also designed and decorated the homes with ornate furniture and sitting areas that replicated elite mansions. This elite propriety and aesthetics made tangible the ethos of Peronist social justice, which entitled the poor to live like the rich.[83]

Likewise, the food served in the Peronist cafeterias and restaurants was abundant and even refined. (This stood in stark contrast to the more modest offerings in somber, state-run dining halls in contemporary Peru and Mexico.[84]) In her inauguration speech for the Argentine Hogares de Tránsito, Eva Perón explained that the Hogar del Tránsito had "dignified lodging, excellent food, [and] effective spiritual, material, and moral guidance."[85] Indeed, the nutritional attention given to each guest was considerable, which was particularly important, as many of the residents were previously undernourished. Each woman received at least 3,000 calories a day divided between breakfast, lunch, and dinner. As one resident later shared with historian Carolina Barry, "We ate like a king [*a cuerpo de rey*]. . . . We would eat two dishes and a dessert and if it was cold, they would make us soup too." In turn, the two restaurants in El Hogar de la Empleada also served elaborate, multicourse meals, in this case for a small fee. In the less expensive of the two, diners enjoyed a live orchestra and a four-course meal for 3.50 pesos. On its opening day, the menu included melon and prosciutto, crepes filled with creamed corn and cheese, grilled entrecôte with French fries, and chocolate cake.[86] This multicourse cosmopolitan feast echoed the culinary preferences of the *porteño* middle and upper classes. In fact, it was a menu that could have easily been drawn from the pages of *El libro de Doña Petrona*.

Rather than proposing a nationalist culinary alternative, during the late 1940s the Peronist government further ingrained the cosmopolitan models of eating embraced by the turn-of-the-century elite. As we have seen, such models had recently been emulated by the nascent middle class during the 1930s and early 1940s. In addition to expanding the ability of the poor to consume, then, the Peronist government also reinforced the model of domesticity that Petrona C. de Gandulfo and her cookbook had come to symbolize.

Popularizing El Libro de Doña Petrona

The celebration of female domesticity and male productivity, along with the government's expansion of consumption, created the potential for Petrona (and her sponsors) to reach a broader audience. One of the key means for expanding her reach continued to be the radio. In 1947, Petrona left Radio Excelsior and moved back to Radio El Mundo, which was now informally under the purview of the Peronist government and reached a broad public.[87] She joined a line-up of largely female hosts, sponsored by Royal baking powder, which was, of course, an international corporation. With Doña Petrona as the headliner, the show, called *Tardecitas de Royal* (Afternoons with Royal), was broadcast every Tuesday and Friday at 3:45 P.M. and targeted *amas de casa*. In announcing the new program, the entertainment magazine *Radiolandia* explained that this "authoritative" expert on culinary matters, along with other "recognized artists," would lead a "refined and agreeable domestic" program.[88] The week after the first performance, *Radiolandia* published a large picture of what it dubbed "Doña Petrona's program" for Royal.[89]

Listeners who tuned into this program heard a wide range of culinary and domestic advice. One woman who as a child listened to this program (which, she recalled, was sponsored by Royal and Aurora stoves) remembered that "Doña Petrona would give suggestions and advice. I remember that my mom would sew; at that time we were accustomed to spending a lot of time in the kitchen practicing reading or doing homework, and I remember hearing her. My mom did not have her book but she would listen to the advice and she would adopt it." For example, she and her mother learned to add sugar to tomato sauce to make it taste less acidic and how to beat egg whites to a peak. Her mother, busy with the sewing, would ask her to jot important things down. "She would say, 'Did you hear that? Take notes.' She would have me take notes sometimes on a piece of paper to remember it." Later, such suggestions, both those written and heard, "were passed person to person."[90]

In this way, Doña Petrona's latest initiative in mass media encouraged the development of shared recipes and techniques. Petrona later recalled her fourteen-year tenure on this program: "Together with . . . other prestigious figures from that period, I brought to life the memorable [program] 'Tardecitas de Royal' [Afternoons with Royal], whose broadcasting had great success and warranted the frank and definitive support of the specialty press in Buenos Aires."[91] For its part, Royal encouraged this support by placing advertisements in a variety of publications. For example, in 1948, this company regularly bought the prime advertising space on the back of *Radiolandia*. Many of these advertisements featured Petrona promoting Royal baking powder.[92] Overlapping promotional efforts among media outlets, corporations, and Argentina's leading culinary expert would continue to flourish during the Peronist era, as they had previously.[93]

Petrona was now joined in this endeavor by her second husband, Atilio Massut. In 1946, three years after Oscar Gandulfo passed away, Petrona remarried. She and Atilio had met through shared friends. From the outset, Atilio took a strikingly different attitude toward her career than had her first husband. Petrona later publicly explained, "Gandulfo never got involved in my work, but this was because he did not even want to know that I was working." In contrast, she recalled, "my second husband, Atilio, helped me a lot, he was an excellent manager."[94] In marrying Atilio Massut, Petrona gained a life partner and also a partner interested in helping build her career. Like Petrona, he was from the provinces (from San Juan) and an entrepreneur.[95] Soon after they married, Atilio left his job with the stock market to manage Petrona's business relationships with publishers, bookstores, and sponsors. He focused especially on increasing the distribution and promotion of her cookbook. The couple's commitment to what one journalist later termed "the Doña Petrona business" was so complete that Petrona C. de Gandulfo kept her first husband's name despite her second marriage, even as her son, Marcelo (about ten years old), took Massut's last name.[96] At this time, women were expected by their peers to take their husband's names, and men were legally entitled to request a divorce if they did not.[97] Apparently, the substantial commercial power of her name outweighed social and legal conventions for this couple.

During the late 1940s, Petrona and Atilio would begin to work together to expand *El libro de Doña Petrona*'s audience. In response to the changing patterns of consumption engendered by the Peronist government, Petrona began to incorporate tips and recipes that would speak to upwardly mobile members of the working class. For example, she added a new, more economical recipe for *pan dulce* to the twenty-third edition of her cookbook. In Pan Dulce de Navidad, sin Huevos (Sweet Christmas Bread without Eggs), she told readers that they could use grated squash in lieu of a dozen eggs and less expensive generic nuts instead of pricier pine nuts and almonds.[98] This type of recipe spoke of her desire to reach a broader audience, including working-class *amas de casa*, who might be interested in making *pan dulce* but were unable to afford all of its original ingredients.

In 1948, Petrona released a new edition of *El libro de Doña Petrona* that adapted advice and recipes to make it even more relevant and accessible beyond the most privileged sectors of society. Most notably, in this edition she acknowledged for the first time that not all of her readers employed domestic servants. She incorporated a new extended section that provided suggestions on how to arrange housework with little or no domestic service help, based upon North American and European models. "In almost all [European and North American] homes," she explained, "*amas de casa* have organized their domestic tasks with domestic help that does not live with them or is there for only a few hours or half days."[99] She asserted that the North American and European solution could be both "comfortable" and "economical," noting that it might, in fact, be a necessity for many Argentines due to the smaller servants' quarters in the most recently constructed Argentine apartments.

In this comment, Petrona hinted at but did not explicitly recognize the upward social mobility engendered by Perón's policies during his first term. Starting in 1946, the government had begun constructing and financing modern apartments, especially in greater Buenos Aires. As historian Anahi Ballent explains, by copying the aesthetics of middle-class homes, the government enabled those living in such modern constructions to imagine themselves to be part of the middle class.[100] Similarly, as Petrona now suggested, this could be the case even if those people could not afford to have full-time help or any help at all. By recognizing this possibility, she broadened her audience to include Argentines whose upward mobility stemmed not from their ability to hire domestic help but rather from Peronist initiatives that enabled them to live in modern homes and cook and eat in modern ways.

In fact, as Petrona's comment suggests, the number of people working in domestic service and the number of households that enjoyed such services decreased (but certainly did not disappear) during the first half of the twentieth century.[101] This trend had accelerated with industrialization, which had increased the number of job alternatives for poor women. Whereas, in 1914, maids and cooks represented almost half of all "economically active" females, by 1947 that number had dropped to around a third. Nearly half of all women who worked for wages were now employed in industry, commerce, and other service jobs.[102]

The background and type of work of those employed in domestic service also changed during this era, becoming more feminized, generalized, and regionally based. In contrast to the substantial number of men in domestic service during the nineteenth century, only .5 percent of economically active men were employed in domestic service by 1947.[103] Likewise, cooks and wet nurses virtually disappeared by 1930, as the number of all-purpose female maids (*mucamas*) grew.[104] Thus the feminization of domestic work occurred for both unpaid homemakers and their modestly paid help.[105] Beginning in the 1940s, more female servants came from the provinces and bordering countries, many of mixed or indigenous ancestry, and a number came from Petrona's home province of Santiago del Estero.[106] As Petrona's advice suggests, a larger number of these new workers did not live with their employers and worked part time for more than one family. Supporting this conclusion, the majority of elderly Argentines I interviewed, many of whom saw themselves as belonging to the middle class during this period, did not employ full-time, live-in domestic help.[107]

While Petrona suggested that the increasing scarcity and part-time employment of domestic servants affected those living in both smaller and larger apartments in the late 1940s, she continued to direct her approach to *amas de casa* who could afford to dedicate their time exclusively to their own homes. When recommending how to organize one's tasks without domestic help, she provided suggestions that would require women to be busy with domestic tasks almost all day—impossible for those who also had to work outside of the home. Even as Petrona recognized for the first time in 1948 that "all families and homes are different," she continued to focus on full-time *amas de casa* and ignored the rest whose extradomestic work still did not excuse them from their presumed domestic responsibilities.[108] Petrona's oversight is particularly ironic in light of the public nature of her own career. However, unlike most women who worked for wages, Petrona could afford to employ a staff of domestic servants, including Juanita Bordoy, whom we will meet in the next chapter.[109]

Going Forward, Scaling Back

By the end of the 1940s, *El libro de Doña Petrona* had been reissued over twenty times since Atlántida began publishing and distributing it in 1941. In 1949, the Mexican publisher Editorial Diana printed an exact replica of *El libro de Doña Petrona* of some 5,000 copies for the local market. While this was a testament to Petrona's growing popularity elsewhere in Latin America, this Mexican edition was not something the author had approved or condoned.[110]

In 1949, Petrona and Atilio decided to regain total control over the cookbook and ended their relationship with Atlántida. After retaking sole control of the publishing process, Petrona and Atilio became even more ambitious in reissuing *El libro de Doña Petrona*, releasing four editions of 15,000 copies each in 1949 alone. These 60,000 books in just one year surpassed the number sold during the entire 1930s. They also equaled about half of what had been sold during the rest of the 1940s. This solo editorial venture was notable not only for its scale but also for the fact that for the first time this cookbook did not include advertisements. In 1949, the twenty-ninth edition of this cookbook was published for the first time without any apparent commercial or government support. Petrona's ability to do this demonstrates that her previous success, second marriage, and growing audience enabled her to expand her profits and exert her autonomy during the Peronist era.

But at the same time that she was seeking control of the culinary advice market, the Peronist government was beginning to reach out to Argentines with its own imperatives about food. On 29 April 1949, Juan Perón established the "first-ever national food policy" at the inauguration of the two-month-long Curso de Política Alimentaria Argentina (Argentine Food Politics Course). He described the implementation of such a policy as the mark of a civilized nation.[111] Explaining that it was not sufficient that the government ensure that Argentines have enough to eat, "What we want is . . . that people, the worker, the mother, the child, eat *well*."[112] Perón emphasized that in the three years since taking office, his market-based policies had already initiated this process. Locating this improvement in the shift away from an export-based economy, he remarked, "Our homeland [*patria*], galvanized by the revolution, has made it so . . . that no one dies of hunger anymore, like in other times, in this country of wheat and meat."[113] He asserted that, due to higher salaries, price limits on food, and the campaign against speculation, "the worker and his family now consume almost double the food ration that they ate six years ago." And, indeed, in the capital and other parts of central Argentina such policies had significantly changed working-class diets (especially by increasing the amount of beef), but they had had little impact on the diets of poor families further to the north and south.[114] Perón was not eager to draw attention to such regional discrepancies; instead he proudly asserted that the government had defended the population's rights to fairly priced goods against "those who wished that the *patria* surrender itself, like pirates' booty, to the voraciousness of imperialisms."[115]

As opposed to those (like Petrona) who had encouraged the consumption of imported goods, Juan Perón thus blamed the gross inequalities before he took office on the liberal economic approach that made such products available. He emphasized that his government sought to increase domestic food production "in order to not have to depend on outsiders and to really earn the fame that our country already has as the land of abundance."[116] In contrast to Doña Petrona's previous advice, Juan Perón now implored Argentines to avoid buying expensive and imported foods, which he described as harmful to the family budget and to national well-being.

This nationalist rhetoric was in keeping with his previous policies, but Perón also began to substantially change his tune about the consumption of nationally produced goods as the economy began to falter in 1949. With post–World War II surpluses drying up, he attempted to steer consumers away from Argentina's main exports of beef and wheat. Noting that Argentines were the largest per capita consumers of beef in the world and the second-largest consumers of bread, he pointed out that rising wages had only exacerbated what he now labeled "over-consumption," especially in working-class communities.[117] The amount of beef produced in Argentina had grown substantially since he took office, but the amount exported had actually declined, due to growing internal consumption.[118] While the government had previously encouraged and celebrated this trend as a mark of Argentina's growing economic sovereignty, it was about to change its tune.[119]

With exports declining and the economy stagnating, Perón now suggested that, per the advice of doctors, Argentines should cut back their consumption of beef and bread and replace them with healthier options like milk, eggs, fish, fruit, and vegetables. He proposed that the state stimulate the production and aid the distribution of these previously "expensive" foods, along with educating consumers about the benefits of consuming them.[120]

Speaking two weeks after Juan Perón, Ramón Carillo reiterated the importance of reconfiguring Argentines' diets to include more "natural," healthier foods. In his comments, he was more openly critical about the role that working-class *amas de casa* played in this problem. While Perón had not directly blamed women for what he understood to be the deterioration of working-class diets, he had implied their complicity. Perón commented that according to reports from the Ministry of Public Health, "the working class tends to abandon traditional food [and] homemade cooking" of provincial dishes featuring corn, squash, and small amounts of meat and replace them "with preserved foods or with the quick and precarious grilled steak [*bife a la plancha*]."[121] Having directed such studies, Carillo openly remarked on how *amas de casa* had been tricked by the "deceitful advantages" of preserved foods, "causing them to prefer [these foods] to fresh foods." He warned that such foods destroyed the "human machine" and failed to take advantage of "the privilege we have as Argentines to obtain with little effort all of the necessary quantity of fresh foods." Carillo decried the fact that entire working-class neighborhoods in Buenos Aires were not using their stoves and instead were eating only cold meats, preserved foods, and cheeses. He concluded that this occurred "only due to habit and comfort," in other words, "due to the lack of a health education *rather* than due to necessity."[122]

Despite women's significant presence in the paid workforce, both Carillo and Perón (like Petrona C. de Gandulfo before them) failed to address the ramifications of this trend in their assessments of working-class habits. In fact, it seems that in critiquing the little amount of time that working-class women spent cooking in Peronist Argentina, they were also expressing their ambivalence about how women's extradomestic work was affecting everyday life. Nonetheless, for a woman like María Roldán, who worked full time in a meat factory, the ability to buy and cook a steak for her family was more practical, and perhaps even more satisfying, than the "traditional foods" the government and the country's leading *ecónoma* encouraged her to cook, which often required more time and ingredients to prepare.[123]

Reactions to this speech and other Peronist food-related initiatives suggested that economics rather than ignorance shaped working-class women's food-related decisions. A month after Perón inaugurated this national food policy, a group of communist women defended themselves (and their female compatriots) publicly against such charges and, in turn, suggested that the Peronist government's own shortcomings were to blame for working-class Argentines' unbalanced diets. In an article published in *Nuestras Mujeres*, the authors directly referred to and rejected Perón's explanation that Argentines' diets had gotten off track due to "comfort, habit, tradition, and poorly understood economy." Instead, they asserted that the popular classes ate more beef, bread, and pastas in lieu of their more healthy counterparts—milk, eggs, fish, fruit, and vegetables—not because they did not know better but because they could not afford these healthier foods. Indeed, such foods were often more expensive than beef, which the government had helped make significantly less expensive in central Argentina.[124]

While the economic downturn of 1949 made such foodstuffs more expensive for those with limited resources, the economic expansion of the previous three years had dramatically expanded Argentina's consumer market. In 1949, it was still unclear whether the economic dip and the government's response to it was an anomaly or part of a larger trend. In either case, the dream of upward social mobility had been spread across social class and region during the course of the decade, and Argentines were not ready to let go of it quite so easily.

Conclusion

During the 1940s, as industrialization intensified, so did the notion that women should fully dedicate themselves to their families and their homes. Even as more women began to study longer and work more before getting married, they were expected to become full-time unpaid homemakers after marriage, if this was a financial possibility. Cooking was something that a respectable woman should know how to do when she married, and to this end, many young women received *El libro de Doña Petrona* as a gift. Some, like Elba, seized the opportunity to develop and display their culinary repertoire, while others, like Emmy, seemed to experience this as an obligation rather than a choice. In either case, being an *ama de casa*, a mother, and a good cook was widely regarded as a respectable woman's highest calling.

This notion persisted and was even reinforced by the Peronist government. At the same time that the state granted women the vote and helped create industrial jobs for men and women, it lauded the male industrial worker while generally ignoring his female counterpart. The government did set up homes for female workers in Buenos Aires and even crowned "queens of work" (*reinas de trabajo*) across Argentina.[125] But it lavished the most praise on women in their roles as *amas de casa* and consumers. As working-class wages and consumption rose from 1946 to 1948, the state celebrated its ability to create a more socially just form of citizenship that enabled Argentines to buy more food, live in more modern homes, cook on gas stoves, and share in the ritual of eating *pan dulce* during the Christmas holiday. In these acts, the government highlighted the working class's newfound right to take a seat at Argentina's expanding common table. Still, while the Peronists brought a new social group to this table, they ultimately reinforced the abundant, cosmopolitan approach to cooking associated with the middle class and Doña Petrona. While *porteños* could now sample provincial fare at the *peñas* (folkloric clubs) popping up in Buenos Aires and the nationalist government occasionally encouraged home cooking of traditional provincial dishes, the government did not forcefully promote a nationalist cuisine.[126]

Nevertheless, as the national economy began to decline in 1949, the government shifted its tone surrounding consumption from one of celebration to one of fiscal responsibility. Using a health-based rationale, it encouraged Argentines to change their diets and eat less of the country's main exports. At the same time, the government decried the lack of time and effort working-class women were putting into cooking, as well as their general ignorance about nutrition. In response, some working-class women pushed back, pointing out that it was not a lack of education or will but rather a simple matter of economics that prevented them from feeding their families the healthier foods the government recommended.

Such critiques were often courageous acts in a climate in which the Peronist government was cracking down on expressions of public dissent. Petrona seemed to recognize this, did not openly criticize Peronist policies, and went along with their imperatives. She incorporated the advertisement for Gas del Estado into her cookbook and provided her signature on a Peronist advertisement touting gas stoves. To do otherwise would have compromised her ability to benefit from the government's expansion of consumption. By Perón's second year in office, she had already revised *El libro de Doña Petrona* with new advice directed toward members of the upwardly mobile working class, some of whom could now aspire to the middle-class domesticity she had come to represent.

But she was not immune from state politics. After a few years of collaboration, Gas del Estado fired Petrona, in 1949 or 1950. She was apparently quite upset by this decision, which meant the end of her more than two-decade-long professional relationship with Argentina's gas providers.[127] While she shared her dismay with her friends and relatives, she did not say anything publicly against the government in the closely monitored and heavily censored media. Other celebrities made different decisions, including film stars Libertad Lamarque and Niní Marshall, both of whom were forced into exile during the Peronist years.[128] A few prominent intellectuals (including Jorge Luis Borges) spoke out, but most did not.[129] As she would throughout her career, Petrona sought to appear "apolitical" and, at the same time, to bridge political divides. Her growing popularity suggests that a number of Argentines were eager to embrace her version of national commensality, despite, or indeed because of, the deepening class divisions and animosity that characterized this period.

While Petrona remained in the public eye, the decision to fire her in the first place reveals the tensions that surrounded corporate success and fame in an era when the Peronist government sought to assert control over, and portray itself as the definitive expert in, Argentina's consumer market. The government emphasized its role above those of all others in creating and enabling domestic "progress" in Argentine homes. It sought to do so by co-opting or removing previous corporate experts like Doña Petrona and replacing them with representatives selected by the state.

But neither Juan nor Eva Perón could push Petrona C. de Gandulfo from the public spotlight. And as her growing sales figures demonstrate, *El libro de Doña Petrona* became even more popular during the course of the 1940s. Part of the story was about the expansion of consumption by the government. But what happened commercially before and during the Peronist era was just as important. Petrona and her sponsors had previously used the rapidly expanding mass media to establish her name and a desire for her cookbook. She established herself not just in Buenos Aires but across the nation. By partnering with Atlántida starting in 1941, she made it possible for people beyond the capital to buy her cookbook.

As we shall see in the next chapter, during the early 1950s, the Peronist government would seek to undermine her influence—as well as scale back its own previous celebration of consumerism—by emphatically directing women to more nutritious and economical meals. Nevertheless, neither nutrition nor economical consumption would elicit the same joy for many Argentines as the ability to enjoy a delicious steak or receive and cook with a copy of *El libro de Doña Petrona*. Ultimately, Argentines were more drawn to messages about upward social mobility through consumption than ones of austerity. But with the economic situation continuing to deteriorate, the

Peronist government would step up its messages about economizing. And as economic crises began to regularly rock the country during the 1950s, the government would be joined by numerous others who sought to professionalize and recognize women in their capacity as thrifty and efficient *amas de casa*.

CHAPTER FOUR

PROFESSIONALIZING A THRIFTIER HOMEMAKER

Supremas de Pollo Maryland (Maryland-Style Chicken)

6 chicken breasts, salt, pepper, beaten egg, breadcrumbs, oil

12 bananas, beaten egg, breadcrumbs, oil

50 grams butter, 1 onion, 1 can of corn, ½ cup of thick white sauce, salt, pepper, nutmeg

6 slices of ham, 6 bundles of spinach, ½ kilo of peas, butter

Prepare the chicken, cut the wing bones, leaving the little part of the bone that is attached to the breast, remove the breast bone, take off the skin too and flatten the [chicken pieces] making them thin; season with salt and pepper, dunk them in beaten egg, then breadcrumbs and fry them in oil over a slow flame.

Peel the bananas, cut them in half lengthwise, dunk them in beaten egg, then breadcrumbs and fry them in oil.

Brown the finely minced onion in butter, add the corn, sauté a moment and add a nice and thick white sauce, salt, pepper and nutmeg.

Heat the slices of ham.

Cook the spinach, strain it and sauté it in butter. Cook the peas, strain them, and sauté them in butter. Once everything is prepared, put the chicken in a serving dish; over each one a slice of ham and two banana halves. Around [it, place] the spinach, corn and peas, everything nice and warm.[1]

Doña Petrona presented this recipe, Maryland-Style Chicken, in her cookbook and on her television program during the 1950s.[2] It was a dish that reflected Argentina's culinary diversity and the growing interest in the cuisine of the Americas. The name of this recipe referred to a classic preparation, Maryland Chicken, a dish from the state of the same name in which the chicken is pan-fried and covered to steam it and then served with white, creamy gravy.[3] Petrona's recipe also called for chicken with a white sauce, but someone from Maryland would have been unlikely to recognize it. This chicken was fried, not steamed, and then topped with ham and two banana slices—and the white sauce was chock-full of corn. Such additions reflected typical Latin American ingredients.

Despite Petrona's attempts to reach a broader audience that included working-class women during the late 1940s, she continued to cater to an audience with ample leisure time and money. As with her previous recipes, her Maryland-Style Chicken involved a lot of steps and ingredients. The cook would debone six chicken quarters and fry them, fry a dozen bananas, make a white sauce with creamed corn, heat the ham, cook the spinach and peas, and then assemble the dish artfully on a platter—making sure to keep "everything nice and warm." During the 1950s, homemakers were expected to have the skills (or at least the desire to learn these skills) and the enthusiasm to prepare this type of dish for their family and friends. Properly executed, such a dish showcased their domestic dedication and expertise as well as their cosmopolitan repertoire.

As the Cold War intensified in the 1950s, the U.S. government and corporate interests stepped up campaigns to promote capitalist consumption throughout the Americas. For its part, the Peronist government would seek to keep U.S. imperialism at bay during the first half of the decade, while subsequent Argentine leaders would aim to roll back nationalist protections. As Argentina turned away from Europe and looked to the United States for investments, it imported not only companies and capital but also cultural notions, including the U.S. image of the idealized 1950s housewife. Since the 1930s, Doña Petrona had kept up-to-date on U.S. ideas about domesticity and consumption by subscribing to magazines published there, such as *Ladies Home Journal* and *Good Housekeeping*. She also faithfully clipped articles by U.S. advice expert Dorothy Dix, which were reprinted in Spanish in the popular women's magazine, *Para Ti*.[4]

Still, Doña Petrona and others selected the parts of the image of the U.S. housewife they wanted to emulate and tailored them to the local environment. Like her counterpart in the United States, the ideal Argentine *ama de casa* was popularly imagined to be efficient, white, self-consciously middle class, and cheerful in catering to her family—and especially to her husband.[5] At the same time, contemporaries expected her to be more dedicated to cooking from scratch than they imagined her U.S. counterpart to be.[6] She was also uniquely Argentine in that she was required to possess the expertise to adjust her consumption in response to frequent waves of recession and recovery. This was especially important due to the growing instability of the Argentine economy. The national economy had grown

8.5 percent annually during the 1946–48 boom, but from 1949 to 1951 it began to languish, and in 1952 it fell into crisis. The government's increasing attention to female consumers represented an attempt to temper the power of the male-dominated unions as their demands for raises and price controls increased along with inflation.[7]

It was not new, of course, for public figures to target Argentine *amas de casa* during economically challenging moments, but there were some important new twists in the early 1950s. Starting in 1950, the government and mass media outlets began to characterize homemaking as work, and even as an occupation. With the Peronist government's demise in 1955 and the shift toward "the free market," a number of private domestic experts would join Doña Petrona in seeking to further professionalize women in their capacity as *amas de casa*. This chapter explores the quandary that many Argentine women faced during an era in which many public figures promoted women's domestic professionalization and a model of middle-class domesticity that was difficult to live up to, especially given the rocky economy and the frequent lack of paid domestic help.

Recognizing Women's Domestic Work

As the economic situation continued to decline during the early 1950s, the Peronist government stepped up its economizing campaigns. While all Argentines were encouraged to be more careful consumers, the government increasingly placed the responsibility for preventing such waste on Argentine *amas de casa*. For example, at an antispeculation conference held in September 1950, Perón characterized *amas de casa* as "extraordinary weapons" essential to the war against economic injustice. In their capacity as "tutelary angels of home economics," Perón remarked, women should take on the responsibility for teaching the men in their lives how to become more frugal.[8] Peronist leaders even urged men to hand over their wages to their wives, based on the assumption that they would spend them more effectively.[9]

The government also targeted a younger demographic through the public schools, paying special attention to young girls' culinary know-how. A sixth-grade text from 1950 explained, "A good *ama de casa* should possess the secrets of the culinary arts." To learn those secrets, girls were not sent to Doña Petrona or even to their female relatives and neighbors, but rather to their teachers. The textbook explained, "At home, girls would do well to start practicing early on, keeping in mind the advice and practices of the home economics courses in the schools."[10]

Home economics classes had encouraged women to focus on domesticity since the early twentieth century, but now the Peronist government used this venue to characterize homemaking as an occupation. For example, a fifth-grade textbook published in 1950 by the government, *The Argentine Woman at Work*, depicted women's unpaid work at home as a complement to men's paid work outside of the home. The introduction explained, "While the man works in the workshop, factory or business setting, the woman is busy with domestic tasks, which are not few in number: she cleans, she washes the clothes, she prepares the food, she cares for her children, she deals with the vendors, etc." Perhaps even more tellingly, on the front cover of this textbook, below the title, "The Argentine Woman at Work," an illustration showed a woman cheerfully serving her two children a lunch of salad, beef, and bread. The scene celebrated whiteness and middle-class manners as well as the woman's role as the queen of the house; there was no father at the table (as he was presumably at work). Only on the back cover and in the second, shorter, part of the text did women appear as workers in extradomestic settings like the textile factory.[11] Women's principal and most important occupation, this textbook suggested, was caring for their families and their homes.

The government was not alone in characterizing women's domestic tasks as work. For example, in 1950, the popular magazine *Mucho Gusto* began to make the argument that homemaking was a "trade" (*oficio*). In a November 1950 interview with a woman named Alicia G. de Caro, this modest, full-time *ama de casa* was lauded for her professionalism and her enthusiasm in taking care of her home and family. According to the magazine, "Her house, her children, and her recipes" spoke for themselves.[12] She was the kind of committed domestic homemaker Petrona had long sought to reach.

Recognizing that the media was necessary to reach women who had already graduated from school, the Peronist government began to more aggressively follow the lead of domestic experts like Petrona C. de Gandulfo during the early 1950s. In April 1951, it initiated a radio program entitled *Cocina de la Salud* (Healthy Cooking). Broadcast across the country on Radio Belgrano under the guidance of Dr. Ramón Carillo, this program sought to promote "rational and scientific diets" so that women could care for their children more effectively under the medical model announced by Juan Perón two years earlier. Designed to address the desire to minimize time spent on cooking, this campaign sought to show women how "easy" it was to cook with little science or time at their disposal.[13]

In conjunction with this radio program, the Ministry of Public Health offered large presentations across Buenos Aires. Apparently, people were

Cover of Peronist fifth-grade textbook La mujer argentina en el trabajo *(The Argentine Woman at Work), published in 1950.*

LA MUJER ARGENTINA
EN EL TRABAJO

quite interested. In the working-class neighborhood of La Boca, for example, the government reported that more than 2,500 were in attendance—"so that many people could not get seats."[14] The primary goal of these large presentations was to get *amas de casa* in Buenos Aires and beyond to sign up for practical cooking classes in neighborhood centers.[15] Like other initiatives by the government and domestic experts, this campaign encouraged women to focus on domestic rather than extradomestic tasks and suggested that the money they saved at home formed the basis of the national economy.[16] Peronist policy thus targeted everyday women as the main audience and agents of its economic and health-related initiatives, leaving men largely off stage.[17]

The culmination of the government's recognition of women's unpaid work in the home was Eva Perón's suggestion that homemakers receive a monthly allowance of "half the average national salary" for their work, "cleaning the house, taking care of clothes, setting the table, bringing up children, etc." Congress apparently considered but did not approve the proposal. In her ghostwritten autobiography, Perón demurred that this issue was not "serious" or "urgent," but rather something she raised for people to consider.[18] This was nevertheless a serious issue, and in her Peronist Women's Party inauguration speech in 1949, Perón had recognized that, despite having suffered "double exploitation," at home and on the job, women enthusiastically joined the working-class struggle.[19]

The Peronist government encouraged women to participate politically by joining the Peronist Women's Party and attending meetings at female-only *unidades básicas*. At these government-sponsored cultural centers, thousands of women across the country gathered to learn more about political and domestic topics. In addition to hearing speeches from the president and first lady, attendees received updates on the government's campaign against speculation as well as instructions on how to sew better and cook with less beef.[20] In this way, the government expanded the home economics curriculum for girls in public schools to include the numerous women who attended these extrascholastic classes or listened to their healthy cooking program on the radio. It sought to shape and to recognize women's agency in the economically important tasks of shopping, sewing, and cooking.

While the Peronist government was remarkable for its acknowledgment of women's domestic work, it continued to echo conservative gender norms within and beyond the *unidades básicas* during the early 1950s. As Eva Perón's 1951 autobiography explained, women "were born to make homes. Not for the street."[21] Despite her extremely prominent role in politics and her accomplishments in the public sphere, the first lady suggested that other women should focus on the home front. She positioned herself and others as properly subservient to Juan Perón. "*He* is the leader," Eva Perón famously said of her presidential husband. "I am only the shadow of his superior presence."[22]

In a similar vein, despite the fact that *she* was the celebrity and principal moneymaker, Doña Petrona later explained that she had also granted ultimate authority, in turn, to both of her husbands. She proudly revealed that she always put the money she made in a joint bank account and asked her husbands' permission to use it.[23] Both women publicly suggested that despite their tremendous influence—the likes of which were unparalleled in Argentina—patriarchy was rightfully alive and well. They emphasized that other women should dedicate themselves to stretching and saving their husband's earnings rather than making money themselves. Such sentiments bespoke the profoundly mixed messages Argentines received with regard to women's proper roles. They watched the first lady and Argentina's leading culinary celebrity build their careers on the public stage, while being told by these very women that other women should not do the same.

A More Economic Ecónoma

As the government stepped up its efforts to reach the public with its own lessons about cooking and consumption, Petrona became more enterprising and resourceful. After being fired from Gas del Estado, she set up her own private "culinary laboratory" in 1950 in downtown Buenos Aires, where she would work for the next four decades developing recipes and preparing for her cooking demonstrations.[24] Faced with a shortage of paper that led many other authors to stop printing, she used the more widely available and economical newspaper-style paper to reissue her cookbook, starting in 1950.[25]

But being resourceful was no longer enough. She now also had to be careful not to upstage the first lady. After the government released Eva Perón's 1951 autobiography, *La razón de mi vida*, and made it required reading in schools, Petrona stopped including the print run (which indicated the number of copies of her book) in new editions of *El libro de Doña Petrona*. "She was afraid that Eva would do something," remarked her granddaughter, because Petrona was selling "more copies of her book."[26] According to scholar Gustavo Castagna, this decision became an Argentine legend, a legend that emphasized and perhaps even contributed to the tremendous popularity of Doña Petrona and her cookbook.[27] Despite the mounting economic challenges of 1950 and 1951, Petrona and her husband, Atilio, issued seven editions of around 30,000 copies each.[28] Even with the economic downturn, Petrona continued to resonate for a cross-class audience attracted to the promise of upward social mobility through consumption she had come to represent.

Of course, Doña Petrona was not the primary figure that most Argentines believed could help improve their country's national economy in 1951. It was an election year, and Argentine voters (including 64 percent of female voters) emphatically reelected Juan Perón to his second term.[29] Eva Perón had hoped to run as his vice president, but military pressure and her failing health forced her from the race. Despite Juan Perón's substantial electoral victory, the second-term president faced a series of droughts and falling world prices that plunged Argentina's economy into crisis in 1952. Argentina's traditional exports of wheat and beef were hit particularly hard; only half the amount of grain was harvested in 1951–52 as had been harvested in 1949–50.

In an attempt to regain control, Perón froze salaries and prices. In February 1952, he announced a new "austerity plan." Explaining this plan, he proclaimed, "Families should organize themselves . . . save not squander . . . economize purchases, acquire necessities, consume essentials."[30] The government blanketed the media with messages about thrifty shopping and also began to distribute free seeds and encourage people to start family gardens to feed themselves.[31] Even today, Isay K. recalls the drama of such initiatives. He remarked, "I remember a famous speech by Perón, encouraging the population to be more careful and more conscious of saving, saying that it was very easy to find good food in the garbage cans."[32]

Argentines often remember 1952 as the year of little meat and brown bread. In response to the declining economy, the government rationed beef, sending the best cuts abroad, and shipped the bulk of the wheat harvest to Europe. For many people, who viewed high-quality beef and white bread as an Argentine birthright, the inability to buy meat one day per week or the indignity of eating brown bread made with unspecified fillers reflected the ineffectiveness of Peronist politics. For example, Emilia S., an eighty-two-year-old descendant of Italian immigrants and a former schoolteacher, began our conversation about food history with this vivid memory: "I remember very well that in Perón's time boats still came from Italy, and there were relatives of my parents who were traveling . . . and they got off the boat . . . with a bag of white bread. And so we called the other relatives and said, 'Come on down, Filippo arrived and brought us white bread.'" She asked her husband, Livio, if he recalled the "brown bread." Livio gestured with his hands: "When I was little, you would press on the crust and it would bounce back because it was so crunchy." In contrast, he recalled that in 1952, "The bread eaten at that time was a calamity. . . . It was really bad, because we had always eaten good bread here." In contrast to previous European immigrants, who had been amazed by the quantities of food available in Argentina, their descendants now experienced the shortage and declining quality of beloved staples in this supposed land of abundance.[33]

As economic challenges continued to mount, Doña Petrona once again demonstrated her responsiveness and resourcefulness. In 1952 alone, she issued four editions of a significantly revamped version of *El libro de Doña Petrona*, with a new section that sought to address the current economic and social climate. Interestingly, despite her ongoing reference to herself as an *ecónoma*, it was not until this point that Doña Petrona "modernized" her cookbook with a section on how to "economize" in the kitchen and the home.[34] Economy, she explained, had become the "motto of the day."[35]

Most striking, Doña Petrona added a new section to the 1952 edition of her cookbook entitled "Something about Leftovers." In it she challenged women to overcome the past "contempt" associated with reusing previously cooked food. She promised that leftovers could, in fact, make "exquisite dishes with a little ingenuity and good taste." She reassured them: "The disguise can be so perfect, that with great satisfaction we see how our fellow diners savor every one of their bites."[36] Making specific suggestions, she recommended livening up previously cooked foods by adding sauces spiked with port or brandy or spices like nutmeg and paprika. She also provided seventeen recipes to make with leftover meat, fish, and noodles.[37] Even as she played up the benefits rather than the necessity of cooking with leftovers, this section reflected the rising cost of living and ongoing Peronist pronouncements that Argentine *amas de casa* should become more careful consumers and not waste food.

In a similar spirit, Petrona would release a new cookbook called *Cómo cocina Doña Petrona con olla a presión* (How Doña Petrona Cooks with a Pressure Cooker) in 1952 as well. Like her previous cookbooks, this new initiative was explicitly dedicated to *amas de casa*, in this case to help those interested in or afraid of the pressure cooker to learn how to use this new technology. A couple of other authors, Marta Beines and Aly Simmons, had recently published similar pressure-cooker cookbooks themselves.[38] Petrona made no mention of these competitors. She explained in her prologue, "I have composed clear, simple recipes, with precise quantities and times. I have tried them one by one, at various times, each dish, trying to make daily menus of common food agreeable and economical, without adding extravagant dishes, as one shouldn't expect that the pressure cooker be something that it is not." As opposed to her original cookbook, then, this was a much more consistently and explicitly thrifty text. There were more basic recipes for stews, vegetables, and fruit preserves and fewer French pastries and stylized presentations. Petrona also included specific tips on how to economize "time, change, and food." Echoing Peronist pronouncements, she instructed women to shop carefully and cook in a thrifty manner by making a shopping list ahead of time, only buying what was needed at the market, and using leftovers quickly and creatively.[39]

Like previous home economists, Petrona now provided more substantive suggestions that went beyond cooking. In *Como cocina Doña Petrona con olla a presión*, she explained how to clean and care for the pressure cooker and set up and stock a kitchen. In *El libro de Doña Petrona*, she added instructions on how to care for kitchen equipment, tablecloths, dishes, glassware, and clothing. This was information that would be particularly useful to the many members of her recently expanded audience. She further addressed herself to such a clientele by providing economizing tips that would impact the "monthly budget." For example, to preserve fuel when cooking on the stovetop, she suggested covering the pot and turning down the burner once the contents had come to a boil. As she had when she was still working for Primitiva, she also recommended cooking several dishes at the same time in the oven to save fuel. She explained, "For example: we can cook an *asado*, a fish or vegetable pie, and if the size of the oven permits it, a dessert and even a vegetable soup."[40]

Some of this information was in keeping with the thrifty and self-sufficient behaviors that the government sought to promote. Still, Petrona's version of economizing presumed the ability to buy certain things—like meat, fish, *and* vegetables—as well as a gas oven in which to cook them. Petrona also provided other "economic" suggestions that would only be applicable to wealthier Argentines. For example, she started off her instructions on cleaning by describing how to clean fine china and crystal.[41] She warned that utensils made of silver should never be washed in the same soapy water used to clean the china—advice that would be practical for only a small sector of her audience.

As opposed to the explicit nature of President Perón's calls for thriftiness and austerity, Doña Petrona highlighted the "spiritual" benefits of economy and suggested that instead of being demeaning, economizing could be liberating for the women who embraced it. She explained that by "economy" she referred to not only tending one's budget but also "economizing physical exhaustion and above all time." Moderating her expectations about how Argentine *amas de casa* should organize their days, she continued, "We must remember that time is gold; we should give ourselves time for everything, not only to carry out everything related to our domestic tasks in an efficient manner, but also in order to entertain our spirit."[42] Thus, for the first time, in 1952 Petrona suggested that Argentine *amas de casa* use shortcuts to spend less time on household chores and more time enjoying themselves. Still, she continued to tout recipes like the Supremas de Pollo Maryland, which required women to spend a significant amount of time cooking.

If Petrona was an inconsistent and sometimes unwilling advocate of economizing, by the early 1950s the Peronist government had become fully committed to this project. In 1953, it published a pamphlet that provided tips and suggestions about how the *ama de casa* could more fully incorporate the "nutritional" and "economical" potato into the family's diet.[43] Eva

Perón was listed as the author, but it is unlikely that she actually wrote this text, especially since she had publicly admitted her inability to cook and had been severely ill the previous year.[44] The Peronist government's decision to focus the recipes on this particular starch represented one of its attempts to find a replacement for wheat-based products, which continued to run short, due to the 1952 harvest shortages.[45] Echoing the platforms of Peronist food policy, this pamphlet began by explaining that it sought to demonstrate "the true importance that the potato has in the family's diet—for children, young people and adults, healthy people and sick people—and the best ways to use them in the kitchen." Like *El libro de Doña Petrona*, it was directed specifically to Argentine homemakers. In the prologue, the director of the National Institute of Nutrition, Enrique Pierangeli, explained that it was "dedicated to the *amas de casa* with the goal of facilitating their difficult work of directing and preparing food for the family."[46]

Over the past couple of years, the Peronist government's recognition of the "difficult work" women did at home had given women's domestic tasks such as cooking and cleaning more visibility. Despite the recognition of the difficulty and importance of this work, it was not deemed worthy of financial compensation. Nor was it suggested that men pick up the slack. Instead, government officials, businesses, and domestic experts bombarded women with advice about how to better carry out their supposedly natural domestic pursuits in an expanding number of venues.

Cooking in the Spotlight

During the early 1950s, television represented the newest form of media. Many Argentines understood televisions to be a "sign of progress," associated with the "American way of life"—a way of life that linked consumption of modern goods to progress.[47] Despite the Peronist government's fervent stance against U.S. imperialism, the first lady felt the time had come in Argentina for this new medium to be imported from the United States, and she facilitated its arrival. The very first broadcast, on 17 October 1951 on LR3 Radio Belgrano TV, showed Eva and Juan Perón giving live speeches in front of the Casa Rosada on the national holiday designated to celebrate "Peronist loyalty." This speech would prove to be one of Evita's last public performances—ten months later she would die of cancer at the age of thirty-three.[48]

From the first year of broadcasting throughout the decade, television programming in Argentina was accessible only in Buenos Aires. And, although many children dreamed of getting a television, only the wealthiest *porteños* could afford to purchase this latest status symbol. For most people, television viewing occurred in public settings like store windows, social clubs, or the Peronist cultural centers. Some went to the homes of wealthy friends to watch. In other words, as Mirta Varela explains, during the 1950s, *porteños* went out to watch television as if they were going to see a movie. At home, they were much more likely to listen to the radio.[49] As a result, the Peronist government continued to broadcast its "healthy cooking" program on the radio rather than beginning a cooking show on television.

Thus, it was not a state-sponsored expert but rather Doña Petrona who became the first to cook on television—in November 1951 on the state-run channel, Canal 7.[50] The only channel in Argentina during the 1950s, Canal 7 primarily showed political events, soccer games, soap operas, and artistic performances. As on the radio, international and Argentine businesses eagerly sponsored programs that targeted female viewers—the U.S. food company Swift, the U.S. glass dish maker Pyrex, and the Argentine kitchenware manufacturer Rómulo Ruffini signed on to support Doña Petrona's program, *Jueves Hogareños* (Thursdays at Home). This program was joined later that year by other corporate-backed programs aimed at women. Fashion designer Jean Cartier promoted his label on the program *El Arte de la Elegancia* (The Art of Elegance), and Elina Colomer, an actress, hosted a beauty program sponsored by Sunlight soap.[51] As this lineup suggests, businesses and media outlets expected women of the early 1950s to follow soap operas and artistic events and also to be interested in learning how to cook, dress, and be beautiful. For their part, men were imagined to be more interested in sports and politics.

With the recovery of the economy in 1953, private sector celebrations of female consumerism took center stage. In 1953, Doña Petrona oversaw a televised cooking contest that emphasized women's interest in cooking and buying the latest technology. The gas stove manufacturer Orbis invited *cocineras criollas* from across the country to send in their recipes. Thousands of letters poured in "from all parts of the country" from women who hoped to win an Orbis stove. In front of a live audience, Doña Petrona, dressed elegantly, with pearls and a fur draped over her shoulders, ceremoniously drew the winning entry for the stove from a large wheel packed with letters. The newscaster exclaimed, "The Argentine woman has demonstrated yet again her proven spirit as an *ama de casa*."[52] As previous sponsors had done, Orbis put Doña Petrona and the numerous homemakers interested in cooking in the spotlight.

Tapping into this interest, Canal 7 would add another cooking show in 1953, this one hosted by Lorenza Taberna. Like Doña Petrona, Lorenza

Taberna was an *económa* who aimed her advice at the middle class. She would continue to broadcast a television program for the rest of the decade. While no one I spoke with suggested that this fellow *económa* posed much of a threat, a handful of Argentines suggested to me that yet another cook, Doña Lola, represented Petrona's most significant competition. Cecilia Hermann (the restaurant owner who preserved her elite forbear's handwritten recipe manuscripts) even expressed her preference for Doña Lola and her cookbook, *El arte de la mesa: Recetario de Doña Lola* (The Art of the Table: Doña Lola's Recipe Book).[53] "She was a woman from a slightly better off family," she explained, and she offered a more refined kind of cooking for a different public.[54]

Like Petrona, Dolores "Lola" Clotilde had previously studied with Angel Baldi at the Cordon Bleu in Buenos Aires. According to Angel's daughter María Adela Baldi, "Doña Lola was part of the *porteña* society," and the "high society people" during the 1950s asked her if she would offer a cooking class for them.[55] María Adela Baldi, who helped her run these classes, explained that "twelve to fifteen students would come, not to learn for themselves but to teach the cook."[56] These well-off women, like the elite ladies who had attended Petrona C. de Gandulfo's culinary lectures in the grand halls of the 1930s, were interested in learning how to cook but not in doing the actual cooking. According to Lola's daughters, their mother never met Petrona and was not interested in appearing on television.[57] This lack of interest in the latest technology made her little match for Doña Petrona in the mass market, but that seemed to be how she wanted it. *El arte de la mesa* would reach its sixth edition by 1955, but it would not significantly diminish the popularity of *El libro de Doña Petrona*.

Over the course of the 1950s, *El libro de Doña Petrona* would reach the peak of its popularity, doubling its sales of the previous decade. Oral histories taken from Argentines who were then in their teens, twenties, and thirties support the conclusion that Doña Petrona and her cookbook became more popular and accessible both during and after the Peronist boom times. Many were obligated to read *La razón de mi vida* in school but chose to buy *El libro de Doña Petrona*—even as such a choice was shaped by consumerism and gender politics. Women bought it for themselves or other women, and men bought it for the women in their lives. Some men and boys also sneaked a peek at it from time to time to consult a recipe or marvel at the illustrations.

But this was not a book that Argentines saw as appropriate for the male sex. For example, as a young boy, Alfredo Arias (now a well-known artist) described how he would escape into a fantasy world while thumbing through the magnificent illustrations of cakes in *El libro de Doña Petrona* during the early 1950s. His parents were less than pleased. "The problem was that I was interested in everything feminine, and it was inconvenient that I was interested in cooking too," he explained. A few years after he tried to make Doña Petrona's *dulce de leche* cake roll, he was sent to military school to learn how to become a proper man. Cooking was not part of the equation.[58]

As during the previous decades, young women were the main audience expected to receive, and then learn how to cook from, *El libro de Doña Petrona*, most often when they were about to get married. Middle- and working-class Argentines shared similar stories of how they had bought or come to possess the cookbook during the 1950s in the oral history workshops I conducted on the outskirts of Buenos Aires. One woman explained, "My brothers and my mom gave me this cookbook when I got engaged, and I used it all the time."[59] Another male participant, who had brought the cookbook with him, held it up and proudly exclaimed, "This is the cookbook that I gave my wife at [our] engagement party."[60] Asked what it meant to have this cookbook in the home, one female participant said that "it was something symbolic."[61] Symbolic in both its presence and its absence. One woman repeated a couple of times that "perhaps I don't have [this cookbook] because I could not buy it."[62] While no one responded to her comment, it pointed to the expectation that women should possess a copy of this cookbook, as well as to the reality that some did not.

Because Doña Petrona's cookbook remained more difficult to obtain outside of Buenos Aires and other urban areas, receiving it as a gift could take on added significance there. Living out in the country with her relatively prosperous family, Etel L. recalled how special she felt when her father ordered Doña Petrona's cookbook for her from the capital for her birthday in the 1950s. Describing how her father spoiled her as his only daughter, Etel remarked, "He was overdoing it to give this kind of book to me, who just barely knew how to beat two eggs, but I felt very important, because my father had given it to me. So when my mom was busy, she would say to me, 'You cook.'"[63] Etel did this, and when she married, she took the cookbook with her and continues to cook with it today.

Several of the women who received this cookbook shared Petrona's belief that it enabled them to surpass former generations of family cooks. For them, preparing food became a way of demonstrating their more comprehensive domestic expertise and even elevating their social position. For example, a woman named Ana C., from Bahía Blanca, shared her joy at receiving a copy of *El libro de Doña Petrona* from her "working-class" fiancé in 1950. Despite the fact that she was not from a "powerful family," she felt that cooking with Petrona allowed her "to improve a little." In contrast to what she perceived as her mother's limited culinary repertoire, Ana used the cookbook to master a wide range of dishes with different presentations. She explained that when she would bring a dish, like the fan-shaped Russian potato salad, to the table, "everyone would applaud."[64]

Doña Petrona had tapped into and helped create this expectation that young women in Argentina needed to learn how to cook from an expert before marrying and that this was an important means of improving their families. A woman of Greek descent from Ingeniero White named Olga also shared her experience to this effect. Her mother died when she was young, and she grew up with her father, who cooked Greek food for the family. After getting engaged, Olga began to learn how to make her fiancé's favorite Italian dishes from his Italian mother. "She would make boiled vegetables and the taste was special, and as much as we wanted to learn to make it, it never turned out like hers. She boiled endive, swiss chard, and potatoes and we would devour it."[65] While Olga could never exactly replicate this or the other ten-or-so dishes her mother-in-law made better than anyone else, she did learn how to make a wider range of dishes. She explained that her range came in large part from cooking with *El libro de Doña Petrona* during the 1950s (and later watching Doña Petrona on television during the next decade).

Like Olga and Petrona's previous magazine correspondents from the mid-1930s, a number of Argentines used the book to learn how and what to cook and also how to serve it. A man who bought the book as a gift for his wife in the mid-1950s explained that its appeal stemmed from the fact that it went beyond the rustic nature of most immigrant dishes and elevated food to a higher standard. He remarked, "This book had different foods because everybody already knew the traditional immigrant foods. But these [recipes] were more elegant and modern." He noted that this elegance and modernity extended beyond the food itself to how it was served—pointing out that Doña Petrona's cookbook provided the knowledge necessary to properly invite people over to eat.[66] Implicit in his and others' decision to give this book as a gift to the women in their lives was the notion that they should take responsibility for implementing this modern, middle-class protocol. As one man put it, its popularity "undoubtedly stemmed from the fact that it was a symbol of upward mobility, of a model family. An orderly family, with a well-set table. It could belong in an immigrant household, which through education and cooking could progress."[67] This text resonated for the children and grandchildren of immigrants eager to find their place at Argentina's literal and metaphorical common table.

In her new prologue to a significantly revised edition of *El libro de Doña Petrona* released in 1954, Doña Petrona emphasized the sense of community and unwavering support she enjoyed from her fans. She explained to her readers that, due to "so many demonstrations of support, affection, and encouragement, I have thought it necessary to modernize this edition, as much in its text as in its artistic presentation, in order to repay in part what my dear readers have given to me." As she had throughout her career, she made an effort to establish a unique connection with each of her fans, despite their ever-growing numbers. She closed the prologue: "One by one please accept my affectionate gratitude."[68] In addition, for the first time in this cookbook, she listed the ingredients and the quantity of each at the top of every recipe, making them easier to follow.[69]

Meanwhile, her television program allowed fans in Buenos Aires to write down her recipes and also to watch her cook up close. As one woman explained, with the transition from radio to television, one could now actually "see her cook."[70] More could do so in 1954 with the continued expansion of this new technology. In 1951, there were just over 4,000 television sets; three years later, they numbered over 60,000.[71] In 1954, Doña Petrona moved her television program to one day later in the week, to a show called *Viernes Hogareños* (Fridays at Home). On the small screen, Doña Petrona showed her viewers how to make a wide range of recipes every Friday at 6:05 P.M. on a special gas stove that had been installed for her program. She emphasized techniques that her fans had been asking her about since the early 1930s, including how to make *hojaldre* (pastry dough) by hand.[72] She also continued to make elaborate cakes, preparing one on air to celebrate a communion and another to celebrate a *quinceañera* (girl's fifteenth birthday).[73] Television allowed her to demonstrate the techniques for such recipes more effectively than print and radio, and more intimately than in her live performances in large halls.

Doña Petrona was joined on-screen by Juana Bordoy, a demure brunette some ten years younger than her boss. Juanita, as she would come to be known, helped Doña Petrona to prepare complicated recipes under significant time pressures. In the 1960s, the authoritative manner in which Petrona treated her assistant on air would become subject to criticism, as we shall see in the next chapter. But during the 1950s, the primary result of their on-screen pairing seemed to be to create a domestic allegory in which Petrona was able to increase her own class standing in comparison to the supposed lower one of her helper.[74] But, in fact, their origins were not that different. As Juanita's nephew pointed out, both women came from relatively modest circumstances and were from the provinces.[75]

Around 1945, Juana Bordoy (later nicknamed "Juanita" by Petrona) came to work as Petrona C. de Gandulfo's *ama de llaves* (head housekeeper).[76] Like many other migrants to Buenos Aires during this era, Juana Bordoy dreamed of a better life in the big city. She had grown up with her seven siblings on the western edge of the province of Buenos Aires. Bocayuva was a classic train-stop town with a school, a church, and a police officer, who as it happens was Juana's father. "And that was it. There were some neighboring houses and farmers."[77] Juana's sister, who goes by the nickname "Porota" (Bean), explained to me that Juana's career began when she and her sister decided, against their parents' wishes, to work for other local families as teenagers during the 1930s to earn some pocket money. After a few years, Juana accepted a full-time job as a maid on a local estancia. Still, she apparently had her mind set on following some of her female friends to the capital to work and hoped to gain employment in a factory or as a hairdresser or seamstress. Instead, Juana met Petrona on a trip with her employers to the capital. According to Juana's family, Petrona liked her so much that she offered her a job with a better salary than she could make in a factory and good accommodations in her home.[78]

Despite subsequent perceptions that Doña Petrona treated her helper badly on television, Juanita's family pointed out that Petrona and her family actually treated Juanita quite well from the outset. This treatment likely stemmed from the similarity of their upbringings and the partial erosion of rigid class stratification during the mid-twentieth century. Perhaps as a result, Petrona gave Juanita the room next to her own (as opposed to a servant's room), shared meals with her, and invited her family to stay in her home when they visited Buenos Aires. As her niece Susana explained to me, Juanita "sat with them at the table, none of this eating in the kitchen with the girls [*chicas*]."[79] As this statement suggests, Juanita's family understood her place at the dining room table as a reflection of her esteemed position within the household, in contrast to that of the other help.

The presence of a staff of female domestic servants, and especially of Juanita Bordoy, who took charge of domestic affairs, allowed Doña Petrona to focus on her career. Petrona later explained to journalists that while she went to her culinary laboratory in the city and although she cooked for guests herself, "Juanita is the one who manages my house and my kitchen every day."[80] Therefore, in Petrona's household, Juanita embodied the model of the ideal homemaker to a greater extent than her employer, who made her living encouraging women to focus on domestic pursuits. In contrast to the *buena ama de casa* (good homemaker) that Doña Petrona publicly revered, Juanita was not married and was paid to play this role for another woman.

Despite the similarities of their backgrounds and even their dress, on television Petrona made clear that she was in charge; she was the *patrona* (female domestic boss or mistress) and Juanita was her assistant. Domestic servants appeared on other Latin American television programs (although most often with a more clearly differentiated dress), but not on television in the United States. There was no on-air equivalent to Juanita on U.S. cooking shows. For example, Julia Child, who would take to the air a decade later, cooked alone or sometimes with another professional cook or chef. The people who helped with food preparation and cleaning remained off stage.

With Juanita by her side on television, Doña Petrona substantially increased her personal network of fans. Two years after she began to appear on television, Doña Petrona claimed to have a personal file with contact information for over 400,000 *alumnas*. Her secretary (who worked with her at her office downtown) sent these students the weekly recipes sponsored by Swift from her television program *Viernes Hogareños*.[81] Such correspondence provided a new kind of opportunity to promote her program and her main sponsor, Swift, and its canned goods.[82] With faithful sponsors and widespread media exposure, Doña Petrona had, by the early 1950s, established herself as *the* definitive domestic expert in Argentina. In 1954, the magazine *Sintonía* announced that "many fans are proposing to create a Nobel Prize of Gastronomy for Doña Petrona C. de Gandulfo."[83]

Even Argentine revolutionary Che Guevara recognized Doña Petrona's importance. From Mexico, in 1955, he wrote to his future in-laws in Peru to ask for their blessing in his marriage to their daughter, economist and political activist Hilda Gadea. Describing their relationship, he explained: "Our married lives probably won't be like yours. Hilda works eight hours a day and, I, somewhat irregularly, around twelve. . . . But our routines work harmoniously together and have turned our home into a free association between two equals. (Of course, señora [Gadea], Hilda's kitchen is the worst part of the house—in terms of order, cleanliness, or food. The saddest part is that even Doña Petrona has not been able to civilize [this] economist.)"[84]

For Che Guevara, as for many of his compatriots, Doña Petrona and her cookbook (which appeared to be in their home, given his reference) represented the high point of culinary expertise. Despite his claim that he and his wife were equals, he (like many other leftist revolutionaries) clearly expected women in general, and Hilda in particular, to do the cooking and cleaning. Recalling the writing of this letter (which Che asked his wife to type), Gadea later explained that "practically everything he said to my parents in the letter was true, except, of course, what he said about my cooking. He was laughing as he dictated that paragraph to me." While Hilda did not have the time to let her parents in on the joke, she made clear in her subsequent book that she was in fact a good cook. Peruvian dishes were her expertise, but "like a good Argentine," Che steered away from spicy foods and "preferred a good steak and salad."[85]

Hilda Gadea and Che Guevara followed not only culinary trends but also political events in Argentina, and they watched with dismay as Perón's presidential authority became more and more tenuous.[86] During the first half of the 1950s, Perón not only lost the political devotion sustained by his charismatic first wife but also depleted the postwar surplus that had initially helped him to raise wages and increase consumption levels. He scaled back some of his earlier initiatives. He also began to publicly criticize the church and the armed forces. In 1954, he infuriated religious leaders by introducing a law that outlawed religious processions, prohibited the teaching of religious education in schools, permitted divorce, and reinstituted brothels. Military leaders who opposed Perón took advantage of the fallout. In 1955, a coalition led by the navy, calling itself the Revolución Libertadora (Liberating Revolution), removed Perón from the presidency by accepting his supposed resignation. Hilda, Che, and the group of Latin American revolutionaries with them in Mexico were disappointed that Perón did not fight back by arming the workers.[87] Still, even as military leaders forced Perón to flee Argentina and made the Peronist Party illegal, they could not suppress Peronism, which was to remain an enduring, powerful political presence. After his departure, Argentines became even more polarized between those who celebrated Peronism and those who vilified it. The series of alternating democratic elections and military coups that followed the 1955 coup highlighted the lack of consensus and political fragmentation of Argentine society.[88]

As previously, Petrona refrained from any explicit political public commentary. Still, after General Pedro Pablo Ramírez moved into the private presidential residence next to her house, his wife apparently invited Petrona over for a private, neighborly chat. She later publicly explained: "The only person who invited me to the President's residence was the wife of General Ramírez in 1955, who wanted to meet me personally. We had tea and talked almost all afternoon."[89]

Despite the intensity of political divisions in the wake of Juan Perón's departure, many Argentines shared a sense of the possibilities for economic development and modernization during the second half of the 1950s.[90] General Pedro Eugenio Aramburu, who headed the 1955 interim military government, quickly established relations with the International Monetary Fund and the World Bank. Along with loans, these institutions provided recommendations for austerity plans that led to the privatization of many sectors of the Argentine economy, beginning to roll back the Peronist government's state-led economic model.

In the wake of this economic crisis and the Peronist government's demise, the number and type of private initiatives aimed at women in their capacity as *amas de casa* would continue to increase. In 1956, Lorenza Taberna published yet another cookbook for the pressure cooker. Like Doña Petrona before her, Taberna implored her readers to make careful use of scraps and leftovers and to cook and clean in such a manner that "the kitchen looks like no one had worked there."[91] Echoing the widespread belief that technology was improving women's lives as well as those of their families, she argued that the pressure cooker was instrumental in helping women cook well and in an economical manner. This was timely advice; in 1956, the economy once again fell into crisis.

In response, in 1956, Elena Zara de Decurgez and a group of other women created the nonprofit Liga de Amas de Casa (Homemaker's League).[92] Confronting the economic instability of the previous seven years as well as the new austerity plans brought on by the latest crisis, they sought to unite Argentine homemakers to find solutions to common problems. Among their founding objectives, they cited the defense of a "fair price" and the support of efforts to provide women with a "better education for the management of their home."[93] They were eager to professionalize as well as to recognize the professional capacity of *amas de casa*. Under a government much less involved in domestic education than the Peronists had been, they joined private *ecónomas* like Doña Petrona and Lorenza Taberna in addressing and seeking to shape homemakers' interests and concerns.

A key issue for many middle-class or upwardly striving working-class women was that of paid domestic help. Most women who did not have help struggled to live up to contemporary domestic expectations, while those who could afford help found themselves faced with new expectations and laws. *Amas de casa* were organizing at the same time that domestic servants were gaining new rights. In 1956, Argentine legislators passed Law

326, which significantly expanded domestic servants' rights. Those working as maids and cooks had gained the right to an annual salary and an annual vacation in 1946, after Juan Perón took office, but it was not until 1956 that full-time domestic servants gained the right to daily and weekly time off, sick leave, and financial compensation for firing.[94] It was also in 1956 that legislators passed Article 1624 of the Civil Code, which brought domestic servants and their employers under municipal and local regulations for the first time.

This was a significant accomplishment, but whether domestic servants could exercise the rights they had won remained in doubt.[95] As mid-twentieth-century legal scholars pointed out, custom had long dictated this work relationship, unique in that it is not intended for profit and occurs in the "intimacy of the home."[96] Still, there was a sense among the upper middle and elite classes that the Peronist government had changed the balance of such relationships by encouraging poor people working in domestic service to be less docile and more rebellious.

Despite scholars' tendency to frame such relationships as paternalistic in nature, women took the lead role in negotiating these domestic work relationships, making them more maternalistic in practice.[97] Thus, although men benefited from women's (paid and unpaid) domestic labor, female rather than male employers generally managed the work and affective qualities of this relationship.[98] While the new 1956 law and expanding number of alternatives allowed domestic servants more power in such negotiations, the female employer continued to hold the upper hand over her help. This was certainly the case in the relationship between Petrona C. de Gandulfo and Juana Bordoy. Perhaps most poignant, Petrona changed Juana's nickname from "la morocha" (the dark-haired, and/or dark-skinned, girl) to "Juanita."[99] Still, Petrona did not go as far as other women, who sometimes completely changed the names of their live-in domestic help.[100] Further, as the 1946 and 1956 laws mandated, Juanita Bordoy made an annual salary, took a yearly vacation, and had time off each week.[101]

While many women (and a small number of men) working in domestic service were unlikely to receive such benefits, a small number of voices began to suggest that those working in domestic service merited a bit more respect from their employers. For example, in 1956, María Adela Oyuela explained to her presumably middle-class readers in her book *Cortesia y buenos modales* (Courtesy and Good Manners) that there "ought to be mutual respect between the home owners and their servants." She advised her readers to be reasonable and not to ask too much of the help. "For this, nothing is more convenient than trying—even with the imagination—to put ourselves—even for an instant—in the place of our servants."[102] Such a suggestion, while clearly grudging, bespoke a new recognition that people working in domestic service had feelings and merited some respect. At the same time, Oyuela did not presume that many of her readers even had such help. She suggested that the middle-class homemaker did most of her housework and entertaining on her own.

Expanding the Professionalization of the Ama de Casa

Doña Petrona continued to increase her fan base with much applause and little critique during the late 1950s. By this point, televisions were becoming much more widely available in Buenos Aires—they were manufactured locally starting in 1956. This allowed the new technology to begin to eclipse films, live theater, and radio in the capital—but not outside of it.[103] During the next couple of years, the number of television sets in Buenos Aires jumped fivefold, from 75,000 in 1957 to 400,000 in 1959.[104] In 1957, Doña Petrona once again gave her television program a new, and this time more elegant, title, *Programa del Arte Culinario* (Program of Culinary Arts).

That same year, she released the fiftieth edition of *El libro de Doña Petrona*. To celebrate this accomplishment, the cover displayed a three-tiered cake covered in pale blue frosting embossed with elaborate designs, pink roses, and golden wheat shafts. The note on the inside of the jacket for the fiftieth edition celebrated the 730,000 copies that had been released since the first edition had come out in 1934. Her collaborators at *Para Ti* applauded this achievement, which they claimed to be "without comparison in Argentina or in the world." They credited this unprecedented success in gaining the "public's favor" to the author's continuous updates and additions to this text as well as her "devoted interest in helping *amas de casa*."[105]

The fiftieth edition testified to the book's previous success and also pointed out Petrona's interest in continuing to improve and update her cookbook. She streamlined the layout by moving the general interest topics to the back of the cookbook, and she added a new chapter about cooking for children, which Lorenza Taberna had also included in her cookbook the previous year. This was a topic that was starting to gain momentum, as psychologists in Argentina and elsewhere argued that children had their own needs, and that the traditional authoritarian model of parenting was harming children.[106] In this vein, Petrona recognized that children had their own preferences and that their mothers should seek to serve them meals that appealed to them. She stressed, however, that ultimately parents should impose discipline. "I have always argued that letting a child get his way all the time is not a demonstration of the best care."[107] Such an idea would come under scrutiny from proponents of new ideas about parenting during the 1960s.[108] But during the previous decade, Petrona and other experts seemed more concerned about the professionalization of homemakers' domestic skills than their parenting skills.

Petrona continued to work closely with her sponsors on television to promote her program and their products to Argentine *amas de casa*. Cooking again under the program title *Viernes Hogareños* (Fridays at Home) in 1958, she prepared dishes with diverse culinary influences, as she had done throughout her career. For example, from September through December 1958, she made dishes that reflected her original French culinary training, like Profiteroles with Chocolate, and others that spoke to the influence of major immigrant populations on Argentine cuisine, like Galician Empanadas. More innovative was her incorporation of her sponsor's products, linked to a new transnational culinary aesthetic.[109] For example, she presented Pasteles de Hojaldre Frita but now filled these traditional *criollo* specialties with Swift-brand Vienna sausages. She also made a fanciful fruit-packed gelatin mold, Fantasias de Gelatina Royal (Royal Gelatin Fantasy), which called for Royal's instant gelatin product. In addition, she included an updated version of Supremas de Pollo Maryland (Maryland-Style Chicken), which reduced the quantity of ingredients from her original recipe in her cookbook (from six to four pieces of chicken and from a dozen to six bananas) and incorporated Swift-brand canned corn into her white sauce.[110] As previously, she sent out a brochure that promoted her television program as well as her sponsors and shared the recipes she had made on air.

Doña Petrona not only used her recipe pamphlets to promote her sponsor's products and share her recipes but also sought to integrate her television program into her cookbook. In 1958, she added thirty pages of new black-and-white photographs of step-by-step cooking procedures photographed during her show. In these photographs, she transformed hard-boiled eggs into bunnies, toads, and (un-self-consciously) "Chinamen"; turned mashed potatoes and almond paste into roses; made a whole chicken into a boneless one; and shaped several types of pastry dough into pastries. These photographs showed her readers the specific steps to making the fanciful modern delicacies she prepared on her television program. They also allowed those without televisions to catch a glimpse of what it was like to watch Petrona on the small screen.

On television, in her cookbook, and on her radio program, Doña Petrona increasingly looked to the United States for models of cooking and living

during the 1950s. This culinary shift reflected a broader shift in the dominant economic paradigm. Starting in the late 1950s, Argentine leaders embraced the idea that Argentina's future depended on its adherence to a model of economic development driven by foreign capital. In keeping with the postwar economic restructuring led by the United States, developmentalism was en vogue in Latin America, not only in Argentina but also in neighboring Brazil.

Despite winning the presidential election with Perón's support, Arturo Frondizi (1958–62) subsequently sought to modernize Argentina and make it one of the "developed" nations in the world by reversing the supposed delay caused by Peronist policies.[111] As opposed to the Peronist celebration of the working class as the backbone of the nation, the Frondicist movement celebrated the middle class and the ways in which its economic policies would ultimately benefit its members.[112] The government implemented the International Monetary Fund's stabilization plan in return for loans—devaluing the peso, freezing wages, and eliminating price controls and state regulations—all of which led to a significant drop in workers' incomes, an increase in unemployment, and another economic crisis in 1959. As promised, this approach also led to a dramatic increase in foreign investment, which grew tenfold in just two years—from just 20 million dollars in 1957 to over 200 million dollars by 1959.[113] Much of the funding, as well as a bevy of new products that the middle class could consume, came from the United States.

During the late 1950s, as household appliances became more available, and, in good economic times, more affordable, domestic experts put an even greater emphasis on the fact that women needed to professionalize by incorporating new technology into their domestic routines. As had been the case throughout her career, Doña Petrona's recommendations to save time and money continued to equate modernity with those who had the resources to acquire the most recent appliances. For example, in the new section on stoves added to her 1958 cookbook, she explained how to cook with several different types of stoves, from those that used fuels such as carbon and coal to "the modern ones," which used gas and electricity. She emphasized the benefits of gas and electric stoves, highlighting their "cleanliness, speed, handling, ease, economy, and comfort in modern homes."[114] However, only those with the purchasing power to buy gas or electric stoves were given recommendations about how to keep cooking costs down.[115] Similarly, she touted the economic benefits that refrigerators could afford in allowing homemakers to buy and store foods ahead of time—while failing to recognize that the refrigerator, while becoming more popular, still represented a "luxury" item for most Argentines.[116]

At the same time that Doña Petrona promoted new technologies for homemakers, she also suggested the possibility that women might professionalize themselves in other ways as well. As in past editions, the fifty-second edition of *El libro de Doña Petrona* instructed readers on whom to seat in the place of honor to the right of the *dueño de casa* (male homeowner). However, in 1958, Petrona now declared that it may be either the "wife of the most important invitee" or "today, a single woman, who has made her name thanks to her work and talent . . . making her more important than the wife of the most important invitee."[117] Such advice seemed to speak to young women's increasing education and professionalization outside of the home during the 1950s. Further, it foreshadowed middle-class women's even greater participation in the job market in the 1960s.

Nevertheless, during the late 1950s, Petrona continued to see the *ama de casa*—and not the professional, single woman—as her target audience. The great majority of her competitors did the same. In fact, most Argentine cookbook authors directed their books to the *ama de casa* and presumed that she was the one responsible for feeding her family—leaving men and domestic servants often unmentioned. In 1958, the Liga de Amas de Casa established 1 December as the Día del Ama de Casa (Homemaker's Day), in recognition of the important work that women, in their capacity as home-makers, were doing at home.

As did members of the Liga de Amas de Casa, publishers and maga-zines that released new general advice books also suggested that women in Argentina were in particular need of a professional domestic education as a result of "modern circumstances." For example, in 1958, the publishing house Aguilar released a book titled simply *El libro del ama de casa* (The Homemaker's Book). Dedicated to helping the *ama de casa* accomplish "the complicated tasks of the modern home," it provided advice to make it easier for women to organize their time, establish a budget, and determine the daily menu.[118] This book was meant to be read but also to be used as a calendar. Most of the pages were dedicated to a day-by-day calendar, with meal suggestions and a listing of the saints' days and a chart to map out each month's budget.

In a similar vein, in 1959, former journalist Alicia Lobstein published a book to help *amas de casa* save time and work. She aimed her text at "mod-ern" women, whom she characterized as educated, middle-class homemak-ers like herself. Borrowing heavily from home economics textbooks from the United States, she attempted to provide her readers with the latest "scientific" advice, which included diagrams of kitchen "work stations" and illustrations of the proper "radius" of arm movements for housework.[119] She explained that despite the fact that being an *ama de casa* represented "the highest and most ancient of human professions," it unfortunately lacked a formal, obligatory education. Echoing one of Doña Petrona's standard lines, Lobstein decried the fact that "millions of young ladies marry without any training." She added that those who have a little training probably learned it "from the mother or the grandmother, who in turn ran their home in accordance with the economic situation and perhaps the old methods com-ing from other countries."[120] She implored the new generation of better-educated women to take on modern responsibilities along with modern rights: "We should not only use our heads to show off modern hats and fashionable hairstyles; but we also should KNOW HOW TO THINK, a possibil-ity that our grandmothers considered only once in a while."[121] Like Doña Petrona before her, Lobstein suggested that traditional female knowledge was not well informed and therefore unworthy of modern women's study or respect.

Lobstein, like many of her contemporaries, saw the modern, middle-class Argentine housewife as lacking domestic help. She titled her book *365 días sin servicio doméstico* (365 Days without Domestic Service) and began her colorful prologue with the sentence, "The maid left me once again." She reported that, in fact, she had gone through three maids in just fifteen days.[122] She attributed this desertion to the other opportunities available to women during this time, like factory work, which she acknowledged gave women more independence.[123]

Around the same time, women's magazines also began to speak to the shortage of help and how to get by without it. For example, in March 1958, an article in *Claudia* suggested that *amas de casa* use their intelligence and the latest technology to "realize their domestic tasks in the most perfect and least time-consuming [manner]."[124] Titled "Mucama perfecta sin sueldo se ofrece" (Perfect Unpaid Maid Offered), this article argued that the efficient *ama de casa* did not need and was perhaps even better off without paid help—she could be the "unpaid maid" herself. Like others during the late 1950s, the author recognized the challenges of doing it all oneself and recommended outsourcing certain tasks, like using a laundry service or buying prepared foods. This piece also championed the latest domestic technology, such as electric mixers and vacuums, as a better long-term investment than a maid. Like Lobstein and Doña Petrona, the author suggested looking to the United States for models, recommending that Argentine couples consider hiring a babysitter for a night out (which never caught on).

Elites continued to enjoy the services of domestic servants during the late 1950s, but many middle-class homes counted on part-time help only or had no paid domestic assistance at all.[125] Part of this trend spoke to upward social mobility. The expansion of education, Peronist policies, and industrial development had allowed a significant number of Argentines to move up the social ladder. Scholars have estimated that by 1960 half of the grown children of working-class migrants to Buenos Aires were working in nonmanual labor, "middle-class" jobs.[126] Such families often had limited resources to hire help. In turn, with expanding job opportunities, fewer poor people were interested in working in domestic service in the first place. In 1947, census takers identified 376,572 women working as domestic servants in Argentina; in 1960, they counted 40,000 fewer women doing so, these making up just a fifth of the "economically active" population.[127] Still, whether this statistical drop in census data represents a real decline in the number of domestic servants remains an open question. Even as the numbers suggest that the number of full-time domestic servants—and the 10 percent or so of households that regularly enjoyed their services[128]—declined during this era, contemporaries often spoke of the shift to part-time domestic work.[129] As with other statistical indications of domestic service, census figures give us only part of the picture for what has long been an often informal, part-time, and undocumented part of the economy.

While the actual number of domestic servants remains hard to determine, it is clear that the changing economic and legal climate shaped the parameters for negotiating new kinds of paid domestic relationships during the mid-twentieth century. As Lobstein and others pointed out, the emergence of alternatives like factory work enabled some domestic servants to exert greater autonomy and request better benefits—like higher salaries and more time off. *Dueñas de casa* accustomed to setting the terms of the relationship were sometimes forced to compete with the factories and provide better benefits in accordance with the new laws to retain their help.[130] A few, like the author of the 1956 book on manners, suggested that these *dueñas de casa* would benefit from making more reasonable requests and encouraging more mutual respect.

Conclusion

Of course, it was homemakers and not domestic servants who received the most attention and adoration from their peers during the 1950s. During this decade, numerous public and private figures celebrated the work of the *ama de casa* and recognized her economic importance in an expanding number of venues. They championed the idea that full-time homemakers needed professional training and merited respect. Public figures like Doña Petrona and Alicia Lobstein suggested that the *ama de casa* without paid help could live up to the middle-class ideal of domesticity by acquiring domestic technology, adopting the practical approach to cooking and housework from the United States, and getting a domestic education, which they were only too happy to provide. They looked to the United States for practical tips and new appliances but continued to stress a local sensibility, expecting women to shop more frequently, cook from scratch, and serve their families and friends meals to enjoy at the table in a more leisurely manner.

The 1950s represented the high point of *El libro de Doña Petrona* and the model of middle-class domesticity it represented. Numerous Argentines literally bought into the vision of the enthusiastic and skilled *ama de casa* who dedicated her time to caring and cooking for her family and entertaining friends, while her husband earned the "family wage." At the same time, domestic servants had recently gained new rights that placed their work under the same legal frameworks as that of other workers. Thus, the 1950s generated some of the first formal proclamations of the possibility that housework might be considered a professional activity, for the glorified but unpaid *ama de casa* and for the less-celebrated, but modestly compensated, domestic helper.

During the first half of the decade, the Peronist government's initiatives aimed at women played a significant role in portraying homemaking as the best professional undertaking for women. During the second half of the 1950s, private individuals and organizations like the Liga de Amas de Casa touted this message as well. For her part, Doña Petrona now faced a more crowded media environment. She made the most of the new medium of television, using it to reach a broader audience while still seeking to preserve an individualized relationship with her fans. For example, in response to the growing number of letters she received, she hired a private car from 1952 through 1957 to bring her responses to the central post office in Buenos Aires.[131] In 1959 and again in 1960 she went to Rosario to give live cooking demonstrations in front of sold-out crowds, sponsored by the magazine *Ecos*.[132] In 1959, an illustration of Petrona C. de Gandulfo appeared on the cover of the Argentine television guide, *Canal TV*. In it, she has a huge smile and holds a mixing bowl in her hand; Royal baking powder is on the counter, with a sleek, silver refrigerator right behind her.[133] As this portrayal suggests, Doña Petrona was not only a culinary celebrity but also an Argentine icon of progress through capitalist consumption.

For many Argentines, Doña Petrona's vision of middle-class domesticity fit the expectations of women's proper roles in a developing nation. One woman explained it this way during the oral history workshop in Puerto Ingeniero White: "I was very small when I watched her . . . but I think that with her classes she tried to demonstrate that as *ama de casa* one could convert herself into the center of the home; through the kitchen it was possible to demonstrate a lot of love for others—the dedication, the effort, I think she tried to demonstrate this, and personally I lived it."[134] Many other women lived it as well, dedicating the majority of their days to caring, cooking, and cleaning for their families. While homemakers enjoyed a newfound public acknowledgment and appreciation, women as a whole experienced a higher level of domestic expectation.

Doña Petrona and her cookbook's intensifying popularity resonated during a decade in which the ideal of women's homemaking expanded in Argentina and elsewhere in the capitalist world. Predictably enough, even socialist revolutionary Che Guevara bought into it, expecting a fellow political activist—his wife—to work outside of the home and to cook like Doña Petrona inside it. In the famous 1959 kitchen debate between Richard Nixon and Nikita Khrushchev, Nixon argued that the superiority of

Cover of Argentina's television guide, Canal TV, *featuring Petrona C. de Gandulfo, 1959.*

capitalism could be found not just in the military but also in the U.S.-style kitchen, which was designed to make things "easier for [our] women."[135]

But, as we shall see in the next chapter, the economic crises that plagued Argentina during the 1960s would make the U.S. model of consumption unattainable for most Argentines. This frustration would be accompanied by the emergence of a new, less domestic model of mainstream womanhood in Argentina and elsewhere. Petrona C. de Gandulfo and other domestic experts would seek to adapt their advice to changing ideas and circumstances, and Argentines would begin to openly question the mainstream, middle-class model of domesticity.

CHAPTER FIVE

SHIFTING PRIORITIES &

ENTERTAINING INEQUALITIES

Empanadas de Carne con Hojaldre Rápida
(Beef Empanadas with a Quick Dough)

Dough: 800 grams flour, 500 grams butter, 1 teaspoon salt, 375 grams water, 4 tablespoons lemon juice

Filling: 1 diced onion, ½ cup oil, 1 can minced beef, 1 hard-boiled egg, 1 tablespoon flour, broth (enough to thicken mixture), chopped parsley, salt, pepper, and nutmeg[1]

In the mid-1960s, Doña Petrona presented a recipe for meat-filled empanadas on the television program *Buenas Tardes, Mucho Gusto*. Wearing a decorative apron and a confident expression, she demonstrated how to make empanadas with a "quick dough" and a canned-meat filling. In her characteristic sing-song cadence and northwestern Argentine provincial accent, she explained how to make the recipe "step-by-step." In grainy black and white, the camera followed Petrona's swollen knuckles and painted nails as she kneaded, rolled out, and folded the empanada dough six times. The camera panned back as she moved to the filling. It followed her as she picked up a can of clearly marked Swift-brand minced beef, emptied the contents into a bowl, and mixed it with the onion, egg, oil, and other seasonings. Adopting the tone of a schoolteacher, Doña Petrona explained to her viewers that she was repeating this recipe because many had not paid good enough attention the first time and had asked her to go over the instructions. She chided her *alumnas* about the importance of paying close attention and practicing the recipes at home. She reminded them that, as always, she would be happy to respond to their questions in writing. She further emphasized the usefulness of this particular recipe, explaining that it was both "quick" and "very appropriate for Mondays and Tuesdays, when there is no meat."[2]

Ever conscious of changing circumstances, Doña Petrona adapted the beef empanada—an emblematic staple of Argentine *criollo* cuisine—to the current economic climate. As during the previous decade, during the 1960s economic crises would continue to rack Argentina about every three years, first in 1963 and then in 1966 and 1969. Expanding a policy originally initiated by Juan Perón, subsequent governments banned the sale of fresh beef two days per week in order to ship more abroad for greater profit. Doña Petrona's decision to use Swift-brand canned beef was therefore not just commercially motivated; it also represented a response to economic policy.

Many Argentines continued to expect women to mitigate the effects of shortages and inflation on their families and, now, also to shop at the new supermarkets, whose shelves were stocked with international brand goods made by companies like Swift. At the same time, more educated, middle-class women in Argentina entered the workforce and fewer chose to be full-time homemakers during the course of the 1960s.[3] Although large numbers of poor women had long worked for wages, the entry of better-off women into the workforce had a major impact on the perception that women's roles were changing dramatically. Social commentators fueled this notion by often conflating middle-class women with all women in this purportedly middle-class nation.[4] Still, the "middle class" itself was not nearly as unified as this term suggested, with people who considered themselves members divided in terms of their socioeconomic standing, as well as their views about the cultural transformations that were taking place.[5]

How would Doña Petrona, who had come to represent the ideal of middle-class domesticity so dominant in 1940s and 1950s Argentina, fare in the 1960s with the emergence of a new, less exclusively domestic model of womanhood? And how would Argentines respond to her treatment of her assistant Juanita on television during a decade when many were becoming more aware of class-based inequalities? As we shall see, Doña Petrona's approach and Argentines' reactions to it reveal that many would make important adjustments to patterns of consumption and domesticity while preserving the idea that female homemakers (or their hired help) should continue to be responsible for cooking and other domestic tasks.

Crafting a New Image

Over the course of the 1960s, many people in the West began to challenge the 1950s cult of female domesticity. In Argentina, this sentiment was inspired by Argentine women's growing access to higher education and better birth control, local experiences with sexism, and exposure to feminist movements from the United States and Europe.[6] While very few Argentine women would come to identify as feminists per se during the 1960s, a broad swath of young middle-class women in Argentina spoke the loudest through their actions—as many in a position to do so chose to continue their educations or seek out extradomestic employment. As a result, during this decade, the number of women deemed "economically active" by census takers would increase significantly for the first time during the twentieth century, bringing women from 20 percent to 25 percent of the official, documented workforce.[7] Even more dramatically, the percentage of women who identified themselves as homemakers would decrease from nearly three-quarters to a little over half of the female population during the course of the 1960s.[8]

Ideas about Argentina and its place in the world would also shift over the course of this decade. As youth movements and members of the left challenged previous forms of hierarchy across the globe, young, politically active Argentines began to criticize the hierarchical nature of their society and to identify Argentina with other Latin American nations more than with European ones. Inspired by the 1959 Cuban revolution leading into this decade and the May 1968 student uprising in France toward its close, many Argentines offered vivid critiques of injustice and poverty in Argentina and the world, often linking these to the dynamics of capitalism. The most dramatic protest in Argentina, the Cordobazo, exploded in the city of Córdoba in 1969.[9] The revolutionary sentiment that was brewing, together with women's increasing professionalization, would generate dramatically new patterns of everyday life, especially in urban settings.[10]

During the 1960s, Doña Petrona would begin to refashion her public image, in part by emphasizing her provincial background and the foods she grew up with in Santiago del Estero. When asked by food journalist and cook Marta Beines in 1960 about her favorite foods to prepare, Petrona responded by saying that although she appreciated European cooking, she preferred "what is ours."[11] This represented a dramatic shift from her self-presentation as a French-trained, cosmopolitan *ecónoma*, and, as with her other adjustments, it reflected changing ideas about Argentina and its (culinary) identity. Two years earlier, the magazine *Mucho Gusto* had published a cookbook of *cocina criolla*. The editors included recipes with both indigenous and Spanish roots from Argentina and other parts of Latin America. While recognizing that their cookbook was not exhaustive, they explained that it represented "the most complete" treatment of *cocina criolla* available to *amas de casa* "in the brother countries [*países hermanos*] of Central and South America."[12]

A new awareness of Argentina's culinary links with other Latin American nations was emerging at this time, and Beines was clearly excited about Doña Petrona's new, more explicit embrace of local, South American cuisine. She wrote, "As a professional [Petrona] is not far from any secret of the diverse cuisines of the world; [still] what is more than true is that she is not, nor does she want to be, a European-style specialist. What is important is not what can be imitated. Doña Petrona is faithful to what is hers."[13] Doña Petrona was particularly suited to tap into this notion of "faithfulness" because of her *santiagueñan* roots. She did so, in part, by increasingly talking about the empanadas from her home province. In her article, Beines included Petrona's recipe for empanadas and described the sensory experience of eating one. "They have a native flavor," she wrote; "they are juicy, spicy enough to excite the palate without destroying it and they are seasoned with spices that perfume the filling without changing the taste of the meat and of the dough, [which is] light and golden."[14] Doña Petrona's empanadas married indigenous flavors with the beef in the inside of the empanada, all the while preserving a civilized, and presumably European, flavor in the "light and golden" crust. Through her characterization, Beines suggested such empanadas to be an apt metaphor for the latest, more indigenous-inflected iteration of *criollo* identity in Argentina.[15]

In addition to beginning to celebrate provincial foods more explicitly during the early 1960s, Petrona continued to present a broad range of cosmopolitan recipes as worthy of women's attention. In contrast, in 1962, well-known Argentine folksinger Margarita Palacios began to use her fame and her culinary roots to exclusively promote *cocina criolla*. In January 1962, this native of the province of Catamarca opened a *peña* (folkloric club) in Buenos Aires featuring "northern foods."[16] Later that year, she published a recipe pamphlet called "Las comidas de mi pueblo" (The Foods of My People) for the Argentine magazine *Folklore*.[17] In 1963, she began her own television program, showing her viewers how to make dishes popular in northern Argentina.[18]

Doña Petrona was attentive to the new interest in provincial foods, but she paid even greater attention to the need to economize—a need that was more important for many of her urban, middle-class fans. In 1962, she released a new text squarely focused on economizing, *Recetas económicas* (Economical Recipes). Some three years earlier, fellow *ecónoma* Chola Ferrer had published *Economía en la cocina* (Economy in the Kitchen).[19] But Doña Petrona did not attribute her desire to publish this new cookbook to this competition. Instead, as with *El libro de Doña Petrona*, she told journalists that her fans deserved credit for the publication of *Recetas económicas*. She explained that she decided to publish a more cost-conscious cookbook "after a man stopped me in the street and told me that I had contributed to destabilizing his family's budget."[20] At other opportunities, she suggested that this happened more than once: "It would happen that I would find myself in the street with wives and their husbands, who would congratulate me for my recipes, but would say, 'Your dishes are so expensive!'" She agreed—at least in this article—recognizing that many Argentines were no longer in the position to serve expensive foods.[21]

The timing of the publication of *Recetas económicas* was sound. Earlier that year, a military coup had ousted President Arturo Frondizi from office due to his inability to control the economy and contain Peronism.[22] In fact, Doña Petrona later described how she heard the commotion and watched as her presidential neighbor was forcibly removed from his official residence across the street.[23] The subsequent civilian government, installed via this coup, also faltered. By 1963, the cost of living had risen 400 percent in monetary terms over its level in 1958, and private consumption was estimated to have fallen off by 10 percent.[24] As it had throughout the twentieth century, food represented a major part of the typical family's budget. For example, a 1962 survey in the city of Córdoba found that residents in a poorer section of town spent about half of their wages on food, and those living in a wealthier neighborhood spent approximately one-third of their income on food.[25]

In explaining the rationale behind *Recetas económicas*, Doña Petrona noted that the "dynamism of modern life" had changed the way people ate. Seeking to get away from the "gluttony of the past," she provided suggestions that centered on reducing the number of dishes in each menu. She encouraged her readers to buy in-season fruits and vegetables and to make a budget before going shopping. She included new, less-expensive recipes such as Torta de Navidad (Christmas Cake) instead of the traditional *pan dulce*, cutting the number of steps and eggs in half.[26] She attributed the subsequent popularity of her thriftier cookbook to not only the "great quantities" of recipes but also the fact that it was "within reach for all budgets."[27] And, in fact, *Recetas económicas* would become her second–best-selling book, with over nineteen editions.

Even as Doña Petrona emphasized more economical recipes for fans who were struggling during the early 1960s, she also continued to emphasize more elaborate ones for those with more resources or aspirations. In 1964, she issued a second edition of *Para aprender a decorar* (To Learn to Decorate), which she described as "my most requested and least found book." She explained in her prologue that she had not been able to reissue it previously due to the "printing costs," which were presumably much higher due to the large number of illustrations. Still, in this fancier cookbook, as in her economical cookbook published two years earlier, she encouraged readers to also purchase *El libro de Doña Petrona* for "an infinity" of recipes.[28] In this way, she helped promote her principal cookbook in her more specialized texts.

El libro de Doña Petrona would continue to sell well during the 1960s, although not quite as well as in the previous decade. About half the number of editions of *El libro de Doña Petrona* were released over the course of the 1960s, compared to the book's high point during the previous decade, when some twenty editions had made their way to the public. Nevertheless, the book continued to enjoy a broad audience, and print runs were still an impressive 35,000 copies each around the middle of the decade, until they began to drop off toward the end of it.[29]

By the mid-1960s, this Argentine "bible for the home," along with *Recetas económicas*, was being sold not only in Argentina and neighboring Uruguay but across the Americas. After several years of pitching the idea, in 1964, Isay Klasse finally convinced Petrona to agree to let his firm, Tres Américas, distribute her cookbooks across the continent. He explained: "I met Doña Petrona as a book distributor because we wanted to have the most successful books, and Doña Petrona's book was perhaps the only cookbook that was in the best-seller category." Even as she was quite accessible to her fans, Isay described how it was "very difficult to get to her to do business, because the book was selling so well that she did not need a distributor." Nonetheless, once she agreed to the idea, she became very committed to the process. She began to consult Isay about the terms used in other Spanish-speaking countries and even considered translating her book into English for the U.S. market before giving up the idea due to the time and expense.[30] The Spanish edition was snapped up by bookstores in Latin American countries like Venezuela and Puerto Rico, as well as in Spanish-speaking markets in the United States, including Miami, New York, and Los Angeles. Referring to the success of *El libro de Doña Petrona* across the Americas, Isay concluded that "it was a phenomenal Argentine ambassador, because [it] was a book that entered into the home, and it was a good book."[31]

As *El libro de Doña Petrona* crossed the globe, so did its author. Following a trip to Bolivia in the previous decade, during the 1960s she went to Brazil, Venezuela, and Peru. She also began a radio and television program in Uruguay.[32] In addition, she traveled to the United States, where she spent two months touring and meeting local domestic experts, including Swift's promoter, Martha Logan, in Chicago. She later explained to journalists that she chose to go to the United States instead of Europe because seeing "the modern interested me more than going to visit the old."[33] Such a sentiment reflected the growing preference for a continental identification with the Americas as opposed to one with Europe.

Doña Petrona and some other Argentines nevertheless continued to express a sense of Argentine cultural dominance within Latin America. Doña Petrona later shared her glee that a North American research firm found her cookbook to be the best-selling book in all of South America during the 1960s.[34] And in the 1962 note to her readers in *Recetas económicas*, she made the grandiose claim that, thanks to their "approval" of *El libro de Doña Petrona*, it had become "the one with the most sales in the whole world."[35] Whether or not these claims were true, they fed into the idea that Doña Petrona in particular, and Argentina in general, had produced an unprecedented success on a regional and global scale.

Making Television Count

Within Argentina, the editorial success of Doña Petrona's cookbooks was tightly linked to her growing presence on the small screen. In 1960, with the privatization of television in Argentina, this *ecónoma* moved to Canal 13, naming her cooking show after herself, *Petrona C. de Gandulfo*. The following year, she initiated a new program, *Magia en la Cocina* (Magic in the Kitchen), which harked back to Primitiva's notion that cooking could be magical.[36]

Cooking on television would reach new heights with the addition of a new women's variety program created by Pedro Muchnik in 1960, *Buenas Tardes, Mucho Gusto*, meaning colloquially, "Good afternoon, pleased to meet you," and literally, "Good afternoon, lots of taste." At first, Doña Petrona maintained her independence and did not participate. In 1961, her program *Magia en la Cocina* was nominated, along with *Buenas Tardes, Mucho Gusto*, for the prestigious Martín Fierro prize for the best televised "home-related program." It won; she lost.[37] By the following year, Doña Petrona had joined the cast of *Buenas Tardes, Mucho Gusto*.

Buenas Tardes, Mucho Gusto began by targeting and reaching mostly urban *amas de casa* of the middle and working classes during the afternoon siesta hour. Its founder, Pedro Muchnik, presumed that these women were not only the most accessible audience but also the most interested one, especially as compared to their male peers.[38] According to Pedro Muchnik's daughter and the host of the program, Annamaría Muchnik, her father originally tailored this program to "the woman in her own home" (*la mujer de su casa*), because "women were not working but were focused on domestic tasks" in 1960 when he created the program.[39]

The numbers of women who worked outside of the home would increase throughout the 1960s, but at the beginning of this decade homemaking still reigned supreme. According to the 1960 census, around three-quarters of women continued to define their occupation as homemaking. Despite the Peronist emphasis on homemakers' economic contributions, this census continued to categorize such women as "economically inactive," along with students and incapacitated people. In contrast, the census registered not a single man as a homemaker, characterizing the 15 percent of "economically inactive" men as retirees, students, or "in other conditions."[40]

In contrast to the 1960 census's labeling of *amas de casa* as nonproductive citizens, the cast members of *Buenas Tardes, Mucho Gusto* (like other domestic experts) emphasized women's work and productivity in the home. The show's slogan reflected this intention, dubbing itself "a television show for the home, made for people whose vocation is housework."[41] During its initial years, the program focused on topics that included cooking, fashion, crafts, sewing, and physical fitness. In addition, Pedro Muchnik selected hosts, including his daughter Annamaría and his former secretary, who projected an image of the "anti-diva" or "domestic woman," who he believed would relate best to his audience.[42] As more and more middle-class women entered the workforce during the course of this decade, *Buenas Tardes, Mucho Gusto* would respond by tailoring some of its advice to this new generation of middle-class professionals, even as it continued to focus its attention on full-time homemakers.[43]

On television, as elsewhere, Doña Petrona directed herself primarily to female *amas de casa*. One of several *económas* who provided cooking lessons on this program, Doña Petrona had three blocks of thirty minutes to prepare her dishes, while the rest of the specialists had only one block of ten minutes. According to Annamaría Muchnik, her father gave Doña Petrona more time than the others had because "she was very important, very famous, a woman with a great career."[44] This was a wise move—Muchnik's ratings soon revealed that the largest number of viewers tuned in when Doña Petrona was on the air.[45] Approximately 1 million people watched the show daily in the capital, an impressive figure, considering that it represented about a third of city dwellers and the same number of households that owned a television.[46] Women represented about 90 percent of the program's viewership, and *Buenas Tardes, Mucho Gusto* was among the first television shows to successfully compete with radio programming for women's attention during the afternoon.[47]

Television access had expanded dramatically since Doña Petrona had appeared on Argentina's first, state-run channel in 1951. Between 1959 and 1965, the number of television sets grew sixfold, from 280,000 to 1.6 million.[48] Argentines did not need to own a television to watch one. Several people recalled that their neighbors would gather together in someone's home to watch *Buenas Tardes, Mucho Gusto* and other television programs.[49] Many continued to watch television in public settings like store windows or social clubs.[50] Argentines' ability to consume this new form of media was largely shaped by where they lived. During the 1960s, provincial channels began to emerge in other large cities beyond the capital.[51] The majority of Argentine viewers and the prime audience for *Buenas Tardes, Mucho Gusto* resided in Buenos Aires, Córdoba, Mar del Plata, and Mendoza.

In these cities, viewers could watch Doña Petrona cook live on television on *Buenas Tardes, Mucho Gusto* on Mondays, Wednesdays, and Fridays.[52] Corporations remained eager backers of this endeavor. In fact, Doña Petrona was the only one on the show who brought her own sponsors with her.[53] At the opening of each cooking segment, the camera panned over a collection of Swift food products and Ruffini's Gamuza brand cutlery placed on the kitchen counter. Doña Petrona often incorporated both of her main sponsors' products into her cooking lessons, taking a spoon off the counter to mix something, or making a recipe with a clearly marked can of Swift Vienna sausages or *dulce de leche* (milk caramel).[54]

Because these broadcasts were live, they were very immediate and personal. The fact that there were no retakes meant that sometimes a recipe might flop on air. Doña Petrona later explained that she tried to cover up any errors, and in her own recollection, she often succeeded. For example, she recalled in her memoirs that once when she was in the middle of explaining how to get a meatloaf out of its pan, she realized that clumps of it were falling out onto the counter. To her relief, the tape inexplicably cut right before the dish fell apart. She used this serendipitous event to reassemble the meatloaf. She explained, "When the camera appeared again after the unexpected break, I de-molded it very naturally, everything came out perfectly. Overcoming the trance, and just getting over my nervousness, it was even possible to hear the sighs of relief from the cameramen." On another occasion, Petrona put a fruit gelatin mold into the freezer "in order to keep it firm until the exact moment." She tried to de-mold it with hot water four times without success and finally, on the fifth try, succeeded. She later realized that foods made with gelatin should go only in the refrigerator and not the freezer. Like her audience, she was still learning about how to cook (and cool) with new products and technologies.[55]

Such moments reveal the extent to which Doña Petrona preferred to maintain the illusion that her recipes always turned out as she expected. In contrast, U.S. television chef Julia Child, whose French cooking program on PBS would premier in 1963, became famous for her decision not to downplay her "delightful mistakes."[56] In one particularly memorable episode, Child flipped a potato pancake into the air and it landed on the counter instead of in the pan. Unflappable, she scooped the pancake back into the pan and looked straight into the camera and famously explained, "Remember, you are alone in the kitchen and nobody can see you."[57] Doña Petrona, on the other hand, preferred to maintain the impression that one should prepare food so well that it would not matter if others—in her case, millions—were watching you in the kitchen.[58]

As with Julia Child, a large part of Doña Petrona's appeal stemmed from her unique delivery and entertaining style. In her gravelly voice, Doña Petrona led a class that was at once serious and entertaining. Adopting a personal and conversational tone, she would explain, "Usté' agarra y estira la masa así, ¿no? [You hold and stretch out the dough like this, no?]."[59] She became infamous for this "no" at the end of her statements and worked hard to get rid of this habit, which many people made fun of. When a journalist asked her if this "no" stemmed from her *santiagueñan* heritage (along with her empanadas), she retorted, "Hold on a second; I don't say it anymore." She went on to explain, "They gave me such a hard time about that everywhere that I had to stop doing it. And don't believe that it was easy. Once someone counted how many times I had said 'no' during a program of a few minutes. Fourteen. A record."[60]

Television highlighted Petrona's manner of speaking and reminded viewers that, although she lived and broadcast in Buenos Aires, she had originally come from the northwestern provinces. Starting in 1962, a comedian on the children's show *Piluso* began to parody this bossy, provincial cook.[61] Even today, *porteños* laughingly recall how Doña Petrona would label an outstanding dish *un puema*, instead of *un poema*, as the word "poem" is spelled and generally pronounced in and around Buenos Aires. They continue to associate what they considered a "mispronunciation" with Petrona's common, provincial upbringing.[62] But while many Argentines I spoke with were clearly aware of Petrona's provincial provenance, most seemed genuinely confused about how they might respond to my questions about their understanding of her (or her assistant Juanita's) racial or ethnic identity. Many stated simply that Doña Petrona was a *provinciana* (from the provinces) or *criolla*, or did not answer at all. Perhaps like other Latin

Americans, some of the people I spoke with regionalized mixed-race identity in Argentina by locating it in the northern provinces.[63]

Doña Petrona's viewers not only were aware of her provinciality, but they were also constantly reminded of her expertise and professionalism. In keeping with her original work promoting gas stoves, Doña Petrona continued to approach her classes as opportunities to teach her female students how to cook correctly. As in her cookbooks, she taught a wide range of cuisine on air. In the one year of extant television programming from the mid-1960s, she explained to her television viewers that she would "teach everything in this class: expensive, economical, easy, and quick cuisine."[64] And she did. She made complicated French-inspired preparations like *media lunas* (croissants) or deboned and roasted a chicken and served it with duchess-style potatoes. She made simple "American" meals, directed to young women, like hot dogs and ham rolls. She also made local favorites like empanadas and *milanesas* (breaded meat cutlets). Her viewers seemed particularly interested in her desserts and frequently asked her to repeat them. She explained in one episode that many had written in with requests for *pan dulce, huevos de Pascua* (chocolate Easter eggs), and meringues. She responded by showing them how to make a recipe for each in the next few programs.

Doña Petrona and some of her viewers continued to be interested in the more complicated preparations, like handmade chocolate Easter eggs, but others were clearly more interested in saving time in order to speed up or "modernize" their domestic practices. Responding to viewers' correspondence, Doña Petrona remarked somewhat defensively on the "quick" empanadas episode: "If I do not modernize a recipe . . . it is because it is not possible. . . . There are classic recipes . . . that cannot be changed." She quickly followed this comment with a statement that showed her commitment to stay up-to-date. She told her viewers about her translator, María Elena Rodríguez Ocampo, who spoke five languages and kept her informed of the "latest [trends] in the world surrounding cooking and home economics."[65]

During the 1960s, Doña Petrona's approach to creating a common table in Argentina reflected the appreciation of traditional values along with the latest iteration of modernity there. As an Argentine psychologist explained in 1963, "Deep down, [Argentine women] think that all this stuff is fine for North Americans, 'who eat everything out of cans,' but not for decent women."[66] As this quote suggests, "decent" women in Argentina were still expected to cook and feed their families from scratch, especially by older generations. Doña Petrona's more expensive and elaborate dishes spoke to this ideal, but her more economical recipes reflected her desire to remain relevant during an unstable economic and political era.

In July 1963, Arturo Illia, a progressive member of the Radical Party, won the presidency with just 25 percent of the votes cast. With only this fragile base of support, the second democratically elected president in over a decade took over a country in economic turmoil. Advocating democracy and free speech, his presidency (1963–66) ushered in a new era of political involvement and questioning of conservative traditions. It also put an emphasis on state regulation and planning, seeking to protect industry and redistribute wealth. At first this approach met with some success, and the economy rallied in 1964 and 1965. But in 1966, the economy floundered, and the press and members of the business community stepped up criticism of President Illia's "inefficiency."[67] On 28 June 1966, a military coup supported by these sectors (and much of society) deposed President Illia and replaced him with General Juan Carlos Onganía. General Onganía's military government applied "authoritarian shock treatment" to the economy, in large part by expanding the interventionist powers of the state and diminishing the reach of the welfare state.[68] It shut down Congress, prohibited political parties, and used intimidation to quell dissent—ushering in what historians have deemed "the most authoritarian regime" up to that time in Argentina.[69]

Ongoing economic crises and recent cutbacks forced more Argentine families to get by with less. Some blamed politicians, and others criticized Doña Petrona. In response to the complaint that her recipes were too expensive, she commonly mentioned on air the "economy" of a particular food that she was using in a recipe or suggested an alternative way to make a dish in order to reduce its costs. She stated on air, "I did not want to give you any reason to call me expensive," for example electing not to use hazelnuts or almonds in her famous Pan Dulce de Navidad (Christmas Sweet Bread).[70] In another television segment, she made it clear that she had intended to use strawberries to make a particular dessert but had found them to be too expensive at the market (at a price of 400 pesos) and decided to replace them with preserved maraschino cherries instead.[71]

Despite her more economical approach in her television series and her latest cookbook, Doña Petrona continued to view Argentina as an essentially middle-class nation in which people could afford to consume for pleasure and for status. But with the deepening economic challenges of the 1960s, more Argentines found even the level of thriftier consumption she now advocated to be too luxurious to emulate. Driving home this point, a woman in her forties recalled as a child watching Doña Petrona prepare a meal with the leftovers from a turkey. Unsure what a turkey was, she asked her mother, who replied, "Don't worry about it; we can't even afford a turkey, never mind the leftovers!"[72] Similarly, a seventy-year-old woman living in one of the poorer sections of Puerto Ingeniero White remarked that Petrona's recipes "were very expensive; she put a lot of ingredients, a lot of egg [in them]."[73] Whether Argentines thought Doña Petrona's recommendations were economical enough often depended on individual socioeconomic situations. As one participant in the oral history workshop in Villa Luro explained, "In order to follow Doña Petrona's recipes during that time, one had to be middle class on up."[74] In other words, Doña Petrona's approach toward economizing was only "economical" for those middle-class Argentines who could afford to follow her advice in the first place.

To further demonstrate her responsiveness to middle-class concerns, Doña Petrona began to address the challenges women faced in balancing their domestic lives with extradomestic work when middle-class women began to pursue careers and advanced education in greater numbers. In the 1960s, she increasingly featured meals on her television program that required relatively little time and effort. Even as she continued to direct these time-efficient recipes to a female audience, she now identified more specific categories of women who might want to try them, namely "young girls," "married women who work outside of the home," and "homemakers who like to spend as little time as possible in the kitchen."[75]

While Doña Petrona recognized women's growing lack of interest in cooking, she spoke most directly, most enthusiastically, and most frequently to the young women of the new generation (especially brides-to-be) about how to prepare meals. This focus reflected her expectations and experiences that a married woman should know how to cook and that many young women, like her, did not know how to do so before marrying. Encouraging her young viewers to practice with and get excited about food, Petrona commented that many of their peers had asked her to teach them how to cook fifteen days to a month before their weddings when there remained no time to learn "little by little."[76]

Expanding on her recent suggestions in *El libro de Doña Petrona*, once a week she presented menus to the *nueva ola* (new wave), a term used to refer to young people in Argentina with new patterns of cultural consumption. She extended the common use of this term, from those who listened to rock, wore jeans, and went out in mixed-sex groups to include those who cooked in a quicker and more Americanized manner.[77] On her weekly program, Doña Petrona advised members of the *nueva ola* that cooking could be easy if they incorporated new types of ingredients and styles of cooking popular in the United States. Her advice was inspired by Argentina's increasingly tight links with this nation and also by her trip there. Following the approach to cooking she found in the United States, she recommended that her fans integrate more canned and processed foods (like Vienna sausages and ketchup) into their meal preparations, in her magazine column in *Para Tí* and on her television program. Because the U.S. company Swift was one of Doña Petrona's main television sponsors, she made a point of regularly incorporating Swift products into the recipes she made on camera, although she did not put many such recipes in her cookbook.[78]

Argentines did not adopt as many canned or processed foods into their diets as did their counterparts in the United States. (And in the United States, culinary celebrities like Julia Child and Alice Waters and their fans rejected such an approach to cooking and eating.)[79] For her part, Doña Petrona added the canned-beef empanadas with "quick dough" recipe that began this chapter to her repertoire but also showed how to make her classic empanada recipe on air. Unlike the "quick" empanadas, the traditional version required a significant amount of time and expertise. When demonstrating how to make the dough for standard empanadas, Petrona described a process of kneading, folding, and letting the dough rest that required two and a half hours of preparation before baking. And in describing how to make the filling, she reiterated her often-quoted remark that one should always cut the meat by hand, as opposed to grinding it or buying it already ground, so that it stayed juicy.

Thus, while Doña Petrona incorporated more time-saving tips and modern recipes into her repertoire during this television series, she (in step with many Argentines) still seemed to prefer traditional recipes that were relatively complicated and labor-intensive. In one segment, Doña Petrona suggested that her viewers could make a sandwich with store-bought *palmeras* (heart-shaped pastries), but in another she encouraged her viewers to make them at home, noting "how tasty" homemade things could be.[80] Additionally, on her television program and in her cookbook, she encouraged her audience to create elaborate garnishes such as piped roses for main dishes and desserts. Of course, such garnishes were diametrically opposed to the idea of cooking as quickly as possible; they were all about spending time to make food look artful and showcasing the skill of the cook.

Doña Petrona had come to love the art of cooking, and she hoped that her fans would do the same. During her television program, she regularly gave out her phone number on the air and told those living in Buenos Aires to call her with any questions.[81] She encouraged people from the provinces, specifically identifying those in other large urban centers like Mar del Plata,

Córdoba, and Mendoza, to write to her. In keeping with her original work promoting gas stoves for Primitiva, she characterized her viewing audience and potential correspondents as her *alumnas*. She encouraged her female students to take notes, practice carefully, and send her their questions. "No letter," she promised, "would remain unanswered."[82]

Two women I interviewed sent Petrona letters and, as promised, received prompt responses. Each saved Doña Petrona's reply for over thirty years—an act that suggests her importance in their lives. The first, Elena T., a sixty-year-old entrepreneur who lives just outside of the capital and loves to cook, wrote Doña Petrona in 1962 when she was in her twenties. In her letter, Elena asked Doña Petrona whether the water used to make the popular Argentine infusion *mate* should be boiling or almost boiling. She excused herself for "bothering" her with this "somewhat insignificant question" but explained that her query had been inspired by a disagreement among friends. Thirteen days later, Doña Petrona sent back her response. She explained that the water should be "removed immediately" from the heat just as it is about to boil but left near the heat source "so that it stays pretty warm."[83] This back-and-forth is interesting not just because it shows that fans actually wrote to Doña Petrona and received individualized responses as Petrona claimed, but also because of the nature of the query. In asking Doña Petrona about *mate*—a traditional drink from precolonial times—Elena demonstrated the extent to which she and her friends saw Petrona as an expert, not only in making complicated recipes but also in preparing a beverage that many enjoyed every day.

Some ten years later, a homemaker named Teresa C. from Puerto Ingeniero White wrote to ask Doña Petrona for clarification about a technique. Specifically, she asked her how to use a pastry sleeve to make roses out of mashed potatoes. In return, she received two letters of reply. In the first, sent the day after Christmas 1972, Petrona encouraged Teresa to call her if she was ever in Buenos Aires, remarking that she would be happy to show her how to make the roses in person because it was too "complicated" to explain in a letter.[84] Six months later, Teresa received another response, letting her know that she would prepare the roses on television. Doña Petrona encouraged her to watch, pointing out, "The only way to be able to make them" is to watch rather than have it explained. She promised that "afterward you will practice them and see how well they come out."[85] Teresa recounted that she was very grateful for the response because she had been intent on learning this procedure for a while.

In fact, three years earlier, Teresa had attended Doña Petrona's live presentation in Bahía Blanca, hoping that Doña Petrona might show her how to make the roses in person. Thinking that many people would not attend on account of the rainstorm that day, she brought a bag with mashed potatoes and a pastry sleeve with her to Petrona's talk. Upon seeing the swelling crowd, Teresa and her sister-in-law boldly decided to knock on Doña Petrona's dressing room door. Teresa warmly recalled that Petrona invited them in and was willing to demonstrate the technique until they realized that Teresa had brought the wrong attachment for the pastry sleeve. Enthusiastic about her interaction with the famous *ecónoma*, Teresa continued to write Doña Petrona with questions and continued to receive replies. As the large crowd at this and other live performances suggests, there continued to be impressive audiences for Doña Petrona during the late 1960s and early 1970s, especially in smaller cities like Bahía Blanca that had recently gained access to her television program and some of the domestic technologies she promoted, like gas stoves and refrigerators.[86]

Some of Doña Petrona's television viewers took their roles as students as seriously as she took her role as a teacher. For them, new ideas about women's extradomestic roles had not made a significant impact on their desire to continue to learn from a domestic expert. Many full time *amas de casa* not only wrote letters but also took notes as they watched. In fact, Teresa and her sister did just that, writing careful notes as they watched Doña Petrona on television. Teresa's niece pointed out that both women tended "to respect the recipe," and whether they used a recipe from Doña Petrona's cookbook or her television program, they made an effort to follow her instructions "step by step."[87] A journalist for the magazine *Siete Días* broadened such a claim, explaining in 1972, "Argentine *amas de casas* take careful notes of the recipes [that appear] at the bottom of the screen and religiously follow the proposed menus."[88]

Not all women shared this level of dedication, ability, or desire to cook like Doña Petrona. For poor Argentines, whose diet remained more about subsistence than variety and presentation, Doña Petrona did not provide relevant advice. At the same time, some more privileged Argentines made clear that they did not aspire to cook or be like Doña Petrona even if they could afford to do so. Specifically, as more women began attending universities (representing 34 percent of all students by 1968), some female students rejected the very idea that it was their duty in life to emulate Doña Petrona.[89] One woman explained to me, "In general, middle-class families had a pretty reverential adoration for . . . Doña Petrona. . . . Therefore, for the women who burst into the university in the sixties, it was necessary to get away from Doña Petrona." She pointed out that she and her peers wanted to distance themselves from the domestic image of women that this *económa* promoted, because it was an obvious example of the "feminine characteristics we were rejecting." She nonetheless noted that she and her classmates did not wholly reject this role, thinking that as women it was still necessary to learn "how to cook something."[90]

Ideas about how much time women should spend doing such cooking had become a point of debate by the late 1960s. Mass media outlets were both responsive to and influential in shaping new ideas—as well as maintaining older ones—about women's changing roles. As historian Isabella Cosse has established, conservative publications aimed at a broad middle-class audience—like *Para Ti*, with which Doña Petrona collaborated—acknowledged women's extradomestic work but continued to celebrate women's domestic roles above all else. In turn, a group of new, more progressive magazines for the upper middle classes—like *Primera Plana, Confirmando*, and *Claudia*—more frequently celebrated the "liberated" young woman who rejected the principal role of homemaker.[91]

In 1966, a journalist for *Confirmando*, who interviewed Doña Petrona, issued such a challenge. The framing of this interview made clear that although Doña Petrona had updated her version of domesticity, this progressive publication still felt it was inadequate. Striking a new, less celebratory tone about women's domestic roles, Doña Petrona now explained that her job was to help women with the "problems of the home." She continued that women were as capable as men and that their extradomestic work was a good thing. When asked whether men should therefore help with housework, Doña Petrona still responded "no," because ultimately a woman prefers "that a man maintains his superiority to a certain extent." The journalist countered, "Then housework makes the one who does it inferior?" Doña Petrona protested, suggesting that rather than asking their husbands to pitch in, working women should leave another woman (presumably a maid) in charge at home. The *económa* then apparently steered the interview to "a topic I like better"—her career. She described her days at her culinary laboratory, the multiple venues in which she gave cooking classes, and the nature of questions she received. Most women, she explained, called to ask how to make meringues. *Confirmando* played along, titling this article with a sarcastic take on what they considered Doña Petrona's unrealistic worldview, "*¡Es tan fácil hacer merengues!* [It Is So Easy to Make Meringues!]."[92]

Even some of Doña Petrona's faithful fans—who tended to be less critical of her explanations—followed her on television with little intent of recreating the recipes at home. For example, Magdalena M., a homemaker in Buenos Aires whose parents had migrated from Spain, recalled that she loved to watch Doña Petrona's program during the 1960s after she acquired

Images of Petrona C. de Gandulfo and Juanita Bordoy from a newspaper article in Mar Tiempo, 1983: top from the late 1950s; bottom from 1963. Courtesy of El Clarín.

her first television set at the start of the decade, but that she never cooked like Doña Petrona "because her dishes were sophisticated and expensive." Still, she explained, "I took away some things. She was very good; she was someone to see. She was someone to watch." What Magdalena seemed to find particularly engaging was how Petrona dressed and interacted with her helper. "Did you see that she always had an embroidered apron [and was always] well put-together, well-coiffed?" she asked me excitedly. And "when Juanita was always removing everything that [Petrona] used, she would say 'Juanita, I'm not done yet!'"[93] Other lower middle-class and working-class Argentines also mentioned that they watched the program more for entertainment than to learn what to cook. Some pointed to their interest in Doña Petrona's and Juanita's elegant outfits, large pearl necklaces, carefully coiffed hairstyles, and embroidered aprons. Others suggested that the drama of the relationship between Doña Petrona and Juanita was what really made the program interesting to watch.[94]

"Pobre Juanita"[95]

Doña Petrona explicitly signaled that the members of her anticipated audience were female and implicitly presumed that they embraced or aspired to middle-class patterns of domesticity. Most obvious, the class-based image that Petrona projected was indelibly marked by the constant presence of her assistant, Juanita, and by their on-screen interaction. Both Juanita and Doña Petrona's husband helped Petrona to prepare for her segments, but Juanita was the one on air with her and became her most important public partner. Cook Emmy de Molina put it simply, "It is unthinkable to remember Petrona without Juanita."[96] And, indeed, articles and conversations with Argentines about Doña Petrona consistently turn to her relationship with Juanita (and only rarely, if ever, to her relationship with her husband).

During and after Doña Petrona and Juanita Bordoy's three-decade-long tenure together on television (1951–83), people have fallen into two camps: those who thought Petrona treated Juanita fairly by soliciting her help, as was only appropriate, and those who thought she treated her unfairly by ordering her around in a condescending fashion. Such reactions were influenced but not entirely determined by class standing. During my hundreds of informal conversations, forty-six formal interviews, and two oral history workshops with Argentines who identified themselves (or would likely be identified by others) as middle class, working class, or elite, some people in each category critiqued this relationship and others complimented it. At the same time that their reactions seemed quite personal, it was striking that the six women I interviewed who had worked (or continued to work) in domestic service tended to express fewer negative sentiments and even to suggest that the relationship between Doña Petrona and Juanita "was very good," as one woman explained.[97] In contrast, in my oral history workshops with a diverse group of people, middle- and working-class participants hotly debated the question of whether such treatment was fair or unfair.

Even today, these two perspectives reveal themselves in the distinct ways people invoke Juanita's name in everyday domestic interactions. For example, Olga G., an enthusiastic home cook in Puerto Ingeniero White now in her seventies, explained that her cousin María B., who dislikes cooking but does not mind cleaning, has been "her Juanita" for years.[98] María told me that she has been happy to play this role, but others said that they have rejected it. Some described how, when being bossed around in the kitchen by friends or family (and not, it is important to note, a *patrona*), they might retort, "What do you think? That you're Petrona and I'm Juanita? [¿Qué te crees, que vos sos Petrona, y yo, Juanita?]"[99] The prevalence of this phenomenon is striking and reveals the extent to which Argentines have incorporated this power-laden domestic relationship into their own domestic interactions. As Juanita's sister proudly explained, in Argentina "the name for a helper in the kitchen became Juanita."[100]

Most Argentines learned about this relationship through watching the pair interact live on television during the 1960s and 1970s. During the approximately 800 minutes of existing taped segments from the mid-1960s, Juanita aided Doña Petrona with tasks such as mixing, kneading, and cutting.[101] She also performed specific duties that Doña Petrona rarely did herself, such as putting things into and taking them out of the oven, or cleaning pans and utensils. Host Annamaría Muchnik explained that Juanita did all the preparatory work: "Petrona did not even have to say anything and it was already done. It was as if it was a surgical operation," and Juanita was the "nurse" (*enfermera*) and Petrona the "doctor" (*médico*).[102] The gendered dynamics behind this analogy are revealing, as Muchnik associates Doña Petrona with the type of power that a male doctor might hold over a female nurse. Another comparison pointed to a more commonly female-to-female relationship of power. A fan named Dora I. explained that Petrona was the "teacher" (*profesora*) and Juanita was the very quiet "helper" (*ayudante*).[103]

Such analogies were likely inspired by the fact that while Doña Petrona spoke to her viewers and to Juanita, Juanita almost never spoke and rarely looked up at the camera. In the one season that exists on tape, Juanita remains silent on all but three brief occasions, when she speaks quickly and quietly to Petrona.[104] Even Doña Petrona addressed the issue of Juanita's silence on air. During an episode in which they made a liver pâté, Petrona looked into the camera and confided to her viewers with a smile, "When Juanita feels like it, she talks too."[105]

Nonetheless, like many *dueñas de casa*, Doña Petrona made it clear that she was the one in charge—modeling behavior for her viewers of how to treat (or not treat) domestic servants. Her reputation as an inconsiderate taskmaster sprang from her tendency to speak to Juanita in a bossy and brusque manner. "¡Basta, eh! [Enough, already!]," Petrona would say to

Petrona C. de Gandulfo and Juanita Bordoy on the set of the television program
Buenas Tardes, Mucho Gusto, 1973. Courtesy of Marcela Massut.

Juanita if she wanted her to stop doing something, such as whipping cream, or "¡Rápido, Juanita! [Quickly, Juanita!]," if she wanted her to hurry up.[106] In the one episode in which Juanita actually spoke audibly to the camera, Petrona commented, "It is hot today and I do not feel like working, you should be the worker, Juanita. Isn't that right, Juanita?" to which Juanita responded, "Bueno, señora [Okay, ma'am]," and resumed working as instructed.[107] In a Christmas Eve episode, Petrona asked Juanita to stop what she was doing so that she could demonstrate where a particular bone she was removing from a turkey would be on Juanita's body.[108] As always, Juanita obliged, this time with a laugh.

Over the past several decades, Argentines have tended to be more critical of or at least more apt to laugh at, rather than applaud, the way Petrona treated Juanita. In many conversations I started about Doña Petrona, one of the first reactions was often a smile followed by the phrase "Ay, pobre Juanita [Oh, poor Juanita]." People would often point out how Petrona ordered her around and portrayed everything as "Juanita's fault and not her [own]."[109] For example, a woman named Elena P. remarked that "poor Juanita" was a "martyr because Doña Petrona was a bossy one."[110] Television scholar Mirta Varela agreed, criticizing the manner in which Doña Petrona "mistreated" her silent helper on air.[111] Journalist and fellow cook Miriam Becker suggested that Petrona's personality made it imperative that she work with someone like Juanita. "Juanita was very respectful, even more than Petrona was tough." Becker continued, "It could not have been any other way for the person playing second to Petrona, because Petrona would not have permitted a single breach of confidence." Nonetheless, despite Petrona's strong will, Becker argued that she was both "generous" and "good."[112]

In other words, those who defended Petrona suggested that her attitude toward Juanita was simply evidence of her strong personality and perhaps even part of what made her successful. A woman now in her seventies explained, "I think that a woman who made it where [Petrona] made it forty or fifty years ago had to establish her authority in order to prevail."[113] Interpreting the criticism of Petrona in this light, Nora L. suggested, "When [Petrona] said 'Bring me that,' people would complain because they thought she didn't treat [Juanita] with much kindness, but no, that was her personality."[114] Several others remarked that if Petrona really had been so cruel, Juanita would not have stayed with her for so many years.[115] Even as she acknowledged that Petrona was "pretty bossy," Juanita's niece, Esther P., explained, "It was [just Petrona's] way of being, it was not that she treated [Juanita] badly, because she loved her and she respected her and she let her make decisions."[116]

For many viewers, Doña Petrona's treatment of Juanita seemed problematic—perhaps because it touched on a larger and long-standing abuse of power in the domestic realm that had been gaining new public recognition. As growing numbers of activists, journalists, and everyday citizens began to question social hierarchies during the 1960s, more people began to suggest that the traditional ways in which *patronas* had treated their paid domestic help were no longer acceptable. Perhaps as a result, magazines began to convey more strongly than the half-hearted entreaties of the previous decade that their (presumably middle-class) readers ought to respect the women they hired to help them cook and clean. For example, in assessing the contemporary "crisis in domestic service," a journalist writing for the relatively conservative middle-class magazine *Femirama* during the 1960s reminded her readers to keep in mind "that the person who helps them is not an inferior being" but rather someone who does "work that is important, useful, and necessary."[117] The journalist continued, "The relationship between *amas de casa* and service personnel has changed because both of their roles have changed. The *ama de casa* of the last century who 'played mom' with the *mucama*, along with the demanding *señora* who treated her like a slave, no longer exists."[118] Of course, as Doña Petrona and Juanita's on-screen relationship demonstrated and my oral histories corroborated, this type of a maternalistic and, at times, domineering relationship did continue to exist—almost always behind closed doors. Because Doña Petrona and Juanita's relationship was so public, it could be publicly scrutinized.

Those who saw Doña Petrona's treatment of her assistant as an abuse of her power began to take Juanita's side, as they perceived it, during the 1960s. This was something that both Juanita and Petrona recognized on some level. Juanita told her niece Susana that when Petrona gave public lectures, she would give Juanita a hard time and say, "Do you realize that they clap harder for you than they do for me?" Juanita confessed to her niece, "It makes me embarrassed, I realize that when we go in to give a lecture that people are clapping so hard for me and it makes me feel I don't know what. . . . It makes me embarrassed." Always aware of (and seemingly more comfortable in) "her place," Juanita concluded, "The star is *la señora*."[119]

As this anecdote suggests, part of what made this pair so compelling and their cooking segment so popular was their very different approaches to stardom. As journalist Matilde Sánchez explained, "The airs of Petrona—married 'to a Gandulfo, who were people of a certain standing,' as she herself would define them—fit with the modesty of Juanita to perfection, almost like a pair of comedians."[120] Eduardo R., who watched Petrona and Juanita on television with his family growing up during the 1960s, also highlighted the comical nature of their interactions. He recalled, "Sometimes you would laugh because [Petrona] treated [Juanita] so badly."[121] Elvira I. remembered that her mother "had a good time" watching Petrona and Juanita interact on *Buenas Tardes, Mucho Gusto*. Elvira explained with a chuckle that her mother would say that Petrona is really "making a scene."[122]

Argentine children also picked up on the tension and the humor of this duo's on-screen relationship by incorporating it into the games they would play. A woman named Marta F. recalled playing "Doña Petrona" with her girlfriends in her middle-class neighborhood of La Plata during the early 1960s, when she was a small child. Marta described how she and her friends would set up a big table in between her neighbor's chicken coop and her yard and "produce" a cooking show. She explained, "The main issue was who [got to be] Doña Petrona. There could be one or a thousand Juanitas but only one Doña Petrona." This honor was generally reserved for the oldest or most powerful girl playing that day. Once elected, "Doña Petrona" would don an apron and a fresh flower. She would proceed to lead the show and order all the other girls—the "Juanitas"—around. Unlike Petrona, the many "Juanitas" did not wear anything special. "The funny thing is," Marta pointed out, "we acted as if we were really on the program." The girl playing Petrona would instruct the Juanitas to bring her the water to mix with the dirt and say, "It's necessary to do this *quickly*, Juanita."[123]

In addition to showing that this group of Argentine girls clearly understood who was in charge, this anecdote also reveals how Doña Petrona and Juanita's television presence made this pair a shared cultural referent. When Marta spoke to her colleagues about this game, many of them said that they played it as well. A female friend who became a member of the

Argentine Congress told Marta that she played "Doña Petrona" and forced one of her cousins to be Juanita. As Marta explained, "The most important thing was to play 'Doña Petrona' and rope someone into being Juanita."[124]

Playing "Doña Petrona" allowed Marta and her friends to boss someone else around and also helped them, as second- or third-generation immigrants, to feel Argentine. Marta explained, "We lived in an Italian neighborhood and no one could say that they were Jewish or Spanish. Everyone wanted to be Argentine. People had to civilize themselves, to know how to eat." By the 1960s, eating and being Italian had been thoroughly incorporated into eating and being Argentine.[125] Feeling Argentine was not only wrapped up in how to eat but also in how to treat presumed inferiors. Doña Petrona's cultural importance and long career in the city made her an emblem of Argentine womanhood, despite her own relatively modest provincial background. As Marta stated, Doña Petrona was "the image of what was the most appropriate for a woman."[126] Her television program taught Argentine girls to cook and also taught them about gender roles and class power.

As these young women and their slightly older counterparts grew up during the 1960s, they also encountered a new, younger, and less domestic model for Argentine womanhood.[127] Many began to dress, talk, and think differently than previous generations, wearing blue jeans and miniskirts, having premarital sex, and peppering their conversations with expletives and English. Some became more politically active.[128] A significant number of girls who grew up during the 1960s chose to pursue professional careers instead of becoming full-time homemakers, including Marta, who became a paleontologist. Of course, Doña Petrona was a career woman herself, even as her attention to domestic matters often obscured this reality and any criticism of it.

Looking back, Argentines tend to disagree about whether the relationship between Doña Petrona and Juanita was typical. For example, when I asked a group of sixteen working- and middle-class women in Puerto Ingeniero White in May 2004 about this issue, some responded that their relationship was not typical, while others argued the opposite. One woman asserted that "every family was unique." Another commented, "We have to try to remember that the relationship of forty years ago was quite different from the one today. The upper class was very clear that the one below [them] was below."[129] In a separate conversation, a feminist named Hilda, who is now in her fifties, further supported this idea that in the past the privileged *ama de casa* (like Doña Petrona) un-self-consciously exercised control over her domestic help. Comparing the way her mother dominated the women who worked for her as maids, Hilda suggested that even though this power play was private, "the relationship between Petrona and Juanita was the most explicit" and therefore the most open to criticism.

Staying on Top, Late 1960s

Doña Petrona's televised treatment of Juanita opened her up to criticism but it also increased her popularity. Though some fans identified with Doña Petrona and others criticized her, many watched because she and Juanita provided an entertaining, if unintentional, parody of a common private domestic relationship between women. By the late 1960s, many more Argentines could observe and comment on this relationship. There were 2 million television sets in Argentina as of 1968, a figure that would continue to grow rapidly over the next few years.[130] And corporations continued to sponsor Doña Petrona, with the dairy company La Serenísima paying her an honorarium of 400 pesos a month (about four times the average worker's full salary) to use their products on television.[131]

As the medium of television expanded, so did media coverage of Doña Petrona and other stars, helping to create a new culture of celebrity. During the 1960s, media outlets began to cover not just people's professional accomplishments but also their personal lives. For example, in May 1967, Doña Petrona was interviewed on a forty-minute radio program about her career and her life.[132] This particular program brought back memories and also people with whom Petrona had worked during the various stages of her career, including former managers from Primitiva and fellow *ecónomas*. Apparently, Juanita was not on the guest list, but a comic who imitated Doña "Patrona" was. Adopting an exaggerated *santiagueñan* accent, he explained, "Juanita couldn't come tonight. She is grounded, because she laughed and my mayonnaise separated."[133] The audience erupted in laughter and continued to chuckle as he peppered his monologue with Petrona's beloved diminutives, deeming a dish he pretended to make with "*papitas*" (little potatoes) to be "*exquisito*" (delicious).

As in this interview, by the late 1960s Doña Petrona was eagerly sharing details about her life story and provincial background and using the new media attention to her personal life to do so. This particular radio program showed the relatively new desire to publicly poke fun at Doña Petrona, but most stories in print continued to be glowing and informative. In 1969, the magazine *Gente* ran an article with a three-page spread featuring photographs in which Doña Petrona and her family (including her son, daughter-in-law, grandchildren, and Juanita) enjoyed empanadas around the traditional outdoor bread oven she had installed on her patio. In this article, Petrona commented, "Empanadas should be eaten spicy and warm. 'In the mouth of the oven,' as they say in Santiago. [This is] a very old, and very wise Indian recipe." By the late 1960s, Petrona was publicly embracing her regional (and perhaps even her indigenous) heritage. She remarked, "Things from the place you were born stay with you."[134]

In this same 1969 interview with *Gente*, Doña Petrona spoke to how ideas about women's roles in Argentina had changed. She now conceded, "At times I think how boring, how tiring, the work of a woman dedicated to her home is. I always say that one should be in the kitchen the smallest amount of time possible."[135] Of course, this was *not* what Petrona had always said, nor what most of her recipes promoted. Instead, it reflected her response to the emergence of a new, less-eager attitude toward cooking held by members of a better-educated and more career-oriented generation of middle-class Argentines.

Doña Petrona's shift was part of a larger and more public discussion about the challenges of being a full-time *ama de casa* that had emerged over the course of the 1960s. For example, even in the relatively conservative magazine *Femirama*, a 1968 article discussed the "difficult trade [*oficio*] of the *ama de casa*." Drawing on U.S. scholarship, it analyzed the psychological afflictions many full-time housewives were purportedly suffering. The piece concluded that housewives' loneliness and the invisibility of women's domestic work in a "modern" society was to blame, and touted women's involvement in extradomestic activities as the answer.[136] In this publication, as opposed to its more progressive peers, such a conclusion was surrounded by those of many other social commentators eager to keep women in their "rightful" unremunerated domestic roles.[137]

Reflecting both new and old ideas about middle-class domesticity, Doña Petrona acknowledged the need to streamline some of her recipes so that women could get out of the kitchen more, even as she continued to tout the more time-consuming recipes that they were expected to know how to cook. She often pointed to technology—things like gas stoves and refrigerators— as the way to save time. She did not (yet) critique the women themselves. In contrast, during the late 1960s a growing number of social commentators began to complain about "liberated" women, critiquing them for their consumption of domestic technologies as a supposed means of escaping their homes and families.[138]

According to her granddaughter, Marcela Massut, Petrona "was an absolutely modern woman, she loved everything that was modern, everything electronic."[139] In fact, this passion showed up even more visibly in her

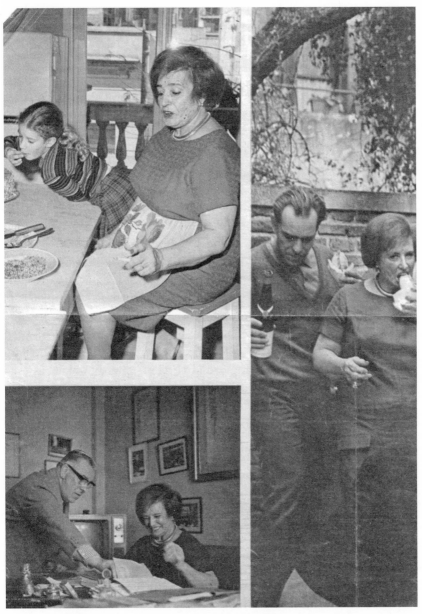

Photographs of Doña Petrona and family accompanying article
"Para comerte mejor," in the magazine Gente, *25 September 1969, 53. Granddaughter,*
Marcela Massut, is on the top left; husband, Atilio Massut, is on the bottom left;
and son, Marcelo Massut (eating empanadas) is on the right.

private life than in her on-screen performances. When Petrona returned to Argentina from the United States, she brought with her a General Electric stove that she had installed in her home. It quickly became "the love of her life."[140] Petrona also returned with many pans and molds, including, for example, some to make train shapes. However, Massut points out that her grandmother realized that other Argentines did not have access to these types of kitchen gadgets, and she therefore sought to adapt what she found in the United States to the Argentine situation, explaining, for example, how to make a train out of different sizes of regular rectangular molds.

Doña Petrona's approach was therefore not just about personal preferences but also about striking a balance between tradition and modernity, as well as between accessible products and those outside her audience's reach. She used various forms of "modern" technology that were available (if not always accessible) in Argentina on the set of *Buenas Tardes, Mucho Gusto*. With the help of Juanita and her second husband, Atilio, Doña Petrona brought a huge basket full of all of her own pans, plates, pastry tools, graters, molds, silverware, utensils, and flatware to the set each time she performed. In addition, permanently on the set, and in view of the camera, sat two gas stoves, a refrigerator, and an electric mixer, which Petrona used frequently on the program. Petrona assumed that certain appliances and tools were a given (such as a refrigerator or a whisk), but she did not assume that everyone owned others, such as an electric mixer.

Doña Petrona used the technology of the television set to display the technology of the kitchen. A perfectionist at her trade, she worked with the cameramen before the show began to make sure that they focused on specific parts of her presentation.[141] One of her unique characteristics, as compared to most of the television chefs who followed her, was her tendency to demonstrate how to use both newer and more conventional forms of technology on camera and to prepare recipes in their entirety during her allotted segment. Annamaría Muchnik commented, "She had the enormous merit of doing everything from the beginning to the end . . . on camera. . . . If she had to mix, she mixed, if she had to beat with an electric beater, she would do that" as well.[142] She made this decision despite the fact that it sometimes meant that she would use a loud electric mixer on camera for five minutes, during which time she was unable to speak over the noise.

Despite her love for technology, Doña Petrona was also willing to use her hands whenever preferable. Many Argentines recalled her penchant to get her hands dirty in order to show the viewer how to replicate every step of a recipe she was explaining. In one graphic example, Petrona cut the head off of a chicken and skinned and deboned it with her fingers. When kneading dough for empanadas or pastries, Petrona would work the mixture while the camera closely followed her hands, showcasing not only her technique but also her knuckles, which were swollen with arthritis by the mid-1960s. Of course, she did not need to do all of this manual labor herself. Juanita did much of it, and many recalled Petrona's assistant whipping cream by hand for what seemed like an eternity.

Indeed, females helping other females do domestic work, as opposed to having the latest technology, has long been what has most aided women in accomplishing their many tasks. The number of appliances grew substantially during the 1960s, but they changed the type of domestic work performed rather than the amount of it. This was something that many women of the 1960s recognized on some level, as historian Inés Pérez concludes.[143] Over the course of the 1960s, the number of registered domestic servants would grow modestly, reversing the trend of the previous decade.[144] Even still, sociologist Carlos Zurita estimates that only 9 percent of Argentine households employed full-time paid domestic help by 1970.[145] While wealthy women could count on such full-time help, most women relied on part-time paid help or the unremunerated assistance of female relatives and neighbors in order to work outside of the home and yet continue to be responsible for the work inside of it.[146]

Conclusion

During the 1960s, Argentine women's changing relationship to domestic work became a matter of intense public discussion and debate. This decade brought a reconsideration of the notion that a woman's only aspiration in life should be to care for her home and family, as more young women who had the opportunity to do so made their educations and their careers a higher priority than their housekeeping and cooking skills. Those older women who had embraced homemaking during the 1950s and before experienced such shifting ideas about the "modern woman" as an implicit criticism of their lives.[147] For her part, Doña Petrona sought to remain relevant for both generations by providing more time- and effort-saving advice, along with her more traditional and labor-intensive recipes—in her cookbooks and on television.

Even as her cookbook sales began to drop, Doña Petrona's success in reaching Argentine women at different stages in life was reflected by the larger amount of correspondence she received. During her television series, Petrona regularly thanked her viewers for the "very lovely letters" and responded on air to some of their requests. She apparently received 400 cards daily and kept a personal file of all of the *amas de casa* who had consulted her.[148] In 1970, she stated that this file held contact information for 600,000 women—a figure that had grown by 200,000 from her estimate of 400,000 in 1952.[149]

In the midst of the new mass media reach allowed by television, she and her fans preserved older ideas about a face-to-face society. They remained deeply committed to personal advice and relationships. When necessary, Petrona enlisted additional secretaries to help her respond to the letters. For example, in 1969, she received so many questions on her *pan dulce* recipe that she hired a secretary just to respond to these questions for five days in a row.[150] She also made herself available to give telephone consultations. She recalled that one day in December she accepted phone calls until one in the morning from her television viewers with questions about the *pan dulce* she had presented on the program that day.[151] Her granddaughter recounts that Petrona would accept calls even on Christmas Eve, getting up from the table with her family to help some stranger on the phone to fix a dish. Massut explained that if your recipe had turned out badly and you had bought eggs, flour, and butter, then Petrona felt that she had the obligation to explain to you how to fix it, because you had spent your money and had tried to make one of her recipes.[152]

As these anecdotes confirm, Doña Petrona's commitment to her public was unflinching and enduring. She compared herself favorably to the new generation of competitors (or, as she preferred to call them, collaborators) by emphasizing the close relationship she had with the women she taught.[153] Responding to a journalist's question about whether Marta Beines was a "good competitor," Petrona remarked, "She is a good journalist and provides good commentary on international cooking. But I am involved with the actual practice [of cooking] and in direct contact with the *ama de casa*."[154] This close relationship, together with technological advances like television, enabled Petrona and her fans to build a larger public culinary community.

Despite the emergence of new competitors and new ideas about domesticity, Doña Petrona's career had reached a high point during the 1960s. At first glance this seems counterintuitive. On reflection, it reveals the continuity of gender-based expectations during this decade. With the boom in psychoanalysis and the professionalization of parenting, some suggested that men should assume a larger parental role.[155] Still, it was the rare voice indeed that suggested that working women should share responsibility for cooking and cleaning with men. Instead, most, like Doña Petrona, suggested that women, even "working" women, not shame their men by asking them to do domestic work. As she explained in 1966, "One cannot imagine a man cleaning, cooking, washing plates."[156] Instead, women should figure out how to do it more quickly themselves or hire other women to help.

Some young women who had different views (like the aforementioned university students) sought to distance themselves from Doña Petrona, but this *ecónoma* remained relevant for many of their contemporaries as well as for older generations of women. Many continued to buy her cookbooks, and growing numbers watched her on television. Across the television airwaves, she and Juanita not only showed Argentines how to cook but also enabled them to watch and to comment upon an increasingly contested and fleeting model of middle-class domesticity. Full-time homemakers with full-time help were growing increasingly rare, but the expectation that modern middle-class women with extradomestic interests should know how to "cook something" persisted. Even the significant changes to sexuality and women's work had not unseated the predominance of this idea.

As we shall see in the next chapter, Doña Petrona would have to work even harder during the 1970s to remain relevant. She and her main cookbook would face competition that was closer in age to the new generation of urban middle-class women who had formed her main fan base for so long. Further, a military dictatorship would unleash an unprecedented reign of terror during the late 1970s and early 1980s. Its rule would alter the gendered patterns of daily life and Doña Petrona's popularity in unexpected ways.

CHAPTER SIX

COOKING IN & OUT OF THE

SPOTLIGHT

Torta Mundial 78 ('78 World Cup Cake)

200 g. butter, 250 g. refined sugar, 6 eggs, 2 tablespoons cognac, 400 c.c. milk, 1 kilo. flour, 100 g. seedless raisins, 100 g. Corinth raisins, 100 g. sultana raisins, 150 g. chopped walnuts, 100 g. candied orange peel, 4 heaping teaspoons baking powder

Put the butter and the refined sugar in a bowl and beat with a wooden spoon until creamy; add the whole eggs one by one and continue beating; add the cognac, the milk, and the sifted flour and baking powder little by little, stirring it constantly; add the raisins, the Corinth raisins, the sultanas, the chopped walnuts and the finely sliced [orange] peels; stir very well until the dried fruit and nuts are well mixed in. Divide [the cake mixture] into the buttered and floured pans and cook them in the oven on low for approximately 1½ to 2 hours. The recipe for each base calls for 2 #22 molds and 1 mold of approximately 15 cm. in diameter, for which it is necessary to prepare 5½ recipes.

Starting from the bottom to the top, place 6 #22 cakes on a cake stand, 5 #15 cakes on the second level, 3 #15 cakes on the third level, one #22 cake on the fourth level, and on the top a #15 cake. Cover it with a light blue or white shiny meringue. On the side of each cake, make the World Cup logo with silver candy balls, placing a little [soccer] ball in the center. Put green "grass" on each cake to imitate the field [along with] a soccer player with a matching [national] flag and a [soccer] ball. On the top level, place the Gauchito Mundialito [Little World Cup Gaucho] and a soccer ball.[1]

To commemorate Argentina's home-field victory in the 1978 World Cup, Doña Petrona elected to put a photograph of her World Cup cake on the cover of the seventy-third edition of *El libro de Doña Petrona*, released one year after the tournament. On five layers of cake, she carefully placed little toy soccer players beside soccer balls and their national flags. She crowned the top of the cake with the Argentine flag, which waved above the 1978 World Cup mascot, the Gauchito Mundialito. Doña Petrona not only celebrated the Argentine footballers' victory with the photograph and recipe in her famous cookbook; she also prepared this cake live on television with the help of her assistant, Juanita Bordoy. It was good television, even if the cake was not something that most viewers would prepare at home. This complicated recipe called for lots of ingredients, many steps, and several knickknacks. It required the ingredients, the time, and the skill necessary to make an English-style wedding cake. To Doña Petrona, an avid soccer fan like most of her compatriots, this homage was well deserved. But this was not an unqualified celebration, as the national team's victory occurred under a repressive and violent military dictatorship.

Prior to the 1976 military coup, the political activity of young people in Argentina continued to accelerate. In 1970, the authoritarian dictatorship installed by retired General Onganía in 1966 came to an end with his execution by the leftist revolutionary group the Montoneros. State-led violence continued to escalate under a series of military governments and the governments of Juan and Isabel Perón (1973–75). While most male and female activists fought to redress class-based injustices and demand the return of democratic liberties, a small number of Argentine women who identified themselves as feminists also sought to challenge gender-based discrimination. Even as the majority of Argentines rejected or ignored feminist activism, broader segments of urban society nevertheless began to embrace or at least accept the model of the "new woman," who was decidedly less domestic than her predecessor. Practices continued to change as well, as a growing number of women studied longer and worked more outside of the home during the 1970s and 1980s.[2] As neoliberal policies of this period widened the gap between the wealthy and the poor, middle-class women who chose to pursue a career were joined by poorer women who had to work in response to the decline in real salaries and male unemployment.[3]

While Doña Petrona elected not to "talk politics" during this politically charged period, she tempered her advice in response to the changing economic situation and shifting gender ideals. But her relevancy remained in doubt. She had been in the public eye since the 1930s and was aging beyond Argentina's most desired consumer demographic. As Argentines' ability to maintain their standard of living fell with the economy during the early 1970s, national politics became increasingly fractious and intense. At the twilight of Doña Petrona's career and life, she faced challenges to her position and her approach to cooking. At the same time, the military dictatorship (1976–83) created new opportunities for Doña Petrona (and

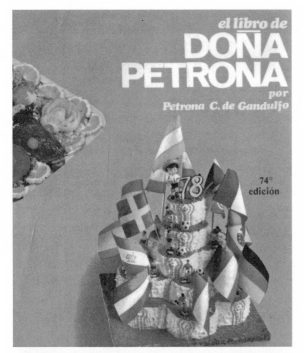

World Cup Cake on the cover of El libro de Doña Petrona, *74th edition, published in 1980); the cake is also on the cover of the 73d edition, from 1979. Courtesy of Marcela Massut.*

Petrona C. de Gandulfo (left) and Juanita Bordoy (right) making World Cup Cake on television on Canal 9, 1978. Courtesy of Marcela Massut.

other *ecónomas*) to remain relevant under a regime eager to promote conservative gender norms and a neoliberal marketplace. Yet, in the wake of this dictatorship, the mainstream model of domesticity would definitively change to incorporate women's extradomestic work more fully.

Staying Current

In 1970, the program on which Doña Petrona presented televised cooking lessons, *Buenas Tardes, Mucho Gusto*, announced its new hosts. Marking a departure from the "domestic woman" embodied by earlier hosts, the program promoted its new hosts, Marta Cerain and Horacio Bustos, as "a modern couple, elegant, and very young."[4] While Doña Petrona did her best to remain "modern," she was now in her seventies and could not pass herself off as being "very young." Nevertheless, she continued to seek out the attention of young (and not-so-young) women, presenting recipes for members of the *nueva ola* (new wave) once a month on television.[5] As she had begun to do the previous decade, during the early 1970s she openly acknowledged the drudgery of spending too much time in the kitchen. But she was willing to go only so far. In response to a journalist's question in 1970 about whether her recipes "obliged *amas de casa* to spend a painfully long time in the kitchen," she replied, "And what do you want? I can't use television to teach how to make a breaded beef cutlet [*milanesa*]."[6] In her view, this staple of the Argentine kitchen was too common and too simple to make for regularly entertaining television.

How Argentines reacted to Doña Petrona's attempts at economizing time and money largely depended on age, region, social outlook, and the current state of the economy. In 1970, the magazine *Para Ti*—which had been running a column by Petrona C. de Gandulfo off and on since 1940 and more consistently since 1966—added a new section with readers' letters entitled "Aquí opina usted" (loosely, Your Opinion Here), which provides us with a rare glimpse into printed reactions to Doña Petrona at the time. Because *Para Ti* was a traditional, Catholic magazine run by the Vigil family (who also owned the publisher Atlántida), these letters suggest how a mainstream audience from across the country related to this domestic icon.[7] More progressive readers who embraced the latest, less domestic iterations of the "modern" woman were more likely to read magazines like *Claudia* or *Vosotras*.[8] These publications outsold *Para Ti* at some points during the 1960s, but during the course of the 1970s *Para Ti* (which, not incidentally, would support the military dictatorship) regularly outsold both of them, releasing some 150,000 issues at a time.[9]

In 1970 and 1971, most of *Para Ti*'s presumably conservative readers were quite complimentary of Doña Petrona's recipe column and dedicated to collecting her recipes. Susana L. de Micieli, for instance, wrote that she prepared many of the menus with "good results."[10] A couple of months later, longtime reader Beatriz Prémoli de Ales explained, "One of the things that interests me the most are the recipes of la señora de Gandulfo, which I always find to be excellent."[11] She followed her praise with a suggestion to make them more easily collectable. Showcasing its responsiveness, *Para Ti* began printing recipe cards by that August. In September, the magazine published several letters that highlighted readers' enthusiasm about this new initiative. For example, Rosalía Demicheli, from the province of Buenos Aires, expressed her delight with the recipe cards, which she characterized as being "easy to understand, well written," and, most important, "created with an exact sense of our taste [*nuestro gusto*]."[12]

Surely this notion that she accurately reflected local taste would have pleased Doña Petrona. As we have seen, since the 1960s she had begun to emphasize both the local roots of her cuisine and her own roots in northwestern Argentina. While the more conservative urban readers of *Para Ti* were probably celebrating her adaptation of international cuisine to "our taste," other more politicized urban Argentines were simultaneously shifting their view of "true" Argentine culture to the provinces.[13] A burgeoning sense of pan–Latin Americanism in Argentina celebrated the native and local culture over that of the United States and Europe. As Valeria Manzano demonstrates, this led to new patterns of consumption of "folkloric" goods at local fairs, as well as travel to, and social work in, the provinces during the early 1970s.[14] For one boy, who traveled to Petrona's native province of Santiago del Estero from the city of Mendoza, the differences were stark. "I could not believe that was also Argentina," he wrote, "but *that* is the true Argentina."[15]

The "true Argentina" was a place one could see and also taste. In 1970, in the northeastern province of Chaco, the provincial capital, Resistencia, hosted what it deemed the "first national festival of creole cooking [*cocina criolla*]." At this festival, men competed to make the best *asado con cuero*—basically a large beef barbecue cooked outside over a stake with its own skin, or "leather," still attached.[16] For her part, Doña Petrona continued to refrain from making *asado* outdoors, explaining that her husband, Atilio, was the "griller of the house" (*asador de la casa*).[17] This reflected her (and many of her contemporaries') gender ideology and not a lack of interest in *cocina criolla*. As she had started to do during the previous decade, during the 1970s she shared specialties like *empanadas santiagueñas, carbonada criolla* (creole beef stew spiked with peaches), and *yema quemada* (a dessert made principally with egg yolks and sugar that has a torched top, like crème brûlée).[18]

Along with this more provincial fare, Doña Petrona also continued to present recipes inspired by the foodways of Europe and the United States, and now Asia as well.[19] The common table in Argentina continued to be additive and eclectic, and during the early 1970s her fans from *Para Ti* suggested that Doña Petrona helped them to serve it effectively. For instance, a woman from Rosario emphasized the importance of her quest to find Doña Petrona's recipe cards, explaining that she saw this collection of recipes as "a very complete guide for the *ama de casa*."[20]

But if most readers were enthusiastic about Doña Petrona's menus and recipe cards in *Para Ti*, not all saw them as infallible. For example, María Esther D. de Figueroa from the capital wrote in just after Easter in 1971 to suggest that even though Doña Petrona's recipes were fantastic, she would have liked to see a fish dish that was more original than the "famous tuna empanadas that I always end up making."[21] As opposed to the direct responses that Doña Petrona had provided to readers during the 1930s in *El Hogar*, *Para Ti* itself now crafted the answers in the magazine—suggesting the growing difficulties of maintaining the face-to-face culture that she and her fans had worked to preserve. In response to María's critique, the editors confessed that their own penchant for sweets had been to blame for the almost exclusive focus on desserts in Doña Petrona's column and promised "more consistent recipes next Easter."[22]

In the face of a worsening economy, Doña Petrona, along with readers of *Para Ti*, devoted much of 1972 to learning how to add more variety to the diet by preparing different types of meals, often by substituting other meats or vegetarian options for beef. During moments of acute economic crisis, the amount of beef shipped abroad increased, causing local prices to rise. In the autumn of 1972, *Para Ti* published an article explaining how to cut meat without wasting any of it. In May, a grateful husband wrote in to thank the magazine for helping his wife save them money. He explained, "I have always told her that she should study this subject, since we were married, twenty-two years ago." He lamented that until now, they had "been spending much more than necessary."[23] His letter suggests some male interest in shopping, especially in a supervisory role. A few months later, Doña Petrona provided more tips to help readers continue to eat beef without spending too much. In July, she wrote a column about how to cook with less expensive cuts—a topic of personal expertise ever since she had written the cookbook for the National Meat Board in 1938. However, as reader

María Teresa Iñigo would point out, it was not always easy to find these cuts at the butcher shops in the capital.[24]

By the end of 1972, the economy was floundering under the direction of General Alejandro Lanusse (1971–73). Salaries fell while unemployment grew and prices for basic foods increased.[25] The readers and the editors of *Para Ti* began more emphatically expressing their frustration about the high prices of food and skyrocketing inflation rates. In September, *Para Ti* published an "economical menu" that cost 2,300 pesos a day.[26] Reader Patricia Millán Acosta from Córdoba responded that even this solution was unrealistic. Doing the math, she explained that "if to the 2,300 pesos we add the daily costs of gas, electricity, and other expenses, without which cooking is impossible, the total (per day) will be above 3,000 pesos." She asked indignantly, "Is this an economical menu? If this figure is needed just to eat, how much is needed to live?"[27] Many other readers sent in similar complaints, suggesting that this was a widespread sentiment. *Para Ti*'s editors largely concurred. They explained, "We are in agreement that money for living [expenses] is lacking today. Every day, inflation grows and the pesos are never enough." Still, they explained that *they* could not be held accountable for this problem. "Our responsibility is to propose the least expensive menu possible [that is] still worthy of our audience. You will understand that it is impossible to recommend pasta or rice every day." They suggested that to make their recipes affordable, one would need to combine some of their recommendations with some even more thrifty homemade options.[28]

While *Para Ti*, like Doña Petrona, defended its stance, other publications began to question such versions of economy, and the mass media culture of celebrity that had begun in the previous decade turned more critical. Increasingly, journalists poked fun at Doña Petrona and her claims. In response to her 1970 claim that she was an ordinary person (*soy muy popular*), for example, a journalist for the magazine *Gente* pointed out the distance of her life from that of most Argentines. "Doña Petrona lives large: she likes to eat very well, and in her home, Juanita, her assistant, cooks. She lives in a comfortable chalet in Olivos."[29] In other words, she was far from the ordinary person she claimed to be.

Two years after this piece in *Gente*, Alicia Gallotti adopted a much more explicitly critical approach in her first interview with Petrona for the satirical magazine *Satiricon*.[30] Gallotti criticized the cost of Doña Petrona's recipes, especially given the current economic climate. She charged, "When you enter in the kitchen, rivers of money start to flow. Your recipes tend to be delicious but in 1972 they are destined for a small very exclusive minority. They are terribly expensive."[31] Doña Petrona protested vehemently, pointing to her many economical recipes and her cookbook *Recetas económicas*. Gallotti refused to concede the point, challenging Argentina's best-selling author not only on the cost of her recipes but also on her gender ideology. Doña Petrona continued to celebrate women as unsung heroes responsible for the important task of "maintaining the home," but Gallotti suggested that women had other more important roles to play. In response to Gallotti's question about the "women's liberation movement," Doña Petrona apparently responded, "I don't understand you. But I will clarify that in my interviews I don't talk about politics."[32] For Gallotti (and presumably for a number of her progressive middle-class readers), Doña Petrona represented an outdated model that was too expensive, too old-fashioned, and too conservative for the current moment.

The small number of women who identified themselves as feminists during the early 1970s would surely have agreed.[33] Inspired by their local experiences, along with the writings of their counterparts in Europe and North America, Argentine feminists sought to fight women's shared oppression and advocate for greater equality between the sexes.[34] At the heart of their claims was the premise that the "personal is political."[35] To drive this point home to the broader public, a number of feminist organizations passed out provocative flyers in plazas across Buenos Aires during the early 1970s. For example, to celebrate Mother's Day, members of the Unión Feminista Argentina (Argentine Feminist Union) handed out flyers with a hand-drawn illustration of a mother frenetically cooking a meal, answering the phone with her foot, and attending her three young children (who were all intent on wreaking havoc) in front of the laundry she had already put on the line to dry. On the table beside her, the television broadcasts an advertisement that encourages her to "Be Beautiful" by using "Sexy" brand lotion. At the bottom of the illustration, the tagline reads: "Mother: a slave or a queen, but never a person."[36] This flyer portrayed the difficult (and often taken for granted) nature of housework. It pointed out that women were expected to cook, clean, care for their children, and, in their spare time, consume products that would make them beautiful. These were, of course, expectations that Doña Petrona had done much to promote. Feminists sought to reveal and to question such ideas as being both unrealistic and unfair.

While feminists were dedicated to questioning existing gender norms during the early 1970s, most Argentines seemed less than eager to follow suit. Even most leftist female activists, who fought to overhaul hierarchies associated with imperialism and social class, tended not to challenge existing gender hierarchies. But this did not mean that women were not taking

Unión Feminista Argentina Mother's Day flyer, ca. 1970.

on more overtly political and public roles. Some participated in armed resistance; for example, one participant in the Montoneros estimated that more than a third of this revolutionary group was female.[37] And even more women participated in nonviolent forms of activism with more traditional gender underpinnings, like establishing women's and children's centers and running *ollas populares* (food kitchens) in poor neighborhoods. For example, during the 120-day strike in the salt mines of La Pampa in 1972, women worked together to literally sustain the movement by cooking huge pots of polenta, stew, and rice soups.[38] Such efforts did not, however, substantially change ideas about men's and women's proper roles. Despite the deepening politicization and professionalization of women, men and women alike generally expected that women should take care of their families, homes, and communities, and men should be the principal breadwinners and political actors.[39] This was especially the case for women of the older generation and those living outside of Argentina's principal cities, many of whom were now Doña Petrona's most faithful fans.

But the rocky economy prevented even the most loyal fans from continuing to regularly follow her recipes. As the economic situation during the first half of 1973 worsened, Doña Petrona once again used her magazine column to recommend less expensive alternatives to beef. She also explained how to make sandwiches and *milanesas*, which she now deemed appropriate for this venue, dubbing them "the little battle horse for women in a hurry."[40] In February 1973, she ran a long column that contained thirty "economical" recipes. In the blurb that accompanied her recipes, Petrona explained, "Yes, Ma'am. It is no longer possible to buy anything cheap today. Potatoes? . . . very expensive; fruit? . . . even bananas are being sold by the kilo. Of meat . . . it's better not to speak." She encouraged her readers to resign themselves to seeking out good deals, in part by buying only in-season fruit and using canned goods.[41]

Apparently some readers found such advice helpful. According to reader Nelly Azcuénaga, "I am about to get married and, even though he and I work, we need to save." She continued, "It is important to save, to excel in the kitchen and to prepare good food. I accomplished this, thanks to these recipes. Congratulations!"[42] But while some young women like Azcuénaga found Doña Petrona's advice important to their success in homemaking just as it was, others began to suggest that Doña Petrona needed to update her advice. For example, in March 1973, Elena González Peña from Mar del Plata (who also was about to get married) stated, "I would love it if you would come out with new recipes by Doña Petrona, [that are] quick to prepare and flavorful."[43] As this letter suggests, even some of her more faithful fans began to suggest that they were ready for a change that would allow them to cook more quickly.

No Politics at the Table

Change was in the air—not just in the kitchen but also in national politics. With inflation spiraling out of control and violence among paramilitary organizations mounting, many Argentines sought a political overhaul. Juan Perón returned from European exile in 1973 to take over in a landslide electoral victory. Many hoped that Perón's wide-ranging political alliances and economic policies would be the answer to Argentina's woes.[44] In the short run, they were. Perón implemented a stabilization program in May 1973 that not only halted inflation but also led to an increase in wages and state spending, stimulating domestic economic activity. He targeted women in particular, labeling them the most important group to "rebuild the country." He also adopted a more positive view of women's extradomestic work, now championing equal pay for equal work, as Karín Grammático has shown. However, he made clear that such work should not compromise women's main responsibilities for taking care of their homes and children.[45]

During much of the second half of 1973, Doña Petrona and fellow Argentines celebrated the fact that the economic slide had abated, with the inflation unleashed in 1972 finally brought under control. In July 1973, *Para Ti* interviewed middle-class *amas de casa* in Buenos Aires about the impact of the government's policy to set maximum prices for close to 6,000 food items. All those quoted were optimistic about the changes. Sixty-two-year-old Francisca de Sigili noted that "today we shop in a better mood because it is clear that prices have gone down." And a thirty-five-year-old mother named señora de Piturro remarked, "Let's pray that things remain this way, that there is work and peace."[46] Doña Petrona also seemed relieved. In October 1973, she noted that at last the price of foods had "begun to drop." She celebrated the fact that one could now prepare recipes for four people with only 8.00 pesos.[47]

Unfortunately, this jubilation was short-lived. By December 1973, signs of inflation began to reappear—a difficult predicament for the Peronist government, which had run on a "zero inflation" campaign.[48] And as Doña Petrona later recalled in a 1985 interview, some "youths" began to march in the neighborhood she shared with the private presidential residence to demand an audience with Juan Perón. Petrona explained that most of the neighbors put down their blinds but that she went out into the street. "Look, *la Petrona* is greeting us," they apparently said, and she gave them "water, bread, and pastries." It was a savvy move. While the other homes in the neighborhood were splashed with paint, hers apparently was not.[49] In part, this was an act of self-protection, but it also suggested Petrona's belief that food and drink helped bring people (including the youthful opposition) together.

Doña Petrona was willing to engage politically active youths in her neighborhood, but she continued to seek to stay out of politics in the public arena. She also claimed to do so when she had guests in her own home. She explained in a 1973 interview with the magazine *Mucho Gusto* that when she had guests over to eat, she put a sign on the table that read *prohibido hablar de política* (no talking politics).[50] This was a sentiment apparently shared by many across Latin America. As U.S. author Charles Henry Baker had explained to potential travelers to Latin America some two decades earlier, "Above all, *leave all arguments and all politics—domestic, local, and world-wide—locked up in your hotel closet. All that sort of needless yak-ity-yak is a veritable profanation over decent food and drink in any Latin house, be it that of a prince or a pauper."[51] That Doña Petrona chose to publicly share her adherence to this philosophy during this period suggests the added weight this idea took on in a politically divided and censored society.

Of course, despite this desire to separate politics from commensality, politics had a major impact on how Argentines could afford to live and eat. In 1974, with the economy declining again, Doña Petrona was back to highlighting the affordability of her recipes in columns for autumn foods and dishes made with pasta.[52] Even fewer readers were convinced that her solutions would really help them to economize effectively, including the self-proclaimed *mujer del pueblo* (common woman), who argued in September 1974 that not everyone could afford "the foods of the señora de Gandulfo."[53] By this point, Doña Petrona was even more clearly not economical enough for many Argentines.

Neither was the government. After a short honeymoon, problems with the economy and among different factions of Peronists began to surface. Then, in July 1974, Juan Perón died, leaving his vice president and third wife, Isabel Perón, as president. The first female president of Argentina sought to continue the policies of her late husband, which had shifted decidedly more to the right. In order to stymie the left, she used paramilitary forces to crack down on "radical" activists, especially those who fought for class-based social change but also feminists.[54] Nevertheless, she began to lose a number of Peronist allies on the right as the economic situation continued to deteriorate.[55]

Doña Petrona became exasperated herself. In 1975, she publicly recognized the shortages of cooking staples like sugar and kerosene and the expense of certain mainstays of the Argentine diet like select cuts of beef.[56] However, in contrast to those who criticized her for the expense of her recipes, she asked women to consider whether *they* were really doing all they could to economize. On 14 April 1975, Petrona took the unusual step of publishing a letter directed to *amas de casa* in her column. She began by recognizing that despite scientific and technological advances, housework remained difficult to do, never-ending, and out of the public eye—as feminists had also recently pointed out. She continued that high prices and the scarcity of certain mainstays of the diet had made homemakers' lives considerably more difficult.[57] Nevertheless, she felt it was important to ask, "Have we exhausted all of our resources before we keep complaining?"[58] Clearly, she thought not. Doña Petrona explained that when she went shopping with her husband she would change her menu if the prices for a certain item were too high. In contrast, she said, she heard other women complaining to the butcher if they could not get the correct cut of beef to make *milanesas*.

Doña Petrona used her magazine column to argue that if *amas de casa* were really concerned about protecting their budget, they needed to replace more expensive foods with less expensive ones and incorporate scientific findings about foods into their decision making. Specifically, instead of making *milanesas*—which required an expensive cut of beef and increasingly scarce cooking oil—they should consider making stews, loafs, meatballs, or even *milanesas* with less-expensive ground beef. She also encouraged her readers not to be so beef-centric and to consider alternative sources of protein like fish, chicken, rabbit, and lentils. In seeking to change Argentines' culinary habits and preferences, Doña Petrona also revealed them. According to Doña Petrona, good eating in Argentina still meant enjoying select cuts of beef with every meal, cooking with a lot of oil or other fat, and serving three courses.[59] Argentina's common table remained abundant, and despite her protests in this piece, it reflected how she served meals in her own home. Just one year earlier, she had explained in this same column that when she had guests over, she served a three-course meal with cocktails before and coffee after, and recommended that her readers do the same.[60] Now she argued that multicourse meals were no longer possible for many Argentines due to the economic situation, nor advisable due to the health concerns linked with a high-fat diet.

During the rest of 1975, Doña Petrona and other contributors to *Para Ti* emphasized the economic challenges Argentines faced under Isabel Perón's government. Such coverage was politically charged, as Paula Bontempo has demonstrated. The magazine had initially supported Isabel Perón—celebrating the fact that a woman had become president of the Argentine nation in 1974—but by 1975 *Para Ti*'s coverage had become much more critical. The editors began to portray Isabel Perón as an incompetent leader who was only capable of creating more havoc in office. In turn, they began to imply that only a military coup could restore order to a populace suffering from ever-worsening economic problems and the escalation of violence.[61] In June 1975, Isabel Perón devalued the peso, sparking runaway inflation and yet another economic crisis. With increasing paramilitary violence, a deepening recession, and a lack of support from the business community and the armed forces with which she sought alliances, Isabel Perón's hold on the presidency was tenuous.

Doña Petrona refrained from explicit political commentary, but her column formed part of the larger portrayal of economic disorder promoted by the magazine. As shortages loomed and inflation spiraled during Isabel Perón's last year in office, Doña Petrona attempted to provide more concrete tips for economizing in the marketplace. In July, she presented a diagram of the cuts of meat (and cooking recommendations for each) of a butchered cow. And in September, food writer Miriam Becker—who had recently been brought on to help produce her column, "to help make it more journalistic"—wrote an article that followed Doña Petrona on a trip to the market in search of good deals.[62] In this column, Doña Petrona further stepped up her warning that if *amas de casa* who "sustain the home, and deal with weighty matters, do not find an immediate and practical solution to everyday cooking . . . NO ECONOMIST CAN HELP US." She called on her fellow *amas de casa* to join her in the "battle against the scarcity of life."[63] This view, though conservative in terms of gender politics, granted women significant economic influence.

Of course, Doña Petrona's personal solutions were only credible if her fans also pretended that she did not have a lot more money and help than most. This article described how Doña Petrona made comments at the market about how she would make do with what she could afford. For example, in talking to the fruit vendor, Doña Petrona apparently explained to those around her that when fruit was expensive and she had only one piece at home, she would use it to make fritters. (She failed to mention here that Juanita did almost all of the cooking at her home and that her husband, Atilio Massut, did much of the shopping.) Whether or not her explanations were believable, the article suggested that her fans at the market still appreciated her advice. Becker noted that several women approached Petrona to compliment her on specific recipes that she had presented on television and in her recipe column. In a subsequent article, Doña Petrona explained that many *amas de casa* had recently come to her with questions about how "to confront the economy of home cooking."[64]

Doña Petrona's efforts to provide homemakers with more easily used tips and recipes once again demonstrated her desire to respond to the changing dynamics of Argentine society. As she stated during her trip to the market, "It is necessary to know how to adapt to reality!"[65] In the early 1970s, Petrona recognized the reality of economic hardship. She also realized that in order to make her advice compelling, she needed to definitively change her approach as well as people's expectations that she could create only complicated and expensive dishes. In 1975, Petrona explained her rationale: "The increase in prices has had repercussions in *all* homes. And if before I used mushrooms or truffles, now I should reconsider my own recipes, adapting them to the [current] reality." Whereas Doña Petrona had once emphasized the idea that women should learn how to cook skill-fully, she now suggested that women learn how to cook (and shop) more purposefully and practically. She explained that "the important thing is to know how to cook with what one has on hand and is the cheapest."[66]

Dieting in a Time of Economic Crisis

At the same time that Doña Petrona tailored much of her advice to the eco-nomic challenges that many of her compatriots were facing, she also sought to capitalize on the increasing culture of thinness in Argentina by publish-ing two diet cookbooks during the 1970s. This decision spoke to the grow-ing appreciation of slim bodies across much of the West during this time and also to the increasing social polarization of society in Argentina dur-ing the 1970s. During this decade, economic conditions led rich and poor Argentines to begin to develop two significantly different types of diets. Up through the 1960s, most Argentines had had access to the same types of region-specific foods—albeit of different quantity and quality. However, during the 1970s, the poor were pushed by economic circumstances to rely on a more limited diet often consisting of *tortas fritas* (fried bread) and the herbal infusion *mate* to fill themselves up.[67] This was the case for one woman I interviewed, Stella, who had grown up poor in Puerto Ingeniero White. Sometimes poor people (especially those living in rural areas) did not know of Doña Petrona, but Stella, who had grown up in the fishing port of Puerto Ingeniero White, clearly stated that "Doña Petrona never mat-tered to me." She continued, saying that Argentina's leading *ecónoma* was not relevant to her experience because she and her siblings had subsisted mainly on *mate* and crackers. But, as her quote suggests, although Doña Petrona was irrelevant in terms of her culinary advice, she had become a potent symbol of the types of food to which Stella and other poor Argen-tines did not have access.

A smaller number of Argentines began to set themselves apart as eco-nomically comfortable enough to choose to diet in the hope of becoming thin. Better-off Argentines ate more fruits and vegetables than meat and more meat than starches, while the poor were forced to do exactly the oppo-site. The poorer sectors of society filled their stomachs with bread, potatoes, and other grains, gradually becoming what anthropologist Patricia Aguirre characterizes as *gordos de escasez* (fat from scarcity). Consequently, like in most of the Western capitalist world, fatness became increasingly associ-ated with poverty and thinness with money and power in Argentina during the last third of the twentieth century.[68]

Attuned to this dynamic, Doña Petrona yet again sought to capitalize on a new trend. In 1972, she partnered with Dr. Alberto Cormillot, a young physician who specialized in dieting, to release the cookbook *Coma bien y adelgace* (Eat Well and Get Thin). "People's tastes are constantly changing," she explained in the preface, "and so I should constantly be updating each ratio [of ingredients] and each recipe." In contrast to the majority of her past recipes, this cookbook presented recipes that were deliberately low in fat and carbohydrates. Readers were encouraged to prepare menus that would create smaller portions, incorporate leaner meats, and use artificial sweeteners to lose weight or maintain their figures. For example, while Doña Petrona's recipe for whipped cream in *El libro de Doña Petrona* still called for 500 grams of whipping cream, 150 grams of powdered sugar, and 1 teaspoon of vanilla, the diet version in *Coma bien y adelgace* called for a half packet of ricotta, 4 tablespoons of nonfat milk, 2 teaspoons of vanilla, and 1 tablespoon of artificial sweetener.[69] In the prologue to this new diet cookbook, Petrona assured women not to feel guilty about serving these types of low-calorie foods to their husbands and friends. Indeed, she promised that her recipes would provide peace of mind: "They will allow you to enjoy eating without having [this experience] darkened by the little cloud of guilt [we feel] when we know that what we are enjoying one minute in our mouth will be in our stomach for an hour and in the 'little rolls' around our waist all of our life."[70]

This admission of a sense of guilt around eating foods high in fat and sugar was a new concept for Doña Petrona to promote. In fact, it was a great distance from the original approach of this culinary legend, who had made her career through presenting foods that put a premium on taste and appearance, such as *pastelitos* (fried quince pastries), empanadas made with beef lard, and elaborate cakes. In reviewing this new cookbook, a journalist for *La Nación* touched on this irony: "For the first time Doña Petrona, without a doubt the most prestigious Argentine *económa*, tackled prickly terrain for someone who, like her, had for years shaped the image of abundance and variety of our table."[71] And, as Argentines pointed out, Doña Petrona had a few *rollitos* herself. Most recalled thinking of her as a large woman. For example, journalist Amalia Iadarola described her as *corpulenta* (heavily built).[72] And, taking this point to the extreme, a man named Eduardo R. suggested that as a child he thought Doña Petrona might have ordered Juanita around so much on television because of her size.[73] In any case, by this point, most people associated Doña Petrona's brand of cooking with *comida que engorda* (fattening foods).[74]

Nevertheless, despite her appearance and association with rich foods, Doña Petrona charged ahead into this latest iteration of culinary modernity and apparently met with some success. As the reviewer of this cookbook suggested, "The colloquial tone of the writing and the wealth of recipes destine it to quickly become a best seller."[75] Doña Petrona's well-established reputation and the respect accorded to doctors both played a part. Doña Petrona and Dr. Cormillot reissued over five editions of *Coma bien y adelgace* throughout the course of the 1970s. And in 1975, Doña Petrona released a similar cookbook on her own, which she titled more simply *Bajas calorías* (Low Calories).[76]

And yet, even as Doña Petrona enthusiastically presented diet foods in these cookbooks, she continued to focus on her traditional strengths in *El libro de Doña Petrona*. Describing the relationship between her first diet cookbook and her previous work, her book distributor explained, "Spurred on by the diet trend, she did *Coma bien y adelgace*, but the famous one and the axis of all of this was [still] the main book."[77] It remained the referent for those with aspirations. For example, María E. P., who had worked as a maid before marrying in the 1970s, recalled receiving *El libro de Doña Petrona* at her wedding.[78] Unlikely to have received this gift while she still worked as a maid (despite the fact that she and others were asked to cook with it by their employers), it served as a testament to her upward social mobility and the fact that she could now cook in her own home.

As she had throughout the course of her career, Doña Petrona added new recipes and tips to successive editions of *El libro de Doña Petrona* during the 1970s. In particular, she included new advice on how to economize and incorporated more simple recipes and a few "low calorie" dishes. However, her earlier recipes, which were often rich and elaborate, remained and continued to occupy the majority of pages, as in her first edition. While some turned to Petrona for modern advice about cooking quickly, economically, or lightly, most continued to associate her with a more old-fashioned and time-consuming cooking style based on rich dishes, large portions, and stylish presentations. Even as fewer people regularly cooked with this cookbook, there was an ongoing attraction to the ideal of abundance it represented, and people continued to turn to it for birthdays and special occasions.

By the 1970s, *El libro de Doña Petrona* had become a culinary encyclopedia with the advantages—and the disadvantages—of having a little bit of every trend in twentieth-century Argentine food history tucked between its covers. On almost 800 pages, one could find a classic French recipe that

Petrona had learned at Le Cordon Bleu forty years earlier or a modern one that she had recently adapted from a foreign magazine. Fans could find recipes with lots of steps and calories and others with fewer steps and less butter and eggs. Readers could learn how to use a now-familiar form of technology—like a gas stove—or a newer one—like a refrigerator. In addition, they could see the original hand-drawn illustrations, together with black-and-white and color photographs of the recipes that Doña Petrona had prepared and added to her cookbook throughout her career. If they paid attention to the print runs (sometimes but not always published on the back page), they might identify the rise and fall in popularity of this cookbook. The sixty-fourth edition published in 1971 had a print run of 10,000 copies, down from print runs more than three times as large in the 1950s and early 1960s.

Sensing the interest in an approach to cooking that would be considered truly modern by Argentine consumers, *Para Ti* (together with its parent company, the publishing giant *Atlántida*) decided to market a different kind of cookbook that reflected new ideas about domesticity. In 1976, they released *Cocina fácil para la mujer moderna* (Easy Cooking for the Modern Woman), written by the *ecónoma* Choly Berreteaga and edited by Miriam Becker. While both women were connected with Doña Petrona, Doña Petrona herself was not tapped for this new, more "modern" initiative.[79] Becker explained the rationale behind the timing: "It was like leaving the history of Petrona behind a little and it was a generational change."[80]

There were beginning to be hints that some felt the time had come to produce an alternative to *El libro de Doña Petrona*. In the prologue to this new cookbook, the editors explained that they wanted to "publish a different [kind of] cookbook" because the dynamics of "modern life" had led to "new schedules, new habits."[81] They related such changes to women's (extra-domestic) work, which had made simplifying cooking all the more important. Choly Berreteaga explained that in lieu of teaching the "professional cooking" of her predecessors, she had decided to introduce a "new" style of cooking in keeping with the hectic demands of future *amas de casa*. She explained that she had tailored it to young women of her daughter's generation, "who wanted to continue studying and working" but also (she implied) needed to continue to do the cooking and homemaking.[82]

This new style of cooking put a premium on economy and speed. Berreteaga and Becker included chapters on how to transform leftovers, use prepared foods, and make an entire meal in less than an hour. Readers were encouraged to take advantage of new products, like the premade disks of empanada dough, to save time and were given instructions on how to make fancy meals for guests with "economical ingredients." The authors ended the cookbook with a chapter titled "Cocina de la salud" (Healthy Cooking), which explained the basic nutritional values of food and recommended that people cut back on sugars and starches to lose weight. Doña Petrona had also incorporated these types of "modern" ideas into her main and more specialized cookbooks on economizing and dieting, but the more compact, 300-page *Cocina fácil para la mujer moderna* presented itself more broadly as an everyday cookbook for women of the new generation.[83]

Like Doña Petrona had before them, Berreteaga and Becker presumed that women of this generation would have little prior cooking knowledge. They were also convinced that they would have scant interest in complicated or time-consuming recipes. A woman named Anahi suggested that they were correct, at least in some cases. She recalled the relief of getting a copy of this cookbook when she went off to the university. She explained that whereas one had to know a fair amount to use *El libro de Doña Petrona*, *Cocina fácil para la mujer moderna* "took off from the idea that one did not know anything."[84] Many of her peers bought into this newer, simpler, and more explanatory approach to cooking—*Cocina fácil para la mujer moderna* was reprinted nine times and sold over 600,000 copies before the second edition was released in 1985, eventually becoming the second-best-selling cookbook in Argentina, after *El libro de Doña Petrona*.[85]

The Safety of the Kitchen Cupboard

Whether Doña Petrona would become a legend rooted in the past or an active figure still relevant to Argentine *amas de casa* in the present would be determined in part by how she reacted to contemporary national politics. From 1976 through 1983, military leaders carried out what they called the Process of National Reorganization, or Proceso, as it was commonly referred to in Argentina. During the Proceso, Minister of the Economy José Alfredo Martínez de Hoz built the free market "by force."[86] The military junta sought to silence any so-called subversives, who included critics or potential critics of the regime, through a brutal campaign of terror, repression, torture, and murder. Military officials "disappeared" some 30,000 Argentines, including many young people who worked as labor activists, academics, and journalists and their families, friends, and acquaintances, as well as the much-reviled "Marxists" and "guerrillas."[87]

The military dictatorship combined these disappearances with an official veil of silence. After seizing power, the government forbade Argentines from making any "reference to subjects related to subversive incidents, the appearance of bodies and the deaths of subversive elements and/or members of the armed or security forces, unless these are announced by a responsible official source."[88] It further suppressed any challenges by definitively ending the freedom of the press and making public gatherings, union organizing, and political parties illegal. These measures created a "culture of fear" in which self-censorship became vital to survival.[89]

The military's campaign shut down most avenues for the public expression of ideas. In a sense, "only the voice of the state remained, addressing itself to an atomized collection of inhabitants," as Luis Alberto Romero has eloquently argued.[90] Yet, while intellectual and political debates were silenced or pushed underground, certain types of non-state-led discourse were allowed. Specifically, it was acceptable, and even encouraged, for Doña Petrona and her fellow *ecónomas* to talk publicly about cooking and consuming. That is, even as the military's crackdown on leftist ideas made activism more dangerous, more traditional female activities like cooking became safer and, therefore, even more important common referents for women and even for a new group of men in Argentina. In fact, Doña Petrona's television cooking program was one of the few (and the only part of *Buenas Tardes, Mucho Gusto*) that the military did not erase or tape over. Indeed, it was the kind of artifact that the cultural authorities might hope to preserve.[91]

In recalling her own experience of exile, a woman named Dora illuminates the extent to which Doña Petrona remained a shared and safe cultural referent for Argentines across the political spectrum. Dora explained that as a militant union activist and member of the university community, she was a clear target for the military. Upon receiving word that interrogators had specifically asked about her during the interrogation of a young woman she knew, Dora decided she must flee to save her life. Before leaving, she thought it important to move her "most dangerous" leftist and Marxist books. She brought these texts to a friend's home where they were put away above the kitchen cabinet. Soon after, her friend's husband called to ask about these books. Almost three decades later, she remembered his question: "What do we do with the books by 'Doña Petroska?'" When asked why he might choose to make a sly reference to Doña Petrona in this instance, Dora explained that "it was safe and above all absolutely innocent. In reality, what it was about was the attempt to convert our collections into innocent international cooking."[92] Cookbooks were, after all, the type of books that women were expected to collect.

The acceptability of culinary materials came from their presumed apolitical nature but also reflected the gender norms that tended to underpin these texts. During its tenure, the military worked hard to maintain conservative notions of men's and, especially, women's places in society. It used its control over the mass media to barrage Argentines with messages about the importance of the family and, especially, the significance of the mother in watching over her family. An Argentine sociologist who had been teaching in the United States returned to Argentina to conduct research and was struck by the omnipresence of such messages in 1977. She explained: "Argentines are bombarded daily by the media coverage of speeches from government and Church representatives as well as by feature articles having one characteristic in common: the praise of the family as the foundation of society and of parental roles as the most important vehicle for the transmission of and control upon the observances of Christian and patriotic virtues."[93] Mothers, who were already broadly assumed to be responsible for the socialization of their children, were now urged by the government to also take responsibility for the political behavior of their children.

Argentines deployed such traditional constructs of motherhood in different contexts and for very different political ends. Taking the government at its word, in 1977 a number of women formed the Madres de Plaza de Mayo (Mothers of the Plaza de Mayo). This group of women whose children had "disappeared" came together to demand that the government tell them where their children were. Facing laws that prevented public assembly and a government predisposed to kidnappings, they protected themselves by emphasizing their maternal roles, enabling them to become an important and unique voice that denounced the government and demanded accountability for its actions.[94]

The great majority of the national media outlets looked the other way and, instead of covering the Madres' protests against the regime, reported official government "news" and pronouncements, along with presumably apolitical content.[95] In addition to emphasizing the importance of mothers' supervision of their families, mass media outlets also highlighted the significance of women's economic roles in improving Argentine society. As Marini noted in 1977, "Does that mean that women are told they should work? Far from it. They are told that their economic importance is in making consumer decisions."[96] As had been the case throughout many of the more economically challenging periods of the twentieth century, the military government encouraged women to become ever-more-efficient consumers of domestic goods.

Perhaps in recognition of this thrust, Doña Petrona took steps to increase her commercial value during the military government's first year at the helm. She started by seeking to trademark her own name. As she explained in June 1976, "I patented my name so that no one could use it except for me and my son, who makes cake pans." The journalist who interviewed her wrote of this decision that "no one doubts that this name, an institution it itself, will reign for many years."[97]

Doña Petrona now had come to portray herself as a "modern" woman who was worldly and relevant. She proudly explained in a 1976 interview that she "spoke Quechua perfectly, read four newspapers a day . . . was interested in politics, soccer, and other things in the world around us."[98] While she refused to publicly talk politics here or elsewhere, her claim that she was fluent in Quechua emphasized her mastery of an indigenous language widely spoken in her native province of Santiago del Estero. At this time, as the provincial and *criollo* was coming to play a larger role in defining Argentine national identity, she pointed to her own mixed-race past even more directly than she had done previously.

For its part, the military dictatorship showed itself to be quite eager to promote *criollo* nationalism and to tap into the tremendous symbolic nature of food to do so.[99] During the winter of 1976, the government joined forces with commercial interests and a charity to benefit children to carry out what they called the first annual Nacional Jornadas de Cocina Criolla (National Conference of Creole Cuisine), making no reference to the event six years earlier in Chaco. This event was held in Córdoba 13–17 August 1976. Doña Petrona was in attendance and was even named "honorary president."[100] As fellow *ecónoma* and participant Choly Berreteaga recalled, her attendance was no small effort. Doña Petrona was already suffering from arthritis at this time and often needed to rest, and her husband, Atilio, accompanied her. Berreteaga fondly recalled, "I spent those days with Atilio, her husband, and with [Petrona], seeing the tenderness with which Atilio took care of her."[101] In addition to this group, participants in the four-day-long conference included cooks, doctors, dieticians, and government officials from across Argentina. Speaking to the links between the military government and commercial interests, Doña Petrona and Choly Berreteaga sat on a panel that judged the empanada competition, along with Roberto Mitchell, administrative director of the Ministry of the Economy, and Héctor Adell, the marketing director for a well-known liquor business.[102]

This event provided the military government with an opportunity to showcase Argentine national pride. The military officials' participation in the conference suggested their interest in showing their government to be authentically Argentine, even *criollo*. This notion was replicated in the diet of military conscripts, who regularly ate traditional *criollo* foods like empanadas and *locro*.[103] Like past political leaders, the military government's interest in female cooking (this was an empanada and not an *asado* competition after all) emphasized the idea that women's domestic duties played an important role in sustaining their families as well as in the national community and economy.

Such a notion was further institutionalized by the creation of the Asociación de Ecónomas y Gastrónomas (Association of Home Economists and Gastronomists) near the end of the military dictatorship's first year in power. At the same time that other professional groups of women and men (including academics and feminists) were forced to disband, a group of fourteen *ecónomas* established themselves as a formal nonprofit organization, with Doña Petrona as the first president. In a nod to the official prohibitions against political parties and public meetings, the *ecónomas* were careful to state in the second article of their charter that their organization "absolutely excludes from all its proceedings questions of a religious, political, or social nature."[104] Instead, they clarified that they intended "to promote the study and knowledge of gastronomical activity, seeking to improve dietary habits for the benefit of the community."[105] They made clear that they would not "talk politics at the table," as Doña Petrona had recently advised her fans.

As had been the case since the hiring of the first *ecónomas* in Argentina, members of this association helped companies to sell their products. Now they did so in the neoliberal marketplace fostered by the military. Being an *ecónoma* was an occupation that was not only in demand but now also safe. One woman recalled how she switched from training in psychology to the culinary arts to protect herself.[106] The new group held its first meetings in the Chandón bodega. At these meetings, members considered whether they might award a stamp of approval for products, similar to the Good Housekeeping label in the United States.[107] Soon after, they decided to focus on leading tours and cooking demonstrations for companies interested in promoting their products. Like Primitiva had done forty years earlier, during the 1970s foreign firms like Knorr Suiza hired *ecónomas* to convince Argentine *amas de casa* to trust in and buy their novel items, in this case bouillon cubes.[108] This sales pitch took on added meaning during the Proceso as the number of successful businesses continued to shrink and the potential for profits for those businesses that succeeded continued to grow.[109]

Ecónoma María Cristina Dillon emphasized the enthusiastic response of both corporations and consumers to the association's initiatives. She recalled that "thousands of people" attended the association's events during the late

1970s and 1980s. In describing the success of the association's own classes, she remembered this period as a "golden age," during which students just showed up ready to learn.[110] It seems that this popularity stemmed in part from the safety and social acceptability of these public gatherings during an era in which social and educational opportunities were severely limited by the dictatorship.

A New Audience

Argentine *ecónomas* primarily directed their advice to women, but they also began to recognize a growing interest in cooking on the part of some men. Not surprisingly, Doña Petrona was eager to capitalize on this trend. In 1977, a journalist explained that Doña Petrona's "new concern is male cooks" and that she planned to hold classes specifically for them. According to this article, men were now more interested in learning how to make more "expensive and difficult foods" than women.[111] This must have been a particularly appealing audience for Doña Petrona, who had been forced to tone down her emphasis on complicated dishes in order to remain relevant to female home cooks dealing with shrinking budgets and growing extradomestic responsibilities. While Petrona was interested in capitalizing on men's interest in high-end cuisine, she was clear about why they were able to embrace this kind of cooking. She explained that, for men, cooking represented a "diversion," while for women it was an "obligation." She continued that if men were free to be more extravagant and detail oriented, it was only because they "spend little time in this work." In contrast, as feminists had also recently pointed out, Doña Petrona now emphasized that women "suffer the everyday obligation of [going to] the market and [making] lunch for the kids."[112]

Doña Petrona was not alone in recognizing men's interest in studying the art of cooking. During the late 1970s, Pelusa Molina also began to teach classes aimed at men at the cooking academy of her mother, Emmy de Molina.[113] These educated, professional men of the 1970s were careful to differentiate themselves from lower-class cooks, echoing the tendencies of their privileged female counterparts from the 1930s. Pelusa Molina explained that her male students approached cooking "not with an attitude like the socially devalued petty cook [*cocinerito*], but rather his opposite, the gourmet who had traveled, the bon vivant, who was up on new things." They were particularly interested in wine and foreign food, topics that she suggested helped make cooking more important in Argentina, "because people started to see it from another perspective."[114] As the interest in Doña Petrona's and Pelusa Molina's classes and the emergence of male culinary celebrity Gato Dumas suggest, some men were indeed becoming more enthusiastic about high-end cooking during the late 1970s.[115] Nevertheless, except in specific circumstances (such as those of a widower or a single man on his own), most Argentines still expected women to do the everyday cooking for their families.[116]

Therefore, even as Doña Petrona and other culinary experts made overtures toward men with culinary interests, they continued to focus on women as their primary audience because they recognized that they still did most of the cooking. On her television program, Doña Petrona continued to see her audience as female, and she sought to keep this audience abreast of the latest trends. For example, on one program, in which she focused on how to use a refrigerator to save time, she pointed out that this would be particularly useful information for women who worked both inside and outside of their home and therefore "needed the most help." She explained that, in response to their continuous correspondence, she felt it important to explain that refrigerators could be used not only for keeping "butter or ice cubes" cold but also for storing dishes that could later be heated up in a few minutes, like *milanesas* and precooked noodles with cheese.[117]

Like her contemporaries, Doña Petrona recognized that women's roles had changed. In a 1978 interview with *Gente*, she explained, "Before the woman was raised to be an *ama de casa*, wife and mother. And nothing more. Today mothers raise their daughters so that they can make a life for themselves outside of the home."[118] Her interviewer finished this thought: "That is to say that the universities are full and the kitchens empty?" Yes, she agreed, and this is the way it ought to be. However, she continued that this did not mean she agreed with feminism or the idea of "equality." Petrona explained: "You will have noticed the quantity of women involved with feminism that attack men. And this is bad, because in trying to be like a man you forget that above everything you are a woman, that you have obligations in your home and with your children."[119] Like many others, Doña Petrona had recently begun to embrace some feminist tenets while seeking to make clear that she was neither a feminist nor a supporter. This important caveat made this a safe gender politics to articulate under a dictatorship that sought to encourage gender norms tightly linking women and domesticity.

In such a context, Doña Petrona enjoyed a boost to her somewhat flagging popularity. She was, as the magazine *Mucho Gusto* (which was affiliated with her television program) reported in 1978, "the most admired *ecónoma* in the country." The editors dubbed her World Cup Cake and a number of other fancy, internationally inflected recipes (like Singapore-Style Shrimp and Sole with Roquefort Sauce) as her greatest successes. "If Doña Petrona did not exist, we'd have to invent her," they explained.[120] But unlike the invented Betty Crocker, Doña Petrona was a real person and one who *Mucho Gusto* and her sponsors believed could continue to help them sell their products.[121]

For its part, the military government was likely quite pleased to see this domestic icon publicly memorializing Argentina's World Cup victory. The military junta was particularly eager to use its hosting of the largest international sporting event in the world to foster national pride and quell international concerns. It had brought the technology for color television to Argentina for this event. But Argentines themselves did not have access to this new color programming in their homes, so the junta sent its color broadcasts abroad to show the world how advanced and civilized Argentina actually was.[122] Within Argentina, the junta mandated massive coverage in black and white of the tournament on the state-controlled media.

Like Doña Petrona, most Argentines were big soccer fans and enthusiastically supported the event and their team. However, there was a notable exception—the Madres de Plaza de Mayo. Seizing on the presence of the international media in Buenos Aires to cover the most-watched sporting event in the world, they boycotted the World Cup in front of international cameras, and their protests were broadcast around the world.[123] But even as international coverage increased, the great majority of media outlets in Argentina did not cover the Madres' protests.[124] Instead, most carried much safer celebratory stories about the World Cup, such as Doña Petrona's presentation of the '78 World Cup Cake.

Doña Petrona's decision to bake the World Cup Cake in the first place suggested her desire to remain a safe and successful public figure during the 1976–83 dictatorship. She did not use her celebrity to speak out against the dictatorship, as some other celebrities, including folklore singer Mercedes Sosa and actress Norma Aleandro, would do, forcing them to flee into exile.[125] But neither did she use her public prominence to speak in favor of the dictatorship, as *Para Ti* had done since the coup, and she ended her column there in 1977.[126] Instead, she maintained a purportedly "apolitical" stance, sticking to her famous proclamation that one should "not talk politics at the table."[127] Of course, as the 1985 film *The Official Story* would demonstrate so poignantly, the decision to remain silent about the military's "Dirty War" was as political as the alternative.[128] Further, food had always been and would continue to be a political issue in Argentina.

The Last Act

In 1982, Doña Petrona replaced the World Cup Cake—which had graced the covers of the seventy-third and seventy-fourth editions—with a culinary testament to her cookbook's own success. On the front cover she placed a large green "75" against a brown background. A five-tiered cake topped with that number and adorned with white dimpled frosting, pink roses, and graceful wheat shafts was on the back cover. This was a remarkable milestone, and Doña Petrona made a point of sharing the story behind her cookbook with journalists. In writing about what would soon become familiar details about the pricing, titling, and publication of this cookbook, journalist Fanny Polimeni explained that she intended to provide readers with the "details that until now have been unknown about the history of this book already established as *the* indisputable publishing phenomenon in this country and many other countries in America."[129]

Nevertheless, even as the success of this now-legendary book was being celebrated, sales were clearly slowing down. In fact, there were only 5,000 copies of the celebrated seventy-fifth edition printed in 1982—just half of what she had printed a decade earlier and only a seventh of the numbers printed at the peak of her fame during the 1950s and early 1960s. *El libro de Doña Petrona* had now returned to the same print run as her first edition in 1934.[130] This "bible of the home" was no longer as dominant as it had once been.

The death of Petrona's second husband, Atilio Massut, in 1979 likely played a part in the declining print runs. Since marrying Petrona in the 1940s, Atilio had taken personal responsibility for the marketing and distribution of the cookbook. In addition to the professional toll of his passing, this loss was quite difficult for Petrona on a personal level. She confided during an interview with Miriam Becker: "I feel lonely because Atilio was a great companion." She continued that she had recently decided to sell her car because "he had driven and now I no longer have anyone to do this."[131]

Still, the loss of her husband was only part of the reason behind the declining print runs. The change in emphasis about the appropriate place of cooking (and other activities) in women's lives, along with the impact of all-too-regular economic crises had taken their toll. The societal embrace of youth since the late 1960s also decreased her appeal, as youth was something that this aging *ecónoma* had a difficult time conveying. That did not mean she did not try. In 1979, she had a face-lift, and in the early 1980s she shared that she was considering going back to "do her neck."[132] As she explained to the journalist who interviewed her about it, "The deal is that television is tremendously revealing"—especially in color, which more and more Argentines had access to starting in 1980.[133] This was something that her contemporary, Julia Child, understood as well, as this seemingly less self-conscious U.S. cook also had cosmetic work done on her face, even as she deliberately kept it from the press.[134]

Doña Petrona's popularity had declined during the early 1980s, but she remained quite popular with certain sectors of society, especially older women. She continued to perform on television and to give live cooking classes to the numerous groups who requested her presence. For example, in 1982 and 1983 alone, over twenty schools and charities, including church groups, retired teacher associations, and female branches of Rotary clubs, asked her if she would be willing to conduct live cooking demonstrations to help them raise funds.[135] On such occasions, she gave out free recipes and also suggestions about relationships. In 1981, she explained to a journalist that she told her *alumnas* that "it is necessary to make a man feel important, support him, accompany him, and know how to respect his place." She reiterated that women could not be equal "even if there are female lawyers, doctors, or architects who perform their jobs as successfully [as men]. A woman shines in her home in a different way than a man, whose authority, on the other hand, has a different strength than a woman's."[136] Despite her own tremendously successful career, Doña Petrona continued to suggest that women should ultimately focus on the home and defer to male authority. And despite her efforts to provide quick and less expensive recipes, she still preferred the rich and elaborate cuisine with which she had built her career.

In 1981, journalist Sibila Camps published an article about Doña Petrona testifying to the culinary transformations that had by then solidified. Aptly titled "Times Have Changed," Camps's piece noted that, on the whole, Argentines (by which she meant middle-class Argentines) spent less time cooking and made fewer and simpler dishes, mainly by incorporating some prepared products and relying on technologies like the refrigerator. Many made their food purchases with considerations of budget, nutrition, or dieting. Those in a position to do so began experimenting with an array of newly available foreign foods and appliances.[137] Additionally, in urban areas, more began to eat some meals out at an expanding array of restaurants.[138] The military junta's economic policies had encouraged this climate of increased consumption, at least for those who could afford it. For the poor, these same policies decreased the amount of food available to them, creating a growing sector of the population that suffered from malnutrition.[139]

During the early 1980s, deepening economic problems, growing discontent among the populace, and international pressure linked to the government's human rights abuses illuminated the military leaders' weaknesses and caused them to begin to slowly loosen their grip.[140] The disastrous decision to invade the Malvinas (Falkland) Islands to try to reclaim them from the British in March 1982 represented a last attempt to bolster national pride. With the failure of this effort, critics forced democratic elections in the fall of 1983.

With the return to democracy, calls abounded for legitimate and enduring political institutions. Human rights groups flourished, and former lawyer and Radical Party candidate Raul Alfonsín was elected president in late 1983 amid great optimism. In the wake of this victory, Doña Petrona joined the calls for political cooperation, publicly remarking that "all of us have to do and fix things. It does not matter who has won, but all of us have to work together for the good of the nation. Not even the Radicals can do everything well [and neither can] the Peronists, and less so [if we are] divided or confrontational."[141] The restoration of democracy seemed to spur her to speak directly and publicly about political matters for the first time. In the wake of the dictatorship, it became fashionable, and even expected, to talk about politics.

Despite the enormous optimism that accompanied President Alfonsín's election, his government took office facing substantial economic challenges. The dictatorship had left behind a 45 billion dollar foreign debt and chronically high rates of inflation. In 1983, the Argentine economy boasted the unfortunate distinction of maintaining the highest rate of inflation in the world. In the previous nine years, the consumer price index had registered annual three-digit increases.[142]

Doña Petrona had been the one to provide advice to *amas de casa* about how to contend with such challenges, but now she would no longer be the main face of the operation. In 1983, she retired from television. In an interview early the next year, she explained that she had recently decided to retire from television because "thirty" was a "round number" and would allow her successors to take her place.[143] Many journalists started to write elegiac pieces thanking her for paving the way for future *ecónomas* and for all she had done for women over the course of her career. For example, Miriam Becker wrote a 1984 article titled, "Thank you, Petrona C. de Gandulfo." Earlier that year, the government awarded her a "silver spoon" in honor of her work.[144]

While most media coverage of Doña Petrona continued to be positive, a 1983 piece in *Panorama* poked fun at her, illustrating the renewal of public skepticism that accompanied the end of military rule. "She says she is honest in her profession. (Honesty is an expensive thing, perhaps because it is not common)," the journalist quipped. "And then she gives me a lecture with a series of proverbs and aphorisms about decency, ethics, etc., that bores the two of us, but fills the voids of conversation that is languishing."[145]

Despite the small number of such public jabs amid a much larger number of celebratory pieces, Doña Petrona made clear that she was not ready to "languish" or to give up her career entirely. In 1984, she publicly expressed her desire to keep working in other venues "as long as the public demands and accepts me."[146] Thus, even as many journalists and culinary figures began to pay homage to Doña Petrona's pathbreaking career as if it had ended, she continued to act as if it had not. Above all, she wished to remain relevant.

To respond to the difficult economic situation in which most Argentines found themselves, Doña Petrona, together with her new business partner, her granddaughter Marcela Massut, issued the fifteenth edition of *Recetas económicas* (Economical Recipes) in 1984. Massut later explained that they published a print run of 20,000 copies (four times the size of the seventy-fifth edition of *El libro de Doña Petrona*) because they felt that this thriftier cookbook was in a position to sell better than Doña Petrona's classic text. Since her husband's death in 1979, Doña Petrona had taken to publishing only the minimum number of copies of *El libro de Doña Petrona* in each print run because of its high cost to print and to buy.[147]

In a 1984 article in celebration of the fifty-year anniversary of *El libro de Doña Petrona*, Doña Petrona commented that it had become prohibitively expensive to publish books. She continued that, in fact, prices for everything were "up in the clouds," noting that even "food has not escaped this phenomenon."[148] In recognition of the truth of this statement, the national government created the Programa Alimentario Nacional (National Food Program) that same year to address the dietary deficiencies of poor people across Argentina, whom the government had recently determined made up over a quarter of the population.[149] It distributed cooking oil, rice, noodles, sugar, powdered milk, beans, corned beef, wheat flour, and corn flour to some 500,000 families, a fraction of the population unable to meet even their "basic needs."[150] For her part, Doña Petrona continued to tailor her approach not for the poorest segments of society but rather for people with some disposable income. Following a tactic that had brought her much past success, she remarked in 1984 that due to the high food prices, "cooking should be adapted to the era in which we live, and I feel obligated to constantly bring myself up-to-date."[151]

Even as *El libro de Doña Petrona*'s popularity waned during these decades, Petrona worked with her granddaughter to revise the cookbook. They trimmed and updated the nearly eighty pages of advice at the beginning of the book. For example, they removed the description of how to wash fine linen tablecloths, about which Marcela commented that "no one used anymore," and added recommendations for how to set a table with colorful place mats. In addition, they added "the latest American and European recipes," for example, cheesecake, apple strudel, and lemon pie. Marcela recalled her grandmother as being remarkably open to change for a woman of her age. "Imagine an eighty-year-old woman learning to work with packaged yeast and a microwave," she remarked with amazement.[152]

Nevertheless, when publicly designated the "official heir" to Doña Petrona in 1984, Marcela Massut shared with a journalist her desire to go beyond her grandmother's "big" cookbook and "traditional" ideas about cooking. She explained: "For me this book is already old, even as it has undergone changes; what was eaten ten or fifteen years ago in our country is no longer consumed for several reasons. Particularly economic reasons, and when it's not that, it's due to a lack of time. For example, I make pastry cream using a powdered mix, and this makes my grandmother's hair stand on end. She is traditional."[153] There were some things that Doña Petrona was willing to do to make her advice more relevant, but she still had reservations about some of the "modern" domestic trends her granddaughter embraced.

The gravity of the economic situation nevertheless enabled Marcela to convince her grandmother to publish several smaller and more inexpensive themed books during the late 1980s and early 1990s. Massut publicly introduced her idea to do so in this same 1984 article. She explained, "My book idea is to make a work that will always be applicable and not just for special occasions. And, in addition, it is not necessary that it be a book exactly, but rather little books that are small and cheap, in installments."[154] Marcela explained that these less-expensive, softcover books sold well during this period because they were more affordable and available not only at bookstores but also at newspaper stands and on supermarket shelves. In contrast, Doña Petrona told a journalist in 1985 that she had prepared a new cookbook focused on *cocina criolla*, or, as she also put it, "our traditional food," but that it was too expensive and difficult to find an editor.[155] Thus, hardcover books, which had become a symbol of middle-class membership over the course of the twentieth century, had become accessible only to the wealthiest sectors of society by the end of the twentieth century, as they had been a century before.[156]

Despite rising publishing costs, Doña Petrona continued to make herself available to a broader public during the mid-1980s. In 1985, she told journalists that she regularly went to her office downtown to take calls from fans who phoned her with questions. She explained proudly that the callers were not only people of her own age but also thirty-year-olds or fifty-year-olds—"and even young ladies who are preparing a special meal for their boyfriends." In response, her interviewer asked if she was not interested in adopting a more relaxed, sedentary lifestyle, to which Doña Petrona replied: "Why? This is my life and I don't plan on changing it."[157]

In this same piece, she suggested that the postdictatorship flourishing of women's and other human rights movements in Argentina had altered some of her views. "The woman has evolved. She has perfected herself because she no longer accepts being only a mother." In particular, she pointed to the right to the vote and *patria potestad*, women's equal parental rights, which were gained in 1985, as important milestones. When asked if feminists were ultimately responsible for such gains, she responded, "Of course they were, because [in this] we were uniting." When asked about her political views, she echoed one of feminism's main tenets, explaining, "Every act of our lives is political."[158] Such a claim bespoke a dramatic shift from her earlier statements that she would not "talk politics" and rejected feminism, and it reflected her latest attempt to remain relevant. Nevertheless, on other occasions, she continued to argue that a woman's first priority should be child rearing and that she should defer to the authority of her husband, who was the rightful "head of the house" (*jefe de la casa*).

For others, it was not only gender but also class that explicitly shaped their views of women's activism and appropriate roles. As Jo Fisher has shown, a group of working-class women formed the Sindicato de Amas de Casa (SACRA) during the early 1980s, with the radical proposals of seeking homemakers' rights to unionize and receive a salary. In response to pressure from the state and male-dominated unions, SACRA eventually backed off of both proposals. Echoing Eva Perón's Women's Party, they recognized women's domestic duties as work but suggested that women's rightful place was in the home. In turn, middle-class feminists emphasized women's domestic and extradomestic lack of equality with men but failed to connect with working-class women's concerns. Fisher concludes that the particularity of the Argentine dictator and postdictator eras stymied both groups' abilities to form the types of cross-class alliances that emerged in other Latin American nations like Brazil during this time.[159] The president of the

Madres de Plaza de Mayo, Hebe de Bonafini, expressed this disjuncture by pointing to the class-based distinctions of domestic work: "We believe in women's struggles, but not in [the struggles of] women who have another woman cleaning their floors."[160]

Over the course of the 1970s and 1980s, the percentage of women that census takers registered as being in domestic service within the "economically active" population returned to the 1960 levels (from the slight increase over the course of that decade). Whereas 20 percent of economically active women were counted in domestic service in 1960, 23 percent were in 1970, 20 percent were in 1980, and 20 percent were in 1991.[161] While Doña Petrona continued to be comfortable with the idea of women paying other women to help with domestic work, she had a much bigger problem with men doing the cleaning. "Personally I don't agree with seeing a man doing the dishes," she explained in 1985. But men cooking was another story: "This I really like."[162]

Despite her fervent desire to keep up-to-date for her fans (who were now both female and male), Doña Petrona was finally forced to withdraw from public life in the late 1980s due to her declining health. Now in her nineties, she began to spend more time at home in the company of Juanita Bordoy, who took care of her. She had to miss the tribute paid to *El libro de Doña Petrona* in 1990 at the annual book fair held in Buenos Aires. An article about this ceremony reported that Doña Petrona was "doing well" at her home in Olivos.[163]

But the same could not be said for the country as a whole. By the late 1980s, the optimism that had accompanied the restoration of democracy had begun to fade. In response to a coup threat in 1987, Alfonsín passed a pair of laws that reestablished the military's position of both political influence and legal immunity.[164] Despite Alfonsín's numerous attempts to adjust his economic stabilization policies, inflation spun hopelessly out of control in 1989. This hyperinflation made basic things like food and housing unaffordable for many across Argentina. During the first five months of 1989, the cost of staples skyrocketed, with the price of bread increasing by 554 percent, milk by 441 percent, and cheese by 1,000 percent.[165] On 24 May 1989, food riots broke out and poor Argentines looted grocery stores across the country, particularly in the suburbs of Buenos Aires, Córdoba, and Rosario. In response, the government declared a "state of siege" and froze food prices. These riots showcased the depths of Argentines' daily suffering and their discontent with the government's attempts to remedy it. In June 1989, Alfonsín announced that he would retire six months early to allow for new elections.[166]

Photograph of Petrona C. de Gandulfo (left) and Juanita Bordoy (right) by Solari, at home, 1986. Courtesy of Marcela Massut .

Conclusion

Petrona C. de Gandulfo's retirement from public life during the late 1980s spoke more to her advancing age than to her loss of popularity. To be sure, her dominance and that of her cookbook was challenged by the recurrent economic crises and the availability of quicker and more "modern" cooking advice, like that offered in the cookbook *La cocina de la mujer moderna*. The desire to streamline cooking was generated by the widespread acceptance of a new model of womanhood in which Argentines expected women to play larger and more important extradomestic roles than had previous generations. In 1985, Doña Petrona explained to a journalist that the ideal woman was "the normal one. The one who lives with her husband, works, and raises her children."[167] This was a new "normal," and it had changed rather recently.

While the notion that women had important extradomestic roles to play first gained traction during the 1960s and early 1970s, the brutal military dictatorship of 1976 to 1983 sought to reinstate the gendered expectations that had reigned during the earlier part of the twentieth century. At first, it seemed relatively successful. Leftist and feminist groups were silenced or forced underground. Safe and presumably apolitical topics like cooking and consumption gained predominance, for both women and men. Doña Petrona and the World Cup Cake took center stage in the national media. But Doña Petrona was no longer the only national domestic expert, and as she neared retirement she began to work with the new generation of *ecónomas* that would succeed her. The ongoing success of this group of *ecónomas* during the course of the Proceso demonstrated the acceptability of the mission to foster women's cooking and consumption during a dictatorship with a conservative and neoliberal approach.

Men also started to take an interest in cooking. As with "respectable" women of the early twentieth century, men's cooking of "gourmet" foods was elevated above other domestic tasks as worthy of their time and interest during the late 1970s and early 1980s. But such men distanced themselves from poorer men who cooked for a living and also from their female peers by seeking out high-end recipes and ingredients rather than everyday cooking and by keeping cleaning out of the equation.

More progressive ideas continued to percolate under a dictatorship, during which conservative gender norms seemed to go largely unchallenged. With the return to democracy, Argentines criticized the dictatorship for not only its campaign of terror but also its imposition of outdated gender ideals. Even as most continued to expect that women should take the primary responsibility for their homes and their families, more began to embrace the idea that women had other important contributions to make as professionals and activists as well. As a result, domesticity was no longer the main goal for those women who claimed or aspired to middle-class status in Argentina.

Shifting ideas about domesticity reflected new gender dynamics and also the changing image of Argentine culture more broadly. During the 1980s, as Doña Petrona was losing her preeminence with the public, the country as a whole was fracturing around the table. Over time, human rights groups like the Madres de Plaza de Mayo forced people to acknowledge that literally thousands had disappeared at the hands of the military junta, leaving empty seats at family tables across Argentina. In addition, the growing disparity between what rich and poor Argentines could afford to eat and how they could afford to live further challenged the idea that Argentina was a land of abundance with shared patterns of sociality. Nevertheless, Argentina's national identity would remain linked with the ideal of such abundance and shared customs. And, despite her withdrawal from public life, Doña Petrona would continue to play a major role in shaping ideas about cooking, eating, and national identity in Argentina.

KEEPING THE TABLE SET

On 6 February 1992, when Petrona C. de Gandulfo was in her late nineties, she passed away, with Juanita Bordoy at her side. All of the major national papers published obituaries celebrating her tremendous career. The journalists who wrote these articles made simple and yet profound claims about her importance. For example, Fernando Muñoz Pace began his article: "She taught half the world to cook."[1] Renata Rocco-Cuzzi described her as a successful career woman who established herself as an *ecónoma* and an important writer.[2] According to Orlando Barone, Doña Petrona was "number one in the mythology of the cooking genre. Everything begins with and follows from her."[3]

Journalists retold many of the stories that Doña Petrona had shared with them and other members of the media throughout the course of her career—her lack of interest in learning how to cook from her mother as a child in Santiago del Estero, her career "start" at Primitiva, her first cooking classes at Le Cordon Bleu, her decision to publish *El libro de Doña Petrona* in 1934 at the behest of her fans, her successful radio and then television programs with Juanita at her side, and her commitment to making herself accessible to fans by publicly sharing her phone number and personally responding to their numerous letters.

Over the course of her long career, Doña Petrona became a widely recognized symbol of the idea that food, and especially women's daily acts of cooking, served to link people across the nation. In her memoirs, she recalled her immense satisfaction in imagining how families' lunches and dinners across Argentina had been inspired by her recipes. She explained that the thousands of letters from *amas de casa* together with media reports about her popularity had led her to consider herself "part of an immense family made up of thousands of sisters of all ages."[4]

Despite many of her contemporaries' interest in joining this "sisterhood" of *amas de casa*, the women to whom she directed her advice have since been overlooked by scholars. This is remarkable, given the importance that fellow Argentines put on women's domestic roles and on food and the unprecedented level of success achieved by Doña Petrona. Journalists frequently compared her to other Argentine greats, like tango singer Carlos

Gardel. Some were amazed to recognize that Argentines had apparently consulted her best-selling cookbook "much more than the Bible."[5] The Argentine National Library reported that *El libro de Doña Petrona* was the most frequently stolen book in its collection and moved it to the *sala de tesoros* (rare book room) with other precious texts.[6] As we have seen, this was all backed up by impressive sales figures. Over the course of the twentieth century, *El libro de Doña Petrona* sold over 3 million copies and its author established herself at the center of Argentine domesticity.[7]

Here she was joined and buoyed by her assistant, Juanita Bordoy. When Juanita Bordoy passed away in 1995, the major newspapers eulogized "Doña Petrona's legendary assistant" who had become the "archetype of the domestic servant in Argentina" and who, only now, at the time of her death, could "recover her full name."[8] Still, as was the case during her career, even today Juana Bordoy continues to be referred to as "Juanita." In fact, at a party in Michigan in 2006, an Argentine expat in her twenties responded to a request from her husband to get him something, "What do you think? That I'm your Juanita?!" And, as had happened so many times before, the discussion, now among a group of Argentines, most of whom were too young to have seen Doña Petrona and Juanita live on television, turned to a critique of Doña Petrona's treatment of her assistant.[9]

During the 1990s, a number of newspaper articles mentioned another critique of Doña Petrona that continued to resonate during this era—that her recipes were too expensive for many Argentines to prepare.[10] In the last years of Petrona's life, Argentines had endured increasingly dramatic bouts of inflation coupled with declining salaries and rising prices. During the 1990s, under President Carlos Saúl Menem (1989–99), economic liberalization policies allowed better-off Argentines to consume new products and travel abroad, while austerity measures contributed to an unprecedented level of poverty in Argentina.[11] By 1996, the percentage of Argentines living under the poverty line, unable to meet basic needs, had risen to 25 percent (from 5 percent in 1960). The gulf that had begun to grow during the 1970s and 1980s had become even wider during the 1990s, as Argentine society became divided between better-off "meat" eaters and poor "noodle" eaters.[12]

The extreme austerity measures taken by Menem and his successors sparked a number of protests—some addressed the absence of food and others responded more broadly to rising rates of unemployment and impoverishment. In 2001, Menem's successor, Fernando de la Rúa (1999–2001), set off a massive wave of protest after he defaulted on foreign loans and froze all bank accounts. In early January 2002, Eduardo Duhalde, who became Argentina's fifth president in two weeks, definitively de-pegged the peso from the dollar (Menem's previous solution to inflation), sending the Argentine currency on a downward spiral and causing many to lose the majority of their savings.[13] In response, middle-class Argentines joined their working-class counterparts in the streets. In a relatively rare moment of cross-class resistance, they marched together, chanting, "Piquete y Cacerola: La Lucha Es Una Sola [Picketing and Pot-Banging: It's All the Same Fight]." As this slogan suggests, in the depths of the recent crisis Argentines made interrelated demands on the government about their right to work *and* their right to food in this supposed land of abundance.[14] In turn, a number of middle-class Argentines suggested their lack of faith in Argentina by leaving (or considering leaving) their birthplace for Europe or the United States.[15]

It was in this context and its aftermath that some Argentines first explained to me that it was "no longer the Day of Doña Petrona." Associating her with the good old days gone by, several people suggested that it was no longer possible to cook with her for economic reasons. For example, in 2004, a sixty-year-old woman named Dora from Puerto Ingeniero White, who loved to cook, explained that "before it was affordable [to cook with Doña Petrona]; when I started to work it was possible to make very tasty things, [but] if you decide to make [her] cake today it will cost you more than twenty pesos."[16] As a result, she no longer made Doña Petrona's cakes very often. Others mentioned that the move away from Doña Petrona also stemmed from women's changing roles in Argentine society. For instance, Annamaría Muchnik, the former host of the television program *Buenas Tardes, Mucho Gusto*, commented: "[Doña Petrona] belonged to an era in this country in which the economic situation was better, women had more time, they were at home more, and as a result they dedicated more time to cooking. It seems to me that today young girls and all women for that matter want to spend less time in the kitchen."[17] This desire to get away from the kitchen, Muchnik and others suggested, stemmed from a lack of time, money, and interest.

Changes and Continuities

The gradual shift away from cooking with (or like) Doña Petrona helps us to appreciate how gendered ideas about domesticity and community both changed and stayed the same over the course of the twentieth century in Argentina. Gender operated as both oppositional and normative. Women's purportedly natural characteristics and roles were distinguished from and seen as complementary to those of men. At the same time, contemporaries compared the "good" *ama de casa* with her often unnamed but nonetheless real opposite, the "bad" woman who neglected her domestic and familial duties.[18] For much of the twentieth century, being a "good" woman meant being a full-time homemaker, but by the 1960s, many "good" women also pursued careers. This was not simply about shifting gender norms, but also about class, because it was middle-class women who entered the workforce in larger numbers beginning in this decade. Poor women had long worked for meager compensation and little respect.

As we have seen, at the turn of the twentieth century, poor women cooked and cleaned while wealthy women managed other women doing such tasks in their homes. Growing up in Santiago del Estero, Petrona was far more interested in employing a cook than in being one. However, after her move to Buenos Aires, she found herself a new career as an *ecónoma*, using the technology of the gas stove and the prestige associated with French culinary techniques to elevate cooking above other domestic tasks, starting in 1928. For their part, women eagerly sought out such lessons, which allowed them to learn a "new" skill in a respectable and sociable public setting with other women. Of course, such cooking demonstrations, gas services, and the cookbook Petrona C. de Gandulfo first released in 1934 were only available for well-off folks in Buenos Aires during the 1930s. As would remain true throughout the rest of the twentieth century, people in other locations frequently had less access to new goods and services. This signals the importance of recognizing the unevenness of history across place and time—especially in a country like Argentina, where the expansion of the consumer and media markets (and gas services and television access) occurred much later outside the capital.

In addition to suggesting the uneven path of "development" in Argentina, tracing the history of Doña Petrona, women, and food enables us to appreciate the ways in which macro-level politics and economics mattered and did not matter to the gendered dynamics of everyday life. For example, as other scholars have shown, Juan Perón's first presidencies (1946–55) had a dramatic impact on improving the material realities and the political weight of the working class and of women after they gained the vote in 1947. Nevertheless, through focusing on cooking and consumption, we see not only women's increasing civic rights and participation in the workforce but also the expansion of the middle-class model of domesticity touted by Doña Petrona under a populist, paternalistic, and maternalistic government.[19] That is, even as the Peronist government invited the working class to the common table that Doña Petrona and her fans had set for the emerging middle class, it continued to be a table set by women and filled with the creolized cosmopolitan fare admired by the upper classes. As throughout the twentieth century, the construction of the ideal of Argentina as a bountiful middle-class nation occurred not just through macrolevel politics and economics but also in quotidian social interactions and patterns of consumption.

Many Argentines literally bought into this version of middle-class domesticity by purchasing millions of copies of *El libro de Doña Petrona* during this cookbook's national expansion in the 1940s, its peak in the 1950s, and its continued success during the 1960s.[20] In other words, in contrast to Mexico, with its nationalist culinary trend that historian Jeffrey Pilcher has revealed in his work, Argentina did not experience the emergence of a nationalist cuisine along with a nationalist government.[21] Instead, the "nationalization" of provincial fare from northwestern Argentina would come later, more gradually, and in a more limited fashion than in Latin American countries with a deeper shared culinary heritage, fewer immigrants, and less of an attachment to a European identity.

Likewise, even as Peronist policies drew more women into higher education and the paid workforce, the mainstream ideal of womanhood would not be challenged until the subsequent decades. During the 1960s and 1970s, as middle-class women studied longer and pursued careers, a new model of the "modern" woman emerged that was decidedly younger, less domestic, and more career oriented. Poor women had long worked for wages in Argentina, but it was not until their better-off counterparts chose to work that the broader society recognized the value of women's paid labor and the need to update the mainstream model of domesticity. In other words, in a country that eagerly claimed a middle-class identity, middle-class women's behaviors played the leading role in defining the norm.

In response to middle-class women's professionalization, Doña Petrona began to offer quicker recipes as well as some diet cookbooks that spoke to the new culture of thinness among the upper echelons of society. She also presented more thrifty recipes in response to the economic crises that began to rock Argentina during the second half of the twentieth century. She was joined by a new generation of *ecónomas* who did the same and who together formed a formal organization under the military dictatorship eager to install a neoliberal marketplace. During this era, Argentine *ecónomas*, who offered general cooking advice along with product promotion and food styling, continued to be more popular than cooks or chefs. Bolstered by an economy that was expanding and yet frequently in crisis during the second half of the twentieth century, *ecónomas*' services were often in demand and their numbers grew.[22]

The fall of the dictatorship was accompanied by the widespread acceptance of a much less domestic model of womanhood in which the ideal woman was expected to be a mother and to work outside of the home in some capacity. Nevertheless, the idea that women should know how to cook persisted, as it does to this day. There are now a number of female and male culinary celebrities who produce television shows, cookbooks, and recipe columns for a more gender-neutral audience, but, as Annamaría Muchnik put it, it is still generally "the woman [who] cooks . . . and goes shopping."[23]

The fact that this expectation continues is not unique to Argentina. Across much of the world today, most people assume that women will do the majority of the daily food preparation and other domestic work. In poorer Latin American countries with a smaller middle sector, relatively well-off families have continued to count on paid female domestic help. In turn, in Argentina, where elite families have continued to enjoy the services of maids and cooks, members of the middle class have increasingly hired part-time help or figured out how to get by without it. Those women who could afford "help" have often asked the women who worked for them to do the "dirty work" of cleaning and then, at least sometimes, have done the more enjoyable and praiseworthy task of cooking themselves. Women have taken the lead in managing such relationships, making them more maternalistic than paternalistic in practice.[24] Nevertheless, as Heidi Tinsman emphasizes, excusing men from domestic work has played a significant role in reinforcing male privilege across the Americas.[25]

In contrast to most domestic "dirty work," cooking can be deeply pleasurable. In Argentina, "respectable" women and men (of the 1930s and 1970s, respectively) discovered this to be the case when taking classes with their peers, using quality ingredients, and employing elaborate techniques that emphasized their artistry. But most Argentines had neither the time nor the resources to cook in this manner, which often drew considerable praise. But some loved cooking anyway. For example, we witnessed the joy that Elba A. took in cooking everyday meals for her family, as well as her wedding cake, with the guidance of Doña Petrona. In turn, others were much less interested, such as María B., who explained that she was willing to play "Juanita" and clean for her cousin Olga G. while she did the cooking.

In every generation, there have been women with a lot of or a little enthusiasm for cooking—what has changed over time is their access to other respectable undertakings and the ideal against which they have been measured. During the 1960s and beyond, as women with educations and resources chose to take up more extradomestic pursuits, many found that they did not have the time or the interest—or the full weight of expectations—to spend their days making elaborate recipes for their families. So that, even as women were still expected to know how to "cook something" during the late twentieth century, neither women's roles nor their actual lives or cooking practices have remained static.

How have women in Argentina managed to work outside of the home as well as inside of it? Technology, which many, including Doña Petrona, touted as the panacea, has never really proved itself able to significantly decrease women's work in caring for their families, in Argentina or elsewhere.[26] Instead, women (especially those with fewer resources) have often turned to female relatives and neighbors for help. Some women in cities have outsourced "their" domestic work by using laundry services, going out to eat, or ordering in. For middle-class women, employing paid domestic help has been essential to their ability to pursue careers and maintain their responsibilities for caring for their children and their homes. Further, in the last couple of decades, some heterosexual partnerships have become more equitable, with men doing some of the cooking, cleaning, and caring for children alongside their female partners. However, as sociologist Catalina Wainerman recently concluded, such men remain the exception. Her study shows that the average Argentine man today does only a tenth of the house-related work and a quarter of the daily child rearing—leaving women to do the great majority of both.[27] Therefore, as in many parts of the world, even as Argentine women's roles have vastly changed over the twentieth century, their double day has not ended. Until the unremunerated or poorly compensated labor of cleaning, cooking, and caring is widely recognized as important work, women, and especially poor women, will continue to carry this burden.[28]

The economic and social importance of *amas de casa* (as well as the domestic servants who work for them) has been overlooked as middle-class women (including scholars) have fought for the right to work on a par with men. But to understand the history of women and gender in twentieth-century Argentina, we must pay attention to the histories of women in the domestic realm, as well as how their roles intersected with other activities and aspirations over time. To do so requires us to ask new questions and bring to the center historical subjects who have generally fallen outside the bounds of labor, economic, and political histories but who, as we have seen, played instrumental roles as domestic workers, consumers, community builders, and citizens.

Studying the trajectory of and responses to Doña Petrona is worthwhile because it brings these roles to the forefront. This is not because Doña Petrona was an average woman but rather because she reached millions of other Argentines—women and, to a lesser extent, men—who followed her cooking lessons, bought her cookbook, and turned to her for advice. Since the 1930s, this *ecónoma* has guided many Argentines in their quest to learn how to make a new dish, "properly" set a table for guests, or make an elaborate birthday cake for their children. In this way, she has helped forge a common table and common practices in a diverse and industrializing nation. To be sure, there were many Argentines who were uninterested in, unable to follow, or unaware of her advice, but even today it is difficult to find an urbanite who is relatively well off who has not heard of her or whose family does not possess a copy of *El libro de Doña Petrona*. Over the course of her seven-decade-long career, Doña Petrona established herself as *the* domestic referent for this demographic.

By following the stories of those who embraced Doña Petrona, along with those who rejected or remained unaware of her, we gain a richer picture of the continuities and changes of daily life in twentieth-century Argentina. We can see which groups were able to take a seat at Argentina's metaphorical common table and which were not. Even today, many middle-class Argentines continue to claim that *El libro de Doña Petrona* is in every home, but in fact a great number of Argentines never owned Argentina's best-selling cookbook. And many poor Argentines have found themselves unable to cook Doña Petrona's typical fare and even eat simple preparations of Argentina's long-favored staple, beef. While the Peronist era enabled many (but not all) Argentines to join the metaphorical common table, the neoliberal era has driven a growing number of poor people from it.

Remaining Relevant

Despite the economic and political tumult that has shaped the second half of the twentieth century and the early part of the twenty-first century, dreams of progress and the desire to share a table with friends or relatives have persisted to this day. Argentines with the ability to do so still spend long hours sitting, eating, and drinking with family and friends. And while specific ideas about how women should spend their time have changed significantly, the notion that women and not men are ultimately responsible for cooking and for organizing social events has not.

Nostalgia for the Argentina of the idealized past perhaps best explains why *El libro de Doña Petrona* and its author continue to resonate even today. Even in the depths of the economic crisis that followed Argentina's 2001 default, the newspaper *El Clarín* decided, in 2002, to release a series of glossy, magazine-like inserts of Doña Petrona's recipes updated by

Blanca Cotta. And in 2011, artist Alfredo Arias opened an exhibition and live show in Buenos Aires that was an homage to the fantasy land that Doña Petrona had created for Argentines. "La Patria Petrona," as he referred to it, was a place where he and other mid-twentieth-century Argentines could escape from the gritty realities of daily life—in his case his parents' constant fighting and the growing poverty of his neighborhood. By staring at Doña Petrona's fanciful illustrations of cakes or watching her and Juanita on television, Argentines like him, many of whom shared dreams of upward social mobility, escaped into a world of art, entertainment, and abundance.[29]

Doña Petrona's grandchildren, Marcela and Alejandro Massut, continue to capitalize on the enduring interest in their grandmother's recipes for Argentina. They have focused on updating and releasing new editions of *Recetas económicas* and *El libro de Doña Petrona*, which is now up to its 103d edition. Argentines at home and abroad continue to snap up this tome, which epitomizes the links between food and national belonging. But these twenty-first-century shoppers are outnumbered by the many more who treasure copies that have been handed down as family heirlooms. As one woman wrote on a blog in response to an article in *La Nación* in 2010, "One of my most prized possessions is *El libro de Doña Petrona*, which was my grandmother's, with my grandmother's notes written in pencil, falling apart and pretty well used." While many of the recipes were from "another era" when women cooked for twenty people at a time and used a "dozen eggs and tons of butter," she explained that a number remain relevant and part of her regular repertoire today.[30]

Testifying to this relevance, along with the desire to update Doña Petrona for a contemporary audience, in 2010 a current star of the Argentine culinary scene, chef Narda Lepes, began filming a new program called simply *Doña Petrona por Narda*. Part of a new generation of male *and* female chefs with international experience and a local fan following, Narda accepted the television channel Utilísima's proposal to move from the high-end culinary channel Elgourmet.com to its homier venue mainly directed to women. Her reason for accepting this offer? Doña Petrona's enduring presence in popular culture. As Narda explained in a 2010 interview, even for people too young to have watched Doña Petrona on television or to have read her cookbook, "when someone says, 'who do you think you are, Doña Petrona?' you understand that you are being [complimented as] a cook because you know that she cooked well." Narda continued, "This is the value of the name itself, the weight of it."[31]

On her program, Narda pays homage to Doña Petrona, whose portrait hangs on the set, not only by updating her recipes (often by cutting out some of the butter and cream) but also by inviting her aunt Viviana to be her "Juanita." Not surprisingly, their on-screen relationship is quite different from that of the original domestic pair, as Narda openly recognizes that her aunt is not a domestic servant but rather an *ama de casa* who cooks well. In contrast, until recently the Argentine actress and television personality Mirtha Legrand (who is now in her eighties) had broadcasted her program *Almorzando con Mirtha Legrand* (Lunching with Mirtha Legrand) with a formally dressed maid standing behind her and attending to her famous guests.[32] But Narda is decidedly part of a new generation of celebrities who prefer the assistant to be behind the scenes or a social peer. And despite her primarily female audience at Utilísima, Narda explains that she "does not talk in the feminine" and hopes to be part of an effort to expand both women's and men's home cooking.[33]

As this latest homage to Doña Petrona attests, while public portrayals of domesticity have changed, the desire to connect with Argentina's leading domestic expert has not. Even at the start of the twentieth-first century, it remains difficult for many people to imagine Argentina without some of the values she came to symbolize. In claiming Argentina's most famous *ecónoma*, citizens with the means to do so implicitly express their right to bountiful food and their commitment to a shared sociability and civility. They also emphasize the enduring importance of women's domestic roles as consumers, cooks, and creators of community.

NOTES

Introduction

1. For a discussion of her date of birth and ancestry, see chapter 1.

2. The etymology of the term *ecónoma* is discussed in chapter 1.

3. Scholars and journalists have put forth different opinions about where exactly *El libro de Doña Petrona* falls in terms of sales records, but all agree that it is in the top three best sellers. See Florencia Ure, "Doña Petrona C. de Gandulfo: 95 años vividos en plenitud," *Todo Chic*, 28 July 1991; Bauer, *Goods, Power, History*, 198; and Toer et al., *Historias del gas*, 27. *Martín Fierro* was published in two installments in 1872 and 1879: Hernández, *El gaucho Martín Fierro*; and Hernández, *La vuelta de Martín Fierro*.

4. "Encuesta sobre alimentación en dos barrios de Córdoba"; Escudero, *La alimentación de la familia en Buenos Aires*, 73.

5. Carol Gold points to the particular success in Denmark of Madame Mangor's cookbooks during this era; her first cookbook came out in forty editions between 1837 and 1910, and her second came out in twenty-nine editions between 1842 and 1901. Gold, *Danish Cookbooks*, especially p. 15.

6. Thomas Lask, "Books of the Times: Making a House a Home," *New York Times*, 30 August 1969, 19; Marcus, "Beeton's Book of Household Management," BR3.

7. Lovera, *Food Culture in South America*, 86.

8. Pilcher, "Josefina Velázquez de León"; Mauricio Velázquez de León, "The Mother of Mexican Cuisine," *Saveur* 89 (December 2005): 69–89.

9. For example, Manuel Caldeiro, "Virtudes y defectos de los argentinos según Petrona C. de Gandulfo," *Gente*, 12 October 1978, n.p.

10. From 1820 to 1932, the great majority of European immigrants (or 57.9 percent) went to the United States, while the second-largest percentage (or 11.6 percent) went to Argentina. Moya, *Cousins and Strangers*, 46.

11. Prieto, *El discurso criollista*, 14.

12. Farmer also wrote a regular column for *Woman's Home Companion* from 1905 to 1915 and published other cookery books. "Fannie Merritt Farmer," *Encyclopaedia Britannica Online* (accessed 26 October 2010).

13. Marks, *Finding Betty Crocker*.

14. Mendelson, *Stand Facing the Stove*.

15. Some two years before commencing her television series, Julia Child released her critically acclaimed 1961 cookbook, written with Simone Becke and Louisette Bertholle, *Mastering the Art of French Cooking*. For more on Julia Child, see Fitch, *Appetite for Life*; Shapiro, *Julia Child*; and Strauss, *Setting the Table for Julia Child*.

16. Chef James Beard was the first to cook on network television in the United States, in 1945. French chef Jacques Pépin moved to the United States, published his first cookbook during the 1970s, and began cooking on television in the 1980s. Emeril

Lagasse joined the Food Network in 1993 and published his first cookbook, *Emeril's New Orleans Cooking*, that year. Like their female counterparts, Emeril and, more recently, Mario Batali have used food channels (and later, the internet) to market their cookbooks and cooking merchandise. In Argentina, Gato Dumas parlayed his culinary training in London with Robert Carrier into a successful series of upscale restaurants established during the 1960s and 1970s. While overseeing these restaurants, he published cookbooks and, starting in the 1990s, produced television programs and started a cooking school in Buenos Aires. For additional information on U.S. chefs, see http://www.kqed.org/food/jacquespepin/; and "James Beard" and "Emeril Lagasse," *Encylopaedia Britannica Online* (accessed 26 October 2010). On Gato Dumas, see Haydeé Lin and Patricio Clavin, "El chef de buen vivir," *Semana Gráfica*, 19 May 2004, 4–8.

17. For further analysis of this topic, see chapter 2; see also Tobin, "Manly Acts," 53–54; and Caldo, "Petrona: Cocinera y educadora." Beef consumption statistics are drawn from Junta Nacional de Carnes, Secretaria de Agricultura y Ganadería, *Junta Nacional de Carnes: Síntesis estadística*, 143.

18. As late as 1999, Michael Jiménez explained that Latin America's "middle classes" were still absent from most studies of Latin America, despite John J. Johnson's book illuminating the importance of studying what he dubbed the "middle sectors" of Latin America some four decades earlier. Ezequiel Adamovsky published the first book-length history of the middle class in Argentina in 2009. And 2012 brought two new important edited volumes that historicize the middle class in Latin America and transnationally. See Johnson, *Political Change in Latin America*; Jiménez, "Elision of the Middle Classes and Beyond"; Adamovsky, *Historia de la clase media*; Parker and Walker, *Latin America's Middle Class*; and López and Weinstein, *The Making of the Middle Class*.

19. See, for example, Germani, "La clase media"; and Rock, "Argentina in 1914," 86.

20. While Ezequiel Adamovsky has argued that a politicized "middle-class" identity emerged in Buenos Aires during the 1920s and 1930s and strengthened during the 1940s in response to Peronism, David Parker describes an earlier process in Lima, Peru (starting in the late 1910s and solidifying in the 1920s), and Brian Owensby identifies a similar trajectory in urban Brazil to that of Buenos Aires. See Adamovsky, *Historia de la clase media*; Owensby, *Intimate Ironies*; and Parker, *The Idea of the Middle Class*.

21. See Míguez, "Familias de clase media"; and Cosse, *Pareja, sexualidad, y familia en los sesenta*.

22. Rocchi, *Chimneys in the Desert*.

23. In contrast to historiographical trends for many other parts of Latin America, histories of race and ethnicity in twentieth-century Argentina have been few in number. Recent work that addresses race includes Adamovsky, *Historia de la clase media*; Garguin, "'Los argentinos decendemos de los barcos'"; Guano, "Denial of Citizenship"; and Margulis and Urresti, *La segración negada*.

24. Chamosa, *Argentine Folklore Movement*, 2; Moya, *Cousins and Strangers*, 56.

25. Recent genetic studies have concluded that around half of the current Argentine population has indigenous heritage and some 10 percent has African heritage. For a discussion and citations, see Adamovsky, *Historia de la clase media*, 64, especially n17.

26. While the European and indigenous culinary trends are better acknowledged by scholars and everyday Argentines alike, Daniel Schávelzon points to *mondongo* (stew made with cow innards) and pureed squash as two clear Afro-Argentine legacies. Schávelzon, *Historias del comer y del beber en Buenos Aires*, 71–72.

27. Ana C. Cara explains that whereas during the colonial era the term *criollo* meant "of the Americas" or "American," by the nineteenth century it had come to identify members of particular national communities like Argentina. In the early twentieth century, she explains, "what was criollo was either romanticized and idealized or considered backward and interfering with progress. It was closely associated with the countryside, orality (illiteracy), with poverty or a lower social class, and yet was considered to embody essential local values and seen as in 'danger' of disappearing." Cara, "The Poetics of Creole Talk," 39.

28. José Juan Arrom provides a useful etymology of the term *criollo* for Latin America up through 1950. In his recent study of Argentine folklore, Oscar Chamosa elected to use the terms *mestizo criollos* or *rural criollos* to refer to mixed-race peasants and rural workers. Arrom, "Criollo;" and Chamosa, *Argentine Folklore Movement*, especially pp. 2, 196n3.

29. I have generally left this term in its original Spanish so as not to conflate it with the historical meanings attached to the terms "housewife" and "homemaker" in English. Historically, the term *ama* referred to women's dominance in their own homes (*casas*), as well as poor women's subservience in the homes of others (that is, a wet nurse was designated an *ama de leche* and a head housekeeper was an *ama de llaves*). The way *ama de casa* was used in twentieth-century Argentina is closest to "homemaker," a term that, unlike the term "housewife," does not implicitly require a husband or necessarily suggest that one does not also do paid work.

30. Guy, "Women, Peonage, and Industrialization."

31. Francois, "Products of Consumption."

32. República Argentina, *Resultados generales del Censo de la población 1947*; República Argentina, *Censo Nacional 1960*; República Argentina, *Censo Nacional de población familias y viviendas 1970*.

33. Dora Barrancos and Marcela Nari explore this issue in Argentina, while Elizabeth Quay Hutchinson makes this point for Chile, and Carolina H. Wainermann and Zulma Recchini de Lattes look at this issue transnationally. See Barrancos, *Mujeres en la sociedad argentina*, 139–48; Nari, *Políticas de la maternidad*, 78–84; Hutchinson, *Labors Appropriate to Their Sex*, 38–47; and Wainermann and Recchini de Lattes, *El trabajo femenino en el banquillo de los acusados*.

34. Guy, "Women, Peonage, and Industrialization"; Liernur, "El nido de la tempestad," 8. For an excellent analysis of the history of women's remunerated work, see Lobato, *Historia de las trabajadoras*.

35. Deutsch, *Crossing Borders, Claiming a Nation*, 4.

36. James, *Doña María's Story*; Lobato, "Lenguaje laboral," 95–115.

37. Adelman, *Frontier Development*; Scobie, *Revolution on the Pampas*; Sabato, *Agrarian Capitalism and the World Market*; Peter Smith, *Politics and Beef in Argentina*.

38. While historians (Caldo, Arcondo, and Remedi) have focused on the nineteenth and early twentieth centuries, anthropologists (Alvarez and Pinotti, Archetti,

and Tobin) have focused on the contemporary period. See Caldo, *Mujeres cocineras*; Arcondo, *Historia de la alimentación en Argentina*; Remedi, *Entre el gusto y la necesidad*; Alvarez and Pinotti, *A la mesa*; Archetti, "Hibridación, pertenencia y localidad en la construcción de una cocina nacional"; and Tobin, "Patrimonializaciones gastronómicas," 27–46.

39. For example, in addition to my work there have been only two other scholarly articles that have focused on Petrona C. de Gandulfo. Caldo, "Petrona: Cocinera y educadora"; and Chesterson, "Chickens Need Hot Ovens." The Argentine company Metro-Gas also commissioned a recent book that focuses on Doña Petrona's relationship to the gas industry; see Tartarini, *Doña Petrona, la cocina y el gas*.

40. For more on masculinity and *asado*, see chapter 2; Tobin, "Patrimonializaciones gastronómicas"; and Tobin, "Manly Acts."

41. Petrona C. de Gandulfo published other specialized cookbooks to respond to the changing interests and preoccupations of Argentines, including *Para aprender a decorar* (Learning How to Decorate) in 1941; *Cómo cocina Doña Petrona con ollas a presión* (How Doña Petrona Cooks with Pressure Cookers) in 1953; *Recetas económicas* (Economical Recipes) in 1962; and two low-calorie collections, *Coma bien y adelgace* (Eat Well and Get Thin) and *Bajas calorías* (Low Calories) during the 1970s. They sold well, but *El libro de Doña Petrona* continued to outsell and outlast them all.

42. Gandulfo, unpublished memoirs, 52.

43. Orlando Barone, "Petrona de Gandulfo: La reina de la cocina," *La Razón*, 19 June 1985, n.p.

44. Ignacio Covarrubias, "La conocida profesora nos habla de su iniciación en el arte culinario," ca. 1931, courtesy of *La Nación*; "Cirugía, como toda una diva," *Crónica*, 14 August 1983, 25; M. B., "La mujer, el hogar, el niño: Acaba de aparecer un nuevo libro de cocina dietética," *La Nación*, ca. 1972, courtesy of *La Nación*.

45. Petrona C. de Gandulfo, "Al margen de las conferencias de 'El Hogar,'" *El Hogar*, 27 September 1935.

46. *Para Ti*, 30 September 1974, 90.

47. For example, the bookseller who first told me about *El libro de Doña Petrona* in 2001 and later Blanca Cotta, who was a colleague of Doña Petrona's, both called this book the "bible of the home." Blanca Cotta, interview by author.

48. Stella M. D., interview by author.

49. During the 1970s, economic conditions led rich Argentines and poor Argentines to develop two significantly different types of diets. For analysis, see chapter 6; and Aguirre, "Gordos de escasez."

50. Portelli, *Battle of Valle Giulia*.

51. Emilia S. and Livio S., interview by author.

52. This collection is analyzed in depth by Eduardo Elena and is also available in the *Archivo General de la Nación*. See Elena, *Dignifying Argentina*; and Elena, "What the People Want."

53. This argument, as well as my approach to oral history, is inspired by the work of historian Ann Farnsworth-Alvear. See Farnsworth-Alvear, *Dulcinea in the Factory*, especially p. 4.

54. Jason Scott Smith (and some other scholars he cites) argues against the use of decades to organize historical studies in U.S. history. However, as Smith himself acknowledges, during the twentieth century these became meaningful ways in which people understood and recalled their lives. Further, attention to gender-based change is something that Alexandra Shepard and Garthine Walker argue has been in short supply, due to many feminist scholars' focus on the continuity of patriarchy. Jason Scott Smith, "The Strange History of the Decade"; Shepard and Walker, "Gender, Change, and Periodisation."

55. I also explore these relationships in my article "Entertaining Inequalities: Doña Petrona, Juanita Bordoy, and Domestic Work in Mid-Twentieth-Century Argentina."

56. As Nara Milanich argues, such gendered expectations were actually relatively new and unique to the mid-twentieth century and therefore not so traditional after all. Milanich, "Women, Gender, and Family in Latin America."

57. Prieto, *El discurso criollista*, especially p. 18.

58. For book-length treatments of commensality, see Anigbo, *Commensality and Human Relationships among the Igbo*; Ohnuki-Tierney, *Rice as Self*; and Sutton, *Remembrance of Repasts*.

59. For a useful explanation of the meanings and scholarly uses of the term "commensality," see Anigbo, *Commensality and Human Relationships among the Igbo*, especially chapter 1. For a different (but still face-to-face) way in which commensality adapts in a different "modern" context, see Traphagan and Brown, "Fast Food and Intergenerational Commensality in Japan."

60. As we shall see, Doña Petrona sought to appeal to fans in Argentina and beyond, responding, for example, to fan mail from Peru and broadcasting a television program in Uruguay. Even so, it was within Argentina that Doña Petrona and her recipes found their greatest and most enduring success.

61. Anderson, *Imagined Communities*. For a critique of Anderson's argument as it pertains to nineteenth-century Latin America, see Castro-Klarén and Chasteen, *Beyond Imagined Communities*.

62. Claude Grignon argues that this exclusionary tendency is even more important than its inclusionary function. Grignon, "Commensality and Social Morphology," 23–33.

Chapter One

1. Gandulfo, *El libro de Doña Petrona*, 1st ed., 340. Unless otherwise stated, all translations are mine.

2. Marcelo Vidales, "Maestra en la cocina y best seller nacional," *La Prensa*, 11 October 1998, 24.

3. As quoted in Cotta, "Los 100 mejores recetas de Doña Petrona," *El Clarín*, insert 5, p. 100; "Dejó de existir Doña Petrona," *La Nación*, 7 February 1992, n.p.

4. Olga C. G., interview by author.

5. As discussed elsewhere, the meaning of the term *criollo* (creole) shifts over time and place. Here it describes particular foods that combine European and indigenous rural influences.

6. Oscar Chamosa's recent book provides the richest account in English to date. Chamosa, *Argentine Folklore Movement*.

7. Conversation with Marcela Massut, January 2004.

8. Sarmiento was president from 1868 to 1874. Sarmiento, *Facundo: Civilización y barbarie*.

9. There are conflicting accounts of when Petrona Carrizo was born, and I have not been able to locate a definitive birth certificate. While she claimed to be born on 29 June 1898 in her memoirs, in some interviews, and even on her *libreta civil* (identity card), there are several other newspaper articles and interviews that list her birth year as 1896. Given her desire to appear younger, I suspect that her birthday was either then or as early as 1890—the 1895 national census records list a "Petrona Carrizo" of Santiago del Estero as five years old. "Argentina National Census, 1895," database, FamilySearch, 2009; from Archivo General de la Nación. Argentina national census 1895. Archivo General de la Nación, Buenos Aires, Argentina; FHL microfilm, Family History Library, Salt lake City, Utah, https://www.familysearch.org (accessed 26 May 2011).

10. Gandulfo, unpublished memoirs, 7. Gandulfo's untitled memoirs were compiled by biographer Oscar Alberto Cejas at some point during the late 1980s.

11. Lullo and Garay, *La vivienda popular de Santiago del Estero*.

12. Gandulfo, unpublished memoirs, 7.

13. In her memoirs, Petrona described her mother as a *criolla oriunda de la provincial* (creole native to the province) on p. 4. For more on the use of the term *criolla/o*, see the introduction.

14. Gandulfo, unpublished memoirs, 68.

15. Given his last name, Manuel Carrizo was likely of Castilian and not Basque origin. Ibid., 4.

16. I have been unable to find a marriage certificate for Petrona's parents, but I have found birth certificates that appear to be for Petrona's siblings Manuel and Carolina, which list "Clementina Carrizo" as the mother and do not list a father. However, because Petrona referred to her mother as Clementina Ramasco in her memoirs, I do the same. Argentina National Census, 1895, database, FamilySearch, 2009; from Archivo General de la Nación. Argentina National Census, 1895. Archivo General de la Nación, Buenos Aires, Argentina. Microfilm, Family History Library, Salt lake City, Utah, https://www.familysearch.org (accessed 15 February 2011).

17. A 1909 government census found that only 48 percent of children ages six to fourteen were attending school in Santiago del Estero. Tenti, "Escuela y centenario el caso de Santiago del Estero," 3.

18. She translated this phrase in Spanish as *bien venido sea señor*, loosely, "You are welcome here." Gandulfo, unpublished memoirs, 85.

19. In 1869, Diego de la Fuente, the director of the first national census in Argentina, characterized the population of Santiago del Estero as largely "descended from the mixture of Indians of Quechua origin [*indios de raza quiche*] and Spaniards." Primer Censo Nacional, 1869, 304, as cited in Tasso, *Ferrocaril, quebracho y alfalfa*, 219.

20. Gandulfo, unpublished memoirs, 10.

21. Torado, *Historia de la familia*, 262–66.

22. Starting in the 1870s, home economics manuals imported from Europe instructed elite women in Argentina on how to more effectively manage their homes and their domestic servants. Liernur, "El nido de la tempestad," 8.

23. Martin y Herrera, *Código de instrucción primaria, colección de leyes, decretos, acuerdos, reglamentos y disposiciones vigentes*, Ley de la educación, Art. 1, 28 July 1884, 16.

24. For an excellent analysis of the ideas, tensions, and politics surrounding women's maternal roles, see Nari, *Políticas de la maternidad*.

25. Law 5.291 in 1907 stipulated a six-hour workday for women. Wainerman and Navarro, "El trabajo de la mujer en la Argentina," 17–18.

26. Email correspondence with Paula Lucía Aguilar, 9 January 2012.

27. In the United States, Megan J. Elias explains that a number of early home economists were also suffragists. Elias, *Stir It Up*, 8–9.

28. Paula Lucía Aguilar notes that this school had limited enrollment and success. Aguilar, "El hogar como problema y como solución."

29. Ibid.; Caldo, "Pequeñas cocineras," 6.

30. The individualist approach, in which each student completed the entire task herself, was popular in England and the United States. Guillen, "Instalación de una cocina escolar," 330–40.

31. Guillen, "Algunas observaciones sobre el funcionamiento de las clases de cocina," 182–86; Guillen, "Enseñanza de la cocina en la escuela primaria," 189.

32. Prinvalle, *Lecciones de economía doméstica*, 7. This book seems to have been in circulation in Argentina, judging from its presence at the Education Ministry.

33. Armus, *The Ailing City*, especially pp. 156–61.

34. He dedicated this book to his wife for her "efficient collaboration on this text." Bassi, *Gobierno: Administración e hiegene del hogar*, especially pp. 9, 17; Caldo, "Pequeñas cocineras."

35. For analysis of Bassi, see Caldo, *Mujeres cocineras*, 73–90; on eugenics, see Stepan, *"Hour of Eugenics."*

36. Nari, *Políticas de la maternidad*, 71–77.

37. Nari, "La educación de la mujer," 45.

38. Petrona's education preceded Bassi's reforms, and Guillen herself had recently acknowledged the lack of actual kitchens in the public schools. Guillen, "Algunas observaciones sobre el funcionamiento de las clases de cocina," 182–86.

39. "Dejó de existir Doña Petrona," *La Nación*, 7 February 1992, n.p.

40. Dr. J. B. Zubiar, "La enseñanza práctica e industrial en la República Argentina," *El monitor de la educación común* 403 (21 July 1906): 437–38.

41. Ibid., 437.

42. Adamovsky, *Historia de la clase media*, 84–89.

43. Consejo Nacional de Educación, *Digesto de instrucción primaria, leyes, decretos, resoluciones vigentes para las escuelas y dependencias del Consejo Nacional de Educación*, 279–80, 292.

44. On the early dynamics of domestic service across Latin America, see Francois, "Products of Consumption."

45. Cecilia Hermann, interview by author.

46. Ibid.

47. Figueredo moved to Buenos Aires around 1870, most likely from Uruguay or Brazil, and worked as a cook for wealthy families there. This and Figueredo's other cookbooks have proven very difficult to find; therefore I rely on Arcondo's analysis of them. Arcondo, *Historia de la alimentación en Argentina*, 223–27.

48. Tobin, "Manly Acts," 53.

49. Iriarte and Torre, "Juana Manuela Gorriti."

50. Arcondo points out that Castex added several recipes to later editions of this cookbook from her travels to Europe. While the tenth edition in 1895 had 413 recipes, her 1940 edition had 1,052, many of which were inspired by European restaurants and travels. Arcondo, *Historia de la alimentación en Argentina*, 227.

51. Caldo, *Mujeres cocineras*, 136.

52. Congregación de Hijas de María y de Santa Filomena de Tucumán, *El arte de cocinar.*

53. Caldo, *Mujeres cocineras*, especially chap. 4.

54. Gandulfo, unpublished memoirs, 7–8.

55. Ibid., 9–10.

56. Modern amenities mentioned by visitors as lacking included paved roads, trolley cars, European cafés, and shops with imported goods. Tasso, *Historia testimonial argentina*; Gandulfo, unpublished memoirs, 10.

57. The 1914 census registered 23,470 people in the city of Santiago, making it the fifteenth-largest city in Argentina at the time. República Argentina, *Tercer Censo Nacional*, 469. For an excellent economic and social history of this province during this era, see Tasso, *Ferrocarril, quebracho y alfalfa.*

58. Tasso, *Historia testimonial argentina*, 58.

59. Fazio, *Memoria descriptiva de la provincia de Santiago del Estero*, as cited in Tasso, *Historia testimonial argentina*, 60.

60. Leandro Losada describes this trend in Buenos Aires, while Fernando Remedi does so for Córdoba. Losada, *La alta sociedad en la Buenos Aires*, 204–8; Remedi, *Entre el gusto y la necesidad*, 141–52.

61. For example, Petrona recalls eating empanadas at her great-grandfather's wedding. Gandulfo, unpublished memoirs.

62. Lullo, *El folklore de Santiago del Estero*, 84.

63. For more on Santiago's migratory workforce, see Faberman, "Trabajar con fuentes parcas en regiones marginales"; Tasso, *Ferrocarril, quebracho y alfalfa*; and Chamosa, *Argentine Folklore Movement.*

64. For analysis of the harvesting of trees and alfalfa, see Tasso, *Ferrocarril, quebracho y alfalfa.*

65. "Alimentación Nacional en las Provincias de Catamarca, Rioja, Santiago del Estero y Tucumán," *Boletin de Sanidad Militar* 7, no. 1 (January 1895): 392.

66. Lobato, *Historia de las trabajadoras*, 36.

67. For complaints about the scarcity and conditions of lodging, see travelers' reports from Tasso, *Historia testimonial argentina*, especially pp. 44, 50.

68. Gandulfo, unpublished memoirs, 50.

69. "Goyo" C., interview by author.

70. Olga C. G., interview by author.

71. "Goyo" C., interview by author.

72. Radio broadcast, 23 May 1967, Rollo 306, Band 1, Pies 125–35, Archivo General de la Nación.

73. Gandulfo, unpublished memoirs, 13.

74. Ibid., 14–15.

75. Ibid., 15.

76. President Sarmiento labeled Manuel Taboada, with disgust, "the President of the North." Lascano, "Los Taboada."

77. While she does not specify exactly what made this marriage "illegitimate," some likely possibilities include a common law marriage or children born out of wedlock. Gandulfo, unpublished memoirs, 14.

78. Ibid., 17.

79. Ibid., 18.

80. In subsequent media interviews, she sometimes referred to Beatriz as her daughter. For example, Mario Mactas, "Para comerte mejor," *Gente*, 25 September 1969, 53.

81. Gandulfo, unpublished memoirs, 19.

82. On women's virginity and honor in Brazil during this period, see Caulfield, *In Defense of Honor*. On gender and honor in nineteenth- and early twentieth-century Latin America more broadly, see Caulfield, Chambers, and Putnam, *Honor, Status, and Law in Modern Latin America*.

83. Gandulfo, unpublished memoirs, 20.

84. Ibid.

85. Ibid.

86. Ibid., 21.

87. As previously mentioned, it is difficult to track the exact dates of some major events in Petrona's early life history, including for this move. I have calculated this date based on her explanation in her memoirs that she moved to the Taboada estancia when she was fifteen years old and stayed there for five years. If this was accurate, and if she was indeed born in 1896, then she would have been twenty years old in 1916 when she moved to Buenos Aires.

88. Whereas the census registered 58 percent of the Argentine population as rural in 1895 and 42 percent as urban, by 1914 these percentages had exactly flipped. Lobato and Suriano, *Atlas histórico*, 568.

89. Ibid., 566.

90. The third national census noted that there were 539 men for every 461 women in the capital city in 1914, a ratio quite similar to that of 1895. República Argentina, *Tercer Censo Nacional*, 131; Romero, *History of Argentina*, 11.

91. Nari, *Políticas de la maternidad*, 71.

92. Deutsch, "Visible and Invisible Liga Patriotica Argentina," 252.

93. This article is a copy of a presentation that María Luisa Mégy gave at the Museo Escolar Sarmiento, sponsored by the Sociedad de Cultural Popular. María Luisa Mégy, "Prácticas del hogar," *El monitor de la educación común* 536, no. 62 (1917): 108, 113.

94. Donna Guy demonstrates that nineteenth-century public hygiene specialists criticized the urban poor for their unsanitary moral shortcomings rather than

recognizing the structural inequalities under which they suffered. Guy, *White Slavery and Mothers Alive and Dead*, especially p. 124.

95. Garguin, "El tardío descrubimiento de la clase media en Argentina"; Adamovsky, *Historia de la clase media*.

96. Adamovsky, *Historia de la clase media*, especially p. 235.

97. Míguez, "Familias de clase media."

98. Sandra McGee Deutsch points out, for example, that Jewish women would replace apple with quince to make the filling for their strudels. Deutsch, *Crossing Borders, Claiming a Nation*, 32.

99. For additional analysis of food history during this era, see Arcondo, *Historia de la alimentación en Argentina*; Caldo, *Mujeres cocineras*; and Remedi, *Entre el gusto y la necesidad*.

100. For analysis of French dining culture and its expansion, see Ferguson, *Accounting for Taste*, especially pp. 3, 33–34; for more on eugenic thought, see Stepan, *"Hour of Eugenics"*; on the upper class, see Losada, *La alta sociedad*.

101. Schávelzon, *Historias del comer y del beber en Buenos Aires*, 54–69.

102. Losada, *La alta sociedad*, 204–8.

103. For the ambivalence of nation making, see Sarlo, *Una modernidad periférica*; on folkloric culture, see Chamosa, *Argentine Folklore Movement*. On gauchos, see Slatta, *Cowboys of the Americas*; and Moya, *Cousins and Strangers*, especially p. 363.

104. Bergero, *Intersecting Tango*, 37–40.

105. Patricio Bernabé, "El Cordon Bleu de Baldi," *Cuisine e Vins* (1990).

106. Bergero, *Intersecting Tango*, 19.

107. Arcondo, *Historia de la alimentación en Argentina*, 194.

108. Caldo, *Mujeres cocineras*.

109. Gandulfo, unpublished memoirs, 21.

110. Recent scholarship in other contexts in Latin America demonstrates the importance of women's (and children's) participation in the informal economy. See, for example, Blum, *Domestic Economies*; Milanich, *Children of Fate*; Putnam, *The Company They Kept*; and Weinstein, *For Social Peace in Brazil*.

111. Gandulfo, unpublished memoirs, 99.

112. From 1914 to 1917, unemployment shot up to 19.4 percent, whereas it had previously been under 7 percent. Lobato and Suriano, *Nueva historia argentina*, 347. For analysis of race and region vis-à-vis employment and social mobility, see Adamovsky, *Historia de la clase media*.

113. Gandulfo, unpublished memoirs, 26.

114. The percentage of female *estancieras* reported by the census dropped from 19.2 percent in 1895 to 7.3 percent in 1914. Lobato, *Historia de las trabajadoras*, 36.

115. Adamovsky points out that government workers enjoyed higher status, if often less pay, than their commercial counterparts. Adamovsky, *Historia de la clase media*, 125.

116. Gandulfo, unpublished memoirs, 27.

117. Enrique O. Sdrech, "Doña Petrona C. de Gandulfo: El sabor de la vida a los 91," *El Clarín*, 29 July 1987, 51.

118. Most male chefs trained in Europe. Angel Baldi had previously studied baking with his uncle in Italy and served as Germain Mairet's assistant in Buenos Aires before buying the academy from his boss when he retired. María Adela Baldi, interview by author.

119. Enrique O. Sdrech, "Doña Petrona C. de Gandulfo: El sabor de la vida a los 91," *El Clarín*, 29 July 1987, 51.

120. Petrona C. de Gandulfo, "La nota que nunca tuvo," *Mucho Gusto*, May 1981, 7.

121. In 1922, for example, the National Department of Work calculated that the average male *obrero* (worker) made 6.50 pesos per day. República Argentina, Dirección General de Estadística de la Nación, "El costo de la vida y el poder de compra de la moneda" (8 February 1924). For quote, see Miriam Becker, "Gracias, Petrona C. de Gandulfo," *Mujer*, 31 January 1984, 15.

122. Gandulfo, unpublished memoirs, 67.

123. "Doña Petrona: El hombre puede ayudar, incluso a encerar," *Tiempo Argentino*, 20 March 1983, 4.

124. Adamovsky, *Historia de la clase media*, especially p. 235.

125. "Cirugía, como toda una diva," *Crónica*, 14 August 1983, 25.

126. "Doña Petrona celebra sus bodas de oro en la cocina profesional," *La Nación*, 8 May 1981, 4.

127. Argentine Law 11.537 on Women's Civil Rights, passed in 1926, stipulated that married women could seek employment and keep income they earned themselves, even as community property was still administered by the husband. Still, it was not until 1968 that Law 17.111 granted married women full civil capacity and equal property rights and significantly modified the administration of marital property so that now both husband and wife held control over the property earned or inherited during marriage. Htun, *Private Lives, Public Policies*.

128. "Doña Petrona: El hombre puede ayudar, incluso a encerar," 4; Lobato, "Lenguaje laboral," 95–115, especially p. 100.

129. Florencia Ure, "Doña Petrona C. de Gandulfo, 95 años vividos en plenitud," *Todo Chic*, 28 July 1991.

130. Gandulfo, unpublished memoirs, 27.

131. Ibid., 2.

132. Lobato, *Historia de las trabajadoras*.

133. Nari, *Políticas de la maternidad*, 78–84; figures as cited in Guy, "Women, Peonage, and Industrialization," 66.

134. Mirta Lobato calculates these particular percentages for the years from 1914 to 1917. The census registered the majority of working women as among the unskilled menial or semiskilled labor force, with 90 percent of those deemed "unskilled" working in domestic service as of 1914. Lobato, "Lenguaje laboral," 108; República Argentina, *Tercer Censo Nacional*, 201–12, as analyzed and cited in Walter, *Politics and Urban Growth*, 12.

135. Argentina, Congreso Nacional, *Diario de Sesiones de la Cámara de Diputados*, 1920, Tomo 1 (Buenos Aires: Imprenta y Encuadernacion de la H. Cámara de Diputados, 1920), 526, as cited in Wainermann and Navarro, "El trabajo de la mujer," 18.

136. Nari, "Maternidad, política y feminismo," 197–243; Nari, *Políticas de la maternidad*, 84–88.

137. For analysis of the changing perception of women's work, see Liernur, "El nido de la tempestad"; and Lattes and Wainerman, "Empleo femenino y desarrollo económico."

138. Barrancos, *Mujeres en la sociedad argentina*, 145. For an in-depth historical analysis of this issue and other women's work, see Lobato, *Historia de las trabajadoras*.

139. Lobato points to the new expectations about beauty, manners, technology, and seduction; my work emphasizes women's roles as consumers and cooks and Petrona's ambassadorial role in this regard. Lobato, *Historia de las trabajadoras*, 106.

140. Winbaum et al., *The Modern Girl around the World*; Cott, "Modern Woman of the 1920s, American Style," 76–91.

141. The logo might also have referred to the significant role that black women played in eviscerating meat. Molina, *Para mi hogar*, 16.

142. Ibid.

143. Toer et al., *Historias del gas*, 21.

144. Primitiva had lost 6 million pesos in business during this period. Ibid., 24.

145. Rocchi, "Inventando la soberanía," 301–21.

146. For these and other examples of advertisements, see Fundación Metrogas, *Historia de la publicidad del gas en la Argentina*, 16–17.

147. Available in Toer et al., *Historias del gas*, 25.

148. Rocchi, "Inventando la soberanía," 308; Borrini, *El siglo de la publicidad*, 12.

149. Adamovsky, *Historia de la clase media*, 69.

150. Available in Toer et al., *Historias del gas*, 25.

151. Clendinning, *Demons of Domesticity*.

152. Salas, *Apuntes para la historia de la cocina chilena*, 153n15.

153. Patricio Bernabé, "El Cordon Bleu de Baldi," *Cuisine e Vins* (1990): 114.

154. In Castilian Spanish, *económo* at first referred to a man in charge of administering church properties and later was extended to mean bookkeepers and accountants more broadly. Alonso, *Enciclopedia del idioma*, entry "ecónomo." The standard-bearer of Castilian Spanish, *Diccionario de la lengua Española de la Real Academica Española*, still does not include an entry for the female version of this term.

155. I found a few dictionaries published in Argentina during the 1990s that included the term *ecónoma* at the Biblioteca Nacional in Buenos Aires. Despite the lack of an earlier dictionary that included this term, it is clear that the female version of this word was in public usage by the late 1920s when Primitiva was publicly promoting its *ecónomas*. A dictionary of *Argentinismos* (Argentinisms) published in 1993 defined an *ecónoma* as a "woman in charge of providing advice about the economy of the home, especially about the purchase and preparation of foods." This exact same definition is also included in the dictionary of *Uruguayismos* but is not included in the dictionary of *Colombianismos* or *Mexicanismos* published by the same institute. Nevertheless, a January 2011 search of the Google books collection for the term *ecónoma* turned up a reference to *ecónoma* as a possible career (with no description) in a 1908 Chilean primary education manual, entitled *Dispociones*

relativas al servicio de instrucción primaria. Further, a 1902 description written by Mexican governor Jose Vicente Villada described an *ecónoma* as a woman who oversaw the domestic work of a school. *Nuevo Diccionario de Argentinismos*, entry "ecónoma."

156. Marcelo Vidales, "Maestra en la cocina y best seller nacional," *La Prensa*, 11 October 1998, 24.

157. Ofelia F., interview by author.

158. Carretaro, *Vida cotidiana en Buenos Aires*, 70.

159. Ofelia F., interview by author.

160. "Nunca me guarde secretos," *La Nación*, 28 February 1988, 16.

161. Enrique O. Sdrech, "Doña Petrona C. de Gandulfo: El sabor de la vida a los 91," *El Clarín*, 29 July 1987, 51.

162. As quoted in Cotta, "Los 100 mejores recetas de Doña Petrona," *El Clarín*, insert 18, p. 417.

163. Petrona C. de Gandulfo, "La nota que nunca tuvo," *Mucho Gusto*, May 1981, 5.

164. María Cristina Dillon, interview by author.

165. Tartarini, *Doña Petrona, la cocina y el gas*, 24.

166. Toer et al., *Historias del gas*, 24.

167. Apparently, President Hipólito Yrigoyen's friend Scarlatto asked Petrona's brother-in-law, Emilio, to pass along this request. Gandulfo, unpublished memoirs, 51.

168. Ballent, "La 'casa para todos.'"

169. Correspondence with Oscar Chamosa, 15 February 2011.

170. Gandulfo, unpublished memoirs, 62.

171. As mentioned in the introduction, Petrona frequently reiterated that she was an *ecónoma* and not a cook, emphasizing that no one could say that they had "had Doña Petrona in their kitchen at any time." Orlando Barone, "Petrona de Gandulfo: La reina de la cocina," *La Razón*, 19 June 1985, n.p.

Chapter Two

1. Gandulfo, *El libro de Doña Petrona*, 1st ed. (1934), 385.

2. As Fernando Rocchi explains, around this time Siam di Tella began selling ice cream machines primarily to bakeries rather than to individual consumers. Rocchi, "La americanización del consumo," 171.

3. Suffrage struggles reached a high point in 1932. The Argentine Senate considered various proposals for female suffrage but, as Gregory Hammond explains, "proved surprisingly reluctant to tackle the issue" (*The Women's Suffrage Movement*, 124). While none of the major parties opposed female suffrage outright, opponents of this legislation ultimately succeeded in stalling it by arguing that the cost to register female voters was too high. For further analysis, see Hammond, *The Women's Suffrage Movement*, especially pp. 121–25; Barrancos, *Mujeres en la sociedad argentina*, 156–71; and Palermo, "El sufragio femenino en el Congreso Nacional."

4. "Charlas sobre la urbanidad," *El Hogar*, 21 August 1931, 18.

5. For analysis of primary and professional schools as well as a generational breakdown of women's work, see Torado, *Historia de la familia*, 199–200, 212. For statistics on university education, see Hollander, "Women: The Forgotten Half," 153.

6. While the decline in male-led foreign immigration is well documented, the rise in female-led migration is much less so for this and subsequent eras. Guy, "Female-Headed Migrant Families in Buenos Aires."

7. República Argentina, *Cuarto censo general, 1936*, 227.

8. "Doña Petrona: El hombre puede ayudar, incluso a encerar," *Tiempo Argentino*, 20 March 1983, 4.

9. Gandulfo, unpublished memoirs, 32–33.

10. In numerous interviews, she described how she initially balked at this promotion because she did not like "to pull the rug out from under anyone." "Doña Petrona a 50 años de su primer libro, habla con Emmy de Molina, su amiga y colega," *La Prensa*, 9 April 1984, 4; Marcelo Vidales, "Maestra en la cocina y best seller nacional," *La Prensa*, 11 October 1998, 24.

11. Ulanovsky, *Paren las rotativas*, 33.

12. Tartarini, *Doña Petrona, la cocina y el gas*, 24.

13. *El Hogar*, 24 April 1931, 60.

14. Gandulfo, unpublished memoirs, 29.

15. Ibid.

16. Ibid., 30.

17. The announcement for *El Hogar*'s "salon de conferencias" specified this number, even as Petrona later recalled this hall as holding 1,000 people; it seems likely that she was referring to the larger hall she performed in for *Caras y Caretas*. *El Hogar*, 24 April 1931, 60; "Nunca me guarde secretos," *La Nación*, 28 February 1988, 16.

18. Florencia Ure, "Doña Petrona C. de Gandulfo, 95 años vividos en plenitud," *Todo Chic*, 28 July 1991; "Doña Petrona a 50 años de su primer libro, habla con Emmy de Molina, su amiga y colega," *La Prensa*, 9 April 1984, 4.

19. For example, *El Hogar*, 24 June 1931, 42.

20. Amalia Iadarola, "Petrona Carrizo de Gandulfo: La sartén por el mango," *Gente*, 2 November 1970, n.p.

21. There are few early photos of the full conference hall at *El Hogar*; the photo from her ca. 1936 performance in Rosario (p. 61) reflects the seating policy.

22. Amalia Iadarola, "Petrona Carrizo de Gandulfo: La sartén por el mango," *Gente*, 2 November 1970, n.p.

23. Gandulfo, unpublished memoirs, 57.

24. "Doña Petrona: El hombre puede ayudar," 4.

25. Tartarini, *Doña Petrona, la cocina y el gas*, 28.

26. *El Hogar*, 22 May 1931, 12. For analysis of ideas about "modern women" and sports, see Bontempo, "Las entusiastas modernas juegan al golf y al tenis."

27. María Angelica del Campo, "La mujer moderna y las conferencias de El Hogar," *El Hogar*, 22 May 1931, 12.

28. "Clausura del primer curso de conferencias de 'El Hogar,'" *El Hogar*, 18 December 1931, 54.

29. Weinstein, "Unskilled Worker, Skilled Housewife," especially p. 91.

30. Correspondence with Ann Farnsworth-Alvear, September 2011.

31. As Anahi Ballent has demonstrated, during the 1930s Argentine architects established the basic traits of the "modern" home in which each room in a single-family home served a unique purpose. Ballent, "La 'casa para todos.'"

32. Bontempo, "'Para aquellas mujeres equivocadamente modernas.'"

33. *El Hogar*, 29 January 1932.

34. Ofelia F., interview by author.

35. Ibid.

36. Most had two last names connected by the honorable "de," which told their contemporaries that they were born to an officially married mother and father and officially married to a man who had the same "legitimate" bearing. *El Hogar*, 8 May 1931, 36–37.

37. Tartarini, *Doña Petrona, la cocina y el gas*, 26.

38. "Clausura del primer curso," *El Hogar*, 18 December 1931.

39. Ibid.

40. Gandulfo, unpublished memoirs, 30.

41. Gastón Lazzari describes this chronology in great detail in "Las recetas de cocina en las revistas argentinas."

42. *El Hogar*, 1933, as cited in Tartarini, *Doña Petrona, la cocina y el gas*, 43.

43. "Doña Petrona: El hombre puede ayudar," 4.

44. "Nunca me guarde secretos," *La Nación*, 28 February 1988, 16.

45. *El Hogar*, 8 September 1933, 46.

46. *El Hogar*, 14 April 1933, n.p.

47. *Para Ti*, 3 October 1933, 46.

48. I am extremely grateful to Christine Ehrick for sharing this announcement and subsequent coverage from entertainment press with me. "Gente Conocida y Escuchada," *Sintonia*, 4 November 1933.

49. Enrique O. Sdrech, "Doña Petrona C. de Gandulfo: El sabor de la vida a los 91," *El Clarín*, 29 July 1987, 51.

50. For a social history of Argentine radio that describes this chronology as well as the process of creating a massive radio audience, see Matallana, *"Locos por la radio,"* especially p. 35, for comparative statistics.

51. For a discussion of the use and meanings of the term "soundscape" for radio scholars, see Ehrick, "'Savage Dissonance,'" especially pp. 71–75.

52. Claxton, *From Parsifal to Perón*, 128.

53. As Ehrick points out, the magazine *Antena* published a June 1931 interview in which Guerrico "described her show's content as 'frivolous,' because it focused on impractical matters such as poetry and poking fun at men rather than recipes and stain removal." For further analysis of Guerrico's rise and demise, see Ehrick, "'Savage Dissonance,'" especially pp. 75–83.

54. "Gente Conocida y Escuchada," *Sintonia*, 4 November 1933.

55. Ibid.

56. For further analysis of the presence and meanings of music, and especially tango, on the radio, see Karush, *Culture of Class*; and Claxton, *From Parsifal to Perón*, 123–25.

57. He moved his show to Radio La Nación's larger stage in 1933. Gallo, *La radio*, 205.

58. Rocchi, "Inventando la soberanía."

59. Claxton, *From Parsifal to Perón*, 122–25.

60. Rocchi, "La americanización del consumo," 176. For a historical sketch of programming directed toward women, see Gallo, *La radio*, 197–206.

61. For an analysis of such programming, see Matallana, *"Locos por la radio,"* 99–101.

62. Gandulfo, unpublished memoirs, 30.

63. As Robert Claxton points out, Radio El Mundo was the first capital city station to deliberately broadcast across the country, starting in 1935. Nevertheless, receiver owners in the provinces reported picking up other channels previously. They also had access to local stations. Claxton, *From Parsifal to Perón*, 66–67.

64. Matallana, *"Locos por la radio,"* 128–29.

65. Florencia Ure, "Doña Petrona C. de Gandulfo, 95 años vividos en plenitud," *Todo Chic*, 28 July 1991.

66. "La penúltima: Esto pasó un 6 de febrero," *El Clarín*, 6 February 2003, n.p.

67. Gandulfo, unpublished memoirs, 31.

68. "Nunca me guarde secretos," *La Nación*, 28 February 1988, 16.

69. Enrique O. Sdrech, "Doña Petrona C. de Gandulfo: El sabor de la vida a los 91," *El Clarín*, 29 July 1987, 51.

70. Gandulfo, unpublished memoirs, 32.

71. Florencia Ure, "Doña Petrona C. de Gandulfo, 95 años vividos en plenitud," *Todo Chic*, 28 July 1991; Gandulfo, unpublished memoirs, 31.

72. Petrona C. de Gandulfo, "La nota que nunca tuvo," *Mucho Gusto*, May 1981, 6–7.

73. Gandulfo, unpublished memoirs, 97.

74. For an in-depth analysis of this cookbook and the women behind it, see Mendelson, *Stand Facing the Stove*.

75. Gandulfo, unpublished memoirs, 32.

76. Doña Petrona's cookbook sold for seven pesos in 1934. A study by the National Institute of Nutrition in Buenos Aires estimated that a working-class family could feed itself properly for about 77 pesos per month. It suggested a breakfast of coffee with milk, bread, butter, and cheese; a mid-morning snack of *mate cocido* with milk, bread, and butter; a lunch of lentil soup, *puchero* (a traditional, modest dish featuring boiled beef and vegetables), bread, and bananas; and a dinner of buttered noodles, potato and Swiss chard *tortilla* (omelet), and bread. According to Cecilia Lanata Briones's analysis of statistics gathered by the Departmento Nacional de Trabajo (1935, 1937), the Dirección de Estadística Social (1947), and the Secretaría Tecnica (1947), the average worker in Buenos Aires made about 126 pesos per month in 1934 and spent more than 60 percent of this income on food. Escudero, *La alimentación de la familia en Buenos Aires*, 73, 77–80; Briones, "Revising the Standard of Living," 7.

77. Gandulfo, unpublished memoirs, 51.

78. Ibid., 32.

79. Enrique O. Sdrech, "Doña Petrona C. de Gandulfo: El sabor de la vida a los 91," *El Clarín*, 29 July 1987, 51.

80. Interestingly, she included a repetition of her explanation about how to keep one's hands clean and white (which she would also include in the first two editions of the cookbook). *Rosalinda*, August 1934, courtesy of Marcela Massut.

81. Petrona C. de Gandulfo, "La nota que nunca tuvo," *Mucho Gusto*, May 1981, 7.

82. Isay K. and Mary T., interview by author; Luis L. C., interview by author.

83. Pilcher, *¡Que vivan los tamales!*, 1.

84. In Argentina, as elsewhere, recipes cannot be copyrighted. For a discussion of the ethics of recipe accreditation, see Heldke, "Let's Cook Thai," 175–98.

85. "Doña Petrona a 50 años de su primer libro, habla con Emmy de Molina, su amiga y colega," *La Prensa*, 9 April 1984, 4. Unfortunately, she never said which cookbooks she consulted, and the remaining collection of Petrona's cookbooks, held by her granddaughter, postdates the first edition of *El libro de Doña Petrona*.

86. Gandulfo, prologue to *El libro de Doña Petrona*, 1st ed. (1934).

87. "El libro de Doña Petrona," *La Nación* (16 December 1934), n.p., courtesy of *La Nación*.

88. Torado, *Historia de la familia*, 194–99.

89. Gandulfo, prologue to *El libro de Doña Petrona*, 1st ed. (1934).

90. Caldo, "De mujer a mujeres."

91. Ibid.

92. As discussed later in the book, only in the 1960s and 1970s would a self-consciously nationalistic *criollo* cuisine emerge in Argentina.

93. See Appadurai, "How to Make a National Cuisine"; and Revel, *Culture and Cuisine*.

94. This is not to suggest that these other places, like France, have entirely bounded cuisines, but rather that they often have deeper and more consistent (if still quite region-specific) shared culinary roots. Gabaccia, *We Are What We Eat*.

95. Caldo, "De mujer a mujeres."

96. Gandulfo, *El libro de Doña Petrona*, 1st ed. (1934).

97. Caldo points to the first explanation and Tobin to the second. Caldo, "De mujer a mujeres"; Tobin, "Manly Acts," 53–54.

98. Gandulfo, *El libro de Doña Petrona*, 1st ed. (1934), 10. Despite the prevalence of female domestic help during this period in all but the most elite households, it is noteworthy that Petrona used the masculine form of the term *mucamo*. When used generically, as in this case, this term could refer to either male or female servants.

99. Gandulfo, *El libro de Dona Petroña*, 20th ed. (1945), 14.

100. As this has long been a frequently undocumented part of the economy, census (and other) statistics tend to underestimate the number of homes with paid domestic help. Germani, "La clase media," 123.

101. Gandulfo, *El libro de Doña Petrona*, 1st ed. (1934), 9.

102. Germani concluded that the *porteño* middle class had grown to 46 percent of the population by 1936, from 36 percent in 1914. Germani, "La clase media," 107–9.

103. Looking back from some four decades later, Manuel Mora y Araujo made a similar argument. Mora y Araujo, "Las clases medias consolidadas," 267; Germani, "La clase media," 127.

104. Enrique Garguin and Ezeqiel Adamovsky agree that a sense of shared middle-class identity did not truly emerge until the 1940s; Adamovsky further challenges the notion of shared upward social mobility prior to this era. See Garguin, "El tardío

descrubimiento de la clase media en Argentina," 3–5; and Adamovsky, *Historia de la clase media*, 43–51.

105. Germani, "La clase media," 112–14.

106. Ibid., 111.

107. Bagú, *La clase media en la Argentina*, 12–15.

108. The ad included a photograph of the author and her cookbook, specifying that it "contains more than 100 color illustrations, exact recipes and clear and precise explanations." Advertisement for *El libro de Doña Petrona*, *El Hogar*, 63, n.d., courtesy of Marcela Massut.

109. "Al margen de las conferecias del 'El Hogar,'" *El Hogar*, 25 May 1934, 73.

110. *El Hogar*, 22 May 1931, 43.

111. The following numbers of people from the various provinces received printed responses in *El Hogar* from June 1934 through November 1935: Santiago del Estero, 5; Tucumán, 4; Salta, 4; La Pampa, 4; Corrientes, 4; Formosa, 3; Chaco, 3; San Juan, 3; San Luis, 2; Rio Negro, 2; Neuqén, 2; Mendoza, 1; and Jujuy, 1.

112. Nine lived in nearby Uruguay, which often shared a media market with Argentina; two lived in Peru; and there was one each from Brazil and Venezuela.

113. Just 13 of her 400 printed responses were addressed to women whose elite status was marked by their use of the honorable "de" and two last names. Perhaps some were embarrassed that they did not know how to cook; or, alternatively, like previous generations of elites, perhaps they feared that their public association with cooking would link them with their supposed inferiors.

114. For example, on 21 December 1934, Petrona C. de Gandulfo replied to one woman with the Spanish surname Iriarte, another with the Italian name Romano, and a third with the possibly Japanese name Miki (which, alternatively, could have been a nickname for Micaela).

115. Response to Carlos A. Morand, "Al margen de las conferencias del 'El Hogar,'" *El Hogar*, 25 January 1935, 73.

116. "Al margen," *El Hogar*, 10 August 1934.

117. For example, see Petrona C. de Gandulfo's column of 11 October 1935 in *El Hogar*.

118. For this new policy, see *El Hogar*, 14 December 1934, 73; and for a typical response from Petrona, see Gandulfo, "Al margen," *El Hogar*, 27 September 1935, 69.

119. "Al margen," *El Hogar*, 18 January 1935.

120. Accompanying a photograph in 1935 from a recent conference, *El Hogar* explained that many of her fans referred to this *ecónoma* as "Doña Petrona." *El Hogar*, 7 December 1935.

121. "Al margen," *El Hogar*, 4 January 1935, 73.

122. For example, ibid., 27 July 1934, 69.

123. Ibid., 20 July 1934, 75.

124. Ibid., 31 August 1934, 75.

125. Ibid., 24 August 1934, 73.

126. She does not mention whether the notebooks were returned to the readers, but this seems probable; otherwise it is surprising that so many women would have been willing to part with them. Gandulfo, unpublished memoirs, 30.

127. It seems from her memoirs that she organized this contest in 1934 or 1935. Ibid., 31.

128. This estimate of over a million is from Karush, *Culture of Class*; for an analysis of the various estimates of radio sets and an explanation of how Karush arrived at this number, see p. 60, n53.

129. Others broadcasting food-related content on the radio during the 1930s and 1940s included Juan Máspero on Radio Prieto, Amanda C. Rosso de Ramella on Radio Exelsior, and Petrona's mentor Angel Baldi on Radio El Mundo. There was also a show called *Para el hogar y la mesa*. Gallo, *La radio*, 205.

130. Gandulfo, unpublished memoirs, 31.

131. Claxton, *From Parsifal to Perón*, 70.

132. Ibid., 32.

133. Gandulfo, unpublished memoirs, 31.

134. For example, Claxton points out that the popular actress Libertad Lamarque earned a mere thirty pesos a month for radio work. Claxton, *From Parsifal to Perón*, 133.

135. Ulanovsky recalled that her first programs were sponsored by firms selling various products, which ranged from "pans to butter." Conversation with Carlos Ulanovsky, 11 November 2003, Buenos Aires.

136. Many men came home for lunch during this period, and some of them listened to this program (and its advertisements) with their wives and, frequently, the rest of the family. For example, a man in his sixties mentioned that he and his siblings used to tune in to Petrona on the radio with their mother when they were growing up during the 1940s. Eduardo R., interview by author.

137. Sutro, "Radio in Latin America (Part 1)," as cited in Claxton, *From Parsifal to Perón*, 38.

138. *Caras y Caretas*, 1936, 16, courtesy of Marcela Massut.

139. This cross-promotion provided a more subtle way for Primitiva to promote its product. *Caras y Caretas*, 1 August 1936, 16.

140. See, for example, *Caras y Caretas*, 19 September 1936.

141. "El arte de cocinar por Petrona C. de Gandulfo," *Caras y Caretas*, 15 August 1936, n.p. Gandulfo, *El libro de Doña Petrona*, 6th ed. (Buenos Aires: Talleres Gráficos Compañía General Fabril Financiera, 1939), after p. 288, ill. no. 19. It is likely that she actually added this recipe sometime before 1939, most likely in 1937, after she began to work with *Caras y Caretas*.

142. "El arte de cocinar," *Caras y Caretas*, 15 August 1936, 100. Further, in future recipe columns she referred readers back to previous recipes in previous editions.

143. Gardella collected recipes from 1935 to 1939 in this beautifully arranged book. Her niece, a professor at the Universidad de la Pampa, generously introduced me to this text and told me a little bit about her aunt, who was originally from Rosario and later moved to Santa Rosa. Among the recipes she collected were Doña Petrona's recipes for *empanadas santiagueñas*.

144. "El arte de cocinar," *Caras y Caretas*, 29 August 1936.

145. Claxton points to the ubiquity of such surveys during this era. Claxton, *From Parsifal to Perón*, 124–25; for quote, see *Caras y Caretas*, 5 September 1936.

146. "El arte de cocinar," *Caras y Caretas*, 16 January 1937, 98.

147. The caption for one photograph showing a woman reading an edition of the magazine explained that "to beneficially follow the lessons, there is no better text than the pages of *'Caras y Caretas'* in which the teacher explains her acts." "El arte de cocinar," *Caras y Caretas*, 4 September 1937, 40.

148. "El arte de cocinar," *Caras y Caretas*, 21 August 1937, 98.

149. *Caras y Caretas*, 12 September 1936 and 26 September 1936, 95.

150. "El arte de cocinar," *Caras y Caretas*, 5 December 1936, 98.

151. This was in the eighth conference advertisement, *Caras y Caretas*, courtesy of Marcela Massut.

152. Each raffle ticket cost twenty cents. See, for example, *Caras y Caretas*, 25 September 1937, 98, and 2 October 1937, 165.

153. Guy, *Women Build the Welfare State*.

154. Ramón Gallardo, "Con El Corazon En Santiago; Petrona Carrizo de Gandulfo," *Fundación Cultural Santiago del Estero* 9 (April 2001). Petrona C. de Gandulfo's relatives in Santigo del Estero confirmed these details. Gallardo speculates that this adoption might have inspired her to be so committed to helping children's charities, like the Patronato de la Infancia, throughout her career.

155. Gandulfo, unpublished memoirs, 100.

156. Ibid., prologue.

157. For more on infertility and adoption, see Guy, *White Slavery and Mothers Alive and Dead*; and Villalta, "La apropiación de 'menores.'"

158. Gandulfo, unpublished memoirs, 34.

159. Junta Nacional de Carnes, Ministerio de Agricultura, *Informe de la labor realizada desde el 1 de octubre 1935 hasta el 30 de septiembre de 1937*.

160. Schleh, "La alimentación en la Argentina," 20.

161. Escudero, *La alimentación de la familia en Buenos Aires*, 3–4.

162. Within these studies, carried out in the 1930s and 1940s, Escudero and his colleagues recommended daily menus to better meet dietary and economic needs.

163. He drew this conclusion based on a 1936 survey of the relationships among economic resources, nutrition, and health in the families of *obreros* (workers) and *empleados* (employees) living in Buenos Aires. Escudero, "Estudio técnico económico de la alimentación de 159 familias de obreros y empleados de la ciudad de Buenos Aires," 225.

164. *Almanaque del Ministerio de Agricultura de la Nación*, 111.

165. Ibid., 112.

166. It was an industry that had supported the 1933 Roca-Runciman Treaty, which guaranteed British consumption of Argentine beef in exchange for much larger economic concessions for British interests in Argentina. For more on this treaty, see Rock, *Argentina, 1516–1987*, 223–27.

167. However, in her main cookbook she accompanied this dish with *papitas a la parisienne* (Parisian Potatoes). Gandulfo, *El libro de Doña Petrona*, 1st ed. (1934), 178.

168. Gandulfo, *Los cortes de carnes y su utilización*.

169. D'Amato, "El problema de la alimentación en la República Argentina," 402.

170. Ortiz died of diabetes-related complications in 1942.

171. Escudero, *La alimentación de la familia en Buenos Aires*, 30.

172. Conversation with Marcela Massut.

173. The number of copies of each edition was not listed after the first, which specified 5,000 copies.

174. *Caras y Caretas*, 28 August 1937, 106.

175. My friend Lorena T., who worked as a maid for the family who owned this cookbook originally at the governor's household, generously gave me this copy of *El libro de Doña Petrona* and shared its history with me. Gandulfo, *El libro de Doña Petrona*, 6th ed. (Buenos Aires: Talleres Gráficos Compañía General Fabril Financiera, 1939).

Chapter Three

1. Gandulfo, *El libro de Doña Petrona*, 23d ed. (Buenos Aires: Atlántida, 1947), 322–23.

2. She included specific instructions about timing for preparations in at least the first through the sixth editions of her cookbook. See, for example, Gandulfo, *El libro de Doña Petrona*, 6th ed. (Buenos Aires: Talleres Gráficos Compañía General Fabril Financiera, 1939), 284.

3. In the oral history workshops I conducted in Villa Luro, a variety of participants expressed how Juan and Eva Perón's approach made them feel like part of a national family. For a thoughtful and well-researched examination of the relationship between the Peronist government and the newspaper industry, see Cane, *The Fourth Enemy*.

4. Ballent, "La 'casa para todos,'" 24.

5. Florencia Ure, "Doña Petrona C. de Gandulfo, 95 años vividos en plenitud," *Todo Chic*, 28 July 1991; "Doña Petrona a 50 años de su primer libro, habla con Emmy de Molina, su amiga y colega," *La Prensa*, 9 April 1984, 4.

6. Miriam Becker, "Gracias, Petrona C. de Gandulfo," *Mujer*, 31 January 1984.

7. She had taken a brief public hiatus from this venue when the magazine *Caras y Caretas* folded in 1938, but in 1940 she began to sign a new recipe column in the magazine *Para Ti*. She apparently consulted for *Para Ti* during this interim, as evidenced by her 1938 letterhead in which she refers to herself as an adviser to this magazine.

8. Bontempo, "'Para aquellas mujeres equivocadamente modernas.'"

9. "Para el menú," *Para Ti*, 15 October 1940 and 3 June 1941.

10. "Para el menú," *Para Ti*, 1 April 1941 (polenta); 6 May 1941 (empanadas and *pastelitos*).

11. Luis L. C., interview by author.

12. Isay K. and Mary T., interview by author. Isay started to distribute Petrona's cookbooks through his company Tres Américas in 1964, as will be discussed in chapter 4.

13. I have calculated this figure based on the exact print runs for the ninth through the thirteenth editions and the twenty-first through the twenty-ninth. I have estimated that there were 6,000 copies printed for the fourteenth through the twentieth editions, since the thirteenth edition, which preceded this period, had 6,600 copies printed, and the twenty-first edition, which succeeded it, had 10,000 copies. It is possible that Atlántida actually published twenty-three new editions, as I have been unable to locate the thirtieth and thirty-first editions to determine the publishers. In the thirty-second

edition, published in 1949, Talleres Gráficos de la Cía Gral is the publisher. Fabril Financiera is once again listed on the last page as the printing house.

14. I have used the same calculations to arrive at this figure for the period 1941 through 1946.

15. As discussed in chapter 4, Lola P. de Pietranera's *El arte de la mesa: Recetario de Doña Lola* offered the greatest threat, but Doña Lola's lack of interest in appearing on radio or television made her and her cookbook less of a household name than that of Doña Petrona. Other cookbooks published during this decade include the Compañía Italo Argentina de Electricidad's *Cocinando con placer: Recetas selectas para cocinas eléctricas* and Eyzaguirre's *El libro del buen comer*.

16. Gandulfo, *El libro de Doña Petrona*, 9th ed. (1941).

17. Rocchi, "La americanización del consumo," 135.

18. Gandulfo, *Para aprender a decorar* (Buenos Aires: Atlántida, 1941). Atlántida printed 10,000 copies of the first edition on 15 July and released the ninth edition of *El libro de Doña Petrona* on 15 December of the same year.

19. As discussed in chapter 5, despite this success, the second edition was not released until 1964, apparently due to the high printing costs for a book with so many illustrations.

20. "6 libros interesantes para la mujer," *Para Ti*, 2 June 1942, 74.

21. Elba A. de B., interview by author. Elba was seventy-six years old in 2003 and described herself as being of *criollo* and German descent. She moved to a suburb of Buenos Aires in the 1970s.

22. Gandulfo, unpublished memoirs, 47.

23. Elba A. de B., interview by author.

24. Rock, *Argentina, 1516–1987*, 236–37, 241.

25. In 1941, the United States passed the Lend-Lease Act, which provided arms to several Latin American nations. The largest number went to Brazil, generating significant concern in Argentina. Ibid., 243.

26. Gandulfo, unpublished memoirs, 35.

27. Lattes and Lattes, *Migraciones en la Argentina*.

28. Gandulfo, *El libro de Doña Petrona*, 20th ed. (1945), 12 (emphasis added).

29. Ibid., 11.

30. Instituto Alejandro Bunge, *Soluciones argentinas a las problemas económicos y sociales del presente*, 162, as cited in Torado, *Historia de la familia*, 166.

31. Oral history workshop in Villa Luro, 3 February 2004.

32. Gandulfo, *El libro de Doña Petrona*, 12th ed. (Buenos Aires: Editorial Atlántida, 1943). The cookbook I consulted in Marcela Massut's personal collection includes Petrona's handwritten edits.

33. Isay K. and Mary T., interview by author.

34. Luis L. C., interview by author.

35. Ibid. Further, in 2003 and 2004 a number of male taxi drivers told me that they sometimes used *El libro de Doña Petrona* to cook, although most said they did so infrequently and had only done so during the past two or three decades, after men's cooking (beyond *asado*) had come into vogue, as discussed in chapter 6.

36. Ofelia F., interview by author.

37. María del Carmen, *Mucho Gusto*, May 1981, 45.

38. Emmy de Molina, "Homenaje a doña Petrona," *La Prensa*, 16 April 1990, 10.

39. Irene Cristina "Pelusa" Molina, interview by author.

40. Ibid.

41. Elba A. de B., interview by author.

42. Royal set up shop in Argentina in 1935. For a list of other international firms that established themselves in Buenos Aires during the 1930s and early 1940s, see Lobato and Suriano, *Atlas histórico*, 369.

43. See, for example, *Para Ti*, 11 November 1947, 62, and 8 June 1948, 66.

44. Carretaro writes that Royal's booklet was the most successful of any such corporate effort. Carretaro, *Vida cotidiana en Buenos Aires*, 89.

45. For analysis of this march as a moment of class consciousness, see James, "October 17th and 18th, 1945," 444.

46. Adamovsky, *Historia de la clase media*, 245–50.

47. James, *Resistance and Integration*; James, "Perón and the People."

48. Rock, "Survival and Restoration of Peronism," 187.

49. For an excellent analysis of such policies, see Elena, *Dignifying Argentina*.

50. Elena, "Peronist Consumer Politics," 120.

51. James, "Perón and the People."

52. James, *Doña María's Story*, 71, 99.

53. Rock, "Survival and Restoration of Peronism," 187.

54. Torre and Pastoriza, "La democratización del bienestar," especially p. 307.

55. For a thoughtful analysis of how such anxiety manifested itself in daily life, see Milanesio, "Peronists and Cabecitas."

56. See, for example, Garguin, "El tardío descrubimiento de la clase media en Argentina"; and Adamovsky, *Historia de la clase media*.

57. For analysis of the self-presentation and reception of Eva Perón, see Julie M. Taylor, *Eva Perón: The Myths of a Woman*; Fraser and Navarro, *Eva Perón*; and Plotkin, *Mañana es San Perón*.

58. Elena, "Peronist Consumer Politics."

59. Galé, *El gas de la Argentina*, 79.

60. Gandulfo, *El libro de Doña Petrona*, 21st ed. (Buenos Aires: Atlántida, 1946), after p. 168.

61. Galé, *El gas de la Argentina*, 97–101.

62. Even more dramatically, by the end of 1960, five years after Perón left office, the state supplied about 1.3 million homes. Toer et al., *Historias del gas*, 28–30.

63. Belini, "La industria durante el primer peronismo," 587. Belini explains that in 1946 the production value of this industry was 45,280 pesos corrientes, which grew to 1,259,845 pesos corrientes by 1957.

64. As Natalia Milanesio has determined, the Peronist government was eager to direct consumers away from electric stoves because natural gas was less expensive than electricity, and the government wished to use electricity for industrial purposes. Milanesio, "Industry, Nation, and Energy in Peronist Argentina."

65. Lazzari, "Carbón, kerosene, gas."

66. Bähler, *La nación Argentina*, 119.

67. This document was published in *Revista Mundo Argentino* on 27 November 1946.

68. She did eventually share the story with her family and some close friends, although she never mentioned it in any media reports that I have seen. Olga C. G. and Olga A. G., interview by author; Isay K. and Mary T., interview by author.

69. See, for example, Eva Perón, *La razón de mi vida.*

70. Navarro, "Evita," 338.

71. The first quote and the reference to the home as the center of the country come from a speech by Eva Perón, "Dedicado a la mujer argentina y su derecho a elegir y ser elegida," given on 12 February 1947, as reprinted in Eva Perón, *Discursos completos*, vol. 1, 42; the second quote from Eva Perón as cited in Liscia, *Mujeres, maternidad y peronismo*, 9.

72. Eva Perón, *La mujer ya puede votar*, 11.

73. For analysis of the early feminist movement, see Lavrin, *Women, Feminism, and Social Change.*

74. Palermo, "El sufragio femenino en el Congreso Nacional."

75. For analysis, see Navarro, "Evita," 353; Deutsch, "Gender and Socio-Political Change," especially pp. 272–76; Hammond, *The Women's Suffrage Movement*, especially pp. 169–87. Quotes are drawn from Eva Perón, *Discursos completos*, vol. 1, 164 and 230.

76. From 1931 to 1940, there was a 74 percent increase in the number of female university students over the previous decade. Statistics as cited in Hollander, "Women: The Forgotten Half," 153.

77. By 1950, nearly 80 percent more women were employed in the industrial sector than in 1939, as compared to around 30 percent more men; this trend was even more pronounced in Buenos Aires. Ministerio de Asuntos Técnicos, Estadística Industrial, Buenos Aires (1939 and 1949–50), as cited in Hollander, "Women: The Forgotten Half," 45; Girbal-Blacha, "El hogar o la fábrica."

78. Walter, *Politics and Urban Growth*, 248.

79. Torado characterizes women's childbearing years as from twenty-five to thirty-four years of age. Torado, *Historia de la familia*, 210–13.

80. For a discussion of the relationship between Catholic and Peronist discourse, see Zabaleta, *Feminine Stereotypes and Roles*, 290–92.

81. As previously mentioned, such statistics should not be taken at face value, as they surely undercounted women's remunerated work.

82. For my discussion of the use of the term "maternalist" to designate domestic relationships of power among women, see Pite, "Entertaining Inequalities."

83. For analysis of these aesthetics, see articles by Barry, Ballent, and acha, in *La fundación Eva Perón y las mujeres.*

84. For analysis of Peru, see Drinot, "Food, Race, and Working-Class Identity"; on Mexico, see Aguilar-Rodriguez, "Cooking Modernity."

85. Speech by Eva Perón, "Al inaugurarse un Hogar de Transito," given on 19 June 1948, as reprinted in Eva Perón, *Discursos completos*, vol. 1, 235.

86. On nutrition, see Ramacciotti, "Las voces que cuestionaron la política sanitaria del peronismo," 190–91; Carolina Barry, interview with Delfina V., as cited in Barry,

"Mujeres en tránsito," 92; the menu from El Hogar de la Empleada is described in "Fueron habilitadas ayer las instalaciones del Hogar de la Empleada," *Democracia*, Buenos Aires, 20 January 1950, as cited in acha, "Dos estrategias," 167.

87. While the state revoked the licenses of a number of other radio stations, Leonardo Mindez explains that Miguel Maranda, "right-hand man to Perón," took over most decisions at Radio El Mundo. Cosse describes Radio El Mundo (and Radio Belgrano) as those with the broadest social reach. Mindez, *Canal siete*, 45; Cosse, "Relaciones de pareja a mediados de siglo en las representaciones de la radio porteña," 134.

88. "Petrona C. de Gandulfo actuará en 'El Mundo,'" *Radiolandia*, 22 February 1947.

89. *Radiolandia*, 8 March 1947.

90. Female participant, oral history workshop in Villa Luro, 10 February 2004.

91. Gandulfo, unpublished memoirs, 88.

92. See, for example, *Radiolandia*, 7 February 1948, 14 February 1948, and 21 February 1946.

93. In a similar vein, Eduardo Elena finds that the Peronist publication *Argentina* included not only state-led undertakings but also corporate advertisements. Elena, "Peronism in Good Taste."

94. "Doña Petrona: El hombre puede ayudar, incluso a encerar," *Tiempo Argentino*, 20 March 1983.

95. She explained in her unpublished memoirs that her second marriage was not as much about love as it was about having a "good companion." Gandulfo, unpublished memoirs, 35. For an excellent analysis of the 1944 earthquake in San Juan and how it changed this province and the nation, see Healey, *The Ruins of the New Argentina*.

96. Florencia Ure, "Doña Petrona C. de Gandulfo, 95 años vividos en plenitud," *Todo Chic*, 28 July 1991.

97. Navarro, "Evita," 366.

98. Gandulfo, *El libro de Doña Petrona*, 23d ed. (1947), 516. But the recipe still called for cognac.

99. Gandulfo, *El libro de Doña Petrona*, 26th ed. (Buenos Aires: Talleres Gráficos Compañía General Fabril Financiera, 1948), 22.

100. Ballent, "La 'casa para todos,'" 39–40.

101. Zurita, *El servicio doméstico en Argentina*, 12–13.

102. Torado, *Historia de la familia*, 211. In the 1914 census, census takers reported 49 percent of economically active women as working in domestic service and 28 percent as working in industry, commerce, and services (which did not include domestic service). In 1947, census takers reported 44 percent of economically active women as working in industry, commerce, and services and 28 percent as working in domestic service.

103. For analysis of this shift in Buenos Aires, see Moya, *Cousins and Strangers*, 247.

104. Pagani, "Aspectos estructurales."

105. This was part of a broader feminization of domestic work across twentieth-century Latin America. Francois, "Products of Consumption."

106. Marshall, "Inmigración, demanda de fuerza de trabajo e estructura ocupacional en la área metropolitana argentina," as cited in Gogna, "Domestic Workers," 84. For

a discussion of the relationship between slavery and early domestic service in Argentina, see Pagani, "Aspectos estructurales."

107. Further, as I discuss in chapter 4, Carlos Zurita argues that only a small minority of Argentine households (or around 9 percent) employed paid domestic help by the 1970s. Zurita, *El servicio doméstico en Argentina*, 13, 48–49.

108. Gandulfo, *El libro de Doña Petrona*, 26th ed. (1948). As of 1947, this "economically active sector" represented nearly a quarter of all Argentine women over the age of fourteen. Torado, *Historia de la familia*, 211.

109. See chapter 4 for a discussion of this staff, including Juanita Bordoy, who joined Petrona's household around 1945.

110. Isay K. and Mary T., interview by author.

111. Juan Domingo Perón, "Política alimentaria argentina," 33.

112. Ibid., 36.

113. Ibid., 37.

114. Ibid. Natalia Milanesio points out that beef consumption remained relatively low in the northern and southern parts of Argentina due to distribution problems, scarcity, and high prices. Milanesio, "Food Politics and Consumption," 86–88.

115. Juan Domingo Perón, "Política alimentaria argentina," 36.

116. Ibid., 37.

117. Ibid., 45.

118. Torre and Pastoriza, "La democratización del bienestar," 282.

119. For analysis of the Peronist government's celebration of Argentines' growing beef consumption prior to 1950, see Milanesio, "Food Politics and Consumption."

120. Juan Domingo Perón, "Política alimentaria argentina," 44–45. He noted that these replacements could be costly because there was greater demand than supply of such foods in Argentina.

121. Ibid.

122. For a thoughtful examination of Ramón Carillo and the politics of pulic health during the Peronist era, see Ramacciotti, *La política sanitaria del peronismo*; this specific quote is drawn from Carillo, "El criterio biológico en el reordenamiento económico de la alimentación en la Argentina," 53–54 (emphasis added).

123. James, *Doña María's Story*.

124. Natalia Milanesio points out that from 1933 to 1949 the amount an average working-class family with three children spent on beef doubled, while the amount it spent on fruit increased almost tenfold. Milanesio, "Food Politics and Consumption," 91. *Nuestras Mujeres* (Buenos Aires) (1 June 1949), 11. I am grateful to Karina Ramacciotti for finding and sharing this primary source with me.

125. For an analysis of these "queens of work," see Lobato, *Cuando las mujeres reinaban*.

126. For a suggestive analysis of a nationalist culinary turn under Perón that merits further research, see Milanesio, "Food Politics and Consumption"; on peñas, see Chamosa, *Argentine Folklore Movement*, 175–77.

127. Conversations with Isay K. and Marcela Massut.

128. In a 1996 interview, Libertad Lamarque (nicknamed *La novia de América*) stated that she was actually "grateful" to Eva Perón, because Lamarque's decision to

leave Argentina allowed her to "triumph." In turn, Niní Marshall's radio comic sketches were censored, beginning with the military government that took office in 1943. She was driven into exile in 1950, most likely at the hands of Eva Perón, whom Niní was rumored to have parodied at a party dressed as a prostitute, as Christine Ehrick recently suggested. Chávez, "Libertad Lamarque," 45; Ehrick, "Chaplin in Skirts?"

129. In early 1946, before Perón's election, Borges signed a petition criticizing the military government. Perón subsequently demoted him from municipal librarian, offering him a job as "poultry inspector for fairs and exhibitions," which Borges refused. However, Flavia Fiorucci has recently demonstrated that the organization of writers in which Borges and other writers participated (SADE) adopted a much less openly resistant or political stance to protect the survival of their organization under Perón. Stabb, *Jorge Luis Borges*, 22; Fiorucci, "Between Institutional Survival and Intellectual Commitment."

Chapter Four

1. Gandulfo, *El libro de Doña Petrona*, 54th ed. (Buenos Aires: Atlántida, 1959), 269.

2. This recipe first appeared in *El libro de Doña Petrona* around 1947 as *Suprema de Pollo Mary Land*. At some point between 1951 and 1954, she changed "Mary Land" to one word. She cooked an updated version of this recipe on the program *Viernes Hogareños* in 1958.

3. Rombauer and Rombauer Becker, *Joy of Cooking*, 397–98; Shields, *Chesapeake Bay Cooking*, 130–31.

4. Petrona faithfully cut out and saved articles by Dix with titles such as "The Place of Women" and "The Advantages of Having a Husband." The first article was published in *Para Ti* on 11 January 1949; the second is not dated; both articles are in her personal papers, held by Marcela Massut.

5. As Enrique Garguin points out, the "middle class" as a self-conscious category grew in importance and ubiquity during the 1950s. Garguin, "El tardío descrubimiento de la clase media en Argentina." For an analysis of the image, as well as the more complicated reality, of the U.S. housewife, see Coontz, *The Way We Never Were*.

6. Laura Shapiro demonstrates that the U.S. food industry tried to take control of what families ate during this decade by encouraging the consumption of their processed products, but that many women (a great many of whom were still quite interested in cooking) and their families did not follow their lead. David Strauss documents the interest in gourmet dining in the United States starting in the 1930s. Shapiro, *Something from the Oven*; Strauss, *Setting the Table for Julia Child*.

7. See, for example, Plotkin, *Mañana es San Perón*, 211–96.

8. Organización de Consumidores, *¡Defienda sus pesos! ¡Vigile los precios! ¡No pague un centavo más!* as cited in Elena, "Justice and Comfort," 234–35.

9. Milanesio, "The Guardian Angels of the Domestic Economy."

10. Bautiza Aizcorbe, Alberto E. J. Fesquet, and Juan Manuel Mateo, *La mujer en la sociedad*, Conocimientos básicos, serie para 6 grado (Buenos Aires: Editorial Kapelusz, 1950), 64, as cited in Billarou, "El ama de casa 'moderna.'"

11. Aizcorbe, Fesquet, and Mateo, *La mujer argentina en el trabajo*, 3.

12. "Mi oficio de ama de casa me depara gratos momentos," *Mucho Gusto*, August 1950, 5–7.

13. Progreso de la medicina sanitaria en la Argentina, Tercera Conferencia del ciclo "Recientes conquistas de la sanidad argentina," given 21 February 1951 in *Contribuciones al conocimiento sanitario: Obras completas II*, 388–89, as cited in Billarou, "Cómo es fácil," 395.

14. *Boletín del Día* No. 347 (5 June 1951): 1007, as cited in Billarou, "Cómo es fácil," 393.

15. In particular, Billarou points to the club Boca Juniors, where reportedly more than a thousand women took cooking lessons. The other clubs where Billarou identified these classes include Huracán, Azul, Corrientes, Santa Fe, Rafaela, Esperanza, Puán, and Sierras Bayas. Billarou, "Cómo es fácil," 393.

16. Nari, "La educación de la mujer," 37–38.

17. Billarou, "Cómo es fácil," 396.

18. Eva Perón, *My Mission in Life*, 192.

19. Eva Perón, "Discurso en el acto inagural de la primera asamblea nacional del movimiento peronista femenino"; Eva Perón, *Discursos completos*, vol. 2, 87–89.

20. Barry, *Evita capitana*, 274–77.

21. Eva Perón, *My Mission in Life*, 190.

22. Eva Perón, *La razón de mi vida*, 114. For analysis, see Deutsch, "Gender and Socio-Political Change," 271–81.

23. Miriam Becker, "Gracias, Petrona C. de Gandulfo," *Mujer*, 31 January 1984, 17.

24. Amalia Iadarola, "Petrona Carrizo de Gandulfo: La sartén por el mango," *Gente*, 2 November 1970, n.p.

25. Conversation with Marcela Massut. An Argentine writing in from Córdoba to the Ministry of Technical Affairs also mentioned this shortage of paper on 20 December 1951. Archivo General de la Nación, Ministerio de Asuntos Técnicos, box 331, no. 6997.

26. Conversation with Marcela Massut. Monica Esti Rein points out that *La razón de mi vida* replaced *Don Quixote* as the required book in public school. Rein, *Politics and Education in Argentina*.

27. Castagna, "Petrona C. de Gandulfo."

28. She published 15,000 copies of the first four print runs (the twenty-ninth through the thirty-second editions) with Fabril Financiera in 1949, after which point she increased the print runs to 30,000 in 1950 and 1951 (the thirty-third through the thirty-ninth editions).

29. Plotkin, *Mañana es San Perón*, 165.

30. As cited in Romero, *Argentina: Una crónica total del siglo XX*.

31. Goldar, *Buenos Aires: Vida cotidiana en la década del 50*, 16–17.

32. Isay K. and Mary T., interview by author.

33. Emilia S. and Livio S., interview by author.

34. See chapter 1 for analysis of the term *ecónoma* and its history.

35. Gandulfo, *El libro de Doña Petrona*, 40th ed. (Buenos Aires: Talleres Gráficos Compañía General Fabril Financiera, 1952).

36. Ibid., 68.

37. The inclusion of fish was particularly interesting because Perón and Carillo had identified it as one of the "protective foods" that Argentines should eat more of. Further, as compared to beef and noodles, it was relatively expensive and difficult to obtain (outside of places near a river), so it seems unlikely that many people would have had leftover fish with which to make a new dish. This is supported by the aforementioned letter in *Nuestras Mujeres*.

38. Beines, *Las recetas de Doña Prestisima*; Simmons, *Cocinando con olla a presión*.

39. Gandulfo, *Cómo cocina Doña Petrona con ollas a presión*.

40. Gandulfo, *El libro de Doña Petrona*, 40th ed. (1952), 36–37.

41. Ibid., 39.

42. Ibid., 68–69.

43. Eva Perón, *La papa*.

44. Milanesio, "The Guardian Angels of the Domestic Economy," 106.

45. Rock, "Survival and Restoration of Peronism," 190.

46. Eva Perón, *La papa*, prologue.

47. Gonzalo Aguilar, "Televisión y la vida privada," 259.

48. For a history of this channel, see Mindez, *Canal siete*; for a description of Eva Perón's role, see Ulanovsky, Itkin, and Sirvén, *Estamos en el aire*, 25.

49. See Varela, *La televisión criolla*, especially pp. 54–58.

50. Unfortunately, we do not have access to this or any program from the 1950s, because the technology to tape television was not present in Argentina until the 1960s. Nielsen, *La magia de la televisión argentina*, 34.

51. *Diario Popular*, 22 September 1990.

52. Television broadcast, 1953, Legajo 1793, Inventario 1736, Tambor 786, 35 mm, S. Argentina, 979, N. Panamericano 902, Archivo General de la Nación.

53. First published in the late 1940s, *El arte de la mesa: Recetario de Doña Lola* had reached its sixth edition by 1955. The earliest edition I have been able to find is the third edition from 1951 and the latest is the thirteenth from 1961. Unfortunately, the print run is not listed on the publication page. Pietranera, *El arte de la mesa*.

54. Cecilia Hermann, interview by author.

55. María Adela Baldi, interview by author.

56. Ibid.

57. They recall the presence of elite students, like Susana Mitre de Pereyra Iraola and Elenita Ibarguren, as well as the "Galician" cooks who worked for these elite families, in an interview with *La Nación*. "Doña Lola: Refinada y familiar," *La Nación*, 16 July 2000, http://www.lanacion.com.ar/213282-dona-lola (accessed 2 April 2011).

58. Alfredo Arias, interview by author.

59. Oral history workshop in Villa Luro, 30 December 2003.

60. Oral history workshop in Villa Luro, 3 February 2004.

61. Ibid.

62. Ibid.

63. Etel L., interview by author.

64. Ana C., interview by author.

65. Olga G. de A., interview by author.

66. Ibid.

67. Oral history workshop in Villa Luro, 3 February 2004.

68. Gandulfo, *El libro de Doña Petrona*, 46th ed. (Buenos Aires: Talleres Gráficos Compañía Fabril Financiera, 1954), prologue. She also thanked God for the success she had achieved. It is possible that she changed her prologue and formatting in an earlier edition from 1953 or 1954.

69. The previous edition I consulted was the forty-first, which was published in 1952 and did not have the ingredients listed at the top. Petrona had previously separated out the ingredients in her 1938 cookbook for the Junta Nacional de Carnes and, more recently, for her 1952 pressure-cooker book, but this was still not the norm. For example, Lola P. de Pietranera's *El arte de la mesa* did not include ingredients lists.

70. Female participant, oral history workshop in Villa Luro, 10 February 2004.

71. Varela, *La televisión criolla*, 43.

72. "Telecocinando con Doña Petrona C. de Gandulfo," August 1954, typed letter (in possession of the author).

73. Ibid.

74. Further testifying to this dynamic, on at least one occasion Doña Petrona was apparently assisted on this program by the actress Mabel Landó, who played "a scatterbrained assistant." This performance played on the familiar cultural trope popularized by Lino Palacio in his comic *Ramona* during the 1930s and 1940s in *La Razón*. Nielsen, *La magia de la television argentina*, 83.

75. Hector B., interview by author.

76. Juanita said she began to work with Doña Petrona in 1945. Juanita's family puts the year between 1943 and 1945, and Petrona claimed it to be the year she started on television (1951) in her unpublished memoirs and as 1945 in other interviews. Miriam Becker, "Gracias, Petrona C. de Gandulfo," *Mujer*, 31 January 1984, 17.

77. Hector B., interview by author.

78. Juana Bordoy's relatives in Santa Rosa suggested that she was interested in working in a factory. Juana explained in a 1981 interview that she arrived in Buenos Aires with the dream of becoming a hairdresser or a seamstress. "Porota" B. (Juana's sister), Susana (her niece), María Lujan (her grandniece), and Luis (her nephew-in-law, married to Susana), interview by author. Hereafter, I refer to this interview as "Porota" B. and specify the person quoted. Cecilia Pardo, "Juanita: Una mano en la cocina y la otra en el corazón," *Mucho Gusto*, May 1981, 29.

79. "Porota" B., interview by author (Susana).

80. As quoted in Cotta, "Los 100 mejores recetas de Doña Petrona," *El Clarín*, insert 6, 132.

81. She explained that they eventually stopped sending out these recipe pamphlets when it became too expensive. The last printed pamphlet I have seen is from 1958. Radio broadcast, 23 May 1967, Rollo 306, Band 1, Pies 125–435, Archivo General de la Nación.

82. Below her recipes, the tagline announced that "the product that deserves the name Swift deserves your trust." "Telecocinando con Doña Petrona C. de Gandulfo," 1954, ephemera found for sale online. http://articulo.mercadolibre.com.ar/MLA-1037 58060-dona-petrona-receta-carta-co n-logo-original-_JM (accessed 14 March 2011).

83. I am grateful to media scholar Jorge Nielsen, who told me that this proposal appeared in *Sintonía* in November or December 1954.

84. Letter from Che Guevara to "Parents," 1955, as transcribed in Gadea, *Mi vida con el Che*, 124; and *My Life with Che*, 154. The first part of the translation is from the English version, while the last sentence is my translation of the original Spanish (especially the term *economistas*, which I think was meant to be singular and to refer to Gadea's profession rather than Doña Petrona's). I thank Ann Farnsworth-Alvear for bringing this reference to my attention.

85. Gadea, *My Life with Che*, 154.

86. Che Guevara was more critical than supportive of Peronism during the early 1950s, but he was ultimately quite dismayed by Perón's downfall. For her part, Gadea was more consistently sympathetic. Gadea, *My Life with Che*, 23, 75, 161; Elena, "Point of Departure," 34–36, 55.

87. Gadea, *My Life with Che*, 151–62.

88. Historians have characterized this period as one of political stalemate or gridlock. Luis Alberto Romero titles his chapter on the period from 1955 to 1966 "The Stalemate." David Rock titles his chapter on the period from 1955 to 1976 "A Nation in Deadlock." See Romero, *History of Argentina*, 131–72; and Rock, *Argentina, 1516–1982*, 320–66.

89. "La vecina de los presidentes," *La Nación*, 18 February 1985.

90. Romero, *History of Argentina*, 133.

91. Taberna, *La cocina de Lorenza Taberna*, 9.

92. Elena Zara de Decurgez, who had received the title of Profesora de Historia y Geografia from the Universidad Nacional de la Plata in 1922 and subsequently directed two schools in Buenos Aires, was the first woman elected to the Ministry of Education, in 1956. http://www.ligadeamasdecasa.org/la-institucion/quienes-somos/elena-zara-la-fundadora/ (accessed 11 April 2001). For analysis of homemakers' organizing during the 1980s and early 1990s, see Fisher, "Gender and the State in Argentina."

93. I found this information at http://www.ligadeamasdecasa.com.ar/index1.html (accessed 6 December 2005).

94. Passed in 1946, Law 12.919 was the first to guarantee domestic servants an annual salary and yearly vacation. See *Anales de la legislación argentina*, 18 December 1946. In turn, decreed Law 326/56 was published in the *Boletin Oficial* on 20 January 1956.

95. See Rojas, "El servicio doméstico, regimen jurídico," especially p. 120; and Cárdenas, *Ramona y el robot*, 124–25.

96. Grinberg, "El servicio doméstico en el derecho argentina," 6.

97. I develop this argument in greater detail in my article "Entertaining Inequalities: Doña Petrona, Juanita Bordoy, and Domestic Work in Mid-Twentieth-Century Argentina."

98. For an excellent discussion of how making domestic tasks appear to be the natural responsibility of women benefits men as a group, see Tinsman, "Indispensible Service of Sisters."

99. Hector B., interview by author. He also mentioned that "La Morocha" was a prototype of the Argentine woman.

100. For example, photographer Sebastián Friedman, who has taken photographs and collected stories of Argentine domestic servants, shared the story of María Concepción Alvarez with me in 2004. She explained to Friedman that as a young girl she was sent to the city to work as a domestic servant and that the family who hired her changed her name from María Concepción because they thought it was too "long and common." They began addressing her as Hilda, a name that remained with her for the rest of her life, in spite of the fact that it was not the one that her mother and father had chosen for her with "love."

101. Elvira P. and Esther P., interview by author; "Porota" B., interview by author.

102. Oyuela, *Cortesia y buenos modales*, 253. My thanks to Beatriz for bringing this book to my attention.

103. Goldar, *Buenos Aires: Vida cotidiana en la década del 50*, 127.

104. According to Mirta Varela, this represented about 19 per 1,000 Argentines. Varela, *La televisión criolla*, 41.

105. "Verdadero Éxito," 20 August 1957, Gandulfo, personal papers.

106. Cosse, "Argentine Mothers and Fathers."

107. Gandulfo, *El libro de Doña Petrona*, 54th ed. (1959), 662.

108. Cosse, "Argentine Mothers and Fathers."

109. Together with her third main sponsor, the cutlery company Gamuza, Swift and Royal helped her produce this recipe pamphlet, which included advertisements for their products. "Recetario: *Viernes Hogareños*, telecocinando con Doña Petrona C. de Gandulfo" (September–November 1958).

110. Ibid.

111. For analysis of the Frondizi government's ideas about modernization and developmentalism, see Altamirano, *Bajo el signo de las masas*, especially pp. 50–72.

112. As historian Valeria Manzano explains, "The middle class family constituted the ideal of respectability and stability that the country needed in order to prevent social chaos and cultural decay, the decay that Peronism allegedly represented." Manzano, "Sexualizing Youth," 441.

113. Romero, *History of Argentina*, 140–42.

114. Gandulfo, *El libro de Doña Petrona*, 52d ed. (1958), 41.

115. Ibid., 43. For example, she recommended cooking as many things as possible in the oven at the same time in order to save fuel and money.

116. Mirta Varela explains that, according to a 1952 report from the company, Siam di Tella had sold 500 percent more refrigerators in the last two years than during the 1940s. Varela, *La televisión criolla*, 51; Sibila Camps, "Los tiempos han cambiado," *El Clarín*, 1 October 1981, 4.

117. Gandulfo, *El libro de Doña Petrona*, 52d ed. (1958), 661.

118. See *El libro del ama de casa* (Buenos Aires: Aguilar, 1958), especially p. 11.

119. Lobstein, *365 días sin servicio doméstico*. For diagram, see after p. 16; for illustration, see p. 28.

120. Ibid., 10.

121. Ibid., 470.

122. Ibid., 9.

123. Carlos Zurita also makes this point in looking back at this period. Zurita, "Trabajo, servidumbre y situaciones de género," 3.

124. "Mucama perfecta sin sueldo se ofrece," *Claudia* (10 March 1958): 41.

125. Cárdenas, *Ramona y el robot*; Szretter, *La terciarización del empleo*, 10.

126. Torre and Pastoriza, "La democratización del bienestar," 277; Germani, "La movilidad social en la Argentina."

127. Gogna, "Domestic Workers," 84; Torado, *Historia de la familia*, 211; Zurita, *El servicio doméstico en Argentina*, 12–13.

128. Even as Gogna shows that the registered numbers of domestic servants would grow during the 1960s, Carlos Zurita estimates that only 9 percent of Argentine households employed full-time paid domestic help by 1970. Szretter finds similar but slightly higher numbers than Zurita, stating that there were around 10 domestic employees for every 100 homes from 1947 to 1970; his statistics do not include people who worked by the hour or in multiple homes. See Gogna, "Domestic Workers," 84; Zurita, *El servicio doméstico en Argentina*, 13, 48–19; and Szretter, *La terciarización del empleo*, 9–10.

129. For an example, see "Relaciones con el servicio doméstico," *Femirama* (ca. 1963–64): 26. I am grateful to Amalia Berardone for sharing this article with me.

130. Cárdenas, *Ramona y el robot*, 115.

131. Amalia Iadarola, "Petrona Carrizo de Gandulfo: La sartén por el mango," *Gente*, 2 November 1970, n.p.

132. In her personal papers, Petrona preserved five articles from the local newspaper from 1959 and extensive coverage in *Ecos* from 1959 and 1960.

133. *Canal TV*, 3 September 1959, 6.

134. Debate, Museo del Puerto Ingeniero White.

135. Nixon, "The Kitchen Debate."

Chapter Five

1. *Las recetas de Doña Petrona*, Volver, Archivo Dario Billani, 21, courtesy of Canal 13. Hereafter, I refer to this program as *Las recetas* followed by the number of the program. According to documentation with the tapes, the television channel Volver believes that this television series was broadcast in 1961. However, due to the presence of Annamaría Muchnik, who did not start to host *Buenas Tardes, Mucho Gusto* until 1964, it seems more likely to be from that or the following year.

2. Ibid., program 21.

3. Rosalia Cortés states that women's participation in the workforce rose "strongly" by 4 percent during the 1960s; David Rock claims that it rose by 5 percent. See Cortés, Dirie, and Braun, *Informe sobre el mercado de trabajo femenino en la Argentina*; and Rock, *Argentina, 1516–1982*, 332.

4. For more on the dynamics and impact of this choice, see Feijoo, Nari, and Fierro, "Women in Argentina during the 1960s," 12.

5. For example, in his anthropological study of the city of Paraná, in northeastern Argentina (for which much of the field work took place in the mid-1960s) Ruben E. Reina describes the disjunction between the popular perception of a homogenous

"middle class" (*clase media*) and the "greater variety of ethnic, occupational, and educational backgrounds" in that class than in the "lower class" (*clase baja*). Most residents considered themselves to be *clase media*, but Reina notes the discursive distinction between the *clase media baja* (lower middle class) and the regular and upper middle class. See Reina, *Paraná*, especially, pp. 102–4; 186–98; quote, p. 186.

6. Alejandra Vassallo argues that the relevance of women's local experiences and insights has been underappreciated by historians and by contemporaries who sought to denounce feminism as imperialist. Vassallo, "'Las mujeres dicen basta.'"

7. Rock, *Argentina, 1516–1982*, 332.

8. CEPAL, *Cinco estudios sobre la situación de la mujer en América Latina*, 152.

9. Brennan and Gordillo, "Working Class Protest, Popular Revolt, and Urban Insurrection in Argentina."

10. For an excellent compilation, which includes recent work on this topic, see Cosse, Felitti, and Manzano, *Los '60 de otra manera*.

11. Marta Beines, "Que prefieren comer los grandes gastrónomos, Doña Petrona: Empanadas Santiagueñas," *La Nación*, 5 June 1960, n.p.

12. *Especialidades de la cocina criolla*, 8.

13. Marta Beines, "Que prefieren comer los grandes gastrónomos, Doña Petrona: Empanadas Santiagueñas," *La Nación*, 5 June 1960, n.p.

14. Ibid.

15. Research I've done for a forthcoming article indicates that meanings of *criollo* changed over the course of the twentieth century and took on a more implicitly indigenous valence associated with the northwestern provinces during the 1960s and 1970s.

16. "Guia de Peñas," *Folklore*, January 1962, 63.

17. "Margarita Palacios: Cantora y cocinera," http://fogon-argentino.com.ar/cocina-criolla.html (accessed 21 August 2011).

18. "Guia nativa: Radio y TV," *Radiolandia*, September 1963, 72.

19. Ferrer, *Economía en la cocina*.

20. She claimed to have written it in three months after this incident. Judith Gociol, "Historia para chuparse los dedos," *El Clarín*, 11 August 1996.

21. "Doña Petrona celebra sus bodas de oro en la cocina profesional," *La Nación*, 8 May 1981, 4.

22. Romero, *Argentina: Una crónica total del siglo XX*, 176.

23. "La vecina de los presidentes," *La Nación*, 18 February 1985.

24. Rock, "Survival and Restoration of Peronism," 205.

25. "Encuesta sobre alimentación en dos barrios de Córdoba."

26. Gandulfo, *Recetas económicas*, 1st ed. (Buenos Aires: Fabril Financiera, 1962).

27. Gandulfo, unpublished memoirs, 36.

28. Likewise, in *Recetas económicas*, she argued that that this thriftier book was a "practical complement" to *El libro de Doña Petrona*. Gandulfo, *Para aprender a decorar*, 2d ed. (Buenos Aires: Fabril Financiera, 1964), prologue; Gandulfo, *Recetas económicas*, 1st ed. (1962).

29. It is difficult to know the exact number of editions during the 1960s, as editions published after 1963 have been very hard to locate. The fifty-eighth edition published in 1963 had 35,000 copies printed, and the sixty-fourth edition published in 1971 had

10,000. Marcela Massut explained during a July 2011 conversation that this decline began to occur during the late 1960s.

30. Mary T. described how Petrona asked her if she would be willing to translate her cookbook into English. This never happened, as ultimately Petrona decided it might not be a profitable undertaking. Isay K. and Mary T., interview by author.

31. Ibid.

32. Gandulfo, unpublished memoirs, 43.

33. Orlando Barone, "Petrona de Gandulfo: La reina de la cocina," *La Razón*, 19 June 1985, n.p.

34. Enrique O. Sdrech, "Doña Petrona C. de Gandulfo: El sabor de la vida a los 91," *El Clarín*, 29 July 1987, 51. Gandulfo, unpublished memoirs, 57. I have not been able to find this survey.

35. Gandulfo, *Recetas económicas*, 1st ed. (1962).

36. Because they were live and not taped, no copies of these programs exist. Jorge Nielsen, information to author via email, 18 May 2002.

37. Igarachi, a chef originally from Japan who had begun broadcasting on television in 1960, was also nominated. "Clasificación de Candidato Para Premios en la TV: Programa Hogareño," *La Nación*, 6 September 1961, 12; "Adjudicáronse los premios en la televisión," *La Nación*, 5 October 1961, 22.

38. Annamaría Muchnik, interview by author.

39. Annamaría Muchnik, interview by Jorge Nielsen.

40. República Argentina, *Censo Nacional 1960*; Estudio Sur, *Potencial económico argentino*, 10.

41. Ulanovsky, Itkin, and Sirvén, *Estamos en el aire*, 144.

42. Annamaría Muchnik, interview by Jorge Nielsen.

43. Annamaría Muchnik, interview by author.

44. Ibid.

45. Ibid. See also Marcelo Vidales, "Maestra en la cocina y best seller nacional," *La Prensa*, 11 October 1998, 25.

46. Annamaría Muchnik, interview by author. One did not need to own a television to watch one. For population figures, see República Argentina, *Censo Nacional de población familias y viviendas 1970*; and for television statistics, see Ulanovsky, Itkin, and Sirvén, *Estamos en el aire*, 129.

47. Pujol, *La década rebelde*, 162–63.

48. Carretaro, *Vida cotidiana en Buenos Aires*, 180; Aguilar, "Televisión y la vida privada," 256.

49. Eduardo R., interview by author; oral history workshops in Villa Luro, 30 December 2003, 3 February 2004, and 10 February 2004.

50. Inés Pérez explains that this was even more likely outside of Buenos Aires in cities like Bahía Blanca, where television arrived in 1960 but was not regularly a part of homes other than elite ones until the second part of the decade. Varela, *La televisión criolla*; Pérez, "La domesticación de la 'tele.'"

51. Ulanovsky, Itkin, and Sirvén, *Estamos en el aire*, 391.

52. Blanca Cotta, as cited in Fernanda Muñoz Pace, "A los 95 años murió Doña Petrona," *El Clarín*, 7 February 1972, 26.

53. Annamaría Muchnik, interview by author.

54. *Las recetas*, especially programs 1, 9, 15, 19, 23, and 28.

55. Gandulfo, unpublished memoirs, 42.

56. Fitch, *Appetite for Life*, 297.

57. Molly O'Neil, "Savoring the World according to Julia," *New York Times*, 11 October 1989, C1.

58. Doña Petrona's viewers did not remember or exaggerate her mistakes as vividly as those who watched Julia Child, but a number of Argentines I spoke with recalled Petrona blaming any mistakes that occurred on Juanita.

59. Marcelo Vidales, "Maestra en la cocina y best seller nacional," *La Prensa*, 11 October 1998, 24.

60. Mario Mactas, "Para comerte mejor," *Gente*, 25 September 1969, 55.

61. Pujol, *La década rebelde*, 35.

62. During the 1950s and 1960s, domestic employees were strongly associated with Santiago del Estero because this region sent many female migrants to the capital to work. Two contemporary articles that spoke to this regional trend are "Un problema de nuestro tiempo: El trabajo doméstico," *Claudia* 44 (January 1961); and "El drama de ser servida," *Claudia* 45 (February 1961).

63. Such terminology neither confirms nor denies their understanding of Doña Petrona as being of mixed race. For an explanation of the term *criollo/a* in Argentina, see the introduction. For discussions of the racialization of region in Latin American history, see Weinstein, "Racializing Regional Difference"; Appelbaum, *Muddied Waters*; and Wade, *Blackness and Race Mixture*.

64. *Las recetas*, program 7.

65. Ibid., program 21.

66. "El argentino de 1963: Un ser que se debate entre polos contradictorios," *Primera Plana*, 11 June 1963, 28.

67. Romero, *History of Argentina*, 148–49.

68. Ibid., 179.

69. Brennan and Gordillo, "Working Class Protest, Popular Revolt, and Urban Insurrection in Argentina," 478.

70. *Las recetas*, program 27.

71. Ibid., program 18.

72. Comment from a participant during the discussion of my paper at the Universidad de Buenos Aires, Instituto de Género, 7 July 2004.

73. Because there were four women speaking with me, I am not sure which one of them made this comment. All of them were about the same age and of similar socioeconomic standing. Nelly F., Isabel T., Milagros M., and Angélica H., interview by author.

74. Oral history workshop in Villa Luro, 3 February 2004.

75. *Las recetas*, program 12.

76. Ibid., program 18.

77. According to Valeria Manzano, this term entered the Argentine vocabulary at the close of the 1950s and start of the 1960s. For more analysis of the *nueva ola*, see Manzano, "Ha llegado la 'nueva ola.'"

78. For example, in the late 1960s, she dedicated one of her weekly recipe columns in the popular women's magazine *Para Ti* to providing recommendations about cooking with canned goods. She advised her readers that even if it was not a good moment for "big purchases," it would still be helpful to stock the pantry with basics like canned tomatoes, peas, corn, and sardines. This type of advice also allowed Doña Petrona to integrate Swift's canned goods into her recipes on television. Petrona C. de Gandulfo, "En abrir latas," *Para Ti*, late 1960s, courtesy of Marcela Massut; Amalia Iadarola, "Petrona Carrizo de Gandulfo: La sartén por el mango," *Gente*, 2 November 1970, n.p.

79. Shapiro, *Something from the Oven*, especially pp. 249–53.

80. *Las recetas*, program 13.

81. Marcelo Vidales, "Maestra en la cocina y best seller nacional," *La Prensa*, 11 October 1998.

82. Unfortunately, the correspondence received by Petrona was eventually thrown away. *Las recetas*, program 5.

83. Elena T. to Petrona C. de Gandulfo, 13 December 1962, Buenos Aires, personal correspondence, courtesy of Elena T.; Petrona C. de Gandulfo to Elena T., 26 December 1962, Buenos Aires, personal correspondence, courtesy of Elena T.

84. Petrona C. de Gandulfo to Teresa C., letter, 26 December 1972, courtesy of Teresa C.

85. Petrona C. de Gandulfo to Teresa C., letter, June 1973, courtesy of Teresa C.

86. For an excellent discussion of domestic technologies in secondary cities, see Pérez, "El trabajo doméstico."

87. Nora A. O. de L., interview by author.

88. "Mi esposa, Doña Petrona," published interview with Atilio Massut, *Siete Días*, 17 November 1972, n.p.

89. Wainerman, *Vivir en familia*, 195.

90. Dora B., interview by author.

91. Cosse also explains that during the early 1970s the magazine *Vosotras*, which had a more popular audience, took women's work as the norm but did not really position this work as liberating, as did magazines directed to upper middle-class women. Cosse, "Los nuevos prototipos femeninos."

92. "Doña Petrona: ¡Es tan fácil hacer merengues!" *Confirmando* (17 November 1966): 74. My thanks to Katherine French-Fuller for sharing this article with me.

93. Magdalena R. D. de M., interview by author.

94. For example, during my interview with Nelly F., Isabel T., Milagros M., and Angélica H. in a poorer section of Puerto Ingeniero White, one of them remarked, in response to my question about the relationship between Juanita and Petrona, "I liked it a lot; I didn't watch [the program much], but the few times I saw it, I liked it because of the aprons they wore, and [their] hairstyles, and necklaces."

95. As previously noted, I have written an article focused on the relationship between Doña Petrona and Juanita Bordoy in relation to that of other *patronas* and their help, entitled, "Entertaining Inequalities: Doña Petrona, Juanita Bordoy, and Domestic Work in Mid-Twentieth-Century Argentina."

96. Emmy de Molina, as cited in Marcelo Vidales, "Maestra en la cocina y best seller nacional," *La Prensa*, 11 October 1998, 25.

97. María E. P., interview by author.

98. Olga G. de A. and María B., interview by author.

99. While often repeated, this phrase came directly from my interview with Marcela A. and her niece María Laura A.

100. "Porota" B., interview by author.

101. These tapes of the only extant year of television segments, which I watched in 2002, are available at Canal 13 and are sometimes replayed on its nostalgic channel, Volver. In addition, some programs are available on YouTube.com.

102. Annamaría Muchnik, interview by author.

103. Dora I., interview by author.

104. In the first of these instances, Juanita mumbled something inaudible; the second time, she quickly acknowledged Petrona's request; and the final time, on the aforementioned Christmas dinner program, she asked Petrona if the marmalade had reduced enough. *Las recetas*, programs 10, 24, 28.

105. Ibid., program 16.

106. Ibid., especially programs 8 and 14.

107. Ibid., program 24.

108. Ibid., program 28.

109. Hilda R., interview by author.

110. Elena P., interview by author.

111. Varela, *La televisión criolla*, 153.

112. Miriam Becker, interview by author.

113. Debate, Museo del Puerto Ingeniero White.

114. Nora A. O. de L., interview by author.

115. Someone made this exact point during the debate at the Museo del Puerto Ingeniero White, commenting: "I think that Juanita would not have stayed with her for so many years if she had treated her badly."

116. Esther A. P., interview by author.

117. "Relaciones con el servicio doméstico," *Femirama* (ca. 1963–64): 26.

118. Ibid.

119. "Porota" B., interview by author (Susana).

120. Matilde Sánchez, "Murió Juanita, la legendaria asistente de Doña Petrona," *El Clarín*, 6 July 1995, 42.

121. Eduardo R., interview by author.

122. Elvira I., interview by author.

123. Marta F., interview by author.

124. Ibid.

125. As elsewhere, Italian immigrants and other locals transformed what "Italian" food meant in Argentina, for example by replacing hard-to-find ingredients like olive oil with vegetable oil.

126. Marta F., interview by author.

127. For analysis of this new, younger female model, see Cosse, "Los nuevos prototipos femeninos"; Feijoo, Nari, and Fierro, "Women in Argentina during the 1960s"; and Manzano, "Sexualizing Youth."

128. Nouzeilles and Montaldo, *The Argentina Reader*, 341–43; Cosse, "Los nuevos prototipos femeninos"; Manzano, "Blue Jean Generation."

129. Debate, Museo del Puerto Ingeniero White.

130. This grew to 4 million by 1973. Statistics as cited in Gonzalo Aguilar, "Televisión y la vida privada," 256.

131. Economists Juan M. Graña and Damián Kennedy calculate the average real salary at 923 pesos in 1968. Graña and Kennedy, "Salario real, costo laboral y productividad," 34. By 1970, with Law 18.188, this would be eqivalent to about 400 pesos. Letter dated 30 September 1968, Gandulfo, personal papers.

132. Radio broadcast, 23 May 1967, Rollo 306, Band 1, Pies 125–435, Archivo General de la Nación.

133. Ibid.

134. Mario Mactas, "Para comerte mejor," *Gente*, 25 September 1969, 53.

135. Ibid.

136. "El difícil oficio de ama de casa," *Femirama* (October 1968): 72–74.

137. Cosse, "Los nuevos prototipos femeninos."

138. French-Fuller, "The Woman Who Works Does Not Create Any Social Problems."

139. Conversation with Marcela Massut.

140. Ibid.

141. "Mi esposa, Doña Petrona," published interview with Atilio Massut, *Siete Días*, 17 November 1972, n.p.

142. Annamaría Muchnik, interview by author.

143. For an article that draws this conlusion for Argentina, see Pérez, "El trabajo doméstico." Ruth Schwartz Cowan was among the first to advance this argument in the context of the United States, in *More Work for Mother*.

144. Gogna, "Domestic Workers," 84.

145. Zurita, *El servicio doméstico en Argentina*, 13, 48–49.

146. Pérez, "El trabajo doméstico."

147. Isabella Cosse and Inés Pérez both develop this argument in their respective works. See Cosse, "Los nuevos prototipos femeninos"; and Pérez, "El trabajo doméstico."

148. Castagna, "Petrona C. de Gandulfo."

149. Iadarola, "Petrona Carrizo de Gandulfo: La sartén por el mango," *Gente*, 2 November 1970, n.p.

150. Ibid.

151. Marcelo Vidales, "Maestra en la cocina y best seller nacional," *La Prensa*, 11 October 1998, 24.

152. Conversation with Marcela Massut, 24 May 2002.

153. She made this distinction during the 1967 radio program focused on her. Radio broadcast, 23 May 1967.

154. Amalia Iadarola, "La sarten por el mango," *Gente*, 11 February 1970.

155. Cosse, "Argentine Mothers and Fathers."

156. "Doña Petrona: ¡Es tan fácil hacer merengues!" *Confirmando* (17 November 1966).

Chapter Six

1. Gandulfo, *El libro de Doña Petrona*, 73d ed. (Buenos Aires: Talleres Gráficos de Sebastián de Amorrortu e Hijos, 13 January 1979), 685.

2. Census statistics (which, as previously discussed, continued to underrepresent women's remunerated work) suggest that females over fourteen years of age increased as a part of the "economically active" population vis-à-vis men, from 22 percent in 1960 to 25 percent in 1970 and 27 percent in 1980. According to Susana Torado, this meant that 23 percent of all women over fourteen were defined "as economically active" in 1960, 26.5 percent were so defined in 1970, and 26.9 percent were so defined in 1980, a figure that rose to 34 percent in greater Buenos Aires in 1970 and 1980. Women who stayed in the workforce after forming a union with a male partner were the main reason for the statistical increase, even as such an increase was limited by young women's longer educations. Wainerman, "Familia, trabajo y relaciones de género," 156; Torado, *Historia de la familia*, 210–16.

3. Torado, *Historia de la familia*, especially p. 215; Wainerman, *La vida cotidiana en las nuevas familias*, especially p. 80.

4. Advertisement, *Paladar* (May 1970): 8.

5. Amalia Iadarola, "La sarten por el mango," *Gente*, 11 February 1970; for analysis of the *nueva ola*, see Manzano, "Ha llegado la 'nueva ola.'"

6. Amalia Iadarola, "La sarten por el mango," *Gente*, 11 February 1970.

7. Many women, along with a number of men, wrote in from big cities like Buenos Aires, Córdoba, and Rosario, as well as from smaller towns from the provinces of Buenos Aires, Catamarca, and Corrientes. Most seemed to be from the middle class, but there was still a considerable socioeconomic range. Some had relatively modest incomes; for example, one woman explained that she was "a woman who worked inside and outside her home and sacrificed to buy the magazine." Others were seemingly well-off, such as the reader concerned about how to properly serve caviar. All letters published in the magazine appeared in the column "Aquí opina usted" unless otherwise noted. Letter, *Para Ti*, 30 July 1973, 90; letter, *Para Ti*, 7 December 1970; Bontempo, "Construcciones culturales bajo autoritarismo y democracia." For analysis of *Para Ti*, see Paola Margulis, "Representación del cuerpo en *Para Ti*"; and Bontempo, "Construcciones culturales bajo autoritarismo y democracia."

8. Cosse, "*Claudia*: La revista de la mujer moderna."

9. Part of this success stemmed from this publication's support of the junta. Ulanovsky, "Noticias de los años del fuego"; Paola Margulis, "Representación del cuerpo en *Para Ti*," 472; Cosse, "*Claudia*: La revista de la mujer moderna."

10. Susana L. de Micieli, letter, *Para Ti*, 7 December 1970.

11. Beatriz Prémoli de Ales, letter, *Para Ti*, 2 February 1970.

12. Rosalía Demicheli, letter, *Para Ti*, 28 September 1970.

13. Amalia Iadarola, "La sarten por el mango," *Gente*, 11 February 1970.

14. Manzano, "The Making of Youth in Argentina," especially the chapter entitled "Close to the Revolution: The Politicization of Youth."

15. "Cartas," *Nuevo Hombre* 25 (March 1972): 12, as cited in ibid. (emphasis added).

16. Emmy de Molina, "Sabor y saber sobre la mesa: Exotismo en nuestro folklore gastronomic," *La Prensa*, 25 November 1972, 2a.

17. Elsa San Martin, "Petrona C. de Gandulfo: Una mujer positiva," *Mucho Gusto*, 12–25 September 1973, 9.

18. For example, she referred to her famous empanadas in Amalia Iadarola, "La sarten por el mango," *Gente*, 11 February 1970; and she shared recipes for *carbonada criolla* and *yema quemada* in a 1973 article, Elsa San Martin, "Petrona C. de Gandulfo: Una mujer positive," *Mucho Gusto*, 12–25 September 1973, 10.

19. For example, she told Amalia Iadarola that she had introduced Asian sweet-and-sour dishes into the Argentine repertoire. Iadarola, "La sarten por el mango," *Gente*, 11 February 1970.

20. Esther Alicia Känel de Ghia, letter, *Para Ti*, 7 February 1972.

21. María Esther D. de Figueroa, letter, *Para Ti*, 12 April 1971.

22. Response, *Para Ti*, 7 December 1970.

23. Juan Ignacio Roboredo, letter, *Para Ti*, 29 May 1972.

24. She does not say whether this was because such cuts were so popular or because they were uncommon, but I presume it to be the latter. María Teresa Iñigo, letter, *Para Ti*, 7 August 1972.

25. Lobato and Suriano, *Nueva historia argentina*, 460.

26. The response to this article in *Para Ti* was dated 9 October 1972. Earlier in this month, on 2 October 1972, *ecónoma* Chola Ferrer had started a cooking supplement, "replete with economic, nutritious, and easy-to-prepare recipes to keep the whole family happy."

27. Patricia Millán Acosta, letter, *Para Ti*, 9 October 1972.

28. Response, *Para Ti*, 9 October 1972.

29. Amalia Iadarola, "La sarten por el mango," *Gente*, 11 February 1970.

30. I thank Valeria Manzano for sharing this source, as well as her knowledge about the author, with me. For more on this genre of satirical and humorous writing, see Manzano, "Contra toda forma de opresión."

31. Alicia Gallotti, "Mitos Argentinos: Una torta llamada Doña Petrona C. de Gandulfo," *Satiricon* 2 (December 1972): 12–13.

32. Ibid.

33. For analysis of feminist activism, see Nari, "Feminist Awakenings"; and articles from the compilation *Historia, género y política en los '70*, including Grammático, "Las mujeres políticas y las feministas en los tempranos setenta"; Vassallo, "'Las mujeres dicen basta'"; and Campagnoli, "El feminismo es un humanismo."

34. As previously mentioned, Alejandra Vassallo convincingly suggests both contemporary and subsequent scholars have tended to overlook the impact of local experiences on Argentine feminism, depicting it as a bourgeois, proimperialist movement. Vassallo, "'Las mujeres dicen basta.'"

35. This concept was also being asserted by feminists elsewhere. As Marcela Nari points out, most Argentine feminists were very familiar with Simone de Beauvoir, Kate Millett, Shulamith Firestone, Carla Lonzi, and Juliet Mitchell. See CECYM, "Feminismo por feministas," 24–26; and Nari, "Feminist Awakenings," 529.

36. Unión Feminista Argentina, Flyer, 1970. I am grateful to Valeria Pita for sharing this and other feminist documents with me.

37. Grammático, "Historia reciente, género y política," 255.

38. Liscia and Lassalle, "Verano del '72."

39. In the early 1970s, Nora Scott Kinzer interviewed 125 professional women in Buenos Aires, many of whom expressed such a sentiment themselves. Scott Kinzer, "Women Professionals in Buenos Aires," 177.

40. For example, on 23 April 1973, she published a recipe column in *Para Ti* that encouraged people to eat well by consuming a "variety" of foods. For the quote regarding *milanesas*, see Petrona C. de Gandulfo, "Milanesas en todas las versiones," *Para Ti*, 5 March 1973.

41. Petrona C. de Gandulfo, "Menús para todos los presupuestos," *Para Ti*, 19 February 1973.

42. Nelly Azcuénaga, letter, *Para Ti*, 2 April 1973.

43. Elena González Peña, letter, *Para Ti*, 19 March 1973.

44. "He who had once been identified with one-half of the country came to be everything to everyone," as Juan Carlos Torre and Liliana de Riz explain. Torre and de Riz, "Argentina since 1946," 311.

45. Grammático, "Historia reciente, género y política," 275; Grammático, "Populist Continuities in 'Revolutionary' Peronism?," 133–34.

46. As cited in "Cuanto cuesta vivir con los precios congelados," *Para Ti*, 30 July 1973.

47. Petrona C. de Gandulfo, "No gastes más que 8.00 pesos," *Para Ti*, 29 October 1973.

48. Romero, *Argentina: Una crónica total del siglo XX*, 206.

49. "La vecina de los presidentes," *La Nación*, 18 February 1985, courtesy of *El Clarín*.

50. San Martin, "Petrona C. de Gandulfo: Una mujer positiva," *Mucho Gusto*, 12–25 September 1973, 10.

51. Charles Henry Baker, *South American Gentleman's Companion*, xiv (emphasis in original).

52. See, for example, Petrona C. de Gandulfo, "Recetas económicas de otoño," *Para Ti*, 18 March 1974; and her column with pasta recipes, *Para Ti*, 29 July 1974.

53. *Para Ti*, 30 September 1974, 90.

54. For example, she prevented a coalition of Argentine feminist groups from holding an international feminist conference in Buenos Aires in 1975. CEYCM, "Feminismo por feministas," 19.

55. María Sáenz Quesada argues that the ridicule surrounding Isabel Perón's presidency is in keeping with what she dubs Argentina's *machista* (male-dominated, sexist) society, in which screaming at a woman driver to "go do the dishes" is a tactic to prevent women from competing against men. As we saw previously, Doña Petrona repeatedly recounted how the famous footballer Angel Labruna once yelled at her to get out of the car and back into the kitchen before realizing who she was. Quesada, *Isabel Perón*, 475.

56. A few of the people I interviewed recalled the shortages of sugar and kerosene in 1974 and 1975. During this period, Doña Petrona mentioned in her column in *Para*

Ti that using artificial sweeteners would allow consumers to circumvent their inability to buy sugar.

57. Petrona C. de Gandulfo, "Petrona habla a las amas de casa," *Para Ti*, 14 April 1975.

58. Ibid.

59. Ibid. Three years later, Petrona made a similar point about the importance of meat within Argentine eating habits, even publicly admitting that she was "tired of beef." Manuel Caldeiro, "Virtudes y defectos de los argentinos según Petrona C. de Gandulfo," *Gente*, 12 October 1978, n.p.

60. "Pasen amigas," *Para Ti*, 22 July 1974, 28–29.

61. Bontempo, "Construcciones culturales bajo autoritarismo y democracia."

62. Miriam Becker, interview by author.

63. Miriam Becker, "Fuimos a la feria con Doña Petrona," *Para Ti*, 8 September 1975, 64.

64. Petrona C. de Gandulfo, "Cocina de la 'verdadera' economía," *Para Ti*, 15 September 1975, 24.

65. As cited in Miriam Becker, "Fuimos a la feria con Doña Petrona," *Para Ti*, 8 September 1975, 63.

66. Ibid. (emphasis added).

67. Aguirre, "Gordos de escasez." For an analysis of the regional diets, see Alvarez and Pinotti, *A la mesa*.

68. Ibid., especially pp. 172–73. For analysis of the links between thinness and Western bourgeois capitalism, see Bordo, *Unbearable Weight*; and Counihan, *Anthropology of Food and Body*.

69. She also included another diet version in *Coma bien y adelgace*, but neither of these low-calorie versions made their way into *El libro de Doña Petrona* during the 1970s. For the respective recipes, see Gandulfo, *El libro de Doña Petrona*, 73d ed. (1979), 463; and Gandulfo and Cormillot, *Coma bien y adelgace*, 257.

70. Gandulfo and Cormillot, *Coma bien y adelgace*, 2d ed. (Buenos Aires: Sebastián de Amorrortu e Hijos, 1974), 196.

71. M. B., "La mujer, el hogar, el niño: Acaba de aparecer un nuevo libro de cocina dietética," *La Nación*, ca. 1972, n.p., courtesy of *La Nación*.

72. Amalia Iadarola, "La sarten por el mango," *Gente*, 11 February 1970.

73. Eduardo R., interview by author.

74. Alicia Gallotti used this term and also poked fun at Doña Petrona for her size, in her satirical piece "Mitos Argentinos: Una torta llamada Doña Petrona C. de Gandulfo," *Satiricon* 2 (December 1972): 12–13.

75. "Acaba de aparecer un nuevo libro de cocina dietética," *La Nación*, ca. 1972, courtesy of *La Nación*.

76. Gandulfo, *Bajas calorías*.

77. Isay K., interview by author.

78. María E. P., interview by author.

79. Choly Berreteaga considered herself to be one of Petrona's *alumnas*, and Miriam Becker continued to produce Petrona's recipe column. In a handwritten dedication in *Cocina fácil para la mujer moderna* to Doña Petrona, Berreteaga wrote, "Para

Petrona, Maestra y ejemplo, con todo cariño, Choly Berreteaga, 5-IX-1985" (For Petrona, Teacher and role model, with much fondness, Choly Berreteaga, 5 September 1985). Courtesy of Marcela Massut.

80. Miriam Becker, interview by author.

81. Berreteaga, *Cocina fácil para la mujer moderna*.

82. Radio interview with Choly Berreteaga, "La otra agenda."

83. Berreteaga, *Cocina fácil para la mujer moderna*, especially pp. 291–99.

84. Anahi B., interview by author.

85. Miriam Becker, interview by author.

86. Romero, *History of Argentina*, 232.

87. About 80 percent of the approximately 30,000 people who "disappeared" were between the ages of sixteen and thirty-five. Roughly 70 percent were male and 30 percent were female. CONADEP, *Nunca más*, especially p. 294.

88. Amnesty International, *Extracts from the Report of an Amnesty International Mission to Argentina, 6–15 November 1976*, 15.

89. Juan Corradi coined this term; see Corradi, *Fitful Republic*.

90. Romero, *History of Argentina*, 219–20.

91. Still, it is curious that the regime kept only one season from the mid-1960s and nothing from the era in which it was in power.

92. Dora B., interview by author.

93. Marini, "Women in Contemporary Argentina," 116.

94. Navarro, "The Personal Is Political."

95. Jerry Knudson points to the silence of the Argentine press (with the two notable exceptions of Jacobo Timmerman's *La Opinión* and the *Buenos Aires Herald*). He argues that even as fear contributed to the decision not to report such atrocities, newspapers were businesses and elected to self-censor in part to protect the significant stream of government advertising support. He also points out that previous governments had stepped up controls of the media since 1970, when a decree made the Ministry of Government responsible for the orientation and control of all radio and television content and stations were instructed to preserve "the national style of life" in their broadcasts. In August 1973, Juan Perón issued an even stricter decree that prohibited "international news agencies from distributing news about Argentina produced elsewhere." Knudson, "Veil of Silence."

96. Marini, "Women in Contemporary Argentina," 116.

97. It is not clear why she chose to patent her name at this time, except perhaps to try to help her son's business in San Isidro, where he ran a bakery and sold these cake pans. "Como Viven Los Argentinos: Petrona C. de Gandulfo; ¿El gardel de las amas de casa?" *El Clarín*, 11 June 1976, n.p., courtesy of *El Clarín*.

98. Ibid.

99. For an analysis of the familial dynamics of this nationalist discourse, see Filc, *Entre el parentesco y la política*.

100. Signed document entitled "1er Jornadas Nacionales de Cocina Criolla a su Presidenta Honoraria," A.P.A.N.E.C., Córdoba, 17 August 1986, courtesy of Marcela Massut.

101. Choly Berreteaga, interview by author.

102. "Sabor y saber sobre la mesa: La cocina criolla en jornadas," n.p., n.d., courtesy of the Association of Ecónomas.

103. Conversation with a former military conscript, who served in 1983, October 2011.

104. Asociación de Ecónomas y Gastrónomas, Libro de actas, article 2, p. 2, courtesy of the Association of Ecónomas.

105. This association was established following two years of informal activity. Asociación de Ecónomas y Gastrónomas, Libro de actas, p. 1, courtesy of the Asociación de Ecónomas y Gastrónomas.

106. The military targeted psychologists and others studying the social sciences, as suggested by this interviewee in June 2004.

107. María B., interview by author. It seems they decided against this approach.

108. María Cristina Dillon, interview by author.

109. Luis Alberto Romero discusses the consolidation of businesses and wealth during this period. Romero, *History of Argentina*, 215–54.

110. During our interview, Dillon contrasted this interest with the need to search for students today. María Cristina Dillon, interview by author.

111. José Tcherkaski, "Para mi, cocinar es una pesadilla," *7 Días*, 10 June 1977, 39.

112. Ibid.

113. Irene Cristina "Pelusa" Molina, interview by author.

114. Ibid.

115. On Gato Dumas, who became a successful restaurant owner during this time, see Haydeé Lin and Patricio Clavin, "El chef de Buen Vivir," *Semana Gráfica*, 19 May 2004, 4–8.

116. I interviewed some people who described to me widowers and single men who did most of their own cooking. For example, Olga G. described how her father cooked for the family after her mother died. Armando S. R. said he cooked because he never married. Olga G. de A., interview by author; Armando S. R., interview by author.

117. On another episode, Doña Petrona also addressed young women, explaining how to make quick meals from leftover beef or chicken.

118. Caldeiro, "Virtudes y defectos de los argentinos según Petrona C. de Gandulfo," *Gente*, 12 October 1978.

119. Ibid.

120. "Si Doña Petrona no existiera, habría que inventarla," *Mucho Gusto*, December 1978, 3.

121. For more on Betty Crocker, see Marks, *Finding Betty Crocker*.

122. Muraro, "La comunicación masiva," 28.

123. The Dutch even elected to broadcast footage of the Madres instead of simultaneous shots of the opening ceremonies. Bonafini and Sánchez, "The Madwomen at the Plaza de Mayo," 436–37.

124. Knudson, "Veil of Silence," especially p. 97.

125. Mercedes Sosa sang protest songs and was driven into exile in France and then Spain in 1979. Norma Aleandro spoke out against the dictatorship during the late 1970s, forcing her into exile in Uruguay and then Spain. She would subsequently star in the 1985 film *La historia official*, which critiqued the military's campaign of terror.

126. Two weeks after the coup, *Para Ti* began to publicly support the military dictatorship's government by praising General Jorge Rafael Videla's rise to the presidency. In contrast, the owner of the more progressive magazine *Claudia* went into exile. For analysis of the latter, see Scarzenella, "Entre dos exilios."

127. San Martin, "Petrona C. de Gandulfo: Una mujer positiva," *Mucho Gusto*, 12–25 September 1973, 10.

128. *La historia official.*

129. Fanny Polimeni, untitled and undated article, courtesy of Marcela Massut. Polimeni wrote for *Mucho Gusto.*

130. For example, in 1963 she released a print run of 35,000 of the fifty-eighth edition and in 1974 a print run of 12,500 of the sixty-eighth edition. Gandulfo, *El libro de Doña Petrona*, 58th ed. (Buenos Aires: Fabril Financiera, 29 June 1963); Gandulfo, *El libro de Doña Petrona*, 68th ed. (Buenos Aires: Artes Gráficas de Amorrortu e Hijos, 1974).

131. Petrona C. de Gandulfo, as cited in Miriam Becker, "Gracias, Petrona C. de Gandulfo," *Mujer*, 31 January 1984, 17.

132. "Cirugía, como toda una diva," *Crónica*, 14 August 1983, courtesy of *El Clarín*.

133. According to Heriberto Muraro, a 1985 survey found that 60 percent of families in Buenos Aires had color televisions. Outside of the capital, color television was much less common. According to a former director of the Secretary of Communications interviewed by Ulanovsky et al., only 2.5 percent of the total population had color sets as of 1990. See "Cirugía, como toda una diva," *Crónica*, 14 August 1983, courtesy of *El Clarín*; Muraro, "La comunicación masiva," 28; and Ulanovsky, Itken, and Sirvén, *Estamos en el aire*, 368.

134. Laura Shapiro explains that Julia Child first had an "eye job" in 1969, followed by a face-lift in 1971 and more plastic surgery in 1977 and 1989. Shapiro, *Julia Child*, 115–16.

135. In Petrona's personal materials held by her granddaughter, Marcela Massut, I found a "libro de solicitudes," in which the following organizations requested a demonstration: Asociación Mujeres de Negocios y Profesionales "Juana Azurduy," Asociación Docentes Jubilados de Lomas de Zamora, Asociación Cooperadora Centro Anticancero, Liga de Madres de Familia Nuestra Señora del Rosario, Club de Leones de Monte Grande, Club de Leones de Remedios de Escalada Este, Sociedad de San Vicente de Paul, La Rueda Rotaria Femenina, and several public schools.

136. "Doña Petrona celebra sus bodas de oro en la cocina profesional," *La Nación*, 8 May 1981, 4.

137. Sibila Camps, "Los tiempos han cambiado," *El Clarín*, 1 October 1981, 4. Speaking to Argentines' adoption of new technologies, Camps explained that the "import opening" had led some soon-to-be-married couples to register for a few new types of appliances, including electric mixers, blenders, coffee machines, crepe machines, juicers, electric grills, refrigerators, electric knives, toasters, and pasta machines. Still, she pointed out that even people who could afford these types of products (who were relatively few in number) did not tend to own freezers and microwaves. Camps argues that freezers and microwaves were "not adopted by Argentines because of their high cost and also the space they take up."

138. Mora y Araujo, "Las clases medias consolidadas," 273.

139. Armstrong, "Hunger and Monetarism in Buenos Aires."

140. Furthermore, internal dissent among different factions of the leadership was exposed through leaks about the controversy surrounding General Roberto Viola's replacement of his boss General Videla at the helm in March 1981, followed by General Leopoldo Galtieri's replacement of General Viola toward the end of that same year.

141. Becker, "Gracias, Petrona C. de Gandulfo," *Mujer*, 31 January 1984, 17.

142. Torre and de Riz, "Argentina since 1946," 347.

143. She had actually been on television for thirty-two years. Petrona C. de Gandulfo, as cited in "Doña Petrona a 50 años de su primer libro, habla con Emmy de Molina, su amiga y colega," *La Prensa*, 9 April 1984, 4.

144. Secretary of Commerce Ricardo Campero presented her with this spoon as part of a 1984 ceremony to analyze the Project CONCOM (Comunicación al Consumidor or Communication to Consumers). *La Nación*, 8 August 1984, n.p., courtesy of *La Nación*.

145. "Doña Petrona: Hay que ser simpática," *Panorama*, June 1983, courtesy of *La Nación*.

146. Miriam Becker, "Gracias, Petrona C. de Gandulfo," *Mujer*, 31 January 1984, 15.

147. Conversation with Marcela Massut, 1 August 2006.

148. "Doña Petrona a 50 años de su primer libro, habla con Emmy de Molina, su amiga y colega," *La Prensa*, 9 April 1984, 4.

149. Specifically, 27 percent. INDEC, La pobreza en la Argentina, 1980, as cited in Récalde, *Mujer, condiciones de vida, de trabajo y salud*, 108.

150. Peronist politician and lawyer Héctor Récalde argues that such efforts failed to reach all the families who needed help or address the root problems of this poverty. Récalde, *Mujer, condiciones de vida, de trabajo y salud*, 87–89, 105.

151. "Doña Petrona a 50 años de su primer libro, habla con Emmy de Molina, su amiga y colega," *La Prensa*, 9 April 1984, 4.

152. Conversation with Marcela Massut, 1 August 2006.

153. "Marcela Gandulfo heredera de Doña Petrona," *El Clarín*, 5 August 1984.

154. Ibid.

155. "Doña Petrona a 50 años de su primer libro, habla con Emmy de Molina, su amiga y colega," *La Prensa*, 9 April 1984, 4.

156. As discussed previously, Adolfo Prieto demonstrates that elites were the main authors and the main audience for hardcover books in late nineteenth- and early twentieth-century Argentina. Prieto, *El discurso criollista*.

157. "Petrona fuera de la cocina," *Crónica*, 8 September 1985, 10.

158. Ibid.

159. Fisher, "Gender and the State in Argentina."

160. Hebe de Bonafini, interview with Marguerite Guzman Bouvard, 1989/1990, as cited in Bouvard, *Revolutionizing Motherhood*, 191.

161. Zurita, "Trabajo, servidumbre y situaciones de género," 2.

162. "Petrona fuera de la cocina," *Crónica*, 8 September 1985, 10.

163. "La cocina y un homenaje especial a Doña Petrona C. de Gandulfo," *El Clarín*, 10 April 1990, 24.

164. The "Full-Stop" Law stipulated that the courts would not hear any additional claims for human rights abuses after 23 February 1987. Three months later, the "Due Obedience" Law absolved all military personnel below the rank of lieutenant colonel of responsibility for the crimes they had committed.

165. *Time*, 12 June 1989, as cited in Serulnikov, "When Looting Becomes a Right."

166. For further analysis of these food riots, see ibid., especially pp. 70–71.

167. "Petrona fuera de la cocina," *Crónica*, 8 September 1985, 10.

Conclusion

1. She apparently died of a heart attack. Fernando Muñoz Pace, "A los 95 años murió Doña Petrona," *El Clarín*, 7 February 1992, 26.

2. Renata Rocco-Cuzzi, "¿Tretas del débil? La profesionalización de un viejo arte," *El Cronista*, 7 February 1992.

3. Orlando Barone, "Doña Petrona: La hazaña de ser mito en la cocina," *El Cronista*, 7 February 1992, 20.

4. Gandulfo, unpublished memoirs, 72.

5. León Bouche was among the first to make this comparison, during a 1967 radio show focused on this *ecónoma*. Radio broadcast, 23 May 1967, Rollo 306, Band 1, Pies 125–435, Archivo General de la Nación.

6. Marcelo Vidales, "Maestra en la cocina y best seller nacional," *La Prensa*, 11 October 1998, 24.

7. Journalists like Vidales frequently referred to this figure, which seems reasonable based on my research into the number of print runs, which, as previously explained, were not consistently printed in the books. The second most popular cookbook, as previously mentioned, appears to be *Cocina fácil para la moderna*, which sold over 1.5 million copies, according to Choly Berreteaga. "Cocinar es un acto de amor," *El Clarín*, 6 July 2010, http://www.clarin.com/ollas-sartenes/Cocinar-acto-amor_0_293970605.html (accessed 19 May 2011).

8. Matilde Sánchez, "Murió Juanita, la legendaria asistente de Doña Petrona," *El Clarín*, 6 July 1995, 42.

9. This happened on 2 December 2006 at a birthday celebration for an Argentine friend in Ann Arbor, Michigan. Most of the people in attendance were Argentine expats in their twenties or early thirties, and most were unaware of my project.

10. See, for example, Fernando Muñoz Pace, "A los 95 años murió Doña Petrona," *El Clarín*, 7 February 1992, 26–27.

11. Aguirre, "Gordos de escasez," 173.

12. Aguirre, "Toda la carne al asador."

13. Petras, "Argentina: 18 Months of Popular Struggle," 28.

14. Nevertheless, many members of the middle class later seemed to lose their sympathy for working-class protestors. By 2003–4, it had become common for people (like taxi drivers and shop owners) to complain about the ways in which the *piqueteros* were making their work more challenging. For media analysis of this trend, see "The Americas: Pickets Unfenced; Argentina's Unemployed."

15. When I was in Buenos Aires in May 2002, almost every middle-class person I spoke with was thinking about leaving or knew someone (a close family member or friend) who was planning to leave or had already left.

16. Dora I., interview by author.

17. Annamaría Muchnik, interview by author.

18. This follows from and, to some extent, echoes Ann Farnsworth-Alvear's findings in Colombia. See Farnsworth-Alvear, *Dulcinea in the Factory*, especially pp. 4, 27–33, 234–35.

19. As discussed previously, scholars Juan Carlos Torre and Elisa Pastoriza argue that while the Peronists radically redrew the social hierarchy, they did not promote a new cultural identity for Argentina, a finding that my research reinforces on the culinary level. Likewise, Sueann Caulfield concludes that paternalism stayed intact and was reinforced by Getulio Vargas's populist government in Brazil. Torre and Pastoriza, "La democratización del bienestar," especially p. 307; Caulfield, *In Defense of Honor*.

20. While the consistent lack of print runs, which were removed during the Peronist era and omitted at other points, makes it impossible to determine the exact number of copies produced, during the 1940s, 1950s, and 1960s, Doña Petrona produced over fifty-five editions of 6,000 to 40,000 copies each.

21. See Pilcher, *¡Que vivan los tamales!*; and Pilcher, "Many Chefs in the National Kitchen."

22. Among the better known were Emmy de Molina, Choly Berreteaga, and Miriam Becker, who joined María Cristina Dillon and Doña Petrona (along with nine others) in founding the original association of *ecónomas* in 1976.

23. Annamaría Muchnik, interview by author.

24. I develop this argument in more detail in my article "Entertaining Inequalities: Doña Petrona, Juanita Bordoy, and Domestic Work in Mid-Twentieth-Century Argentina."

25. Tinsman, "Indispensible Service of Sisters," 55.

26. Ruth Schwartz Cowan was among the first to advance this argument in the context of the United States, while Inés Pérez has developed it for Argentina. The washing machine is the one appliance that has been recognized by scholars including Katharine French-Fuller to have significantly cut down on work across the Americas. Cowan, *More Work for Mother*; Pérez, "El trabajo doméstico"; French-Fuller, "Gendered Invisibility, Respectable Cleanliness."

27. See Wainerman, "Familia, trabajo y relaciones de género," especially p. 164.

28. Two compilations (one book and one journal) that address this trend across Latin America are Chaney and Castro, *Muchachas No More*; and articles by Hutchinson, Milanich, Olcott, and Pite in *Labors of Love: Production and Reproduction in Latin American History* (special issue, *Hispanic American Historical Review* 91, no. 1 [February 2011]).

29. Alfredo Arias, interview by author; "Arias y la patria petronista," ADN, La Revista de *La Nación*, 17 June 2011, 3–9; "Cien ediciones después de su mítico libro, el arte rinde homenaje a Doña Petrona a través de Alfredo Arias," VIVA, La Revista del El *Clarín*, 19 June 2011, 52–56.

30. This blog is found at http://blogs.lanacion.com.ar/archivoscopio/archivos copio/dona-petrona-la-reina-de-la-cocina-argentina/ (accessed 19 May 2011).

31. "Narda es utilísima," 22 May 2010, http://www.tvshow.com.uy/blog/5543-narda-es-utilisima/ (accessed 19 May 2011).

32. Despite her friendship with Mirtha Legrand and her sister Silvia Legrand, Doña Petrona never appeared on this program, or vice versa, according to Marcela Massut, who suggested that they would not have wanted to upstage one another. *Almorzando* went off the air in February 2011.

33. "Narda es Utilísima," 22 May 2010, http://www.tvshow.com.uy/blog/5543-narda-es-utilisima/ (accessed 19 May 2011).

BIBLIOGRAPHY

Oral Histories by Author

Interviews with Public Figures

Arias, Alfredo, 12 July 2011, Paris–Easton, Pa., via telephone
Baldi, María Adela, 15 April 2004, Buenos Aires
Becker, Miriam, 10 June 2004, 7 August 2005, Buenos Aires
Berreteaga, Choly, 18 June 2004, Buenos Aires
Cotta, Blanca, 16 May 2002, 15 December 2003, Quilmes
Dillon, María Cristina, June 2004, Buenos Aires
Hermann, Cecilia, 3 December 2003, Buenos Aires
Massut, Marcela, 24 May 2002, 22 October 2003, 9 July 2004, 14 January 2004, 1
    August 2006, Greater Buenos Aires
Molina, Irene Cristina "Pelusa," 11 June 2004, Buenos Aires
Muchnik, Annamaría, 22 May 2002, Buenos Aires
Ulanovsky, Carlos, 11 November 2003, Buenos Aires

Interviews with Large Groups

Debate, 22 May 2004, Museo del Puerto Ingeniero White
Oral history workshops in Villa Luro, 30 December 2003, 3 February 2004, 10
    February 2004, Buenos Aires

Interviews with Individuals and Families

Ana C., 19 May 2004, Bahía Blanca
Anahi B., 28 May 2002, Buenos Aires
Armondo S. R., 20 May 2004, Puerto Ingeniero White
"Chacha" D., 21 May 2004, Bahía Blanca
Dora B., 26 June 2004, Buenos Aires
Dora I., 17 May 2004, Puerto Ingeniero White
Eduardo R., 23 May 2002, Buenos Aires
Elba A. de B., 26 November 2003, Greater Buenos Aires
Elena P., 27 May 2004, Buenos Aires
Elena T., 5 November 2003, Greater Buenos Aires
Elvira B. P. and Esther A. P., 25 November 2003, La Plata
Elvira I., 18 June 2004, Buenos Aires
Emeteria T. and Lorena T., 7 February 2004, Buenos Aires
Emilia S. and Livio S., 6 November 2003, Buenos Aires
Esther A. P., 25 November 2003, La Plata

Etel L., 17 May 2004, Bahía Blanca
"Goyo" C., 6 May 2004, Santiago del Estero
"Gugu" A., 6 May 2004, Santiago del Estero
Hector B., 4 December 2003, Buenos Aires
Hilda R., 17 June 2004, Buenos Aires
Isay K. and Mary T., 12 June 2004, Buenos Aires
Luisa P., 21 May 2002, Buenos Aires
Luis L. C., 21 June 2004, Buenos Aires
Magdalena R. D. de M., 16 January 2004, Buenos Aires
Marcela and María Laura A., 4 July 2004, Greater Buenos Aires
María B., 15 April 2004, Buenos Aires
María C. D., 8 June 2004, Buenos Aires
María E. P., 22 July 2004, Buenos Aires
Marta F., 4 April 2004, La Plata
Nelly F., Isabel T., Milagros M., and Angélica H., 18 May 2004, Puerto Ingeniero
    White
Nora A. O. de L. and Teresa S. de C., 21 May 2004, Puerto Ingeniero White
Ofelia F., 31 December 2003, Buenos Aires
Olga C. G. and Olga A. G., 4 May 2004, Santiago del Estero
Olga G. de A. and María B., 18 May 2004, Puerto Ingeniero White
"Porota" B., Susana, María Lujan, and Luis, 26 July 2004, Santa Rosa
Stella M. D., 19 May 2004, Puerto Ingeniero White

Cookbooks and Domestic Advice Literature

Bachofen, Elisa. *Enseñanza técnica para la mujer: Su influencia en la conducción científica del hogar y en las diversas actividades*. Buenos Aires, 1932.

Bassi, Angel C. *Gobierno: Administración e hiegene del hogar*. Buenos Aires: Cabaut, 1914.

Beeton, Isabella. *The Book of Household Management*. 1859–61. Reprint, New York: Farrar, Straus, and Giroux, 1969.

Beines, Marta. *Las recetas de Doña Prestisima*, 2d ed. Buenos Aires: Imprenta López, 1952.

Benavento, Teofila. *La perfecta cocinera argentina*. Buenos Aires: Jacobo Peuser, n.d.

Berreteaga, Choly. *Cocina fácil para la mujer moderna*. 1976. 9th ed., edited by Miriam Becker. Buenos Aires: Editorial Atlántida, 1983.

Compañía Italo Argentina de Electricidad. *Cocinando con placer: Recetas selectas para cocinas eléctricas*. Buenos Aires, ca. 1940.

Conferencias sobre arte culinario dictada por la señora Petrona C. de Gandulfo (pamphlet). Courtesy of Marcela Massut.

Congregación de Hijas de María y de Santa Filomena de Tucumán. *El arte de cocinar*. Tucumán Argentina Imp. La Commercial de Anibal L. Medina, 1920.

Cotta, Blanca. "Los 100 mejores recetas de Doña Petrona." *El Clarín* (1999), inserts 1–20.

Dotto, Isadora Canale de. *La cocina moderna*. Santa Fe, Argentina: Ediciones Colmegna, 1962.

El libro del ama de casa. Buenos Aires: Aguilar, 1958.

Eyzaguirre, José. *El libro del buen comer*, 2d ed. Buenos Aires: Editorial Saber Vivir, 1946.

Ferrer, Chola. *Economía en la cocina*. Buenos Aires: Fabril, 1959.

Gandulfo, Petrona C. de. *Bajas calorias: Coma bien y adelgace*. Buenos Aires: Editorial Atlántida, 1975.

———. *Cómo cocina Doña Petrona con ollas a presión*, 2d ed. Buenos Aires: Compañía General Fabril Financiera, 1953.

———. *El libro de Doña Petrona*, 1st–103d eds. Buenos Aires: 1934–2011.

———. *Los cortes de carnes y su utilización: Recetas de cocina preparadas por la señora Petrona C. de Gandulfo*. Buenos Aires: Junta Nacional de Carnes, Ministerio de Agricultura, publication no. 9, 1938.

———. *Mis mejores recetas para fiestas*. Buenos Aires: Sainte Claire Editora, 1989.

———. *Para aprender a decorar*, 1st–2d eds. Buenos Aires: Atlántida, 1941; Fabril Financiara, 1964.

———. *Recetas económicas*, 1st–15th eds. Buenos Aires: 1962–84.

Gandulfo, Petrona C. de, and Dr. Alberto Cormillot. *Coma bien y adelgace*, 2d ed. Buenos Aires: Sebastián de Amorrortu e Hijos, 1974.

Gorriti, Juana Manuela. *Cocina ecléctica*. Buenos Aires: Lajouane, 1890.

Lobstein, Alicia. *365 días sin servicio doméstico*. Buenos Aires: Editorial Sudamericana, 1959.

Molina, Luis Barrantes. *Para mi hogar: Síntesis de economía y sociabilidad domésticas; Escrita expresamente para la Compañía Sansinena de carnes congeladas*. Buenos Aires: 1923.

Mucho Gusto. *El horno familiar*. Buenos Aires: Compañía General Fabril Editora, 1967.

———. *Especialidades de la cocina criolla: Seleccionadas por el personal técnico de la revista Mucho Gusto*. Buenos Aires: Fabril Financiera, 1958.

Oyuela, María Adela. *Cortesia y buenos modales*. Buenos Aires: Biblioteca de Mucho Gusto, 1956.

Perón, Eva. *La Papa: Valor alimenticio, su preparación en la cocina* 2, no. 42. Provincia de Buenos Aires: Ministerio de Asuntos Agrarios, July 1953.

Perry, Maria Della. *La cocina de mi hogar*. Buenos Aires: Talleres Gráficos Argentinos/L. J. Rosso, 1941.

Pietranera, Lola P. de. *El arte de la mesa: Recetario de Doña Lola*, 3d and 4th eds. Buenos Aires: Talleres Gráficos Guillermo Kraft, 1949–50.

Rombauer, Irma S., and Marion Rombauer Becker. *Joy of Cooking*. Indianapolis: Bobbs-Merrill, 1953.

Shields, John. *Chesapeake Bay Cooking*. New York: Broadway Books, 1998.

Simmons, Aly. *Cocinando con olla a presión*. Buenos Aires: El Ateneo, 1950.

Taberna, Lorenza. *La cocina de Lorenza Taberna: Manual práctico de cocina moderna*. Buenos Aires: Editorial Salus, 1957.

Newspapers and Magazines

Multiple Editions

Antena (1951–62, selectively)
Caras y Caretas (1936–38)
El Clarín (1934–2011, selectively)
El Hogar (1931–35)
La Nación (1934–2011, selectively)
Mucho Gusto (1950–81, selectively)
Para Ti (1932–83, selectively)
Radiolandia (1933–92, selectively)
Teleastros (1953)

Specific Articles

Claudía (1958, 1961)
Confirmando (1966)
Crónica (1983, 1985)
El Cronista (1992)
Cuisine e Vins (1990)
Diario Popular (1990)
Femirama (1963–64)
La Fundación: Revista Bimestral de la Fundación Cultural Santiago del Estero (2001)
Gente (1969, 1970, 1978)
Mujer (1984)
New York Times (1969, 1989)
Nuestras Mujeres (1949)
Paladar (1970)
Panorama (1983)
La Prensa (1984, 1998)
Primera Plana (1963)
La Razón (1985)
Revista de Arquitectura (1931)
Revista Mensual de Le Cordon Bleu de Buenos Aires (1932)
Rosalinda (1934)
Satiricon (1972)
Saveur (2005)
Semana Gráfica (2004)
7 Días (1972, 1977)
Sintonia (1933)
Tiempo Argentino (1983)
Todo Chic (1991)

Film, Radio, and Television

"Canasta familiar, bolsa de comidas básicas." Informativo Cinematográfico Provincial, Noticiario Bonarense, Edición Sene 2, #30, Instituto Nacional Juan Domingo Perón, no. 471, videocassette.

La historia oficial [The Official Story]. Luis Puenzo, director, Argentina, 1985, videocassette.

Radio broadcast, 23 May 1967. Rollo 306, Band 1, Pies 125–435, Archivo General de la Nación, tape recording.

Radio interview with Choly Berreteaga, "La otra agenda," 16 June 2010. Tape recording. Available at http://www.alejandrazuccoli.com (2 May 2011).

Las recetas de Doña Petrona. Volver, Archivo Dario Billani. Courtesy of Canal 13, ca. 1964, videocassettes.

Government and Medical Reports and Documents

Aizcorbe, Bautista, Alberto E. J. Fesquet, and Juan Manuel Mateo. *La mujer argentina en el trabajo.* Conocimientos básicos, serie para 5 grado, no. 511. Buenos Aires: Editorial Kapelusz, 1950.

Alberdi, J. B. *Bases y puntos de partida para la organización política de la República Argentina.* Buenos Aires, 1928.

"Alimentación Nacional en las Provincias de Catamarca, Rioja, Santiago del Estero y Tucumán." *Boletin de santidad militar* 7, no. 1 (January 1895).

Almanaque del Ministerio de Agricultura de la Nación, Dirección de Propaganda y Publicaciones. Buenos Aires, 1938.

Anales de la legislación argentina, 18 December 1946, Law 12.919, 1946.

Archivo General de la Nación, Ministerio de Asuntos Técnicos, letters, 1951.

Bähler, Luis Guillermo, ed. *La nación Argentina: Justa, libre, soberana.* 3d ed. Buenos Aires, 1950.

Boletin Oficial, Law 326/56, 20 January 1956.

Carillo, Ramón. "El criterio biológico en el reordenamiento económico de la alimentación en la Argentina." Speech given in the Teatro Cervantes, Buenos Aires, 14 May 1949, as reprinted in *Hechos e ideas* 1, no. 4 (Buenos Aires) (May–June 1974).

Consejo Nacional de Educación. *Digesto de instrucción primaria, leyes, decretos, resoluciones vigentes para las escuelas y dependencias del Consejo Nacional de Educación.* Buenos Aires, 1920.

D'Amato, Dr. Hugo J. (Secretario General del Departamento Nacional de Higiene). "El problema de la alimentación en la República Argentina." *Revista oral de ciencias medicas* 66 (31 August 1941).

"Encuesta sobre alimentación en dos barrios de Córdoba." *Revista médica de Córdoba* 50, nos. 7–9 (July–August–September 1962): 203–7.

Escudero, Pedro. *La alimentación de la familia en Buenos Aires* 1–2. Buenos Aires: Ministerio de Relaciones Exteriores y Culto, Instituto Nacional de la Nutrición, 1938–39.

———. "Estudio técnico económico de la alimentación de 159 familias de obreros y empleados de la ciudad de Buenos Aires." *Trabajos y publicaciones* 4 (Buenos Aires: Publicaciones del Instituto Nacional de Nutrición) (1939): 225.

Estudio Sur. *Potencial económico argentino*. Buenos Aires: Editorial Estrada, 1972.

Everett, Ruth. "El arte de la cocina: Su importante papel en las escuelas públicas de los Estados Unidos de América." *El monitor de la educación común* 375 (translated by María Antonia Solano) (30 April 1904): 918–21.

Guillen, Clotilde. "Algunas observaciones sobre el funcionamiento de las clases de cocina." *El monitor de la educación común* 403 (3 July 1906): 182–86.

———. "La educación doméstica en las escuelas europeas." In *Informe sobre la educación común en la capital, provincias y territorios nacionales, presentado al Ministerio de Instrucción Pública*, edited by Dr. Ponciano Vivanco. Buenos Aires: Guillermo Kraft, 1907.

———. "Enseñanza de la cocina en la escuela primaria." *El monitor de la educación común* 424 (30 April 1908): 189.

———. "Instalación de una cocina escolar." *El monitor de la educación común* 426 (20 June 1908): 330–40.

Instituto Alejandro Bunge. *Soluciones argentinas a los problemas económicos y sociales del presente*. Buenos Aires: Editorial Kraft, 1945.

Junta Nacional de Carnes, Ministerio de Agricultura. *Informe de la labor realizada desde el 1 de octubre 1935 hasta el 30 de septiembre de 1937*. Buenos Aires, 1937.

———. Secretaria de Agricultura y Ganadería. *Junta Nacional de Carnes: Síntesis estadística*. Buenos Aires, 1983.

Lechuga, Julia, et al. *Estadísticas de Argentina, 1913–1990*. Buenos Aires: INDEC, April 1983.

Liga Patriótica Argentina. *Sus escuelas de obreras en las fábricas*. Buenos Aires, 1922.

Martin y Herrera, Félix. *Código de instrucción primaria, colección de leyes, decretos, acuerdos, reglamentos y disposiciones vigentes*. Buenos Aires: Angel Estrada, 1890.

Mégy, María Luisa. "Prácticas del hogar." *El monitor de la educación común* 536, no. 62 (31 August 1917).

———. "Prácticas del hogar, contribución al desarrollo del programa de economía doméstica." *El monitor de la educación común* 574 (31 October 1920).

Ministerio de Educación. *La escuela y el problema de la nutrición del escolar, ciclo de conferencias dedicadas al personal directivo de las escuelas secundarias y primarias*. Buenos Aires, 1949.

Organización de Consumidores. *Defienda sus pesos! Vigile los precios! No pague un centavo más!* Buenos Aires, 1950.

Perón, Eva. *Discurso en el acto inagural de la primera asamblea nacional de movimiento peronista feminino*. Buenos Aires, 26 July 1949.

———. *Discursos completos*. Vol. 1, *1946–1948*. Buenos Aires: Editorial Megafón, 1985.

———. *Discursos completos*. Vol. 2, *1949–1952*. Buenos Aires: Editorial Megafón, 1986.

———. *Escribe Eva Perón*. Buenos Aires: Subsecretaria de Informaciones de la Presidencia, 1950.

———. *La mujer ya puede votar*. Buenos Aires, 1950.

———. *La razón de mi vida*. Buenos Aires: Ediciones Peuser, 1951.

———. *My Mission in Life*. Translated by Ethel Cherry. New York: Vantage Press, 1953.

Perón, Juan Domingo. "Política alimentaria argentina." Speech given in the Teatro Colon, Buenos Aires, 29 April 1949. As reprinted in *Hechos e ideas* 1, no. 4 (May–June 1974).

Prinavalle, Emma Catalá de. *Lecciones de economía doméstica: Obra adoptada por la Dirección General de Instrucción Primaria para servir de texto en las escuelas publicas*, vol. 1. Montevideo: El Siglo Ilustrada de Turenne, Varzi, y Compañía, 1905.

Progreso de la medicina sanitaria en la Argentina. Tercera Conferencia del ciclo "Recetas conquistas de la sanidad argentina." Speech given on 21 February 1951. As reprinted in *Contribuciones al conocimiento sanitario: Obras completas II*. Buenos Aires: Eudeba, 1974.

República Argentina. *Anuario estadístico de la República Argentina, 1957*. Buenos Aires: Dirección Nacional de Estadística y Censos, 1957.

———. *Censo de la República Argentina*. Buenos Aires: Imprenta del Porvenir, 1872.

———. *Censo nacional 1895*. Microfilm. Family History Library. Salt Lake City, Utah, https://www.familysearch.org (accessed 15 February 2011).

———. *Censo nacional 1960*. Prepared by Secretaria de Estado de Hacienda. Buenos Aires, 1963.

———. *Censo nacional de población familias y viviendas 1970*. Prepared by Ministerio de Economía. Buenos Aires, 1973.

———. *El costo de la vida y el poder de compra de la moneda*. Prepared by Dirección General de Estadística de la Nación. Buenos Aires, 1924.

———. *Cuarto censo general, 1936*, vol. 1. Buenos Aires, 1938.

———. *Informe de mográfico de la República Argentina, 1944–1954*. Prepared by Dirección Nacional de Estadística y Censos. Buenos Aires, 1956.

———. *La población de la República Argentina al 31 de diciembre de 1934*. Prepared by Dirección General de Estadística de la Nación. Buenos Aires, 1934.

———. *Resultados generales del censo de la población 1947*. Prepared by Dirección Nacional de Servicios Técnicos del Estado. Buenos Aires, 1951.

———. *Segundo censo de la República Argentina*. Buenos Aires: Taller tip. de la Penitenciaria nacional, 1898.

———. *Tercer censo nacional*, vol. 4. Buenos Aires: Rosso, 1916.

Schleh, Emilio J. "La alimentación en la Argentina: Cómo se alimenta el habitante de la Argentina." *Anales biotipología, eugenesia y medicina social* (1 February 1935).

Secretaria de Salud Pública de la Nación. *Almanaque de la salud*. Buenos Aires: Talleres Anglo Argentinos, 1948.

———. *Plan analítico de salud pública*, prepared by Prof. Dr. Ramón Carillo, vol. 2. Buenos Aires, 1947.

Szretter, Héctor. *La terciarización del empleo en la Argentina: El sector del servicio doméstico*. Buenos Aires: Ministerio de Trabajo y Seguridad Social, 1985.

Other Primary Sources

Amnesty International. *Extracts from the Report of an Amnesty International Mission to Argentina, 6–15 November 1976.* 1977.

Asociación de Ecónomas y Gastrónomas. *Libro de actas.* Buenos Aires, 1976. Courtesy of Asociación de Ecónomas y Gastrónomas.

Baker, Charles Henry. *The South American Gentleman's Companion.* New York: Crown, 1951.

Bonafini, Hebe de. "Historia de las Madres de Plaza de Mayo" (talk). 6 July 1988, available at www.mothers.org.

Elena T. Letter to Petrona C. de Gandulfo, 13 December 1962, Buenos Aires, personal correspondence. Courtesy of Elena T.

Gandulfo, Petrona C. de. Letter to Elena T., 26 December 1962. Courtesy of Elena T.

———. Letters to Teresa C., 26 December 1972 and June 1973. Courtesy of Teresa C.

———. Personal papers. Courtesy of Marcela Massut.

———. Unpublished memoirs, compiled by Oscar Alberto Cejas, ca. 1980. Courtesy of Marcela Massut.

Muchnik, Annamaría. Interview by Jorge Nielsen, transcript, January 2001. Courtesy of Jorge Nielsen.

Nixon, Richard. "The Kitchen Debate." In *The Challenges We Face: Edited and Compiled from the Speeches and Papers of Richard Nixon*, 219–27. New York: McGraw-Hill, 1960.

Sarmiento, Domingo Faustino. *Facundo: Civilización y barbarie.* 1845. Reprint, Barcelona: Editorial Planeta, 1986.

Sutro, Victor. "Radio in Latin America (Part 1)." *Bulletin of the Pan American Union* 68 (October 1934): 649.

Unión Feminista Argentina. Flyer. 1970. Courtesy of Valeria Pita.

www.guisabor.homestead.com/files/e_mag_Nov_2_2.pdf, emag, November 2001.

www.ligadeamasdecasa.com.ar/index1.html (accessed 16 December 2005).

http://www.ligadeamasdelasa.org (accessed 11 April 2011).

Scholarly Works

acha, omar. "Dos estrategias de domesticación de la mujer joven trabajadora: La Casa y el Hogar de la Empleada." In *La fundación Eva Perón y las mujeres: Entre la provocación y la inclusión*, edited by Carolina Barry, Katrina Ramacciotti, and Adriana Valobra. Buenos Aires: Editorial Biblios, 2008.

Adamovsky, Ezequiel. *Historia de la clase media: Apogeo y decadencia de una illusion, 1919–2003.* Buenos Aires: Planeta, 2009.

Adelman, Jeremy. *Frontier Development: Land, Labour, and Capital on the Wheatlands of Argentina and Canada, 1890–1914.* Oxford: Clarendon Press, 1994.

———. *Republic of Capital: Buenos Aires and the Legal Transformation of the Atlantic World.* Palo Alto, Calif.: Stanford University Press, 1999.

Aguilar, Gonzalo. "Televisión y la vida privada." In *Historia de la vida privada: La Argentina entre multitudes y soledades; De los años treinta a la actualidad,* vol. 3, edited by Fernando Devoto and Marta Madero. Buenos Aires: Taurus, 1999.

Aguilar, Paula Lucía. "El hogar como problema y como solución. Una mirada genealógica de la domesticidad a través de las políticas sociales (1890–1940)." Ph.D. diss, Universidad de Buenos Aires, 2012.

Aguilar-Rodriguez, Sandra. "Cooking Modernity: Nutrition Policies, Class, and Gender in 1940s and 1950s Mexico City." *The Americas* 64, no. 2 (October 2007): 177–205.

Aguirre, Patricia. "Gordos de escasez: Las consecuencias de la cocina de la pobreza." In *La cocina como Patrimonio (in)tangible*. Buenos Aires: Comisión para la Preservación del Patrimonio Histórico Cultural de la Ciudad de Buenos Aires, 2002.

————. "Toda la carne al asador." *Todo el historia* 380 (March 1999): 92.

Alberto, Paulina. *Terms of Inclusion: Black Intellectuals in Twentieth-Century Brazil*. Chapel Hill: University of North Carolina Press, 2011.

Aldaburu, María Inés, Inés Cano, Hilda Rais, and Nené Reynoso. *Diario colectivo*. Buenos Aires: Ediciones La Campana, 1982.

Alonso, Martín. *Enciclopedia del idioma*, vol. 2. Madrid: Aguilar, 1968.

Altamirano, Carlos. *Bajo el signo de las masas, 1942–1973*. Buenos Aires: Editorial Ariel, 2001.

Alvarez, Marcelo, and Luisa Pinotti. *A la mesa: Ritos y retos de la alimentación argentina*. Buenos Aires: Grijalbo S.A., 2000.

"The Americas: Pickets Unfenced; Argentina's Unemployed." *Economist*, 20 December 2003, 77–79.

Anderson, Benedict. *Imagined Communities: Reflections on the Origin and Spread of Nationalism*. New York: Verso, 2006.

Anigbo, Osmud A. C. *Commensality and Human Relationships among the Igbo*. Nsukka: University of Nigeria Press, 1987.

Appadurai, Arjun. "How to Make a National Cuisine: Cookbooks in Contemporary India." *Comparative Study of Society and History* 30, no. 1 (1982): 3–24.

Appelbaum, Nancy P. *Muddied Waters: Race, Region, and Local History in Colombia, 1846–1948*. Durham, N.C.: Duke University Press, 2003.

Appelbaum, Nancy P., Anne S. Macpherson, and Karin Alejandra Rosemblatt, eds. *Race and Nation in Modern Latin America*. Chapel Hill: University of North Carolina Press, 2003.

Archetti, Eduardo. "Hibridación, pertenencia y localidad en la construcción de una cocina nacional." In *La Argentina en el siglo XX*, edited by Carlos Altamirano and Fernando Aliata. Quilmes: Ariel, Universidad de Quilmes, 1999.

Arcondo, Aníbal. *Historia de la alimentación en Argentina: Desde los orígenes hasta 1920*. Córdoba: Ferreyra Editor, 2002.

Armstrong, Warwick. "Hunger and Monetarism in Buenos Aires, 1976–1983: A Food Systems Approach." *Boletín de estudios latinoamericanos y del caribe* 45 (December 1988): 29–49.

Armus, Diego. *The Ailing City: Health, Tuberculosis, and Culture in Buenos Aires, 1870–1950*. Durham, N.C.: Duke University Press, 2011.

Arrom, José Juan. "Criollo: Definición y matices de un concepto," *Hispania* 34, no. 2 (May 1951): 172–76.

Bagú, Sergio. *La clase media en la Argentina*. 1950. Reprint, Buenos Aires: Librería Nueva Visión, n.d.

Baily, Samuel. *Immigrants in the Land of Promise: Italians in Buenos Aires and New York City, 1870 to 1914*. Ithaca, N.Y.: Cornell University Press, 1999.

Ballent, Anahi. "La 'casa para todos': Grandeza y miseria de la vivienda masiva." In *Historia de la vida privada: La Argentina entre multitudes y soledades; De los años treinta a la actualidad*, vol. 3, edited by Fernando Devoto and Marta Madero. Buenos Aires: Taurus, 1999.

———. "El lenguaje de bibelot." In *La fundación Eva Perón y las mujeres: Entre la provocación y la inclusión*, edited by Carolina Barry, Katrina Ramacciotti, and Adriana Valobra. Buenos Aires: Editorial Biblios, 2008.

Barrancos, Dora. *La escena iluminada: Ciencias para trabajadores, 1890–1930*. Buenos Aires: Plus Ultra, 1996.

———. *Mujeres, entre la casa y la plaza*. Buenos Aires: Editorial Sudamericana, 2008.

———. *Mujeres en la sociedad argentina: Una historia de cinco siglos*. Buenos Aires: Editorial Sudamericana, 2007.

Barry, Carolina. *Evita capitana: El Partido Peronista Feminino, 1949–1955*. Buenos Aires: EDUNTREF, 2009.

———. "Mujeres en tránsito." In *La fundación Eva Perón y las mujeres: Entre la provocación y la inclusión*, edited by Carolina Barry, Katrina Ramacciotti, and Adriana Valobra. Buenos Aires: Editorial Biblios, 2008.

Barry, Carolina, Katrina Ramacciotti, and Adriana Valobra, eds. *La fundación Eva Perón y las mujeres: Entre la provocación y la inclusión*. Buenos Aires: Editorial Biblios, 2008.

Bauer, Arnold. *Goods, Power, History: Latin America's Material Culture*. Cambridge: Cambridge University Press, 2001.

Belasco, Warren. "Food Matters: Perspectives on an Emerging Field." In *Food Nations: Selling Taste in Consumer Societies*, edited by Warren Belasco and Phillip Scranton. New York: Routledge, 2002.

Belini, Claudio. "La industria durante el primer peronismo (1946–1955): Un análisis de las políticas públicas y su impacto." Ph.D. diss., Universidad de Buenos Aires, 2003.

Bergero, Adriana J. *Intersecting Tango: Cultural Geographies of Buenos Aires, 1900–1930*. Pittsburgh: University of Pittsburgh Press, 2008.

Bertaux, Daniel, ed. *Biography and Society: The Life History Approach in the Social Sciences*. Beverly Hills, Calif.: Sage, 1981.

Billarou, María José. "El ama de casa 'moderna': Los mensajes de la política sanitaria en los primeros gobiernos peronistas." *La aliaba: Revista de estudios de la mujer* 5 (Santa Rosa, Argentina) (2000).

———. "'Cómo es fácil preparar cualquier comida, sin tener mucha ciencia ni mucho tiempo disponible': La cocina de la Salud, 1951–1955." In *Mujeres en escena*, edited by María Herminia Beatriz di Liscia. Santa Rosa, Argentina: Universidad Nacional de la Pampa, 1988.

Blum, Ann S. *Domestic Economies: Family, Work, and Welfare in Mexico City, 1884–1943.* Lincoln: University of Nebraska Press, 2009.

———. "Speaking of Work and Family: Reciprocity, Child Labor, and Social Reproduction, Mexico City, 1920–1940." *Hispanic American Historical Review* 91, no. 1 (February 2011): 63–95.

Bonafini, Hebe de, and Matilde Sánchez. "The Madwomen at the Plaza de Mayo." Translated by Patricia Owen Steiner. In *The Argentina Reader: History, Culture, Politics,* edited by Gabriela Nouzeilles and Graciela Montaldo. Durham, N.C.: Duke University Press, 2002.

Bontempo, Paula. "Construcciones culturales bajo autoritarismo y democracia: Cono sur 1960–2000." Unpublished paper. Courtesy of author.

———. "'Las entusiastas modernas juegan al golf y al tenis': Una mirada a la práctica deportiva desde la revista *Para Ti*," http://www.efdeportes.com, Revista Digital 8, no. 55 (December 2002).

———. "'Para aquellas mujeres equivocadamente modernas' o 'Para aquellas mujeres que cruzáis la ciudad': *Para Ti* y *Vosotras*; Tensiones entre trabajo, matrimonio y maternidad." Paper presented at the VII Jornadas Interescuelas y Departamentos, Salta, September 2001.

Bordo, Susan. *Unbearable Weight: Feminism, Western Culture, and the Body.* Berkeley: University of California Press, 1993.

Borrini, Alberto. *El siglo de la publicidad 1898–1998: Historias de la publicidad gráfica Argentina, 100 años de 1000 anuncios.* Buenos Aires: Editorial Atlántida, 1998.

Bouvard, Marguerite Guzman. *Revolutionizing Motherhood: The Mothers of the Plaza de Mayo.* Wilmington, Del.: Scholarly Resources, 1994.

Boydston, Jean. "To Earn Her Daily Bread: Housework and Antebellum Working-Class Subsistence." In *Unequal Sisters: A Multi-cultural Reader in U.S. Women's History,* 2d ed., edited by Vicki Ruiz and Ellen Dubois. New York: Routledge, 1994.

Brennan, James P., and Mónica B. Gordillo. "Working Class Protest, Popular Revolt, and Urban Insurrection in Argentina: The 1969 'Cordobazo.'" *Journal of Social History* 27, no. 3 (Spring 1994): 477–98.

Briones, Cecilia Lanata. "Revising the Standard of Living of the Working Class of Capital Federal, 1933–1945," available at http://www2.lse.ac.uk/economicHistory/seminars/EH590Workshop/papers/briones.doc (accessed 6 July 2012).

Butler, Judith. *Gender Trouble: Feminism and the Subversion of Identity.* New York: Routledge, 1999.

Caldo, Paula. "De mujer a mujeres . . . un diálogo mediado por las prácticas culinarias: El recetario de doña Petrona; Argentina en la década de 1930." Unpublished paper. Courtesy of author.

———. *Mujeres cocineras: Hacia una historia sociocultural de la cocina argentina a fines del siglo XIX y primera mitad del XX.* Rosario, Argentina: Prohistoria, 2009.

———. "Pequeñas cocineras para grandes amas de casa . . . la propuesta de Angel Bassi para las escuelas argentinas, 1914–1920." *Temas de mujeres* 5, no. 5 (Universidad Nacional de Tucumán) (2009): 6.

———. "Petrona: Cocinera y educadora; El aporte de Petrona C. de Gandulfo en el proceso de la subjectividad de las mujeres argentinas, años 1930." *Revista zona franca* 16 (Rosario, Argentina) (2007): 54–62.

Campagnoli, Mabel. "El feminismo es un humanismo: La década del '70 y 'lo personal es político.'" *Historia género y política en los '70.* Buenos Aires: Femirama, 2005.

Cane, James. *The Fourth Enemy: Journalism and Power in the Making of Peronist Argentina.* University Park: Pennsylvania State University Press, 2011.

Cara, Ana C. "The Poetics of Creole Talk: Toward an Aesthetic of Argentine Verbal Art." *Journal of American Folklore* 116, no. 459 (Winter 2003): 39.

Cárdenas, Isabel Laura. *Ramona y el robot: El servicio doméstico en barrios prestigiosos de Buenos Aires, 1895–1985.* Buenos Aires: Ediciones Búsqueda, 1986.

Carlson, Marifran. *Feminismo! The Women's Movement in Argentina from Its Beginnings to Eva Perón.* Chicago: Academy Chicago Publishers, 1988.

Carretaro, Andrés. *Vida cotidiana en Buenos Aires: Desde la sociedad autoritaria hasta la sociedad de masas (1918–1970).* Buenos Aires: Grupo Editorial Planeta, 2001.

Castagna, Gustavo. "Petrona C. de Gandulfo." Canal 13, 1996. Courtesy of Canal 13.

Castro-Klarén, Sara, and John Charles Chasteen, eds. *Beyond Imagined Communities: Reading and Writing the Nation in Nineteenth-Century Latin America.* Baltimore: Johns Hopkins University Press, 2003.

Caulfield, Sueann. *In Defense of Honor: Sexual Morality, Modernity, and Nation in Early-Twentieth-Century Brazil.* Durham, N.C.: Duke University Press, 2000.

———. "The History of Gender in the Historiography of Latin America." *Hispanic American Historical Review* 81, nos. 3–4 (2001): 451–92.

Caulfield, Sueann, Sarah C. Chambers, and Lara Putnam, eds. *Honor, Status, and Law in Modern Latin America.* Durham, N.C.: Duke University Press, 2005.

CECYM. "Feminismo por feministas: Fragmentos para una historia del feminismo argentino 1970–1996." *Travesías* 5 (Buenos Aires) (1996).

CEPAL. *Cinco estudios sobre la situación de la mujer en América Latina.* Santiago de Chile: Estudios e Informes de CEPAL, Naciones Unidos, 1982.

Chaloub, Sydney. *Ciadade febril: Cortiços e epidemias na corte imperial.* São Paulo: Companhia das Letras, 1996.

Chamosa, Oscar. *The Argentine Folklore Movement: Sugar Elites, Criollo Workers, and the Politics of Cultural Nationalism, 1900–1955.* Tucson: University of Arizona Press, 2010.

Chaney, Elsa M., and Mary Garcia Castro, eds. *Muchachas No More: Household Workers in Latin America and the Caribbean.* Philadelphia: Temple University Press, 1998.

Chasteen, John Charles. *Born in Blood and Fire.* New York: W. W. Norton, 2001.

Chávez, Armando. "Libertad Lamarque: Adiós a las divas." *Memorias de papel.* Havana, Cuba: Editorial José Martí, 2001.

Chelala, César A. "Woman of Valor: An Interview with Mothers of Plaza De Mayo." In *Surviving beyond Fear: Women, Children, and Human Rights in Latin America*, edited by Marjorie Agosín. New York: White Pine Press, 1993.

Chesterson, Bridget. "Chickens Need Hot Ovens: Doña Petrona and the Making of the Argentine Middle Class." *Latin Americanist* 52, no. 2 (June 2008): 61–79.

Chuchuy, Claudio. *Diccionario del Español de Argentina, Español de Argentina— Español de España*. Madrid: Editorial Gredos, 2000.

Claxton, Robert. *From Parsifal to Perón: Early Radio in Argentina, 1920–1944*. Gainesville: University of Florida Press, 2007.

Clendinning, Anne. *Demons of Domesticity: Women and the English Gas Industry, 1889–1939*. Hampshire, England: Ashgate, 2004.

Comisión Nacional sobre La Desaparición de Personas (CONADEP). *Nunca más: Informe de la Comisión Nacional sobre La Desaparición de Personas*. Buenos Aires: EUDEBA, 1984.

Coontz, Stephanie. *The Way We Never Were: American Families and the Nostalgia Trap*. New York: Basic Books, 1992.

Corradi, Juan E. *The Fitful Republic*. Boulder, Colo.: Westview, 1985.

Cortés, Rosalía, Cristina Dirie, and Miguel Braun. *Informe sobre el mercado de trabajo femenino en la Argentina*. Subsecretaría de la Mujer de la Nación, UNICEF, 1988.

Cosse, Isabella. "Argentine Mothers and Fathers and the New Psychological Paradigm of Child Rearing (1958–1973)." *Journal of Family History* 35, no. 180 (2010): 180–202.

———. "*Claudia*: La revista de la mujer moderna en la Argentina de los años sesenta (1957–1973)." *Mora: Revista del Instituto Interdisciplinario de Estudios de Género* 17, no. 1 (Buenos Aires) (2011), available online at http://www.scielo.org.ar.

———. *Estigmas de nacimiento: Peronismo y orden familiar, 1946–1955*. Buenos Aires: Universidad de San Andres, 2006.

———. "Los nuevos prototipos femeninos en los años 60 y 70: De la mujer doméstica a la joven 'liberada.'" In *De minifaldas, militacias y revoluciones: Exploraciones sobre los 70 en la Argentina*, edited by Adriana Andujar, Déborah d'Antonio, Fernanda Gil Lozano, Karin Grammático, and Ana María Laura Rosa. Buenos Aires: Luxemburg, 2009.

———. *Pareja, sexualidad, y familia en los sesenta: Una revolución discreta en Buenos Aires*. Buenos Aires: Siglo Veinteuno Editores Argentina, 2010.

———. "Relaciones de pareja a mediados de siglo en las representaciones de la radio porteña: Entre sueños románticos y visos de realidad." *Estudios sociológicos* 23, no. 73 (January–April 2007): 134.

Cosse, Isabella, Karina Felitti, and Valeria Manzano, eds. *Los '60 de otra manera: Vida cotidiana, género y sexualidades en la Argentina*. Buenos Aires: Promoteo Libros, 2010.

Cott, Nancy. "The Modern Woman of the 1920s, American Style." In *A History of Women in the West: Toward a Cultural Identity in the Twentieth Century*, edited by Francoise Thébaud. Cambridge, Mass.: Belknap Press of Harvard University Press, 1994.

Counihan, Carole. *The Anthropology of Food and Body: Gender, Meaning, and Power.* New York: Routledge, 1999.

Courtis, Corina, and María Inés Pacecca. "La operatoria del género en la migración: Mujeres migrantes y trabajo doméstico en el AMBA." In *Investigaciones e antropología social*, edited by Mabel Grimberg, María Josefina Martínez, and María Inés Fernández Álvarez. Buenos Aires: Facultad de Filosofía y Letras UBA, 2008.

Cowan, Ruth Schwartz. *More Work for Mother: The Ironies of Household Technology from the Open Hearth to the Microwave.* New York: Basic Books, 1983.

Crenshaw, Kimberly. "Intersectionality, Identity Politics, and Violence against Women of Color." In *Critical Race Theory: The Key Writings That Informed the Movement*, edited by Kimberly Crenshaw. New York: New Press, 1995.

Deutsch, Sandra McGee. *Counterrevolution in Argentina, 1900–1932: The Argentine Patriotic League.* Lincoln: University of Nebraska Press, 1986.

———. *Crossing Borders, Claiming a Nation: A History of Argentine Jewish Women, 1880–1955.* Durham, N.C.: Duke University Press, 2010.

———. *Las derechas: The Extreme Right in Argentina, Brazil, and Chile, 1890–1939.* Stanford, Calif.: Stanford University Press, 1999.

———. "Gender and Socio-Political Change in Twentieth Century Latin America." *Hispanic American Historical Review* 71, no. 2 (May 1991): 259–306.

———. "The Visible and Invisible Liga Patriotica Argentina, 1919–28: Gender Roles and the Right Wing." *Hispanic American Historical Review* 64, no. 2 (May 1984): 233–58.

Drinot, Paulo. "Food, Race, and Working-Class Identity: Restaurantes Populares and Populism in 1930s Peru." *The Americas* 62, no. 2 (Oct. 2005): 245–70.

Ehrick, Christine. "Chaplin in Skirts? Niní Marshall and the Female Comic Radio Voice in Argentina, 1937–1943." Paper presented at the annual meeting of the American Historical Association, Boston, 9 January 2011.

———. "'Savage Dissonance': Gender, Voice, and Women's Radio Speech in Argentina, 1930–1945." In *Sound in the Age of Mechanical Reproduction*, edited by David Suisman and Susan Strasser. Philadelphia: University of Pennsylvania Press, 2010.

Elena, Eduardo. *Dignifying Argentina: Peronism, Citizenship, and Mass Consumption.* Pittsburgh: University of Pittsburgh Press, 2011.

———. "Justice and Comfort: Peronist Political Culture and the Search for a New Argentina, 1930–1955." Ph.D. diss., Princeton University, 2002.

———. "Peronism in Good Taste: Culture and Consumption in the Magazine *Argentina*." In *The New Cultural History of Peronism: Power and Identity in Mid-Twentieth-Century Argentina*, edited by Matthew B. Karush and Oscar Chamosa. Durham, N.C.: Duke University Press, 2010.

———. "Peronist Consumer Politics and the Problem of Domesticating Markets in Argentina, 1943–1955." *Hispanic American Historical Review* 87, no. 1 (2007): 111–49.

———. "Point of Departure: Travel and Nationalism in Ernesto Guevara's Argentina." In *Che's Travels: The Making of a Revolutionary in 1950s Latin America*, edited by Paulo Drinot. Durham, N.C.: Duke University Press, 2010.

————. "What the People Want: State Planning and Political Participation in Peronist Argentina, 1946–1955." *Journal of Latin American Studies* 37, no. 1 (February 2005): 81–108.

Elias, Megan J. *Stir It Up: Home Economics in American Culture*. Philadelphia: University of Pennsylvania Press, 2008.

Espínola, Cristina. "La mujer y la política con la llegada del peronismo." *Historia de revistas argentinas* 4, http://www.learevistas.com/notaHistoria.php?nota=1 (accessed 20 July 2011).

Faberman, Judith. "Trabajar con fuentes parcas en regiones marginales: Reflexiones metodológicas acerca del estudio de las poblaciones indígenas rurales en el noroeste argentino, siglos XVII y XIX." *Revista de historia de América* 127 (July–December 2000): 35–62.

Farnsworth-Alvear, Ann. *Dulcinea in the Factory: Myths, Morals, Men and Women in Colombia's Industrial Experiment, 1905–1960*. Durham, N.C.: Duke University Press, 2000.

Fazio, Lorenzo. *Memoria descriptiva de la provincia de Santiago del Estero*. Buenos Aires: Compañía General de Billetes de Banco, 1889.

Feeley-Harnik, Gillian. *The Lord's Table: The Meaning of Food in Early Judaism and Christianity*, 2d ed. Washington, D.C.: Smithsonian Institution Press, 1994.

————. "Religion and Food: An Anthropological Perspective." *Journal of the American Academy of Religion* 63, no. 3 (1995): 565–82.

Feijoo, Maria del Carmen, Marcela M. A. Nari, and Luis Fierro. "Women in Argentina during the 1960s." *Latin American Perspectives* 23, no. 1, Part 2, Women in Latin America (Winter 1996): 7–26.

Feitlowitz, Marguerite. *A Lexicon of Terror: Argentina and the Legacies of Torture*. New York: Oxford University Press, 1998.

Ferguson, Priscilla Parkhurst. *Accounting for Taste: The Triumph of French Cuisine*. Chicago: University of Chicago Press, 2004.

Filc, Judith. *Entre el parentesco y la política: Familia y dictadura, 1976–1983*. Buenos Aires: Editorial Biblios, 1997.

Fisher, Jo. "Gender and the State in Argentina: The Case of the Sindicato de Amas de Casa." In *Hidden Histories of Gender and State in Latin America*, edited by Elizabeth Dore and Maxine Molyneux. Durham, N.C.: Duke University Press, 2000.

————. *Mothers of the Disappeared*. Boston: South End Press, 1989.

Fitch, Noel Riley. *Appetite for Life: The Autobiography of Julia Child*. New York: Anchor Books, 1999.

Franco, Jean. "Going Public: Reinhabiting the Private." In *On Edge: The Crisis of Contemporary Latin American Culture*, edited by George Yudice et al. Minneapolis: University of Minnesota Press, 1992.

Francois, Marie Eileen. "The Products of Consumption: Housework in Latin American Political Economies and Cultures." *History Compass* 6, no. 1 (2008): 207–42.

Fraser, Nicholas, and Maryssa Navarro. *Eva Perón*. New York: W. W. Norton, 1981.

French, John D., and Daniel James. "Introduction." In *The Gendered Worlds of Latin American Women Workers: From Household and Factory to the Union Hall and*

Ballot Box, Comparative and International Working-Class History, edited by John D. French and Daniel James. Durham, N.C.: Duke University Press, 1997.

French-Fuller, Katharine. "Gendered Invisibility, Respectable Cleanliness: The Impact of the Washing Machine on Daily Living in Post-1950 Santiago, Chile." *Journal of Women's History* 18, no. 4 (Winter 2006): 79–100.

———. "'The Woman Who Works Does Not Create Any Social Problems': Discourses about Women, Work, and Consumerism in 1960s Argentina." Paper presented at the annual meeting of the American Historical Association, Boston, 9 January 2011.

Fundación Metrogas. *Historia de la publicidad del gas en la Argentina*. Buenos Aires: Grupo Abierto, 2008.

Gabaccia, Donna. *We Are What We Eat: Ethnic Food and the Making of Americans*. Cambridge, Mass.: Harvard University Press, 1998.

Gadea, Hilda. *Mi vida con el Che*. Lima, Peru: Arteidea Editores, 2005.

———. *My Life with Che: The Making of a Revolutionary*. 1972. Reprint, New York: Palgrave Macmillan, 2008.

Galé, Nidia Elsa. *El gas de la Argentina: Más de un siglo de historia*. Buenos Aires: Ediciones Cooperativas, 2005.

Gallo, Ricardo. *La radio: Ese mundo tan sonoro*, vol. 2. Buenos Aires: Corregidor, 2001.

Gálvez, Lucía. *Las mujeres y la patria: Nuevas historias de amor de la historia argentina*. Buenos Aires: Grupo Editorial Norma, 2001.

Garguin, Enrique. "'Los argentinos decendemos de los barcos': The Racial Articulation of Middle Class Identity in Argentina (1920–1960)." *Latin American and Caribbean Ethnic Studies* 2, no. 2 (2007): 161–84.

———. "El tardío descrubimiento de la clase media en Argentina." *Nuevo topo/ Revista de historia y pensamiento crítico* 4 (September–October 2007): 85–108.

Germani, Gino. "La clase media en la ciudad de Buenos Aires." 1942. Reprinted in *Desarollo Económico* 21, no. 81 (April–June 1981).

———. "La movilidad social en la Argentina." In *Movilidad social en la sociedad industrial*, edited by Seymour Lipset and R. Bendiz. Buenos Aires: EDUEBA, 1963.

Girbal-Blacha, Noemí. "El hogar o la fábrica: De costureras y tejedoras en la Argentina Peronista (1946–1955)." *Revista de ciencias sociales* 6 (Universidad Nacional de Quilmes) (September 1997): 217–30.

Gogna, Mónica. "Domestic Workers in Buenos Aires." In *Muchachas No More: Household Workers in Latin America and the Caribbean*, edited by Elsa M. Chaney and Mary Garcia Castro. Phildelphia: Temple University Press, 1998.

Gold, Carol. *Danish Cookbooks: Domesticity and National Identity, 1616–1901*. Seattle: University of Washington Press, 2007.

Goldar, Ernesto. *Buenos Aires: Vida cotidiana en la década del 50*. Buenos Aires: Plus Ultra, 1992.

Grammático, Karin. "Historia reciente, género y política: El caso de la agrupación Evita." In *Los '60 de otra manera: Vida cotidiana, género y sexualidades en la*

Argentina, edited by Isabella Cosse, Karina Felitti, and Valeria Manzano. Buenos Aires: Promoteo, 2010.

———. "Las mujeres políticas y las feministas en los tempranos setenta: ¿Un diálogo (im)posible?" In *Historia, género y política en los '70*, edited by Andrea Andújar, Déborah D'Antonio, and Nora Domínguez. Buenos Aires: Femirama, 2005.

———. "Populist Continuities in 'Revolutionary' Peronism? A Comparative Analysis of the Great Discourses of the First Peronism (1946–1955) and the Montoneros." In *Gender and Populism In Latin America: Passionate Politics*, edited by Karen Kampwirth. University Park: Pennsylvania State University Press, 2010.

Graña, Juan M., and Damián Kennedy. "Salario real, costo laboral y productividad: Argentina 1947–2006." *Documentos de trabajo* 12 (Universidad de Buenos Aires, CEPED) (November 2008).

Grinberg, Oscar. "El servicio doméstico en el derecho argentina." Thesis, Universidad de Buenos Aires, 1951.

Gringnon, Claude. "Commensality and Social Morphology: An Essay on Typology." In *Food, Drink, and Identity: Cooking, Eating, and Drinking in Europe since the Middle Ages*, edited by Peter Scholliers. Oxford: Berg, 2001.

Guano, Emanuela. "The Denial of Citizenship: 'Barbaric' Buenos Aires and the Middle Class Imaginary. *City and Society* 16, no. 1 (2004): 69–97.

Guy, Donna. "Female-Headed Migrant Families in Buenos Aires, 1930–1950." Paper presented at the annual meeting of the American Historical Association, Boston, 8 January 2011.

———. *Sex and Danger in Buenos Aires: Prostitution, Family, and Nation in Argentina*. Lincoln: University of Nebraska Press, 1991.

———. *White Slavery and Mothers Alive and Dead: The Troubled Meeting of Sex, Gender, Public Health, and Progress in Latin America*. Lincoln: University of Nebraska Press, 2000.

———. "Women, Peonage, and Industrialization: Argentina, 1810–1914." *Latin American Research Review* 16, no. 3 (1981): 65–89.

———. *Women Build the Welfare State: Performing Charity and Creating Rights in Argentina, 1880–1955*. Durham, N.C.: Duke University Press, 2009.

Hammond, Gregory. *The Women's Suffrage Movement and Feminism in Argentina from Roca to Perón*. Albuquerque: University of New Mexico Press, 2011.

Healey, Mark. *The Ruins of the New Argentina: Peronism and the Remaking of San Juan after the 1944 Earthquake*. Durham, N.C.: Duke University Press, 2011.

Hébrard, Jean. "The Writings of Moïse (1898–1985): Birth, Life, and Death of a Narrative of the Great War." Translated by Rebecca J. Scott. *Comparative Studies in Society and History* 44, no. 2 (April 2002): 263–92.

Heldke, Lisa. "Let's Cook Thai: Recipes for Colonialism." In *Pilaf, Pozole, and Pad Thai: American Women and Ethnic Food*, edited by Sherrie A. Inness. Amherst: University of Massachusetts Press, 2001.

Hernández, José. *El gaucho Martín Fierro*. Buenos Aires: G. Kraft, 1872.

———. *La vuelta de Martín Fierro*. Buenos Aires: Libreria del Plata, 1879.

Hoffnung-Garksof, Jesse. *A Tale of Two Cities: Santo Domingo and New York after 1950*. Princeton: Princeton University Press, 2008.

Hollander, Nancy Caro. "Si Evita viviera." *Latin American Perspectives* 1, no. 3 (Autumn 1974): 42–57.

———. "Women: The Forgotten Half of Argentine History." In *Female and Male in Latin America*, edited by Ann Pescatello. Pittsburgh: University of Pittsburgh Press, 1973.

hooks, bell. *Feminist Theory: From Margin to Center*. 1984. 2d ed., Cambridge, Mass.: South End Press Classics, 2000.

Htun, Mala Nani. "Private Lives, Public Policies: Divorce, Abortion, and Family Equality in Latin America." Ph.D. diss., Harvard University, 1999.

Hutchinson, Elizabeth Quay. *Labors Appropriate to Their Sex: Gender, Labor, and Politics in Urban Chile, 1900–1930*. Durham, N.C.: Duke University Press, 2001.

———. "Shifting Solidarities: The Politics of Household Workers in Cold War Chile." *Hispanic American Historical Review* 91, no. 1 (February 2011): 129–62.

Iriarte, Josefina, and Claudia Torre. "Juana Manuela Gorriti: Cocina ecléctica." In *Mujeres y cultura en la Argentina del siglo XIX*, compiled by Lea Fletcher. Buenos Aires: Feminaria Editora, 1994.

James, Daniel. "The Apogee of Perón, 1946–1955." In *Argentina, 1516–1987: From Spanish Colonization to Alfonsín*, edited by David Rock. Berkeley: University of California Press, 1987.

———. *Doña María's Story: Life History, Memory, and Political Identity*. Durham, N.C.: Duke University Press, 2000.

———. "October 17th and 18th, 1945: Mass Protest, Peronism, and the Argentine Working Class, 1946–1976." *Journal of Social History* 21 (Spring 1988): 441–61.

———. "Perón and the People." In *The Argentina Reader: History, Culture, Politics*, edited by Gabriela Nouzeilles and Graciela Montaldo. Durham, N.C.: Duke University Press, 2002.

———. *Resistance and Integration: Peronism and the Argentine Working Class, 1946–1976*. Cambridge: Cambridge University Press, 1988.

Jiménez, Michael F. "The Elision of the Middle Classes and Beyond: History, Politics, and Development Studies in Latin America's 'Short Twentieth Century.'" In *Colonial Legacies: The Problem of Persistence in Latin American History*, edited by Jeremy Adelman. New York: Routledge, 1999.

Johnson, John J. *Political Change in Latin America: The Emergence of the Middle Sectors*. Stanford, Calif.: Stanford University Press, 1958.

Kaplan, Amy. "Manifest Destiny." In *No More Separate Spheres*, edited by Cathy N. Davidson and Jessamyn Hatcher. Durham, N.C.: Duke University Press, 2002.

Karush, Matthew B. *Culture of Class: Radio and Cinema in the Making of a Divided Argentina, 1920–1946*. Durham, N.C.: Duke University Press, 2012.

Knudson, Jerry W. "Veil of Silence: The Argentine Press and the Dirty War, 1976–1983." *Latin American Perspectives* 24, no. 6 (November 1997): 93–112.

Labors of Love: Production and Reproduction in Latin American History. Special issue, *Hispanic American Historical Review* 91, no. 1 (February 2011).

Lascano, Luis C. Alén. "Los Taboada." *Todo es historia* 47 (March 1971): 9–29.

Lattes, Zulma L. Recchini de. *Aspectos demográficos de la urbanización en la Argentina, 1869–1960*. Buenos Aires: Editorial del Instituto Torcuato di Tella, 1973.

Lattes, Zulma L. Recchini de, and Catalina H. Wainerman. "Empleo femenino y desarollo económico: Algunas evidencias." *Desarrollo económico* 66 (1977): 301–17.

———. *El trabajo feminino en el banquillo de los acusados: La medición censal en América Latina*. Mexico City: Terra Nova, 1981.

Lattes, Zulma Recchini de, and Alfredo E. Lattes, comps. *Migraciones en la Argentina: Estudio de las migraciones internas e internacionales, basado en datos censales, 1869–1960*. Buenos Aires: Centro de Investigaciones Sociales, Instituto Torcuato di Tella, 1969.

———. *La población de Argentina*. Buenos Aires, 1975.

Lauderdale Graham, Sandra. *House and Street: The Domestic World of Servants and Masters in Nineteenth-Century Rio De Janeiro*. New York: Cambridge University Press, 1988.

Lavrin, Asunción. *Women, Feminism, and Social Change in Argentina, Chile, and Uruguay, 1890–1940*. Lincoln: University of Nebraska Press, 1995.

Lazzari, Gastón E. de. "Carbón, Kerosene, Gas: Artefactos de cocina en la publicidad gráfica argentina (1940/1970)." *Opción* 21, no. 46 (January–March 2005): 39–54.

———. "Las recetas de cocina en las revistas argentinas (1915–1940)." In *La cocina como Patrimonio (in)tangible*. Buenos Aires: Comisión para la Preservación del Patrimonio Histórico Cultural de la Ciudad de Buenos Aires, 2002.

Leavitt, Sarah A. *From Catherine Beecher to Martha Stewart: A Cultural History of Domestic Advice*. Chapel Hill: University of North Carolina Press, 2002.

Liernur, Jorge Francisco. "Casas y jardines: La construcción del dispositivo doméstico moderno." In *Historia de la vida privada: La Argentina plural*, vol. 2, edited by Fernando Devoto and Marta Madero. Buenos Aires: Taurus, 1999.

———. "El nido de la tempestad, la formación de la casa moderna en la Argentina a través de manuales y artículos sobre economía doméstica, 1870–1910." *Entrepasados: Revista de historia* 13 (1997): 7–36.

Liscia, María Hermina B. di. *Mujeres, maternidad y peronismo*. Santa Rosa, La Pampa, Argentina: Fondo Editorial Pampeano, 2000.

Liscia, María Hermina B. di, and Ana María Lassalle. "Verano del '72: Ollas populares en la huelga de Salinas Grandes." In *Historia, género y política en los '70*, edited by Andrea Andújar, Déborah D'Antonio, and Nora Domínguez. Buenos Aires: Femirama, 2005.

Lobato, Mirta Zaida. "Lenguaje laboral y de género en el trabajo industrial, primera mitad del siglo XX." In *Historia de las mujeres en la Argentina, siglo XX*, edited by Fernanda Gil Lozano, Valeria Silvina Pita, and María Gabriela Ini. Buenos Aires: Taurus, 2000.

———. *Historia de las trabajadoras en la Argentina (1869–1960)*. Buenos Aires: Edhasa, 2007.

———, ed. *Cuando las mujeres reinaban: Belleza, poder, y virtud en la Argentina del siglo XX*. Buenos Aires: Editorial Libros, 2005.

Lobato, Mirta Zaida, and Juan Suriano. *Atlas histórico*. Buenos Aires: Editorial Sudamericana, 2004.

———. *Nueva historia Argentina*. Buenos Aires: Editorial Sudamericana, 2000.

Losada, Leandro. *La alta sociedad en la Buenos Aires de la Belle Epoque: Sociabilidad, estilos de vida e identidades*. Buenos Aires: Siglo Veintiuno Editorial Iberoamericana, 2008.

López, A. Ricardo, and Barbara Weinstein, eds. *The Making of the Middle Class: Toward a Transnational History*. Durham, N.C.: Duke University Press, 2012.

Lovera, José Rafael. *Food Culture in South America*. Translated by Ainoa Larrauri. Westport, Conn.: Greenwood Press, 2005.

Lullo, Orestes di. *El folklore de Santiago del Estero*. Tucumán, Argentina: Universidad Nacional de Tucumán, 1943.

Lullo, Orestes di, and Lewis G. B. Garay. *La vivienda popular de Santiago del Estero*. Tucumán: Universidad Nacional de Tucumán, 1968.

Manzano, Valeria. "The Blue Jean Generation: Youth, Gender, and Sexuality in Buenos Aires, 1958–1975." *Journal of Social History* 42, no. 3 (Spring 2009): 657–76.

———. "Contra toda forma de opresión: Sexo, política y clases medias juveniles en las revista de humor de los primeros 1970." *Sociohistoria* (forthcoming).

———. "Ha llegado la 'nueva ola': Música, consumo y juventud en la Argentina, 1956–1966." In *Los '60 de otra manera: Vida cotidiana, género y sexualidades en la Argentina*, edited by Isabella Cosse, Karina Felitti, and Valeria Manzano. Buenos Aires: Promoteo Libros, 2010.

———. "The Making of Youth in Argentina: Culture, Politics, and Sexuality." Ph.D. diss., Indiana University, 2009.

———. "Sexualizing Youth: Morality Campaigns and Representations of Youth in Early 1960s Buenos Aires." *Journal of the History of Sexuality* 14, no. 4 (2005): 433–61.

Marcus, Steven. "Beeton's Book of Household Management." *New York Times*, 14 December 1969.

Margulis, Mario, and Marcelo Urresti. *Le segración negada: Cultura y discriminación social*. Buenos Aires: Editorial Biblios, 1998.

Margulis, Paola. "Representación del cuerpo en *Para Ti* durante la década del '70." In *Historia, género y política en los '70*, edited by Andrea Andújar, Déborah D'Antonio, and Nora Domínguez. Buenos Aires: Femirama, 2005.

Marini, Ana María [pseudonym]. "Women in Contemporary Argentina." *Latin American Perspectives* 4, no. 4 (Autumn 1977).

Marks, Susan. *Finding Betty Crocker*. New York: Simon and Schuster, 2005.

Marshall, Adriana. "Inmigración, demanda de fuerza de trabajo e estructura ocupacional en el área metropolitana argentina." *Desarrollo ecónomico* 17, no. 65 (Buenos Aires) (1997): 3–37.

Matallana, Andrea. *"Locos por la radio": Una historia social de la radiofonía en la Argentina 1923–1947*. Buenos Aires: Promoteo Libros, 2008.

Mead, Teresa A. *"Civilizing" Rio: Reform and Resistance in a Brazilian City, 1889–1930*. University Park: Pennsylvania State University Press, 1997.

Mendelson, Anne. *Stand Facing the Stove: The Story of the Women Who Gave America the Joy of Cooking*. New York: Scribner, 2003.

Míguez, Eduardo J. "Familias de clase media: La formación de un modelo." In *Historia de la vida privada: La Argentina plural*, vol. 2, edited by Fernando Devoto and Marta Madero. Buenos Aires: Taurus, 1999.

Milanesio, Natalia. "Food Politics and Consumption in Peronist Argentina." *Hispanic American Historical Review* 90, no. 1 (2010): 75–108.

———. "'The Guardian Angels of the Domestic Economy': Housewives' Responsible Consumption in Peronist Argentina." *Journal of Women's History* 18, no. 3 (Fall 2006): 108.

———. "Industry, Nation, and Energy in Peronist Argentina." Paper presented at the annual meeting of the American Historical Association, Boston, 9 January 2011.

———. "Peronists and Cabecitas: Stereotypes and Anxieties at the Peak of Social Change." In *The New Cultural History of Peronism: Power and Identity in Mid-Twentieth-Century Argentina*. Durham, N.C.: Duke University Press, 2010.

Milanich, Nara. *Children of Fate: Childhood, Class, and the State in Chile, 1850–1930*. Durham, N.C.: Duke University Press, 2009.

———. "Women, Children, and the Social Organization of Domestic Labor in Chile." *Hispanic American Historical Review* 91, no. 1 (February 2011): 29–62.

———. "Women, Gender, and Family in Latin America, 1820–2000." In *A Companion to Latin American History*, edited by Thomas Holloway. Malden, Mass.: Blakewell, 2008.

Miller, Francesca. *Latin American Women and the Search for Social Justice*. Hanover, N.H.: University Press of New England, 1991.

Mindez, Leonardo. *Canal siete: Medio siglo perdido; La historia del Estado argentino y su estación de televisión*. Buenos Aires: Ediciones Ciccus, 2001.

Mintz, Sidney. *Sweetness and Power: The Place of Sugar in Modern History*. New York: Viking, 1985.

———. *Tasting Food, Tasting Freedom: Excursions into Eating, Culture, and the Past*. Boston: Beacon Press, 1996.

Molyneux, Maxine. "No God, No Boss, No Husband: Anarchist Feminism in Nineteenth-Century Argentina." *Latin American Perspectives* 13, no. 1 (Winter 1986): 132.

Mooney, Jadwiga E. Pieper. *The Politics of Motherhood: Maternity and Women's Rights in Twentieth-Century Chile*. Pittsburgh: University of Pittsburgh Press, 2009.

Mora y Araujo, Manuel. "Las clases medias consolidadas." In *Buenos Aires: Historia de cuatro siglos*, vol. 2, edited by José Luis Romero and Luis Alberto Romero. Buenos Aires: Editorial Abril, 1983.

Moya, Jose C. *Cousins and Strangers: Spanish Immigrants in Buenos Aires, 1850–1930*. Berkeley: University of California Press, 1998.

Muraro, Heriberto. "La comunicación masiva durante la dictadura militar y la transición democrática en la Argentina, 1876–1983." In *Medios, transformación, cultura y política*, edited by Oscar Landia. Buenos Aires: Editorial Legasa, 1987.

Museo del Puerto Ingeniero White. *Cocina a leña y darle al hacha*. Bahía Blanca: Editorial La Cocina del Museo, 1999.

Nari, Marcela. "La educación de la mujer o acerca de cómo cocinar y cambiar los pañales a su bebé de manera científica." *Mora* 1 (August 1995).

———. "Feminismo por feministas: Fragmentos para una historia del feminismo argentino 1970–1996." *Travesias* 5 (Buenos Aires) (1996): 24–26.

———. "Feminist Awakenings." In *The Argentina Reader: History, Culture, Politics*, edited by Gabriela Nouzeilles and Graciela Montaldo. Durham, N.C.: Duke University Press, 2002.

———. "Maternidad, política y feminismo." In *Historia de las mujeres en la Argentina, siglo XX*, edited by Fernanda Gil Lozano, Valeria Silvina Pita, and María Gabriela Ini. Buenos Aires: Taurus, 2000.

———. *Políticas de la maternidad y maternalismo politico, Buenos Aires, 1890–1940*. Buenos Aires: Editorial Biblios, 2004.

Nash, June. *We Eat the Mines and the Mines Eat Us: Dependency and Exploitation in Bolivian Tin Mines*. New York: Columbia University Press, 1979.

Navarro, Maryssa. "Evita." In *Nueva historia Argentina, Tomo 8, Los años peronistas*, edited by Juan Carlos Torre. Buenos Aires: Editorial Sudamericana, 1998.

———. "The Personal Is Political: Las Madres de Plaza de Mayo." In *Power and Popular Protest*, edited by Susan Eckstein. Berkeley: University of California Press, 1989.

Needell, Jeffrey D. *A Tropical Belle Epoque: Elite Culture and Society in Turn-of-the-Century Rio de Janeiro*. New York: Cambridge University Press, 1987.

Newman, Kathleen, et al., eds. *Women, Culture, and Politics in Latin America*. Berkeley: University of California Press, 1990.

Nielsen, Jorge. *La magia de la television argentina: 1951–1960; cierta historia documentada*. Buenos Aires: Ediciones del Jilguero, 2004.

Nouzeilles, Gabriela, and Graciela Montaldo, eds. *The Argentina Reader: History, Culture, Politics*. Durham, N.C.: Duke University Press, 2002.

Novaro, Marcos, and Palermo Vicente. *La dictadura militar 1976–1983: Del golpe de estado a la restauración democrática*. Buenos Aires: Paidós, 2003.

Nuevo Diccionario de Argentinismos. Santa Fe: Instituto Caro y Cuervo, 1993.

Ohnuki-Tierney, Emiko. *Rice as Self: Japanese Identities through Time*. Princeton: Princeton University Press, 1993.

Olcott, Jocelyn. "Introduction: Researching and Rethinking Labors of Love." *Hispanic American Historical Review* 91, no. 1 (February 2011): 1–27.

———. *Revolutionary Women in Postrevolutionary Mexico*. Durham, N.C.: Duke University Press, 2005.

Owensby, Brian P. *Intimate Ironies: Modernity and the Making of Middle-Class Lives in Brazil*. Stanford, Calif.: Stanford University Press, 1999.

Pagani, Estela. "Aspectos estructurales, tipológicos, evolutivos, y reglamentarios del servicio doméstico en Buenos Aires, 1870–1940." In *III jornadas de historia de Buenos Aires "El trabajo en Buenos Aires."* Buenos Aires: Instituto Histórico de la Ciudad de Buenos Aires, Secretaria de Cultura, 1988.

Page, Joseph. *Perón: A Biography*. New York: Random House, 1983.

Palermo, Silvana. "El sufragio femenino en el Congreso Nacional: Ideologías de género y de ciudadanía en la Argentina, 1916–1955." *Boletín del Instituto de Historia Argentina y Americana* 16/17 (1997–98): 151–78.

Parker, David Stuart. *The Idea of the Middle Class: White-Collar Workers and Peruvian Society, 1900–1950*. University Park: Pennsylvania State University Press, 1998.

Parker, David S., and Louise Walker, eds. *Latin America's Middle Class: Unsettled Questions and New Histories*. Lanham, Md.: Lexington Books, forthcoming.

Peden, Margaret Sayers, ed. *A Woman of Genius: The Intellectual Autobiography of Sor Juana Inés de la Cruz*. Salisbury, Conn.: Lime Rock Press, 1982.

Pérez, Inés. "La domesticación de la 'tele': Usos del televisor en la vida cotidiana; Mar del Plata, 1960–1970 (Argentina)." *Histórica Crítica* 39 (Bogotá) (September–December 2009): 84–105.

———. "El trabajo doméstico y la mecanización del hogar: Discursos, experiencias, representaciones; Mar del Plata en los años sesenta." In *Los '60 de otra manera: Vida cotidiana, género y sexualidades en la Argentina*, edited by Isabella Cosse, Karina Felitti, and Valeria Manzano. Buenos Aires: Promoteo, 2010.

Pérez, Louis A., Jr. *On Becoming Cuban: Identity, Nationality, and Culture*. Chapel Hill: University of North Carolina Press, 1999.

Petras, James. "Argentina: 18 Months of Popular Struggle." *Canadian Dimension* 37, no. 4 (June–August 2003).

Pilcher, Jeffrey M. "Josefina Velázquez de León: Apostle of the Enchilada." In *The Human Tradition in Mexico*, edited by Jeffrey M. Pilcher. Wilmington, Del.: Scholarly Resources, 2003.

———. "Many Chefs in the National Kitchen: Cookbooks and Identity in Nineteenth Century Mexico." In *Latin American Popular Culture: An Introduction*, edited by William H. Beezley and Linda A. Curcio-Nagy. Wilmington, Del.: Scholarly Resources, 2000.

———. *¡Que vivan los tamales! Food and the Making of Mexican Identity*. Albuquerque: University of New Mexico Press, 1998.

———. "Vivan tamales! The Creation of a Mexican National Cuisine." Ph.D. diss., Texas Christian University, 1993.

Pita, Valeria Silvina. *La casa de las locos: Una historia social del Hospital de Mujeres Dementes, Buenos Aires, 1852–90*. Rosario: Prohistoria, 2012.

Pite, Rebekah E. "Biography of Petrona Carrizo de Gandulfo." In *Culinary Biographies*, edited by Alice Arndt. Houston, Tex.: Yes Press, 2006.

———. "Entertaining Inequalities: Doña Petrona, Juanita Bordoy, and Domestic Work in Mid-Twentieth-Century Argentina." *Hispanic American Historical Review* 91, no. 1 (February 2011): 97–128.

———. "The Force of Food: Life on the Atkins Family Sugar Plantation, Cienfuegos, Cuba, 1884–1900." *Massachusetts Historical Review* 5 (2003): 58–93.

Plotkin, Mariano Ben. *Mañana es San Perón: A Cultural History of Perón's Argentina*, translated by Keith Zahniser. Wilmington, Del.: Scholarly Resources, 2002.

Portelli, Alessandro. *The Battle of Valle Giulia: Oral History and the Art of Dialogue.* Madison: University of Wisconsin Press, 1997.

Prieto, Adolfo. *El discurso criollista en la formación de la Argentina moderna.* 1988. Reprint, Buenos Aires: Siglo XXI Editores Argentina, 2006.

Pujol, Sergio. *La década rebelde: Los años 60 en Argentina.* Buenos Aires: Emecé, 2002.

Putnam, Lara. *The Company They Kept: Migrants and the Politics of Gender in Caribbean Costa Rica, 1870–1960.* Chapel Hill: University of North Carolina Press, 2002.

Quesada, María Sáenz. *Isabel Perón: La Argentina en los años de María Estela Martínez Perón.* Buenos Aires: Planeta, 2003.

Quiroga, Hugo. *El tiempo del "Proceso": Conflictos y coincidencias entre políticos y militares, 1976–1983.* Rosario, Argentina: Fundación Ross, 1994.

Ramacciotti, Karina. *La política sanitaria del peronismo.* Buenos Aires: Editorial Biblos, 2009.

———. "Las voces que cuestionaron la política sanitaria del peronismo (1946–1949)." In *Las políticas sociales en perspectiva histórica, Argentina 1870–1952,* edited by Daniel Lvovich and Juan Suriano. Buenos Aires: Promoteo Libros, 2006.

Ramacciotti, Karina Inés, and Adriana María Valobra. "Relaciones de género en la propaganda de la Secretaria de Salud pública de la Argentina, 1946–1949." Unpublished manuscript. Courtesy of authors.

Ramacciotti, Karina Inés, Adriana María Valobra, and omar acha, eds. *Generando el peronismo: Estudios de cultura, política y género, 1946–1955.* Buenos Aires: Proyecto Editorial, 2003.

Recalde, Héctor. *Mujer, condiciones de vida, de trabajo y salud,* vol. 1. Buenos Aires: Centro de América Latina, 1998.

Rein, Monica Esti. *Politics and Education in Argentina, 1946–1962,* translated by Martha Grenzeback. Armonk, N.Y.: M. E. Sharpe, 1998.

Reina, Ruben E. *Paraná: Social Boundaries of an Argentine City.* Austin: Institute of Latin American Studies, University of Texas Press, 1973.

Remedi, Fernando J. *Entre el gusto y la necesidad: La alimentación en la Córdoba de los principios del siglo XX.* Córdoba: Centro de Estudios Históricos, 1998.

———. "Inventando la soberanía del consumidor: Publicidad, privacidad y revolución del mercado en Argentina, 1860–1940." In *Historia de la vida privada: La Argentina entre multitudes y soledades; De los años treinta a la actualidad,* vol. 3, edited by Fernando Devoto and Marta Madero. Buenos Aires: Taurus, 1999.

Revel, Jean-François. *Culture and Cuisine: A Journey through the History of Food,* translated by Helen R. Lane. Garden City, N.Y.: Doubleday, 1982.

Robert, Karen Joyce. "The Argentine Babel: Space, Politics, and Culture in the Growth of Buenos Aires, 1856–1890." Ph.D. diss., University of Michigan, 1997.

Rocchi, Fernando. "La americanización del consumo: Las batallas por el mercado argentino, 1920–1945." In *Americanización, Estados Unidos y América Latina en el siglo XX: Transferencias económicas, tecnológicas y culturales,* edited by María I. Barbero and Andrés M. Regalsky. Buenos Aires: Universidad Nacional de Tres de Febrero, 2003.

————. *Chimneys in the Desert: Industrialization in Argentina during the Export Boom Years, 1870–1930*. Stanford, Calif.: Stanford University Press, 2006.

————. "Inventando la soberanía del consumidor: Publicidad, privacidad y revolución del mercado en Argentina, 1860–1940." In *Historia de la vida privada de los años treinta a la actualidad*, vol. 3, edited by Fernando Devoto and Marta Madero. Buenos Aires: Taurus, 1999.

Rock, David. *Argentina, 1516–1982*. Berkeley: University of California Press, 1985.

————. *Argentina, 1516–1987: From Spanish Colonization to Alfonsín*. Berkeley: University of California Press, 1987.

————. "Argentina, 1930–1946." In *Argentina since Independence*, edited by Leslie Bethell. New York: Cambridge University Press, 1993.

————. "Argentina in 1914: The Pampas, the Interior, Buenos Aires." In *Argentina since Independence*, edited by Leslie Bethell. New York: Cambridge University Press, 1993.

————. "The Survival and Restoration of Peronism." In *Argentina in the Twentieth Century*, edited by David Rock. Pittsburgh: University of Pittsburgh Press, 1975.

Rojas, Julio C. "El servicio doméstico, regimen jurídico." Thesis, Universidad de Buenos Aires, 1956.

Romero, Luis Alberto. *Argentina: Una crónica total del siglo XX*. Buenos Aires: Aguilar, 2000.

————. *Breve historia contemporánea de Argentina*. Buenos Aires: Fondo de Cultura Económica, 1994.

————. *A History of Argentina in the Twentieth Century*, translated by James P. Brennan. University Park: Pennsylvania State University Press, 2002.

Rosemblatt, Karin Alejandra. *Gendered Compromises: Political Culture and the State in Chile, 1920–1950*. Chapel Hill: University of North Carolina Press, 2000.

Ruddick, Sara. *Maternal Thinking*. Boston: Beacon Press, 1989.

Sabato, Hilda. *Agrarian Capitalism and the World Market: Buenos Aires in the Pastoral Age, 1840–1890*. Albuquerque: University of New Mexico Press, 1990.

————. *The Many and the Few: Political Participation in Republican Buenos Aires*. Stanford, Calif.: Stanford University Press, 2001.

Salas, Eugenio Pereira. *Apuntes para la historia de la cocina chilena*. Santiago de Chile: Editorial Universitaria, 1977.

Sarlo, Beatriz. "The Modern City: Buenos Aires, The Peripheral Metropolis." In *Through the Kaleidoscope: The Experience of Modernity in Latin America*, edited by Vivian Schelling. New York: Verso, 2000.

————. *Una modernidad periférica: Buenos Aires, 1920 y 1930*. Buenos Aires: Ediciones Nueva Visión, 1988.

Scarzenella, Eugenia. "Entre dos exilios: Cesare Civita, un editor italiano en Buenos Aires desde la segunda posguerra hasta la dictadura militar (1941–1975)." *Revista de Indias* 69, no. 14 (2009): 65–96.

Schávelzon, Daniel. *Historias del comer y del beber en Buenos Aires: Arquelogía histórica de la vajilla de mesa*. Buenos Aires: Aguilar, 2000.

Schirmer, Jennifer. "'Those Who Die for Life Cannot Be Called Dead': Women and Human Rights in Latin America." In *Surviving beyond Fear: Women, Children, and Human Rights in Latin America*, edited by Marjorie Agosín. New York: White Pine Press, 1993.

Scobie, James. *Buenos Aires: Plaza to Suburb, 1870–1910*. New York: Oxford University Press, 1974.

———. *Revolution on the Pampas: A Social History of Argentine Wheat, 1860–1910*. Austin: University of Texas Press, 1964.

Scott, Joan W. "Gender: A Useful Category of Analysis." *American Historical Review* 91, no. 5 (December 1986): 1053–75.

Scott, Nina M. "Juana Manuela Gorriti's *Cocina ecléctica*: Recipes as Feminine Discourse." In *Recipes for Reading: Community Cookbooks, Stories, Histories*, edited by Anne L. Bower. Amherst: University of Massachusetts Press, 1997.

Scott, Rebecca J. "Reclaiming Gregoria's Mule: The Meaning of Freedom in Arimao and Caunao Valleys, Cienfuegos, 1880–1909." *Past and Present* 170 (February 2001): 181–216.

Scott, Rebecca J., and Jean M. Hébrard. *Freedom Papers: An Atlantic Odyssey in the Age of Emancipation*. Cambridge, Mass.: Harvard University Press, 2012.

Scott Kinzer, Nora. "Women Professionals in Buenos Aires." In *Female and Male in Latin America*, edited by Ann Pescatello. Pittsburgh: University of Pittsburgh Press, 1973.

Serrano Redonnet, María Luisa Olsen de, and Alicia María Zorilla de Rodríguez. *Diccionario de los usos correctos del español*. Buenos Aires: Angel Estrada, 1996.

Serulnikov, Sergio. "When Looting Becomes a Right: Urban Poverty and Food Riots in Argentina." *Latin American Perspectives* 21, no. 3 (Summer 1994): 69–89.

Shapiro, Laura. *Julia Child*. New York: Viking, *2007*.

———. *Something from the Oven: Reinventing Dinner in 1950s America*. New York: Penguin, 2004.

Shepard, Alexandra, and Garthine Walker. "Gender, Change, and Periodisation." *Gender and History* 20, no. 3 (November 2008): 453–62.

Slatta, Richard. *Cowboys of the Americas*. New Haven, Conn.: Yale University Press, 1990.

Smith, Jason Scott. "The Strange History of the Decade: Modernity, Nostalgia, and the Perils of Periodization." *Journal of Social History* 32, no. 2 (Winter 1998): 263–85.

Smith, Peter. *Politics and Beef in Argentina: Patterns of Conflict and Change*. New York: Columbia University Press, 1969.

Steedman, Carolyn. *Landscape for a Good Woman: A Story of Two Lives*. New Brunswick, N.J.: Rutgers University Press, 1987.

Stepan, Nancy Leys. *"The Hour of Eugenics": Race, Gender, and Nation in Latin America*. Ithaca, N.Y.: Cornell University Press, 1991.

Stern, Steve. *The Secret History of Gender: Women, Men, and Power in Late Colonial Mexico*. Chapel Hill: University of North Carolina Press, 1995.

Strauss, David. *Setting the Table for Julia Child: Gourmet Dining in America, 1934–1961*. Baltimore: John Hopkins University Press, 2011.

Sutton, David. *Remembrance of Repasts: An Anthropology of Food and Memory*. Oxford: Berg, 2001.

Szuchman, Mark D., and Eugene F. Sofer. "The State of Occupational Stratification Studies in Argentina." *Latin American Research Review* 11, no. 1 (1976).

Tartarini, Jorge. *Doña Petrona, la cocina y el gas*. Buenos Aires: Fundación Metrogas, 2009.

Tasso, Alberto. *Ferrocarril, quebracho y alfalfa: Un ciclo de agricultura capitalista en Santiago del Estero*. Santiago del Estero: Alción Editora, 2007.

————. *Historia testimonial argentina: Documentos vivos de nuestro pasado*. Buenos Aires: Centro Editor América Latina, 1984.

Taylor, Diana. *Disappearing Acts: Spectacles of Gender and Nationalism in Argentina's "Dirty War."* Durham, N.C.: Duke University Press, 1997.

Taylor, Julie M. *Eva Perón: The Myths of a Woman*. Chicago: University of Chicago Press, 1979.

Tenti, María Mercedes. "Escuela y centenario el caso de Santiago de Estero." *Trabajo y sociedad* 9, no. 9 (Santiago del Estero) (Winter 2007): 1–4.

Theophano, Janet. *Eat My Words: Reading Women's Lives through the Cookbooks They Wrote*. New York: Palgrave, 2002.

Tinsman, Heidi. "The Indispensible Service of Sisters: Considering Domestic Service in United States and Latin American Studies." *Journal of Women's History* 4, no. 1 (Spring 1992): 37–59.

————. *Partners in Conflict: The Politics of Gender, Sexuality, and Labor in the Chilean Agrarian Reform, 1950–1973*. Durham, N.C.: Duke University Press, 2002.

Tobin, Jeffrey P. "Manly Acts: Buenos Aires, 24 March 1996." Ph.D. diss., Rice University, 1998.

————. "Patrimonializaciones gastronómicas: La construcción culinaria de la nacionalidad." In *La cocina como patrimonio (in)tangible*. Buenos Aires: Comisión para la Preservación del Patrimonio Histórico Cultural de la Ciudad de Buenos Aires, 2002.

Toer, J. C., et al., eds. *Historias del gas en la Argentina, 1823–1998*. Buenos Aires: Trasportadora de Gas del Sur S.A., 1998.

Torado, Susana. *Historia de la familia en la argentina moderna (1870–2000)*. Buenos Aires: Ediciones de la Flor, 2003.

Torre, Juan Carlos, and Elisa Pastoriza. "La democratización del bienester." *Nueva historia Argentina, Tomo 8, Los años peronistas*, edited by Juan Carlos Torre. Buenos Aires: Editorial Sudamericana, 1998.

Torre, Juan Carlos, and Liliana de Riz. "Argentina since 1946." In *Argentina since Independence*, edited by Leslie Bethell. New York: Cambridge University Press, 1993.

Traphagan, John W., and Keith L. Brown. "Fast Food and Intergenerational Commensality in Japan: New Styles and Old Patterns." *Ethnology* 41, no. 2 (Spring 2002): 119–34.

Traversa, Oscar. *Cuerpos de papel: Figuraciones del cuerpo en la prensa 1918–1940*. Barcelona: Gedisa Editorial, 1997.

Trillo, Mauricio Tenorio. "1910 Mexico City." *Journal of Latin American Studies* 28, no. 1 (1996).

Ulanovsky, Carlos. "Noticias de los años del fuego." In *Paren las rotativas: Una historia de las grandes diarios, revistas y periodistas argentinos*. Buenos Aires: Edhasa, 1997.

———. *Paren las rotativas: Diarios, revistas y periodistas (1920–1969)*. Buenos Aires: Emecé, 2005.

Ulanovsky, Carlos, Silvia Itkin, and Pablo Sirvén. *Estamos en el aire, una historia de la televisión en la Argentina*. Buenos Aires: Editorial Planeta Argentina, 1999.

Ulrich, Laurel Thatcher. *A Midwife's Tale: The Life of Martha Ballard, Based on Her Diary, 1785–1812*. New York: Knopf, 1990.

Varela, Mirta. *La televisión criolla: Desde sus incicios hasta la llegada del hombre a la luna, 1951–1969*. Buenos Aires: Edhasa, 2005.

Vassallo, Alejandra. "'Las mujeres dicen basta': Feminismo, motivación y política de los setenta." In *Historia, género y política en los '70*, edited by Andrea Andújar, Déborah D'Antonio, and Nora Domínguez. Buenos Aires: Femirama, 2005.

Villalta, Carla. "La apropiación de 'menores': Entre hechos excepcionales y normalidades admitidas." *Revista estudios* 16 (Universidad Nacional de Córdoba) (2005): 129–47.

Wade, Peter. *Blackness and Race Mixture: The Dynamics of Racial Identity in Colombia*. Baltimore: Johns Hopkins University Press, 1993.

Wainerman, Catalina. "Familia, trabajo y relaciones de género." In *Entre familia y trabajo: Relaciones, conflictos y políticas de género en Europa y América Latina*, edited by María Antonia Carbonero Gamandí and Silvila Levín. Rosario, Argentina: Homo Sapiens Ediciones, 2007.

———. *Sexismo en los libros de lectura de escuela primaria*. Buenos Aires: Ides, 1987.

———. *La vida cotidiana en las nuevas familias: ¿Una revolución estancada?* Buenos Aires: Lumiere, 2005.

———, ed. *Vivir en familia*. Buenos Aires: UNICEF/Losada, 1994.

Wainerman, Catalina H., and Marysa Navarro. "El trabajo de la mujer en la Argentina: Un analysis preliminar de las ideas dominantes en las primeras décadas del siglo XX." *Cuaderno del Cenep* 7 (1979): 17–18.

Walter, Richard. *Politics and Urban Growth*. New York: Cambridge University Press, 1993.

Weinstein, Barbara. *For Social Peace in Brazil: Industrialists and the Remaking of the Working Class in São Paulo, 1920–1964*. Chapel Hill: University of North Carolina Press, 1996.

———. "Racializing Regional Difference: São Paulo versus Brazil, 1932." In *Race and Nation in Modern Latin America*, edited by Nancy Appelbaum, Anne Macpherson, and Karin Rosemblatt. Chapel Hill: University of North Carolina Press, 2003.

———. "Unskilled Worker, Skilled Housewife: Constructing the Working-Class Woman in São Paolo, Brazil." In *The Gendered Worlds of Latin American Women Workers: From Household and Factory to the Union Hall and Ballot Box*, edited by John D. French and Daniel James. Durham, N.C.: Duke University Press, 1997.

Winbaum, Alys Eve, Lynn M. Thomas, et al., eds. *The Modern Girl around the World: Consumption, Modernity, and Globalization.* Durham, N.C.: Duke University Press, 2008.

Winn, Peter. *The Americas: The Changing Face of Latin America and the Caribbean.* 1992. Reprint, Berkeley: University of California Press, 1999.

———. *Weavers of Revolution: The Yarur Workers and Chile's Road to Socialism.* New York: Oxford University Press, 1986.

Zabaleta, Marta Raquel. *Feminine Stereotypes and Roles in Theory and Practice in Argentina before and after First Lady Eva Perón.* Lewiston, N.Y.: Edwin Mellen, 2000.

Zurita, Carlos. *El servicio doméstico en Argentina: El caso de Santiago del Estero.* Santiago del Estero, Argentina: Instituto Central de Investigaciones Científicas, Universidad Católica de Santiago del Estero, 1983.

———. "Trabajo, servidumbre y situaciones de género: Algunas acotaciones sobre el servicio doméstico en Santiago del Estero, Argentina." Paper, Universidad Nacional de Santiago del Estero, n.d.

INDEX

Abanico of hot and cold tongue, 86

Adell, Héctor, 204

Afro-Argentines, 10, 230 (n. 25), 231 (n. 26)

Aguilar (publishing house), 146

Aguirre, Patricia, 197

Aleandro, Norma, 208, 273 (n. 125)

Alejandro Bunge Institute, 100

Alfonsín, Raul, 211, 215

"Al margen de las conferencias" (magazine column), 76–79, 88

Almorzando con Mirtha Legrand (TV show), 228, 278 (n. 32)

Amas de casa (homemakers), 10–12, 57, 231 (n. 29); advice books for, 146–47; advice for in *El libro de Doña Petrona*, 71, 74; cookbooks for, 68, 70, 145; Doña Petrona speaking to, 77–78, 114, 129, 145, 148, 176; Doña Petrona's popularity with, 12, 15, 166; early twentieth century, 10, 29–30; economic importance of, 225; home management and, 29–30, 74, 245 (nn. 98, 100); Liga de Amas de Casa, 140, 145–46, 149; nineteenth century, 10–11; Peronist government and, 109, 116, 118, 123–27, 129, 131, 252 (n. 71); professionalizing, 1950s to 1960s, 18, 123–27, 145–49, 158; Sindicato de Amas de Casa (SACRA), 1980s, 214; translation of term, 231 (n. 9). *See also* Domesticity; Home economics

Anderson, Benedict, 19

Ankerman, Ortiga, 69

Antipasto, 78

Aramburu, Pedro Eugenio, 140

Aremengol, Tita, 66

Argentina: censorship of press, 1970s, 202, 203, 272 (n. 95); Christmas and, 92–93; disappearances, 201–2, 203, 208, 272 (nn. 87, 95), 273 (nn. 106, 125); domestic servant rights legislation, 140–41, 259 (n. 94); early twentieth-century schooling, 26–29, 234 (n. 17); Great Depression and, 8–9, 56–57; map of, 2; mass media and, 5, 14, 55–56, 65, 119, 167, 203, 247 (n. 145); military governments, 9, 18, 57, 87, 99, 106, 139, 155, 162, 181, 184, 201–2, 217–18; modernizing of homes, 1920s and 1930s, 51, 62, 243 (n. 31); nationalism and, 19–20, 21, 58; poverty and, 8–9, 16, 20, 39, 104, 155, 197, 210, 226, 232 (n. 49), 237–38 (n. 94); radio broadcasting and, 65–67, 79, 80, 94, 110, 244 (n. 63), 247 (nn. 128, 134), 253 (n. 87); Soccer World Cup, 1978, 183–84, 208, 273 (n. 123); social classes of, 75, 104, 105, 174, 245–46 (n. 104), 276 (n. 14); U.S. influences on, 147, 150; women's suffrage, 57, 107–8, 117, 222, 241 (n. 3); working men in, 43, 239 (n. 121)

—economy: 1940s to 1950s, 98–99, 116, 117, 122–23, 127, 139, 140, 144–45; 1960s, 152, 155, 162; 1970s, 189, 193, 194, 195; 1980s, 210–11, 215; 1990s to 2000s, 220–21, 276 (n. 14), 277 (n. 15); early twentieth century, 38, 39, 77; twentieth-century overview, 8–9, 13, 17

—food: and poverty, 1980s, 212, 215, 220, 275 (n. 150); consumption patterns, late 1940s, 115, 254 (n. 114); shortages, 16, 128, 194, 270–71 (n. 56); government interest in health and, 85–87, 88, 248 (nn. 162–63)

—politics: 1940s, 99, 103–6, 250
(n. 25); 1950s to 1960s, 139, 140,
144–45, 153, 259 (n. 88); 1970s to
1980s, 184, 189, 192–93, 201–2,
211–12, 215, 275 (n. 140), 276 (n. 164)
—vis-à-vis other Latin American nations: culinary repertoire, 6, 40, 109,
139, 153–54, 223, 277 (n. 19); domestic instruction, 61–62; Doña Petrona's
popularity, 14, 76, 114, 156, 209,
233 (n. 60); early cookbooks, 5–6,
30–31; education/literacy, 6, 7, 71;
elites, 40, 62; Eurocentrism, 40, 223;
Eurocentrism's decline, 153, 157, 187;
European immigration, 6, 9, 223;
male privilege, 224; middle class, 8,
224, 230 (nn. 18, 20); native culture,
9, 10, 153, 187, 230 (n. 23); pan–Latin
Americanism, 153, 187; perceived
dominance of, 6, 9, 157; perceived
exceptionalism of, 9; popularity of
radio, 66; prohibition on politics at
the table, 193–94; publishing industry, 95; use of term *criollo*, 10, 231
(nn. 27, 28); use of term *ecónoma*, 48,
240 (n. 155); women's roles/experi-
ences, 7, 11–12, 41, 61–62, 214, 224
See also Buenos Aires; Community
building; Elites; Immigration; Men in
Argentina; Middle classes; Peronist
government; Race in Argentina;
Television—in Argentina; Women in
Argentina; Working class
Argentine Association of Biotypology,
Eugenics, and Social Medicine, 85
Argentine Woman at Work, The, 124, 125
Arias, Alfredo, 133–34, 227
Armus, Diego, 28
Article 1624 of the Civil Code, 141
Asado (beef barbecue), 12, 74, 187; Asado
al Horno, 74
Asociación de Ecónomas y Gastrónomas,
205–6, 273 (nn. 105, 107)
Atlántida (publishing house), 69, 95–96,
114, 119, 186

Bagú, Sergio, 75
Bajas calorías (Doña Petrona), 199
Baker, Charles Henry, 193
Baldi, Angel, 42, 48, 65, 106–7, 133, 239
(n. 118), 247 (n. 129)
Baldi, María Adela, 133
Ballent, Anahi, 112–13
Barone, Orlando, 219
Barrancos, Dora, 45
Barry, Carolina, 110
Bassi, Angel, 28, 235 (n. 34)
Beatriz (adopted "daughter" or *criada* of
Petrona), 35, 42, 237 (n. 80)
Becker, Marion Rombauer, 69
Becker, Miriam, 94, 171, 196, 200–201,
209, 211, 271–72 (n. 79)
Beef, 11, 50, 271 (n. 59); Argentine
export of, 8, 86, 98, 115–16, 127, 128,
248 (n. 166); *asado* (beef barbecue),
12, 74, 187; domestic consumption
of, 7, 86; Doña Petrona, promotion
of cuts of meat and, 84–85, 86–87,
188; *El libro de Doña Petrona* and,
73–74; immigrant preparations of,
40; National Meat Board, 84–87;
Peronist government policies and,
115–16, 126; reserving of for export,
115–16, 152, 269 (n. 24); shortages of,
128, 188, 194–95; working-class consumption of, 115, 116–17, 254 (nn. 114,
124). *See also* Empanadas
Beeton, Mrs., 5
Beines, Marta, 129, 153, 154, 180
Benavento, Teófila (Susana Torres de
Castex), 31, 236 (n. 50)
Berreteaga, Choly, 200–201, 204, 271–72
(n. 79)
Betty Crocker, 6, 208
Bible, 4, 18, 220
Bifes de lomo a la maitre d'hotel, 86
Bonafini, Hebe de, 215
Book of Household Management, The
(Mrs. Beeton), 5
Bordoy, Juana "Juanita": children's
games based on relationship with

Petrona, 173–74; death of, 220; as
Doña Petrona's servant, 35, 114,
137–38, 141, 196, 215, 216, 219,
254 (n. 109), 258 (nn. 76, 78), 265
(n. 95); Doña Petrona's treatment
of, 14, 136–38, 152, 168–75, 220, 264
(n. 58), 265 (n. 95), 266 (n. 115); as
Doña Petrona's TV show assistant,
18, 136, 138, 168, 169, 170–72, 178,
179, 184, 185, 258 (n. 74), 264 (n. 58),
265 (n. 94), 266 (n. 104); homage to,
2000s, 227–28; popularity of, 173
Borges, Jorge Luis, 119, 255 (n. 129)
Brazil, 61–62, 156
Bread, 16, 33, 128, 131
Britain, 48, 98, 211, 248 (n. 166)
Buenas Tardes, Mucho Gusto (TV show),
151, 157–59, 173, 178–79, 186, 202,
221
Buenos Aires: cooking and, 31–32,
42–43, 48, 50, 76–77, 134–35, 222;
cost of living, 1930s, 69, 244 (n. 76);
domestic servants, early twentieth
century, 41, 47, 48, 74; early twentieth century, 27, 31–32, 38–43;
government workers, early twentieth
century, 42, 238 (n. 115); males to
females ratio, 1930s, 57, 242 (n. 6);
males to females ratio, early twentieth century, 38, 237 (n. 90); middle
classes of, 8, 39, 75, 245 (n. 102),
245–46 (n. 104); modernizing of
homes, 1920s and 1930s, 51, 62;
population growth, 1930s and 1940s,
57, 99; provincial immigrants to, 14,
25, 38, 41, 57, 99, 237 (n. 88); television and, 142, 159, 274 (n. 133)
Bunge, Augusto, 44
Bustos, Horacio, 186

Cabecitas negras, 105
Cakes, 82, 97–98, 136, 142, 183, 185, 198
Caldo, Paula, 11
Camps, Sibila, 210, 274 (n. 137)
Canal 7 TV channel, 132–33

Canal 9 TV channel, 185
Canal 13 TV channel, 157
Canal TV, 149, 150
Cannelloni, 73, 103
Caras y Caretas, 46, 80–83, 89, 247
(n. 141), 249 (n. 7)
Carbonada criolla, 86, 187–88
Carillo, Ramón, 116, 124
Carmen, María del, 101
Carrizo, Manuel, 26, 234 (n. 16)
Cartel Sonoro (radio show), 66
Cartier, Jean, 132
Casa D'Huicque, 96
Castagna, Gustavo, 127
Castillo, Ramón, 99
Catholic Church, 109
Cejas, Oscar Alberto, 25, 84
Celebrity: culinary, 5–7, 126; culture
of, 1960s and 1970s, 176, 189; and
outspoken opposition to government,
119, 208, 273 (n. 125), 254 (n. 28)
Censorship. *See* Argentina: censorship of
press, 1970s
Centro Azucarero, 68
Cerain, Marta, 186
Chamosa, Oscar, 10
Chicken, 70, 73, 121–22, 143, 178, 195,
255 (n. 2)
Child, Julia, 6, 138, 160, 164, 210, 229
(n. 15)
Chile, 48, 240–41 (n. 155)
Christmas, 92–93, 118
Claudia, 147, 186, 274 (n. 126)
Claxton, Robert, 80
Clotilde, Dolores "Lola" (Doña Lola),
133
Cocina criolla (creole cooking), 7, 30,
33, 40, 153, 204–5, 233 (n. 5), 262
(n. 15); Doña Petrona and, 10, 24, 63,
72, 86, 143, 152, 154, 187–88
Cocina ecléctica (Gorriti), 31
Cocina fácil para la mujer moderna,
200–201
Colombia, 62
Colomer, Elina, 132

Coma bien y adlegace (Eat Well and
Get Thin) (Petrona and Cormillot),
198–99
Comisión para el Estudio y Propaganda
de la Carne, 86
Commensality, 19, 20, 233 (n. 62)
Community building: and cooking/eat-
ing practices, 19–21, 54, 56, 76; and
Doña Petrona, 12, 20–21, 56, 136, 181,
205; and mass media, 19–20, 56, 180;
and women's domestic activities, 12,
19–21, 54, 76, 205, 221–22, 225, 228
*Como cocina Doña Petrona con olla a
presión*, 129
Confirmando, 167
Consumer market: growth of, 5, 50,
56–57, 88, 105, 117–18, 222; Peronist
government efforts to control, 9, 94,
103, 105, 106, 107, 115–16, 119–20,
127, 251 (n. 64). *See also* Consumption
Consumers, women: businesses' targeting of, 4, 15, 45–46, 53–54, 55–56, 76,
85, 103, 132; and domestic advice, 88;
Doña Petrona's relationship with, 15,
18, 54, 58, 94, 107, 129, 184; and gender dynamics, 5, 53; mass media and,
68, 88; Peronist government and, 94,
105, 116, 118, 123, 132, 222; Primitiva
and, 45, 46–48, 50, 62, 63, 65, 68;
role of in modernizing, middle-class
Argentina, 4–5, 11, 19, 53, 57, 103,
203, 225, 228
Consumption: contraction of, 155, 162;
critique of "liberated" women and,
176; Doña Petrona and changing
patterns of, 14, 89, 122, 127, 150, 152,
162, 163–64; Doña Petrona and ideal
of progress through, 21, 45, 74–75,
89, 93–94, 110, 112, 119, 127, 149,
222; and food/cooking, 7, 84–85, 88,
115–16, 118, 127, 254 (n. 114); growth
of, 74–75, 101, 210; Peronist government and expansion of, 93–94, 110,
112, 117, 118, 119, 139; and social class,

75; and social mobility/progress, 21,
89, 93–94, 117, 119, 131, 223; U.S.
promotion of, 122, 131, 150, 255
(n. 6). *See also* Consumer market;
Consumers, women
Cookbooks: *amas de casa* and, 68, 70,
145; *Bajas calorías* (Doña Petrona),
199; of *cocina criolla* (creole cooking), 153; *Cocina fácil para la mujer
moderna*, 200–201; competition for
Doña Petrona, 95, 133, 250 (n. 15);
diet cookbooks, 198–201, 213, 271
(n. 69); of Doña Petrona, 13, 17,
96–97, 129, 198–99, 213, 223, 227,
232 (n. 41), 271 (n. 69); *El arte de la
mesa: El recetario de Doña Lola*, 133;
nineteenth to twentieth century, 5–7,
30–32, 70, 229 (nn. 5, 12, 15), 236
(nn. 47, 50); *Para aprender a decorar*
(Learning How to Decorate), 96–97,
155–56, 250 (nn. 18–19); politics and,
202–3; for pressure cookers, 129, 140;
Royal baking powder free booklet,
103, 251 (n. 44); U.S. vs. Argentine,
6–7, 68–69, 229 (nn. 12–15), 229–30
(n. 16). See also *El libro de Doña
Petrona*; *Recetas económicas*
Cooking: Afro-Argentine influence, 10,
231 (n. 26); in Argentina, 1980s,
3–4, 210, 274 (n. 137); *asado* (beef
barbecue) prepared by men, 12,
74, 187; Buenos Aires and, 31–32,
42–43, 48, 50, 76–77, 134–35, 222;
dirty fuels for, 30, 32, 33, 47, 62, 106;
económa vs. *cocinera* and, 13, 24,
29, 48, 53, 82–83; gas vs. other fuels
for, 47, 49–50, 59, 62, 63, 106, 145;
male chefs, 5, 6–7, 30, 42, 48, 67, 207,
215, 217, 239 (n. 118), 273 (n. 116);
modern approach to, 89, 113, 176, 178,
213, 225; new style for the modern
woman, 1970s, 200–201; respectability and, 43, 51–52, 53, 58–61, 62–63;
from scratch vs. using processed

foods, 122, 255 (n. 6); women's collection of Petrona's recipes, 78, 79, 82, 102, 103, 188, 246 (n. 126), 247 (nn. 142–43). *See also* Cookbooks; Cuisine; *El libro de Doña Petrona*; Gandulfo, Petrona Carrizo de—cooking and cookbooks; Recipes

Copa "El Hogar" ("El Hogar" Sundae), 55

Cordero wine, 69

Cordobazo protest, 153

Cormillot, Alberto, 198, 199

Cornstarch, 101

Corporations, targeting women consumers, 45–46, 53–54, 55–56, 85, 103, 132

Cortesia y buenos modales (Oyuela), 141

Cosse, Isabella, 167

Cotta, Blanca, 227

Criollo/a, 10, 26, 231 (nn. 27–28), 233 (n. 5), 234 (n. 13)

Cuisine: of Argentine elite, early twentieth century, 32–33, 40–41; Asian, 188, 269 (n. 19); British, 97–98; Doña Petrona and, 7, 72–73, 153, 154, 161–62, 199–200, 269 (n. 19); in *El libro de Doña Petrona*, 7, 72–73, 199–200, 213; French, 7, 33, 40, 41, 43, 53, 62–63, 72, 245 (n. 94); immigrant groups and, 39–40, 238 (n. 98); Italian, 40, 95, 174, 266 (n. 125); national Argentine, 10, 72, 73, 95, 118, 187, 223, 245 (nn. 92, 94); poverty and, 16, 33, 40, 232 (n. 49); South American, 154; Spanish, 40, 72. See also *Cocina criolla*

Cullen de Aldao, Mercedes, 31

Curso de Política Alimentaria Argentina, 114

DairyCo, 69

Decurgez, Elena Zara de, 140, 259 (n. 92)

Desserts, 50, 55, 77, 97–98

Día del Ama de Casa, 145–46

Dieting, 197–201

"Dirty War," 18, 184–86, 201–1, 217–18

Dillon, María Cristina, 50, 205–6

Disappearances. *See* Argentina: disappearances

Dix, Dorothy, 122, 255 (n. 4)

Domesticity: changing views of beginning in 1960s, 19, 123, 150, 152, 181, 186, 218; cooking as component of, 53, 221, 222; Doña Petrona as purveyor of middle-class ideal of, 7, 18, 19, 21, 93–94, 118, 148, 149, 152, 169, 176, 180–81, 220, 222–23; Doña Petrona as purveyor of updated ideal of in 1960s, 152, 167, 176; and gender roles/expectations, 5, 7, 11–12, 53, 110, 123, 150, 152, 180–81, 207, 221, 222, 223, 228; influence of U.S. ideas about, 122, 148; modernization of in 1920s and 1930s, 51, 53, 62; Peronist government and, 18, 93–94, 110, 124; social class distinctions in regard to, 29–30, 93–94, 110, 169–70; and women's extradomestic work, 11, 186, 223

Domestic servants: changes through twentieth century, 11, 113, 147, 245 (n. 100), 254 (nn. 107–8), 261 (n. 128); changing names of, 141, 260 (n. 100); Doña Petrona's advice about, 74, 112, 113–14; early twentieth century, Buenos Aires, 41, 47, 48; *El libro de Doña Petrona*, use of by, 15; growth of, 1960s, 179, 261 (n. 128); lack of, 1940s and 1950s, 112, 113, 146–48; late 1950s and, 140–42, 146–48, 264 (n. 62); legal protection for, 140–41, 148, 259 (n. 94); men vs. women as, 113, 141, 245 (n. 98), 253 (n. 105); 1980s and, 215, 224; respect suggested for, 141–42, 148; social inferiority of, 20, 29–30; women managing, 30, 48, 74, 141, 171, 179

Domestic work: Doña Petrona's early avoidance of, 34–35; feminization

of, 11, 113, 224; as inappropriate for men, 27, 167, 180–81, 215, 224; as part-time work, 147; and social class distinctions, 29, 214–15
—women's: vs. men's extradomestic work, 24, 27; Peronist government's recognition of, 123–27; women as both employer and employee in, 29, 114, 141, 179, 215; vs. women's extradomestic work, 18, 44, 58, 100, 114, 116, 163, 167, 179, 186, 192–93, 200, 225
See also *Amas de casa*; Domestic servants; Household appliances: changing domestic work
Doña Lola (Dolores "Lola" Clotilde), 133
Doña Petrona. *See* Gandulfo, Petrona Carrizo de
Doña Petrona por Narda (TV show), 227–28
Duhalde, Eduardo, 220–21
Dulce de leche, 73
Dumas, Gato, 7, 207, 229–30 (n. 16)
Durione y Sesia, Emilia, 28

Eating practices: in Buenos Aires, 40, 116; Doña Petrona and efforts to change, 185, 198 (*see also* Gandulfo, Petrona Carrizo de—cooking and cookbooks); and *ecónomas*, 50; elite, 32–33, 40; government interest in, 1930s, 85; and immigrants, 174; Peronist government interest in, 110, 116; and processed foods, 164; and sense of community, 19, 226 (*see also* Commensality); in Santiago del Estero, 32–33; working-class, 33, 116. *See also* Argentina—food; Beef; *Cocina criolla*; Cooking; Cuisine; Dieting; Nutrition
Ecónomas: vs. *cocineras*, 13, 24, 29, 48, 53, 82–83; *El libro de Doña Petrona*, influence on, 101–2; during military government, 205, 223, 273 (nn. 105–7), 277 (n. 22); origin of term, 48,

240 (n. 154), 240–41 (n. 155); radio broadcasting and, 79; respectability and, 44–45; term defined, 3. *See also* Gandulfo, Petrona Carrizo de—cooking and cookbooks; Primitiva
Economía en la cocina (Ferrer), 154
Economy. *See* Argentina—economy
Ecos, 149, 261 (n. 132)
Editorial Diana, 114
Editorial Haynes, 79–80
Education, for women in Argentina, 26–29, 57, 71, 108–9, 252 (n. 76)
Ehrick, Christine, 66
El arte de cocinar, 31–32
"El arte de cocinar por Petrona C. De Gandulfo" (lectures), 81–82
El Arte de la Elegancia (TV show), 132
El arte de la mesa: El recetario de Doña Lola, 133, 257 (n. 53)
El Ateneo (bookstore), 101
El Clarín, 226–27
Elena, Eduardo, 104
El Hogar, 56, 57, 68, 72; cooking demonstrations in lecture halls, 58–61, 62–64, 65, 242 (nn. 17, 21); Doña Petrona writing for, 55, 64, 65, 70, 76–79, 246 (n. 120); *El libro de Doña Petrona* and, 76, 246 (n. 108); letters to Doña Petrona in, 76–79, 246 (nn. 111–15, 118); ownership of, 79–80
Elites (upper class): as audience for early cookbooks, 5, 30–31, 32, 70; in Buenos Aires, 7, 41, 70, 72, 84, 97; cooks/cooking in homes of, 5, 30, 32, 41, 49, 133, 246 (n. 113), 257 (n. 57); culinary preferences of, 7, 33, 40–41, 49, 72, 97, 110, 233; and domestic instruction, 27, 29, 133, 235 (n. 22); and domestic servants, 29–30, 141, 147, 174, 224, 235 (n. 22); Doña Petrona and, 29–30, 59–60, 70, 74–75, 84; and Peronist government, 109, 141; and race, 9, 105; in Santiago del Estero, 33, 34–35, 37, 52; and support for military governments, 57;

vis-à-vis lower and middle classes, 8, 39, 40–41, 58, 74, 75, 105, 246 (n. 113)

El libro de Doña Petrona: advertisements and, 69, 96, 106, 114, 260 (n. 109); advice on appliances and kitchen equipment, 129–30, 145; Atlántida collaboration for, 95–96, 249–50 (n. 13), 250 (n. 18); beef recipes in, 73–74; as bible of the home, 3, 14, 89, 156, 209, 232 (n. 47); chicken and fish recipes in, 73–74; competition for, 95, 133; contents of, besides recipes, 69–70, 71–72, 99–100, 213, 244 (n. 80); cooking for children in, 142–43; corporate products and, 143, 260 (n. 109); cuisines used in recipes, 7, 72–73, 199–200, 213; distribution and promotion of, 111–12, 114, 156, 209; domestic servants, advice about, 74, 112, 113–14; domestic servants consulting, 15; Doña Petrona's gratitude expressed in, 136, 258 (n. 68); Doña Petrona's self-presentation in, 96, 97; economizing advice in, 128–29, 130, 145, 260 (n. 115); elaborate recipes of, 16, 70, 82, 86, 91–92, 121–22, 130, 142, 183–84, 198; fame of Doña Petrona and, 76; fifty-year anniversary of, 212; illustrations in, 72, 73, 134, 143, 200, 246 (n. 108); immigrants and, 135–36; ingredients list at top of recipe and, 136, 258 (n. 69); meal presentation and, 72, 143; men and, 15, 101, 133–34, 250 (n. 35); menus in, 100, 163; popularity of, 4, 6, 13, 18, 20, 69, 89, 127, 133, 157, 220, 223, 226, 229 (n. 3), 276 (n. 7), 277 (n. 20); publication of, 3, 4, 55, 67–69, 95–96, 219; recipe instructions, 71–72, 249 (n. 2); sales of, 1940s, 95, 101, 119, 249–50 (n. 13), 250 (n. 14); successors to, 200, 201; table seating arrangements and, 74, 145; targeting middle-class women,

69, 70, 95, 223; translation possibility for United States, 156, 263 (n. 30); as wedding gift, 101–2, 199; women's collection of recipes from, 102, 103; working-class women and, 70, 97, 112, 118, 122, 134–35

—edition(s): early, 18, 55, 67–70, 89, 246 (n. 108), 249 (nn. 173, 175); early, price of, 69, 244 (n. 76); fiftieth, 142; in 1940s, 95–98, 99, 100–101, 112, 114, 119, 249–50 (n. 13), 250 (nn. 14, 18, 32); in 1950s, 121, 127, 128–30, 133, 136, 142, 145, 148, 255 (n. 2), 256 (nn. 25, 28), 258 (nn. 68–69); in 1960s, 156, 262–63 (n. 29), 274 (n. 130); in 1970s, 183–84, 185, 198, 199–200, 271 (n. 69), 274 (n. 130); in 1980s, 209, 212, 213; in 1990s, 215; seventy-fifth, 209; in 2000s, 227 *See also* Gandulfo, Petrona Carrizo de—cooking and cookbooks; Recipes

El libro del ama de casa, 146

Empanadas, 33, 63, 72, 95, 143, 154, 164, 175–76, 177, 198, 204, 205, 236 (n. 61)

Empanadas de Carne con Hojaldre Rápida, 151–52

Empanadas santiagueñas, 187, 269 (n. 18)

Escudero, Pedro, 85, 86, 87, 88, 248 (nn. 162–63)

Escuela Técnica del Hogar, 27, 235 (n. 28)

Ethnicity, 10, 39–41, 72, 76, 160–61, 239 (nn. 22, 25)

Eugenics, 28, 85

Evita. *See* Perón, Eva

Falklands War, 211

Fantasias de Gelatina Royal, 143

Farmer, Fanny, 6, 229 (n. 12)

Feminism in Argentina: Doña Petrona and, 207, 210, 214; Eva Perón and, 107–8; home economics and, 27; 1960s, 152–53, 184, 262 (n. 6); 1970s,

190–91, 194, 217–18, 269 (nn. 34–35), 270 (n. 54); suffrage and, 57, 107–8

Femirama, 171, 176

Ferrer, Chola, 154, 269 (n. 26)

Figueredo, Francisco, 30, 236 (n. 47)

Fish, 13, 50, 73, 129, 188, 257 (n. 37)

Fisher, Jo, 214

Flit bug repellent, 69

Fogón (fire pit), 33

Folklore, 154

Food. *See* Argentina—food; Beef; *Cocina criolla*; Cooking; Cuisine; Dieting; Eating practices; Nutrition

French cuisine, 7, 33, 40, 41, 43, 53, 62–63, 72, 245 (n. 94)

Frondizi, Arturo, 144, 155

Gadea, Hilda, 138–39, 259 (n. 84)

Galician Empanadas, 143

Gallotti, Alicia, 189–90, 271 (n. 74)

Gandulfo, Emilio, 42

Gandulfo, Oscar, 37–38, 41, 83–84; death of, 99; Doña Petrona working and, 43–44, 58; work of, 42, 43

Gandulfo, Petrona Carrizo de (Doña Petrona)

—cooking and cookbooks: *Bajas calorías*, 199; beef and, 7, 73–74, 84–85, 86–87, 188, 194–95, 196, 269 (n. 24), 271 (n. 59); as large woman, 198, 271 (n. 74); *cocina criolla* (creole cooking) and, 10, 24, 63, 72, 86, 143, 152, 154, 187–88, 204, 213; *Coma bien y adlegace* (Eat Well and Get Thin) (Petrona and Cormillot), 198–99; *Como cocina Doña Petrona con olla a presión*, 129; competition for, 133, 180, 267 (n. 153), 278 (n. 32); cookbook collection of, 70, 245 (n. 85); cookbooks of, 13, 17, 232 (n. 41); cuisines used in, 7, 72–73, 153, 154, 161–62, 199–200, 269 (n. 19); demonstrations, 1960s, 149, 165–66; demonstrations, 1980s, 210, 274 (n. 135); demonstrations in Rosario,

80, 81, 89, 149, 242 (n. 21); demonstrations with *Caras y Caretas*, 81–83; demonstrations with *El Hogar*, 58–61, 62–64, 65, 242 (nn. 17, 21); demonstrations with Primitiva, 3, 17, 49–51, 52–53; diet, 198–99, 223, 271 (n. 69); domestic advice for women and, 7–8, 12, 13–14, 67, 111; *ecónoma* vs. *cocinera* and, 13, 24, 29, 53, 82–83, 241 (n. 171); economical recipes, 95, 151–52, 154–55, 162, 188, 192, 193, 194, 196–97, 223; economizing advice and, 188–89, 192, 194–97, 212–13, 270 (n. 40); elaborate recipes used in, 7, 95, 161, 183–84, 198, 199; expense of ingredients used in, 14, 16, 189–90, 194, 210, 213, 220, 221; fan base, 15, 56, 68, 76–79, 82, 89, 136, 191, 214, 233 (n. 60), 247 (n. 136); fan diversity, 76, 246 (nn. 111–12, 114); fans of, provinces vs. Buenos Aires, 14, 76–77, 164–66, 246 (n. 111); feminism and, 207, 210, 214; food and community and, 19–20; Gas del Estado and, 118–19, 127; *Los cortes de carnes y su utilización: Recetas culinarias preparadas por la señora Petrona C. de Gandulfo*, 86–87; media presence of, 95, 96, 250 (n. 15); middle-class women and, 8, 21, 69, 70, 80, 95, 152, 162–63, 222–23; modern approach to, 89, 176, 178, 213, 225; nostalgia for, 13, 16, 221, 226–28; oral history workshops and, 14–15; *Para aprender a decorar* (Learning How to Decorate), 96–97, 155–56, 250 (nn. 18–19); politics at the table and, 193–94, 205, 208; popularity of, 4, 12, 15, 18–19, 135–36, 200, 213, 233 (n. 60); presenting style, 3, 59–60, 63, 64, 160, 161; promoting corporate products, 6, 55, 65, 69, 103, 106–7, 110–11, 119, 132; provincial upbringing and, 153, 154, 160–61, 175–76, 187, 204; publishing, 1980s, and, 212, 213–14,

275 (n. 156); reticence to cook, 17, 24, 29, 32, 42, 53, 219, 241 (n. 171); scholarship on, 12–13, 14–15, 219–20, 232 (n. 39), 276 (n. 5); successors to, 200, 211, 217, 271–72 (n. 79); teaching men, 1970s, 206–7; time-consuming nature of recipes used in, 14, 16, 55, 122, 176, 186, 192, 199, 206; time-saving recipes for, 163, 223; travels to other countries and, 14, 156–57; U.S. domestic roles and, 122, 255 (n. 4); U.S. influences on, 143–44, 157; women's roles and, 122, 126–27, 145, 158, 176, 180–81, 190, 194–95, 210, 214, 215, 217, 222–23, 225–26. See also *El libro de Doña Petrona*; *Recetas económicas*; Recipes

—life events: adoption of son, 83–84, 248 (n. 154); aging and, 209–10; Juanita Bordoy as domestic servant for, 35, 114, 137–38, 141, 196, 215, 216, 219, 254 (n. 109), 258 (nn. 76, 78), 265 (n. 95); Buenos Aires, early years in, 38, 41–42, 237 (n. 87); career, 3–5, 6, 12, 13, 17–18, 93–97, 152, 184–86, 222, 226; career, early, 17, 23–24, 32; career, 1930s, 55, 56, 58–60, 88–89, 242 (n. 10); claiming professional and social status as *ecónoma*, 53, 54; death, 219, 276 (n. 1); early life, 3, 23–24, 25–27, 29, 32, 34, 222, 234 (nn. 9, 16, 18), 235 (n. 38), 236 (n. 61); early reticence about cooking, 17, 24, 29, 32; Oscar Gandulfo and, 37–38, 41–42, 43–44, 58, 99; marriage and name, 41–42, 68; multimedia empire of, 7, 13; National Meat Board association with, 84–85, 86–87, 188; ownership of house and car, 84; Eva Perón and, 127; Peronist government and, 93–94, 95, 106–7, 112, 118–19, 193, 252 (n. 68); politics and, 139, 184, 190, 195–96, 202, 204, 208, 211; provincial upbringing, 10, 25–27, 32; racial identity of, 10, 26, 176, 204,

264 (n. 63); second husband, 111–12, 127, 177, 187, 196, 204, 209, 253 (n. 95); Taboada family ranch and, 34–35, 36, 37–38, 237 (nn. 77, 80, 87); trademarking her name, 203–4, 272 (n. 97); tributes to, after death, 219; unpublished memoirs and, 13, 25, 234 (n. 10)

—magazines, 3, 18; articles about, 175–76, 177, 189–90, 207–8; *Caras y Caretas* and, 80–83, 249 (n. 7); cuisines used in recipes for, 187–88; economical recipes for, 188, 192, 193, 194, 196–97; economizing advice and, 188–89, 192, 194–97, 270 (n. 40); *El Hogar* articles about, 64, 246 (n. 120); *El Hogar* column and, 55, 64, 65, 70, 76–79; *El Hogar* cooking demonstrations, 58–61, 62–64, 65, 242 (nn. 17, 21); *El Hogar* recipes, 64, 70; fan base, 76–79, 89; fan letters sent to, 187, 188, 246 (nn. 111–15, 118); *Para Ti* and, 97, 186–87, 249 (n. 7), 265 (n. 78); *Para Ti* column, 94–95, 103, 164, 208; U.S. women's magazines and, 122; women saving recipes from, 78, 82, 103, 246 (n. 126), 247 (nn. 142–43)

—Primitiva work: cooking demonstrations, 3, 17, 49–51, 52–53; cooking demonstrations with *El Hogar* and, 58–61, 62–64, 65, 242 (nn. 17, 21); as *ecónoma*, 3, 17, 24, 42, 43–45, 49, 50, 54, 56, 58–60, 62–63, 65, 103, 241 (n. 167); heading home economics division, 58, 242 (n. 10); presenting style, 59–60, 63, 64

—radio, 3; contests, 79, 247 (n. 127); domestic advice for women and, 67, 111; fan base, 82, 247 (n. 136); interviews, 175; National Meat Board association and, 86; programs, 1930s, 17–18, 65–67, 79–80, 81, 82, 88, 247 (nn. 135–36); programs, 1940s, 94, 110–11; promoting corporate products

on, 110–11, 247 (n. 135); women's collection of recipes from, 79, 82
—television, 6; Juanita Bordoy, as assistant, 18, 136, 138, 168, 169, 170–72, 178, 179, 184, 185, 258 (n. 74), 264 (n. 58), 265 (n. 94), 266 (n. 104); Juanita Bordoy, treatment of by, 14, 136–38, 152, 168–75, 220, 264 (n. 58), 265 (n. 95), 266 (n. 115); *Buenas Tardes, Mucho Gusto*, 151, 157–59, 173, 178–79, 186, 202, 221; competition for, 132–33; cooking live on, 159–60, 178, 263 (n. 36), 264 (n. 58); cooking shows, independent, 157; cooking shows, 1950s, 17, 121–22, 149, 150; cooking shows, 1960s, 170, 266 (nn. 101, 104); cooking shows, 1970s, 207; cooking shows, 1980s, 210; cooking shows, retirement from, 211–12, 275 (nn. 143–44); cuisines taught, 161–62; economical recipes for, 151–52, 162; elaborate garnishes and, 164, 165–66; elaborate recipes for, 121–22, 161, 186; expense of ingredients in recipes for, 162–63, 164, 168; fan base, 3, 14, 15, 138, 142, 149, 164–66, 167–69; fan letters sent to, 164–65, 179–80; *Jueves Hogareños*, 132, 136, 257 (n. 50); menus for younger people, 163–64; popularity of, 3–6, 15, 18, 81–82, 94, 114, 127, 175, 199, 207, 210, 217, 219; presenting style, 3, 160, 161; processed food and, 164, 265 (n. 78); *Programa del Arte Culinario*, 142; promoting corporate products on, 132, 138, 143, 151, 159, 164, 175, 258 (n. 82), 260 (n. 109), 267 (n. 131); provincial upbringing and, 160–61, 175–76; recipe pamphlets from, 143, 144, 258 (n. 81), 260 (n. 109), 261 (n. 1); time-saving recipes for, 163; U.S. vs. Argentine styles of cooking, 163–64; *Viernes Hogareños*, 136, 138, 143, 144, 255 (n. 2), 258 (nn. 81–82), 260 (n. 109)

García, Luis J., 68
Gardel, Carlos, 219–20
Gas, after nationalization of companies, 106, 251 (nn. 62–64)
Gas del Estado, 106–7, 118, 127
Gas lighting, 46
Gas stoves, 46–49, 51, 59, 62, 65, 74, 132, 145; baking and, 50, 97; manufacture of, with Peronist policies, 106, 251 (n. 64)
General Electric, 79
Gente, 175–76, 189, 207
Germani, Gino, 75, 245 (n. 102)
Gonzaga, Antonio, 67, 243 (n. 57)
Good Housekeeping, 122
Gorriti, Juana Manuela, 31
Grammático, Karín, 193
Great Depression, 8–9, 56–57
Grierson, Cecilia, 27
Guerrico, Silvia, 66, 243 (n. 53)
Guevara, Che, 138–39, 149, 259 (nn. 84–86)
Guillen, Clotilde, 27–28
Guy, Donna, 83

Harrod's, 96
Hermann, Cecilia, 30, 133
Hogar de la Empleada, 109, 110
Hogares de Tránsito, 109
Hojaldre dough, 77, 136
Home(s): and class identity, 8; Doña Petrona and role of *amas de casa* in, 67, 70, 89, 90, 100, 112, 113, 114, 128, 145, 149, 163, 167, 196; gas as fuel in, 48, 51, 145; location of kitchens within, 30, 41, 51; modern, cooking in, 50, 51, 62, 99, 145; Peronist government and, 109, 112–13, 117, 119; in Santiago del Estero, 32–33; and women's domestic instruction, 28, 29, 67, 123, 235 (n. 22), 240 (n. 155); women's economizing in, 38, 128, 196; women's power over, 28, 108, 231 (n. 29); as women's primary focus, 10, 11–12, 28, 43, 44, 57, 70,

100, 108, 117, 124, 126, 149, 158, 190, 191, 193, 196, 210, 214, 218, 225; and women's work outside of, 12, 43, 100, 108, 114, 145, 149, 158, 163, 179, 184, 207, 224, 225. *See also* Domesticity; Kitchen(s)

Home economics: corporations and, 45–48; early twentieth century, 27–29, 235 (nn. 22, 27, 30, 32, 34, 38); in Latin America, 61–62; Peronist government and, 123–24, 126, 149, 256 (n. 15). See also *Ecónomas*

Home economists. See *Ecónomas*

Homemakers. See *Amas de casa*

Household appliances, 166, 274 (n. 137); availability, 1950s, 145, 260 (n. 116); changing domestic work, 147, 179, 225, 267 (n. 143), 277 (n. 26); Doña Petrona and, 176, 178, 207, 225. *See also* Refrigerators

Housewives. See *Amas de casa*

Humita, 73

Iadarola, Amalia, 198

Ice cream, 55, 241 (n. 2)

Illia, Arturo, 162

Immigration: European immigrants to Argentina, 9–10, 38, 39–40, 174, 266 (n. 125); provincial Argentines to Buenos Aires, 14, 25, 38, 40, 41, 57, 99, 237 (n. 88); United States vs. Argentina, 6, 229 (n. 10)

Import substitution industrialization (ISI), 57

"Infamous Decade" (1930s), 57

Ingeniero White, 15, 16

International Monetary Fund, 140, 144

James, Daniel, 104

Jockey Club, 41

Joy of Cooking, The (Rombauer), 6, 68–69

Jueves Hogareños (TV show), 132, 136, 257 (n. 50)

Julia R. Esteves company, 96

Junta Nacional de Carnes (National Meat Board), 56, 84–87, 188

Khrushchev, Nikita, 149–50

Kitchen(s): and gender roles, 12, 17, 53, 60–61, 68, 74, 149, 270 (n. 55); improvements in, 32–33, 51, 62, 106, 149–50, 178; location of within homes, 30, 41, 51; in schools, 28, 235 (n. 38); and social class attitudes, 29, 30, 31, 102, 137, 170; staffing of in elite homes, 41, 51

—Doña Petrona and: early avoidance of, 17, 24, 29, 35, 53; economizing in, 128, 140, 154–55, 189–90; limiting time spent in, 163, 176, 186, 192, 221; setup and equipment for, 129–30, 146, 178

"Kitchen debate," 149–50

Klasse, Isay, 95, 101, 156, 249 (n. 12)

Knorr Suiza, 205

Labruna, Angel, 84

La cocina y la pastelería de América (Figueredo), 30, 236 (n. 47)

La cocinera criolla ("Marta"), 31, 70

La Compañía Primitiva de Gas. *See* Primitiva

La Cueva, Luis, 101

La Cupertina (restaurant), 30

Ladies Home Journal, 122

Lagasse, Emeril, 6, 229–30 (n. 16)

La Liga Argentina de Damas Católicas, 83

Lamarque, Libertad, 119, 254–55 (n. 128)

La Nación, 71, 103, 198, 227

La Negra, 45–46, 240 (n. 141)

Lanusse, Alejandro, 189

La perfecta cocinera argentina (Torres de Castex), 31, 70, 236 (n. 50)

La razón de mi vida (Eva Perón), 127, 133, 256 (n. 26)

"Las comidas de mi pueblo" (Palacios), 154

La Serenísima, 175

Latin America. *See* Argentina—vis-à-vis other Latin American nations

Law 326, 140–41

Lazzari, Gastón, 64–65

Le Bréton, Tomás, 70

Le Cordon Bleu: in Buenos Aires, 1920s, 24, 41, 42–43, 48, 50; Doña Petrona as student of, 43, 70, 200; for respectable women, 53, 59, 133

Leftovers, 77, 129, 140, 200, 273 (n. 117)

Legrand, Mirtha, 228, 278 (n. 32)

Lepes, Narda, 227–28

Levarol baking powder, 69

Liga de Amas de Casa, 140, 145–46, 149

Liga Patriótica, 39

Lobato, Mirta, 44

Lobstein, Alicia, 146–47, 148

Locro, 63, 205; Locro de Maíz "Mamita Cleme," 70

Logan, Martha, 156

Los cortes de carnes y su utilización: Recetas culinarias preparadas por la señora Petrona C. de Gandulfo, 86–87

Lower class. *See* Working class

Lullo, Orestes di, 33

Madres de Plaza de Mayo, 203, 208, 215, 218, 273 (n. 123)

Magazines, 18, 62, 147; food-related articles, 13–14, 64–65; progressive, 1960s, 167, 186, 265 (n. 91); U.S. women's, 122. See also *Caras y Caretas*; *El Hogar*; Gandulfo, Petrona Carrizo de—magazines; *Para Ti*

Magia en la Cocina (TV cooking show), 157

Maids. *See* Domestic servants

Mairet, Germain, 41, 239 (n. 118)

Manzano, Valeria, 187

Marini, Ana María (pseud.), 203

Marshall, Niní, 119, 254–55 (n. 128)

"Marta" (Mercedes Cullen de Aldao), 31

Martinetas en Bella Vista, 72

Martínez de Hoz, José Alfredo, 201

Martín Fierro (poem), 4, 13, 18, 229 (n. 3)

Martín Fierro prize, 157, 263 (n. 37)

Mashed potato roses, 165–66

Massut, Alejandro, 227

Massut, Atilio, 111–12, 127, 177, 178, 187, 196, 204, 209, 253 (n. 95)

Massut, Marcela, 13, 25, 89, 176, 177, 178, 180; continuing Doña Petrona's cookbooks, 227; as Doña Petrona's business partner, 212, 213

Massut, Marcelo, 112, 177, 204, 272 (n. 97)

Maternalism, 106–9, 141, 172, 222, 224, 252 (n. 82)

Mate tea, 16, 165, 197

Mayonnaise, 58–59, 77

Media. *See* Argentina: censorship of press; Argentina: mass media and

Media lunas, 161

Mégy, María Luisa, 39, 237 (n. 93)

Menem, Carlos Saúl, 220

Men in Argentina: and *asado* preparation, 12, 74, 187; as beneficiaries of women's domestic work, 12, 122, 141, 225; and broadcasting, 66; as cookbook authors, 30, 224; cookbooks not addressed to, 133–34, 145; as culinary celebrities, 6–7, 207, 224, 227, 229–30 (n. 16); as domestic servants, 11, 29, 113, 245 (n. 98); domestic work as inappropriate for, 131, 133–34, 167, 180–81, 215, 225, 226; and education, 27, 57; elite, 37, 41; and factory labor, 45, 108, 117, 252 (n. 77); as family heads/providers, 10, 12, 24, 27, 46, 57, 124, 126, 145, 191, 214; as home cooks, 206–7, 217, 224, 250 (n. 35), 273 (n. 116); as limited segment of Doña Petrona's audience, 76, 134, 226, 247 (n. 136), 250 (n. 35), 268 (n. 7); and middle-class respectability, 24, 29, 43; and national identity, 18, 27; and Peronist economic and health-related initiatives, 123, 125; and production of food commodities, 11; as professional chefs, 7, 30, 48, 50–51, 227, 239 (n. 118); as proportion of Buenos Aires population, 38, 57; and shopping, 188, 196; and women's extradomestic work, 43, 44. *See also* Paternalism

Mexico, 5–6, 41, 223

Middle classes, 102, 261–62 (n. 5); Argentina, 1950s, 9, 122, 255 (n. 5); Buenos Aires, 1920s, 8, 39, 230 (n. 20); Buenos Aires, 1930s, 8, 75, 230 (n. 20), 245 (n. 102), 245–46 (n. 104); Doña Petrona and, 8, 21, 69, 70, 80, 95, 152, 162–63, 222–23; Frondicist movement and, 144, 260 (n. 112); immigrants in, 147; of Latin America, 8, 230 (nn. 18, 20); Peronist government and, 104, 110, 222–23; working women, 19, 152

Milanesas, 192, 195, 207

Military governments. *See* Argentina: military governments

Mitchell, Roberto, 204

Molina, Emmy de, 102, 169, 206

Molina, Luis Barrantes, 45–46

Molina, Pelusa, 102, 206, 207

Montoneros group, 184, 191

Muchnik, Annamaría, 157–58, 170, 178, 221, 224

Muchnik, Pedro, 157–58

Mucho Gusto, 124, 153, 193, 207–8

Nari, Marcela, 28

National Institute of Nutrition, 85, 88, 131

Nationalism, 19–20; 21, 58

National Jornadas de Cocina Criolla, 204

National Meat Board, 56, 84–87, 188

Nixon, Richard, 149–50

Nuestras Mujeres, 117

Nueva ola ("new wave" of young people), 163, 186, 264 (n. 77)

Nutrition: general interest in, 119, 201, 210; government interest in, 85, 86, 88, 118, 130–31, 248 (n. 163); home economics and, 28; and malnourishment, 109–10, 210, 212

Ocampo, María Elena Rodríguez, 161

Official Story, The (film, 1985), 208

Ollas populares (food kitchens), 191

Onganía, Juan Carlos, 162, 184

Orbis gas stoves, 132

Ortiz, Roberto M., 87, 99, 248 (n. 170)

Oyuela, María Adela, 141

Pace, Fernando Muñoz, 219

Palacios, Margarita, 154

Palmeras, 164

Pan dulce, 92–93, 105, 118, 155, 180

Pan Dulce de Navidad (Christmas Sweet Bread), 91–92, 162, 249 (n. 2)

Pan Dulce de Navidad, sin Huevos (Christmas Sweet Bread without eggs), 112, 253 (n. 98)

Panorama, 211–12

Panqueques, 35, 37

Para aprender a decorar (Learning How to Decorate), 96–97, 155–56, 250 (nn. 18–19)

Para Ti, 62, 65; Doña Petrona and, 94–95, 97, 103, 164, 208, 249 (n. 7), 265 (n. 78); Doña Petrona's economizing advice in, 188–89, 192, 195, 196, 270 (n. 40); Doña Petrona's recipe cards and, 187, 188; *El libro de Doña Petrona* and, 142; new style of cooking and, 200; opinion about food policies and, 193, 269 (n. 26); opinion letters, 1970s, 186–87, 188, 268 (n. 7); politics and, 208, 274 (n. 126); readership, 186, 268 (n. 9); U.S. women's magazines and, 122; women's domestic roles and, 167

Parrilla, 32

Parrillada, 86

Pasta recipes, 194
Pasteles de Hojaldre Frita, 143
Pastelitos, 17, 32, 50, 95, 198
Pastelitos de Dulce (Quince-Filled Pastries), 23, 24
Pastoriza, Elisa, 105
Paternalism, 109, 141, 222, 224, 277 (n. 19). *See also* Maternalism
Patronato de la Infancia, 83, 248 (n. 154)
Pépin, Jacques, 6, 70, 229–30 (n. 16)
Pepitas, 103
Pérez, Inés, 179
Perón, Eva, 12, 20, 254–55 (n. 128); *amas de casa* and, 125–26, 252 (n. 71); Christmas and, 92–93; Doña Petrona and, 12, 18, 93, 107, 119, 126–27; illness and death of, 127, 131; maternalism and, 108, 109; patriarchy and, 126–27; public presentation of, 18, 105, 107–8; television and, 131; women's rights and protection and, 107–8, 109–10
Perón, Isabel, 184, 194, 195, 270 (nn. 54–55)
Perón, Juan, 18, 20; *amas de casa* and, 123; Christmas and, 92–93; death of, 194; Doña Petrona and, 93, 107, 119, 252 (n. 68); downfall of, 123, 139, 259 (n. 86); election of, 103–4; Eva Perón and, 126; food policies and, 9, 16, 114–17; government of, 184, 192–93, 270 (n. 44), 272 (n. 95); reelection of, 127; rise of, 99; television and, 131; women's roles and, 192–93, 222
Peronist government: *amas de casa* and, 109, 116, 118, 123–27, 129, 131, 252 (n. 71); corporations and advertising and, 111, 253 (n. 93); Doña Petrona working within, 93–94, 95, 106–7, 112, 118–19, 193, 252 (n. 68); economic policies of, early 1950s, 127–28; economizing campaigns, 123, 128, 130–31; "the family table" and, 108, 252 (n. 71); food policies, 104, 109–10, 114–17, 119–20, 124–25,

193, 257 (n. 37); food shortages, 1950s, 131; Che Guevara and, 139, 259 (n. 86); home economics and, 123–24, 126, 149, 256 (n. 15); nationalizing businesses, 105–6; opposition to, 119, 255 (n. 129); paternalism and, 92–93, 277 (n. 19); Peróns as parents of Argentina, 92–93, 109; radio broadcasting and, 110, 124, 253 (n. 87), 254–55 (n. 128); reserving beef for export, 115–16, 128; targeting women consumers, 123, 222; television and, 131–32; U.S. government and corporate interests and, 122; women's roles and, 110, 117–18, 119–20, 141; working-class diet recommendations, 116–17, 118, 254 (n. 124); working class and, 9, 18, 20, 62, 92–93, 104, 105, 109, 112–13, 115, 116–18, 126, 144, 222
Peronist Women's Party, 126
Petrona C. de Gandulfo (TV cooking show), 157
Pierangeli, Enrique, 131
Pilcher, Jeffrey, 223
Piluso (children's TV show), 160
Pirés de Burguez, G. María, 58, 64
Pius XII (pope), 109
Plus Ultra, 46, 47
Polenta, 95
Polimeni, Fanny, 209
Politics. *See* Argentina—politics
Porteños, 14. *See also* Buenos Aires
Potatoes, 130–31, 165–66
Poverty. *See* Argentina: poverty and
Presidente Perón gas pipeline, 106
Pressure cookers, 129, 140
Primitiva: advertising campaign for gas stoves, 46–48, 62, 63, 65; *Caras y Caretas* and, 82, 247 (n. 139); cooking demonstrations, 48, 49–50, 51, 59–60, 61; Doña Petrona as *ecónoma* for, 3, 17, 24, 42, 43–45, 50, 56, 58–60, 62–63, 65, 103; Doña Petrona heading home economics division

of, 58, 242 (n. 10); Doña Petrona's cookbook and, 69, 96, 106; *ecónomas* and, 45, 46, 48, 49–50, 51, 52, 53, 54, 56, 58–60, 64; gas lighting and, 46, 240 (n. 144); male executives of, 48, 49; nationalization, 106; recipes of *ecónomas*, 50, 62–64, 70; targeting women consumers, 45, 46–48, 50, 62, 63, 65, 68. *See also* Gandulfo, Petrona Carrizo de—Primitiva work

Proceso, 201

Process of National Reorganization, 201

Profiteroles with Chocolate, 143

Programa Alementario Nacional (PAN), 212

Puchero, 40, 77–78, 86, 87

Pyrex, 132

Quechua language, 26, 234 (nn. 18–19)

"Queens of work," 118

Quesada, Josué, 58

Race in Argentina, 9, 10, 124, 160–61, 230 (nn. 23, 25); *criollo/as*, 10, 26, 231 (nn. 27–28), 233 (n. 5), 234 (n. 13); indigenous people, 15–16, 20, 26, 234 (n. 19)

Radio, 247 (nn. 128, 134); *Cocina de la Salud*, 124; cooking shows, 66–67, 243 (n. 57), 247 (n. 129); gender and, 66, 243 (n. 53); national audience for, 80, 244 (n. 63); Peronist government and, 110, 124, 253 (n. 87), 254–55 (n. 128); vs. television, 158. *See also* Gandulfo, Petrona Carrizo de—radio

Radio Argentina, 66, 80

Radio El Mundo, 79–80, 81, 110, 244 (n. 63), 247 (n. 129), 253 (n. 87)

Radio Excelsior, 80, 82, 86, 94, 95, 110, 247 (nn. 129, 135–36)

Radiolandia, 110, 111

Radio Mitre, 67

Radio Prieto, 66, 67, 247 (n. 129)

Ramasco, Clementina, 25–26, 33–34, 234 (nn. 13, 16)

Ramírez, Pedro Pablo, 139

Ray, Rachel, 7

Recetas económicas (Doña Petrona), 154–55, 156, 157, 190, 212, 227, 262 (nn. 20, 28)

Recipes: Asado al Horno, 74; beef and, 73–74, 86; *Copa* "El Hogar" ("El Hogar" Sundae), 55; of *ecónomas* at Primitiva, 50, 62–64, 70; *El libro de Doña Petrona* and, 70, 102–3, 156, 199–200, 245 (n. 84), 247 (nn. 141–42), 248 (n. 167), 255 (n. 2); *Empanadas de Carne con Hojaldre Rápida*, 151–52; Fantasias de Gelatina Royal, 143; Galician Empanadas, 143; Locro de Maíz "Mamita Cleme," 70; in magazines, 64–65, 94–95; *Pan Dulce de Navidad* (Christmas Sweet Bread), 91–92, 162, 249 (n. 2); *Pan Dulce de Navidad, sin Huevos* (Christmas Sweet Bread without eggs), 112, 253 (n. 98); Pasteles de Hojaldre Frita, 143; *Pastelitos de Dulce* (Quince-Filled Pastries), 23, 24; Profiteroles with Chocolate, 143; pamphlets of from TV, 143, 144, 258 (n. 81), 260 (n. 109), 261 (n. 1); Suprema de Pollo a la Carolina, 70; Supremas de Pollo Maryland, 121–22, 143, 255 (n. 2); Torta "Caras y Caretas," 82, 247 (n. 141); *Torta Mundial 78*, 183, 185; *tortitas*, 35, 37; on TV cooking shows, 143, 151, 161; wedding cake, 97–98; whipped cream, 198; women's collection of Petrona's, 78, 79, 82, 102, 103, 188, 246 (n. 126), 247 (nn. 142–43). See also *El libro de Doña Petrona*; Gandulfo, Petrona Carrizo de—cooking and cookbooks

Refrigerators, 145, 159, 166, 207, 210, 260 (n. 116). *See also* Household appliances

Revista Aconcagua, 62

Revolución Libertadora, 139

Rocchi, Fernando, 46

Rocco-Cuzzi, Renata, 219
Rojas, Absalón, 32
Roldán, Doña María, 104, 116
Rombauer, Irma S., 6, 69
Romero, Luis Alberto, 202
Rómulo Ruffini, 132, 159
Rosalinda (magazine), 69
Rosario, 80, 81, 82, 149, 242 (n. 21)
Royal baking powder, 103, 110–11, 149, 251 (nn. 42–44), 260 (n. 109)
Royal instant gelatin, 143
Rúa, Fernando de la, 220
Ruiz, Ida P. de, 79

Sánchez, Matilde, 173
Sansinena, 45–46
Santiago del Estero, 3, 7, 10, 187, 222; association with domestic servants, 264 (n. 62); early twentieth century, 17, 25, 26, 33–34, 35, 234 (nn. 17, 19), 236 (n. 57); late nineteenth century, 32, 33, 236 (n. 56)
Sarmiento, Domingo F., 25, 234 (n. 8), 237 (n. 76)
Satiricon, 189
Schleh, Emilio J., 85
Siete Días, 166
Simmons, Aly, 129
Sindicato de Amas de Casa (SACRA), 214
Sintonía, 66, 138
Smith, Lucía Vergara, 48
Soccer World Cup (1978), 183–84, 185, 208, 273 (n. 123)
Social class. *See* Argentina: social classes of; Elites; Middle classes; Working class
Sosa, Mercedes, 208, 273 (n. 125)
Spanish Civil War, 95
Spanish culinary influences. See *Cocina criolla*; Immigration
Stewart, Martha, 7
Suffrage for women in Argentina, 57, 107–8, 117, 222, 241 (n. 3)
Sunlight soap, 132
Suprema de Pollo a la Carolina, 70

Supremas de Pollo Maryland, 121–22, 143, 255 (n. 2)
Swift, 132, 138, 143, 151, 152, 156, 159, 164, 258 (n. 82), 260 (n. 109), 265 (n. 78)

Taberna, Lorenza, 132–33, 140, 142
Taboada, Antonio, 35
Taboada, Gaspar, 35
Taboada, Leandro Antonio, 34–35, 37–38
Taboada, Manuel, 35, 237 (n. 76)
Tango, 67, 219–20
Tardecitas de Royal (radio program), 110–11
Television: in Buenos Aires, 142, 159, 274 (n. 133); color, 208, 210, 274 (n. 133); cooking shows, 6, 7, 132–33, 154, 224, 227–28, 229 (n. 15), 229–30 (n. 16), 263 (n. 37); live taping of, 159; Peronist government and, 131–32
—in Argentina: 1950s, 3, 15, 131–32, 136, 142, 260 (n. 104); 1960s, 158, 159, 263 (nn. 46, 50); 1960s to 1970s, 15, 175, 267 (n. 130); 1970s to 1980s, 208, 210, 274 (n. 133)
See also Gandulfo, Petrona Carrizo de—television
365 días sin servicio doméstico (Lobstein), 146–47
Tinsman, Heidi, 224
Torre, Juan Carlos, 105
Torres de Castex, Susana, 31, 236 (n. 50)
Torta "Caras y Caretas," 82, 247 (n. 141)
Torta de Navidad, 155
Torta Mundial 78, 183, 185, 207–8, 209
Tortas fritas, 197
Tortillas del campo, 32
Tortitas, 37
"Tragic Week" of 1919, 38
Tres Américas, 156, 249 (n. 12)
Tucumán province, 33

Unidades básicas, 126
Unión Feminista Argentina, 190, 191

United States, 47, 70, 77, 131, 138, 187, 221; Argentina turns from Europe to, as source of investments and ideas, 61, 122, 143–48, 150, 157; Argentine political and military relations with, 98–99, 122, 131, 250 (n. 25); Argentine women compared with women in, 27, 61, 122, 146, 152–53; Doña Petrona compared with culinary celebrities in, 6–7, 68–69, 160, 210; Doña Petrona looks to as model for cooking and domesticity, 122, 143–44, 147, 148, 156–57, 163–64, 178, 188; Doña Petrona sponsored by companies from, 103, 132, 164; Doña Petrona visits, 156–57; immigration to (vs. Argentina), 6, 229 (n. 10)

Universidad de la Pampa, 82, 247 (n. 143)

Universidad de la Plata, 28

Upper class. *See* Elites

Uruguay, 48, 156

Varela, Mirta, 132, 171

Velazquez de Léon, Doña, 5

Viernes Hogareños (TV show), 136, 138, 143, 144, 255 (n. 2), 258 (nn. 81–82), 260 (n. 109)

Vitel Tonne, 103

Vol-au-vents, 72

Vosotras, 62, 186

Wainerman, Catalina, 225

Waters, Alice, 164

Wedding cakes, 97–98

Weinstein, Barbara, 61–62

Women in Argentina: class-consciousness and, 59–60, 64, 243 (n. 36), 246 (n. 113); dieting and poverty/wealth, 197; economic hardships and, 39, 42, 203, 237–38 (n. 94), 238 (n. 112); education and, 26–29, 57, 71, 108–9, 252 (n. 76); elite, and cooking, early twentieth century, 30–32; helping in kitchen, 170, 179; home economics and, 27–29, 123–24, 126, 149, 235 (nn. 22, 27, 32, 38); household appliances changing domestic work of, 147, 179, 225, 267 (n. 143), 277 (n. 26); of indigenous descent, 15–16, 20, 26; infertility and adoption, 83–84; "la marocha" types, 141, 259 (n. 99); married and working, 43–44, 45, 239 (n. 127); middle-class, and cooking, 69, 70, 80, 95, 102, 223, 250 (n. 21); "modern women" of 1920s and, 45, 51, 57, 240 (n. 139); as homemakers not remunerated, 109, 252 (n. 81); nationalism and, 39; respectability and, 39, 41, 43–45, 52, 53, 57, 58, 59, 62; scholarship on, 11, 12–13; suffrage, 57, 107–8, 117, 222, 241 (n. 3); taking husband's name, 41, 112, 243 (n. 36)

—domestic roles of: current, 224–25; in early twentieth century, 27, 28–30, 38–39; in 1930s, 71, 74, 75; in 1940s, 100, 109, 117; in 1950s, 123–27, 233 (n. 56); in 1960s, 158, 167–68, 179, 223; in 1970s, 18, 191, 203, 205, 217–18, 223, 270 (n. 39); nineteenth century, 10–11, 235 (n. 22); through twentieth century, 4–5, 7–8, 11–12, 18–19, 24–25, 221–22, 233 (n. 54)

—learning cooking: in 1920s to 1930s, 17, 51, 52–53, 61–63, 65, 71–72, 83, 88, 89, 248 (n. 147); in 1940s to 1950s, 97–98, 102, 124–25, 133, 140, 256 (n. 15); in 1960s, 161–62, 224–25; well-off women and, 83, 133, 257 (n. 57)

—working extradomestically: during childbearing years, 109, 252 (n. 79); early twentieth century, 33–34, 41, 42, 43–45, 238 (n. 114), 239 (n. 134); in 1940s to 1950s, 100, 108–9, 113, 134–35, 145, 252 (n. 77), 253 (n. 102); in 1960s, 152, 153, 163, 166–67, 179, 223, 261 (n. 3); in 1970s to 1980s, 174, 184, 191, 268 (n. 2), 270 (n. 39);

through twentieth century, 11–12, 238 (n. 110)
See also *Amas de casa*; Community building: women's domestic activities and; Consumers, women; Cooking; Domesticity; Domestic servants; Domestic work; *Ecónomas*; Feminism in Argentina; Gandulfo, Petrona Carrizo de—cooking and cookbooks; Peronist government

Working class, 140–41, 169, 206; definition/identity of, 75, 261–62 (n. 5); diet of, 85, 115, 116–17, 118, 254 (nn. 114, 124); and domestic instruction, 28, 61–62, 125; food costs within budgets of, 4, 69, 104, 118, 244 (n. 76), 253 (n. 124); Peronist government and, 9, 18, 20, 92–93, 104, 105, 109, 112–13, 115, 116–18, 126, 144, 222; in political struggles, 126, 214, 221, 276 (n. 14); rising consumption/living standard for, 9, 18, 20, 104, 109, 115, 118, 147, 222; women, and Doña Petrona's books and TV shows, 70, 97, 112, 118, 122, 134–35, 157–58

World Bank, 140
World Cup. *See* Soccer World Cup
World War II, 87, 98

Yema quemada, 188
Yrigoyen, Hipólito, 39, 50, 57, 241 (n. 167)

Zubiar, J. B., 29
Zurita, Carlos, 179